A Short History of South Africa

GAIL NATTRASS

A Short History of South Africa

Jonathan Ball Publishers
Johannesburg & Cape Town

For Rhona, Ashley and Errol

Originally published in South Africa in 2017 by
JONATHAN BALL PUBLISHERS
A division of Media24 (Pty) Ltd
PO Box 33977
Jeppestown
2043

ISBN 978-1-86842-783-3
EBOOK ISBN 978-1-86842-784-0

Twitter: www.twitter.com/JonathanBallPub
Facebook:www.facebook.com/JonathanBallPublishers
Blog:http://jonathanball.bookslive.co.za/

Cover by MR Design
Cover photograph courtesy of Mapungubwe Museum, University of Pretoria.
Back cover photograph © Gallo Images.
Design and typesetting by Triple M Design
Printed and bound by CTP Printers, Cape Town
Set in 10,75pt/15 pt Minion Pro

Contents

Maps

Abbreviations

AMCU	Association of Mineworkers and Construction Union
ANC	African National Congress, originally the South African Native National Congress (SANNC), formed in 1912, and the ruling party in South Africa since 1994
ANCYL	ANC Youth League, established in 1944
APO	African People's Organisation
AWB	Afrikaner Weerstandsbeweging
COSATU	Congress of South African Trade Unions
DA	Democratic Alliance, formed in 2000 through the merger of the Democratic Party, the New National Party (which withdrew from the alliance after only a year) and the Federal Alliance. The Democratic Alliance became the official opposition party to the ANC.
DP	Democratic Party
EFF	Economic Freedom Fighters
FEDSAW	Federation of South African Women
GNU	Government of National Unity
GWU	Transvaal Garment Workers Union
ICU	Industrial and Commercial Workers' Union
IFP	Inkatha Freedom Party
KZN	KwaZulu-Natal (formerly the kingdom of Zululand and the colony of Natal)
MK	Umkhonto we Sizwe, the underground, armed wing of the ANC

NP	National Party. The first National Party was established by JBM Hertzog in 1914.
NMC	Native Military Corps
NNP	New National Party, formed in 1997
NUM	National Union of Mine Workers
NEHAWU	National Education, Health and Allied Workers Union
OFS	Orange Free State, now called the Free State
PAC	Pan Africanist Congress, started by Robert Sobukwe in 1959
PFP	Progressive Federal Party
PNP	Purified National Party, the more extreme national party established under DF Malan in 1934. When Hertzog's National Party fizzled out, the PNP became known as the NP.
SACP	South African Communist Party
SADF	South African Defence Force, established in 1948 by the nationalist government of DF Malan; the SADF replaced the Union Defence Force (UDF).
SADTU	South African Democratic Teachers Union
SAIC	South African Indian Congress
SANDF	South African National Defence Force. Established in 1994 after the first democratic elections had taken place, this was the first national defence force in our country.
SANLC	South African Native Labour Contingent
SANNC	South African Native National Congress and forerunner of the ANC, established in 1912
SACP	South African Communist Party
SAP	South Africa Party, the political party that won the first general elections after the formation of the Union of South Africa in 1910. The SAP was a merger of the South African Party and the Afrikaner Bond of the Cape Colony, Het Volk of Transvaal and Orangia Unie of the Orange Free State. The SAP existed until 1934.
UDF	Union Defence Force, started soon after the establishment of the Union of South Africa in 1910 and active during the First and Second World Wars

UDF	United Democratic Front, established in 1983
UNESCO	United Nations Educational, Scientific and Cultural Organisation
UP	United Party, formed by old rivals JBM Hertzog and Jan Smuts in 1934
VOC	Verenigde Oost-Indische Compagnie, or Dutch East India Company
ZAR	Zuid-Afrikaansche Republiek, or SAR (South African Republic), later called the Transvaal, and now constituting Gauteng, Mpumalanga, Limpopo and part of the North West province

Timeline

3 MILLION YEARS AGO

Hominids

200 000 YEARS AGO

Homo sapiens

10 000 YEARS AGO

Later Stone Age

2–3 000 YEARS AGO

Khoikhoi herders migrate to SA

300–1 000 YEARS AGO

Crop farmers and herders migrate to SA

800 AD

Iron Age: evidence of trade

1000

Later Iron Age

1100

1150 Mapungubwe, SA's first town, extensive trade network

1400

1488 White people, Portuguese traders, visit the Cape en route to India

1500

Thulamela: evidence of gold, copper, iron and tin mining in various parts of SA

1600

1601 Fleets of the English East India Company round the Cape en route to India

1602 Fleets of the Dutch East India Company round the Cape en route to India

1652 Dutch establish a refreshment station for passing ships at the Cape

1657 Large-scale settlement by the Dutch, at the Cape

1658 First slaves brought to the Cape

1688 Arrival of French immigrants at the Cape

1700

1795 First period of British occupation of the Cape

1800

1801 First missionaries from Britain arrive at the Cape

1806 Second British occupation of the Cape; £6 million paid to Dutch; Cape becomes British colony

1820 Arrival of many British settlers; turmoil in Natal and rise of Shaka; turmoil spreads to interior; leads to rise of large centralised kingdoms: the Zulu (Shaka), Thlokwa (Manthatisi), Ndebele (Mzilikazi) and Sotho (Moshoeshoe)

1836 Start of white Dutch/Afrikaans-speaking migrations from eastern Cape into interior (so-called Great Trek)

1838 Battle of Blood River

1843 Natal becomes a British Colony

1852–1854 Establishment of two Boer republics: Transvaal and Orange Free State

1860 Arrival of Indian people to work on sugar cane fields in Natal

1867 Discovery of diamonds at Kimberley

1870 Start of incorporation of black chiefdoms under British control

1879 Anglo-Zulu War and Anglo-Pedi War

1880–1881 First Anglo-Boer War

1886 Discovery of main Witwatersrand gold reef

1893–1914 Mohandas Gandhi in South Africa. NIC (National Indian Congress) and TIC (Transvaal Indian Congress) formed

1899–1902 Second Anglo-Boer (South African) War

1900

1901 Establishment of APO (African People's Organisation) by coloured (mixed-race) people

1904 Arrival of Chinese people to work on gold mines

1905 Start of pass laws and segregation policies for black people

1910 Establishment of the Union of South Africa within the British Commonwealth; former British colonies, Boer republics and black chiefdoms incorporated into the Union; Louis Botha becomes Prime Minister, Jan Smuts his deputy

1912 Establishment of SANNC (South African Native National Congress; in 1923 this becomes the ANC)

1913 Land Act

1913 First women's protest against passes, led by Charlotte Maxeke

1914 Outbreak of World War I; Afrikaner Rebellion against SA's participation in World War I; formation of Afrikaner NP (National Party) under JBM Hertzog

1918 Start of the Afrikaner Broederbond (Afrikaner nationalism accelerates)

1919 Jan Smuts becomes prime minister of the Union

1921 Formation of SACP (South African Communist Party)

1922 White miners' strike

1923 Urban Areas Act

1924 PACT government under JBM Hertzog

1926 Start of Hertzog's Civilised Labour Policies to assist poorer whites

1928 Formation of first multiracial union, GWU (Garment Workers Union), which lasted until 1935

1929–1930s Depression; growing number of poor whites

1930 White women given the vote

1934 Formation of the UP (United Party); Jan Smuts and JBM Hertzog merge; formation of the Purified National Party under DF Malan

1936 Second Land Act

1938 Centenary celebrations of Battle of Blood River; foundation laid of Voortrekker Monument; Afrikaner economic and cultural organisations advance

1939 Outbreak of World War II

1939–1948 Jan Smuts becomes prime minister and leader of the UP

1943 Women's branch of ANC formed

1944 ANC Youth League is formed with the young Nelson Mandela, Walter Sisulu and Oliver Tambo

1948 NP defeats UP and comes to power; beginning of apartheid policies

1949 Nelson Mandela, Oliver Tambo and Walter Sisulu elected to executive of ANC

1950 Hendrik Verwoerd becomes Minister of Native Affairs; Group Areas Act; Population Registration Act; Immorality Act; Mixed Marriages Act

1951 Bantu Self-Government Act creates 10 homelands for black people

1952 ANC joins SAIC (South African Indian Congress) and SACPO (SA Coloured People's Organisation) to stage Defiance Campaign against unjust laws

1953 ANC, SAIC and SACPO adopt the Freedom Charter at Kliptown; Bantu Education Act establishes separate inferior education facilities for black children

1954 Tomlinson Commission reports on poor economic condition of the homelands; FEDSAW (Federation of South African Women) established

1955 Establishment of the Black Sash

1956 Women march to Pretoria against the carrying of passes for black women

1956–1961 Treason Trial

1958 Hendrik Verwoerd becomes prime minister

1960 Harold Macmillan's 'Wind of Change' speech; Robert Sobukwe breaks away from ANC and forms Pan Africanist Congress (PAC); PAC organises pass-burning demonstration at Sharpeville; ANC and PAC banned; activists exiled, Sharpeville organisers imprisoned

1961 South Africa becomes a republic and leaves the British Commonwealth

1963–1964 Rivonia Trial

1966 Hendrik Verwoerd assassinated: succeeded by BJ Vorster

1970 Black representation in Parliament and black citizenship in South Africa taken away; black people have to identify with one of the homelands

1971 Steve Biko starts Black Consciousness Movement

1975 Chief Mangosuthu Buthelezi resists homelands; builds Inkatha movement

1976 Soweto uprising

1976–1977 First two homelands, Transkei and Bophuthatswana, become independent

1982 Formation of first union for black people, NUM (National Union of Mine Workers); activist Ruth First killed by parcel bomb

1983 UDF United Democratic Front establishment

1984 Tricameral (3–part) Parliament set up, with separate houses for whites, coloureds and Indians; black people still have to identify with homelands

1986 COSATU (Congress of South African Trade Unions) established; calls for sanctions against SA; some relaxation of segregation laws; pass laws repealed; Immorality and Mixed Marriages Act repealed

1986–1987 Successive states of emergency

1987 Talks held at Dakar between ANC and white (mainly Afrikaans-speaking) people

1989 Secret meetings between ANC and white leaders held in Lusaka, Zambia and Switzerland; FW de Klerk succeeds PW Botha as prime minister

1990 FW de Klerk announces agenda for negotiations for a democratic constitution; ANC, PAC and SACP unbanned; ANC leaders including Nelson Mandela released from prison and/or return from exile

1991 Group Areas Act repealed; South Africa readmitted to world sport

1993 Chris Hani assassinated; former white schools open to all races

1994 First democratic elections held; the ANC wins majority and becomes the new government; Nelson Mandela elected president; GNP (Government of National Unity) established; former independent homelands reincorporated into SA

1995 TRC (Truth and Reconciliation Commission) appointed to investigate apartheid-era crimes

1996 A new constitution for SA drawn and signed into law as Act 108

1999 Thabo Mbeki succeeds Nelson Mandela as president

2000

2000 DA (Democratic Alliance), formerly Democratic Party, established under Helen Zille as formal opposition party and governing body of the Western Cape

2003 Thabo Mbeki elected for second term as president

2005 Thabo Mbeki fires his deputy, Jacob Zuma, on corruption charges

2007 Thabo Mbeki ousted as ANC president in favour of Jacob Zuma

2008 Thabo Mbeki resigns as president of country

2009 Jacob Zuma elected as president

2012 Violence at Marikana platinum mine between striking workers, the police and the government; ANC celebrates its 100th anniversary

2013 Julius Malema founds EFF (Economic Freedom Fighters) in opposition to the ANC

2014 ANC wins elections and Jacob Zuma is elected president for a second term

2015 Julius Malema and EFF protest against the cost of Jacob Zuma's Nkandla home; Mmusi Maimane succeeds Helen Zille as leader of DA

Introduction

This book is an attempt to give a brief, general account of South African history from the very beginning to the present day. It is not aimed at professional historians but rather at all who have an interest in history – people from both South Africa and other countries.

Some time ago, a friend from the UK, Robin Turnbull, asked if there was something he could read about South Africa that was accurate (as accurate as one could hope to be in a subject as controversial and subjective as history) but readable, and not too long. There are some brilliant histories out there of specific time periods, people and places, but not for some time has there been a general history book that tries to cover it all.

I hope to some extent I have achieved that with this book. For me, writing it is the culmination of almost a lifetime of researching and teaching the broad spectrum of South African history, collecting stories, taking students on tours around the country and working with distinguished historians, whose specialist studies are acknowledged in the text. I have learnt so much from all of these people. It is also my sincere hope that in touching on some of the specific studies of other historians, the more serious reader will want to seek them out and read more.

The story of South Africa is one of struggle and the struggle has assumed many forms – from competition over land and resources in the early years to more sophisticated armed conflict in more recent times. Even when relative peace has prevailed, it has generally been an uneasy peace. Wars, rebellions, strikes and protests have divided our people and highlighted the

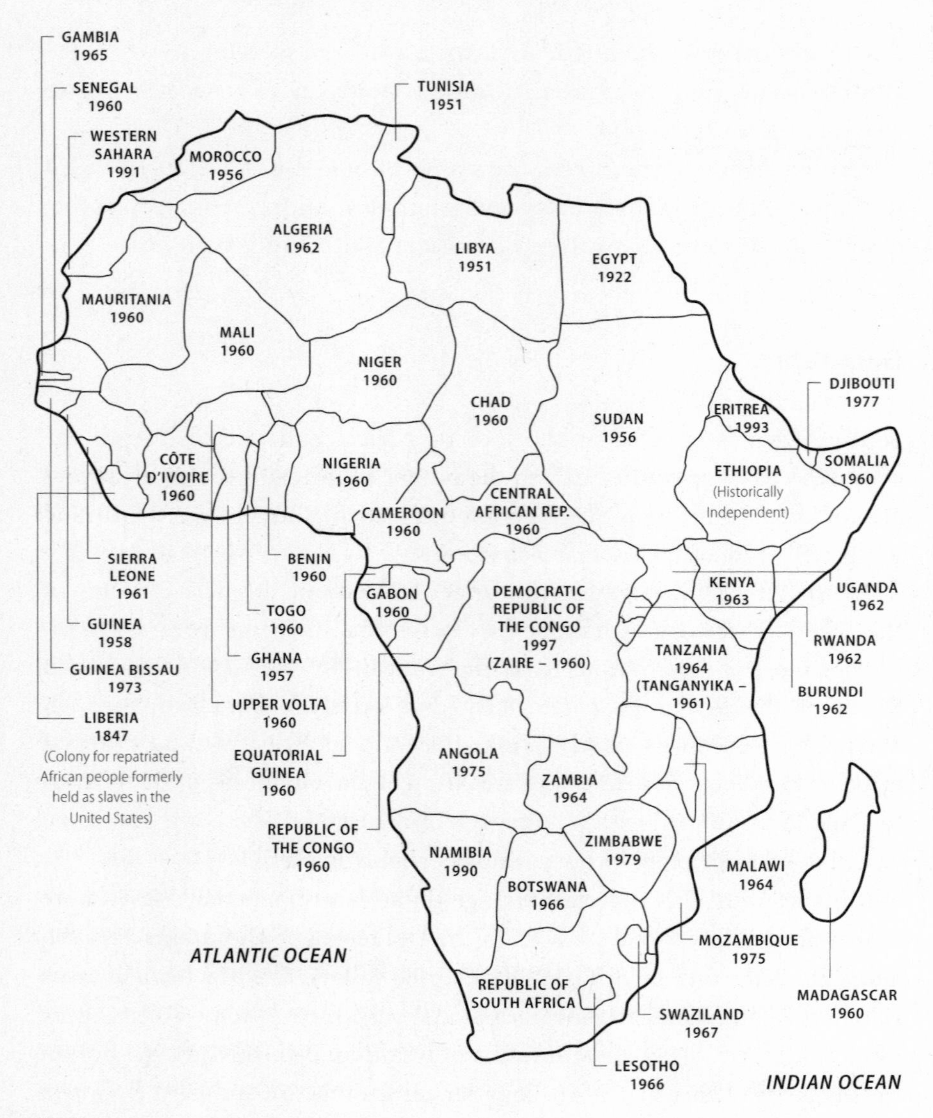

MAP 1

South Africa and its neighbouring countries. Most of these countries were colonised by European powers in what was referred to as 'the Scramble for Africa' between approximately 1881 and 1914. The dates when these countries achieved their independence are shown on the map. South Africa only achieved full democratic status in 1994. Before that it was ruled by a series of white minority governments. Our country shares common boundaries with Lesotho, Mozambique, Zimbabwe, Botswana and Namibia, and within our borders are the independent kingdoms of Swaziland and Lesotho.

differences between us;[1] South Africans are also of mixed ancestry, class and culture, a 'rainbow nation'[2] of diverse people who nevertheless have characteristics in common.

Mainly, this book tries to tell the stories of our people – deeply divided in the past, still striving for unity and solutions in the present. People who, despite the problems that still exist, consider South Africa their home.

Geography

South Africa is situated at the foot of Africa, and stretches from the southern coastline northwards to the border of Zimbabwe, a total surface area of almost 1 223 000 square kilometres, which is larger than the United Kingdom, France and Germany combined.

South Africa has a single time zone, and one of the best climates in the world. There are at least seven ecosystems, ranging from subtropical (for most of the country) to Mediterranean (in the Cape region), with the result that we have a particularly large variety of flora and fauna. In 2004, UNESCO (the United Nations Educational, Scientific and Cultural Organisation) declared the 60km area from Signal Hill north of Cape Town to Cape Point in the south a floristic World Heritage Site. Some species of vascular sap-bearing plants occur nowhere else on earth

Most of South Africa is a plateau ringed by an escarpment that rises to more than 3 000 metres above sea level in the Drakensberg Mountains between KwaZulu-Natal and Lesotho. We have fertile valleys, fine beaches and areas rich in precious stones and metals, but also vast tracts of semi-desert. Some of our cities are world class in terms of wealth and infrastructure, but on the outskirts of those cities are squatter camps that are among the poorest in the world. Barely an hour or two's drive from our cities are rural areas where amenities are few and poverty is rife, but there is also bushveld where wild animals roam freely in game reserves the size of small countries.

Johannesburg, together with its satellites, Randburg and Sandton, is South Africa's largest city. It is the youngest major city in the world and the only major city not built close to the sea, a river or another major source of

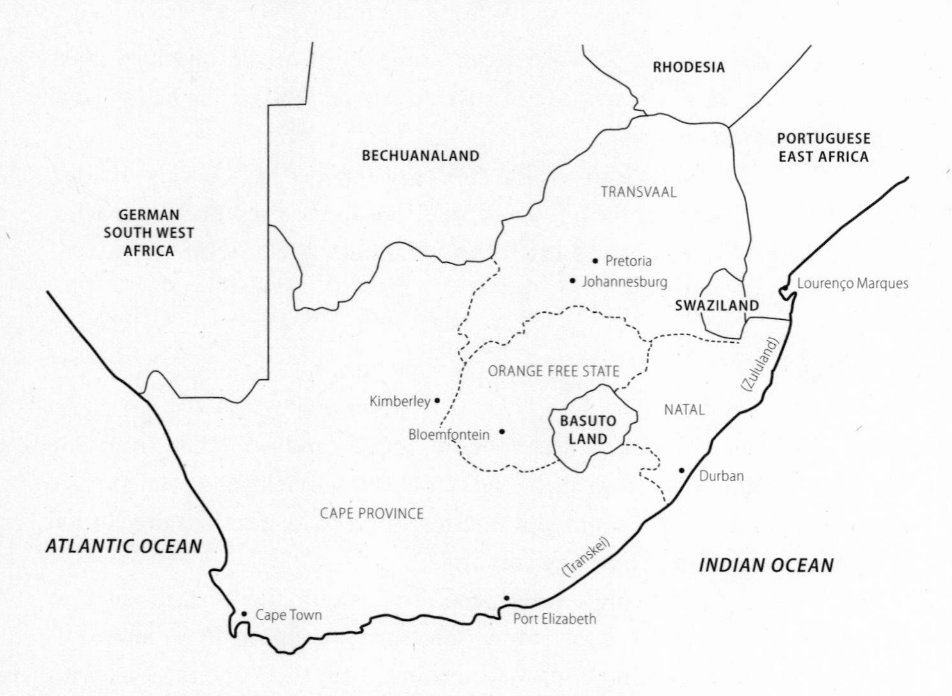

MAP 2 *South Africa in 1910, showing the four provinces of South Africa and their capitals. Swaziland and Basutoland were separate British Crown territories.*

water. The reason for its existence is the gold that was found there in 1886.

Early Johannesburg was a treeless place, where dust storms were common. Quick-growing trees (oaks, planes, bluegum and jacaranda) were planted because wood was needed for the mining industry. Today there are an estimated six million trees in Johannesburg's parks and gardens; in satellite pictures Johannesburg now looks like an urban jungle.[3]

Likewise the country's history is one of contrasts, contradictions and change. Even the concept of South Africa as a country is fairly new. Before 1910, the southern part of Africa consisted of a series of British colonies (the Cape and Natal), Afrikaner republics (the Orange Free State and the Transvaal, established by descendants of the early British and Dutch settlers), and black chiefdoms (Zulu, Xhosa, Sotho and others).

In 1910, these former colonies, republics and chiefdoms were brought together in the Union of South Africa under the British Crown, and the

MAP 3 *South Africa in 1994, showing the new nine provinces and their capitals.*

concept of a united 'South Africa' was born. A white-minority government was set up to rule the new Union. Four provinces were created: the Transvaal, Orange Free State, Cape Province and Natal. Two small areas – Basutoland[4] (now Lesotho[5]) and Swaziland[6] – remained apart as British Crown Colonies.

In 1994, South Africa became a democracy for the first time, and the concept of a 'new' South Africa was born. Nine provinces were created from the original four. These are Gauteng, North West, Mpumalanga, Limpopo, Free State, Western Cape, Eastern Cape, Northern Cape and KwaZulu-Natal, and each has its own legislature, premier and executive council. Having gained independence from Britain in 1966, Basutoland became the Kingdom of Lesotho, and Swaziland achieved independence and became the Kingdom of Swaziland in 1968. Swaziland and Lesotho are still separate, and both are monarchies.

Many towns, cities, buildings and roads in South Africa have had name changes, especially if their previous names were considered inappropriate or undesirable. These changes are shown in brackets in the text.

People

In August 2016, Statistics South Africa estimated that South Africa has a total population of 55.9 million people. The smallest province, Gauteng, had the biggest population, with 13.5 million people (about 24% of the total).[7] KwaZulu-Natal had the second-biggest population with 11 million (about 20%). The Northern Cape had the smallest population with 1.2 million people (about 2.2%). Available figures for the other provinces suggest that the Eastern Cape has approximately 6.5 million people, the Western Cape almost 6 million, Limpopo 5.5 million, Mpumalanga 4 million, North West 3.5 million and Free State 2.7 million.[8]

It is estimated that about 80% of our people are black,[9] 9.6% are white, almost 9% are coloured and 2.6% are of Asian descent (predominantly Indian and Chinese).

In the South African context, the term 'coloured' refers to mixed-race people: the descendants of the early inhabitants of the Cape (the Khoikhoi and San), slaves imported from Madagascar, Mozambique and Asia in the late 1700s, and interracial relationships between white, black and coloured people over a long period of time. People tend to see broad categories of black, white, coloured, Indian and Chinese when they refer to South African people, but these are not homogenous groups.

South Africa has 11 official languages, which is among the highest number in the world. They are English, Afrikaans (the language which evolved from the Dutch settlers in the 1700s), Ndebele, Northern Sotho (Pedi), Sotho, Swazi, Tswana (sometimes referred to as Western Sotho), Tsonga, Venda, Xhosa and Zulu.[10] Only Bolivia and India have more official languages.

The three languages most spoken at home are Zulu (23%), Xhosa (16%) and Afrikaans (13.5%). English only ranks fourth of the languages spoken at home (9.6%), but it is the language of business and commerce. In round figures, these percentages represent the fact that there are approximately

12 million Zulus, 8 million Xhosa, almost 7 million Afrikaners and almost 5 million English. The remaining official languages are spoken at home by between 5% and 9% of the population in each case.[11]

Coloured people constitute about 4.2 million of the population. They speak mainly Afrikaans, and the majority live in the Western Cape. Referring to his coloured heritage, former vice-chancellor of the University of the Free State, Professor Jonathan Jansen, says: 'The trouble with history is that you are part of it. I owe my very existence to black and white entanglements that gave me the name Jansen, a common surname in the Netherlands!'[12]

Indian South Africans constitute about 1.2 million of our population and are largely English speaking, although many also retain the languages of their ancestors. There are approximately 350 000 Chinese South Africans.

Although South Africa has been a democracy under a single government since 1994, tax payers' money is still used to pay ten African kings, a 'Rain Queen',[13] hundreds of chiefs and thousands of headmen who enact laws that run parallel to the official laws of the land.[14] South Africa is also one of the most unequal societies in the world. There is an enormous gap between the haves and the have-nots, the legacy of a succession of white-minority governments whose policies of segregation and apartheid[15] left the majority of people disadvantaged. Regrettably, even since the fall of the old systems, there has not been much narrowing of the gap between the rich and the poor, and corruption abounds.

Refugees from war-torn countries elsewhere in Africa have found refuge in South Africa, where there are large numbers of immigrants, especially those from neighbouring Zimbabwe. This is not always tolerated by locals, who see outsiders as taking away jobs. In 2008 and again in 2015 these concerns led to xenophobic attacks and some brutal crimes.

Since the early 1990s, South Africans of all races can legally work together, live together and socialise in a way they were denied from doing in the past. Despite many stories of friendship and cooperation, divisions still run deep, and people sometimes struggle to find common ground. We cannot yet say that we have a single story.

Note from the author

In 1955, historian Leo Marquard wrote a book entitled *The Story of South Africa*, which was reprinted several times until 1973. Since then, much has changed in the country, not least that after many years of white-minority rule there is now a majority government that is essentially black.

There is a saying: New politics, new history. South African history has been rewritten many times since the 1980s. Evidence has increasingly been collected about previously neglected 'black' stories; new interpretations are being offered on old topics, and more points of view are being considered. In this book, questions are asked about how some groups have been able to dominate others, and why some societies have been able to resist domination whereas others have not. The book traces the long road to democracy, along with the roles of the various players.

Any attempt to write a study of this kind is of course bound by the needs and perceptions of the time. There is more than one story that can be told about South Africa, and this story will certainly change again. The story in this book may be of interest to anyone concerned with class and racial tensions in a diverse society. It is not unlike the stories of many other countries, although solutions have been sought in ways peculiar to South Africa.

By necessity, this story also has to be part conjecture, especially for South Africa's early history, because it was not until the 19th century that we have substantive written records. Until fairly recent times, black history was recorded by men whose special job it was to remember and recount their tribe's traditions and thereby settle disputes about lineages, succession and other issues. Sadly, this oral tradition was not generally considered in early writings by whites.

In the last forty years or more, the use of archaeological, paleo-anthropological, anthropological, pictorial, linguistic, oral, aerial and other sources – both written and not – has enabled us to achieve a much more balanced version of the past. There is still, however, a paucity of sources of black history and that from other racial groups. It should also be noted that much of our early recorded history was dominated by white men. Since the 1980s, historians have tried to integrate gender and race for a more complete picture, but the divisions are still apparent in the way much of this book is structured.

We will never know the stories of all of South Africa's people, especially the disadvantaged and the rural poor. At best, we must be aware of how much we do not and cannot know.

CHAPTER 1

How it all began

Early humans

The story of South Africa may be as old as that of man himself. Archaeological research suggests that southern Africa may well have been the birthplace of the first hominids (humanlike creatures) millions of years ago. The conditions in Africa are generally favourable: the continent comprises almost a quarter of the earth's habitable land surface, and almost three quarters of that lies between the Tropics of Cancer and Capricorn, a large, warm area conducive to evolutionary change.

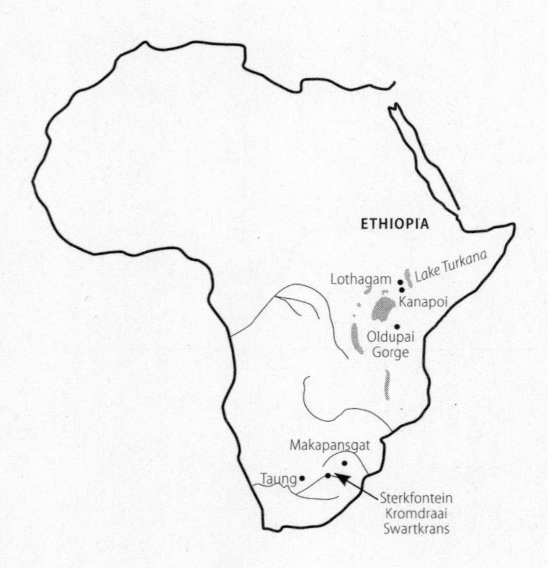

MAP 4 *Some of Africa's early hominid sites.*

KEY

Lothagam and Kanapoi: located south-west of Lake Turkana in northern Kenya

Lake Turkana: formerly known as Lake Rudolf; located in the Kenyan Rift Valley

Oldupai Gorge: located in Tanzania

Makapansgat: located north-east of Mokopane (formerly Potgietersrus) in Limpopo

Sterkfontein, Kromdraai, Swartkrans, Gladysvale: located in the Muldersdrift area close to Krugersdorp, about 40-50km north-west of Johannesburg

Taung: small town located north of Kimberley in the North West

Hominid fossils are extremely rare. There are only a few places on earth where they have been found. Among them are Ethiopia in east Africa, where the famous fossils dubbed 'Lucy' and 'Ardi' were discovered, and South Africa. Some of the oldest and most important hominid sites in the world have been found in caves at Sterkfontein, Swartkrans, Kromdraai and Gladysvale, all about 40 to 50 kilometres from Johannesburg, and Makapansgat, about 22 kilometres north-east of Mokopane (formerly Potgietersrus) in Limpopo. Hominids moved around in these areas some 3 million years ago.

The first hominid fossil discovery of major significance took place in 1924, when the almost complete remains of a skull estimated to be between 2 and 3 million years old were found in a limestone quarry near Taung, north of Kimberley in North West. The word 'tau' means 'place of the lion' and was named after Tau, chief of the Tswana-speaking BaTaung tribe.

The skull was that of a child creature from the transition period when the hominid line split between man and ape. It had a full set of small canine teeth, quite unlike those of apes. The brain cavity was small, but the base of

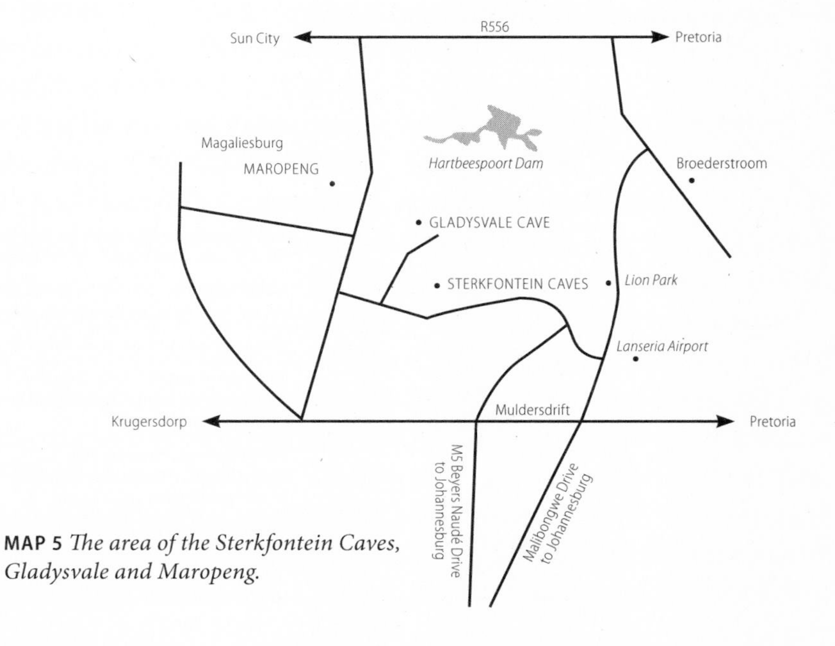

MAP 5 *The area of the Sterkfontein Caves, Gladysvale and Maropeng.*

the cranium showed that the head must have been fairly well balanced on a virtually upright spine. It was undoubtedly a species intermediate between apes and man, the 'missing link'[1] that had eluded scientists from all over the world. Professor Raymond Dart of the University of the Witwatersrand, who examined the skull, named it A*ustralopithecus africanus*, although it has come to be called simply the 'Taung Child'. The discovery has been heralded as one of the 20 most important scientific discoveries of the 20th century.

Other significant finds followed, including the discovery in 1947 of another *Australopithecus africanus* skull – this time an adult – at Sterkfontein. The skull was almost perfectly preserved and came to be known as Mrs Ples. Archaeologists then began to concentrate their efforts on the caves nearby, and in 1994 a hominid skeleton estimated to be at least 3.5 million years old was found. The significant discovery was made by Professor Ron Clarke, assisted by Stephen Motsumi and Nkwane Molefe of the University of the Witwatersrand. The skeleton had a complete hand, arm and leg, as well as a complete set of adult teeth. The big toe still diverged markedly from the other toes and was capable of the grasping movements of apes, but it also showed features of the human foot and was suitable for two-legged gait. Dubbed 'Little Foot', this human creature would have walked upright and spent a lot of time in trees. The foot bones are the oldest and most complete set from a member of the *Australopithecus* hominid family ever found.

The skeleton has never been completely excavated, and parts of it are still entrapped in the Sterkfontein Caves. When interviewed about his work, Professor Clarke explained that in palaeontology, it takes years to excavate something as important as this, and that no one knows what may still lie hidden in the rocks at this and other sites.[2]

At the time that Little Foot died, the Sterkfontein Caves would have been in the middle of a tropical forest with huge trees. Bones fossilised by lime in the caves have been found of lion-sized sabre-toothed cats, large monkeys, and long-legged hunting hyenas. Little Foot might have fallen to its death in these caves while trying to escape from these predators. For millions of years it lay there, becoming fossilised as time passed. Now it is in the process of being brought into our modern world.[3]

In 1999, the area around the Sterkfontein Caves was declared a World

Heritage Site and became referred to as the Cradle of Humankind. In December 2005, a state-of-the-art visitors' centre called Maropeng was opened on the site, where visitors can trace the story of humankind and see models of how their ancestors looked. In Tswana, the main indigenous language in this part of South Africa, the word '*maropeng*' means 'returning to the place of origin'.

In April 2010, palaeoanthropologist Professor Lee Berger and his son, Matthew, found another fossil in the Sterkfontein Caves area, which they named *Australopithecus sediba*, and which they believe may be a direct ancestor of *Homo erectus*. They estimate it would have been about 1.3 metres tall. Five years later, in September 2015, another dramatic announcement was made. In a remote, previously hidden chamber at Sterkfontein, a significantly large number of fossils had been found of a previously unknown branch of the human tree. At least 15 individuals were identified, ranging in age from newborn, to toddler, to adult. The fact that they were all found together – and that there were no signs of claw marks, bites or the nearby presence of predators or scavengers – suggested that this was a burial chamber, and that this branch of hominids had buried their dead.

Professor Berger and a team of scientists from Wits University and the National Geographic society had spent two years working in what was described as some of the most difficult and dangerous conditions ever encountered in the search for human origins. The six main excavators had to be small enough to crawl through a 17.5 centimetre crack in a rock into the cave chamber where the fossil remains were found. The adult hominids were small (about 1.5 metres tall), thin creatures who walked on two legs with humanlike size 7 feet, and humanlike hands. They have been named *Homo naledi*, which means 'star' in the Sotho language.[4]

Professor Francis Thackeray of the Evolutionary Studies Institute at Wits University debates the fact that the *Homo naledi* fossils were in a hidden burial chamber. He says there is evidence of lichen on the bones, which could not have grown without daylight, and suggests that maybe a family of these hominids was in the cave when the roof collapsed. Professor Berger's theory nevertheless remains firm, and the discovery has been heralded as a great moment for science because it indicates the level of human consciousness that had been reached: the concept of mortality. Rituals surrounding death are one of the characteristics that distinguish humans from other animals. The news that this branch of hominids had buried their dead captured human imagination all over the world and in April 2016 Professor Berger was named one of *Time Magazine*'s 100 most influential people of the year. Both Professor Thackeray and Professor Berger have enormous respect for each other, despite their differing opinions.[5]

It has been speculated that it is not just the transitional stage in the evolution to modern man but also the final stage – that of *Homo sapiens* – that originated in South Africa and other parts of the African continent about 100 000 years ago. Fossil finds at Border Cave at Ingwavuma on the Swaziland border in KwaZulu-Natal, at Fish Hoek in the Western Cape and at the Springbok Flats near Naboomspruit (near the borders of Limpopo and North West) are estimated to be about 100 000 years old, several thousands of years older than examples of *Homo sapiens* of a similar evolutionary stage found in Europe and Asia.

There can be no hard-and-fast theories about the exact location of the origins of man, but it is nevertheless apparent that South Africa's human history has its origins millions of years ago, and there is a case for saying that the story of South Africa should begin with the hominids. It is thought that the first human creatures in the southern part of Africa practised a primitive form of hunting and gathering, an evolutionary stage South Africa has in common with the rest of the world. At some point in time, at least a few hundred thousand years ago, these human creatures started using crude stone tools, heralding what is still regularly referred to as the Stone Age.

Hunter-gatherers: the San (Bushmen)

About 10 000 years ago a Later Stone Age period in Africa is discernible by the more sophisticated use of stone, bone and ivory tools and ornaments. About 8 000 years ago, some of these Later Stone Age people migrated into southern Africa from areas further north, probably via what is now

Botswana. These were the ancestors of what are called in South Africa the San or Bushmen people. They shared the same genetic origins as the Khoikhoi and Bantu-speaking groups who came later.

South Africa has no navigable waterways, but river valleys could have supported small dispersed populations of these hunter-gatherers. There was a variety of edible plants in most areas and the land teemed with game: elephant, rhinoceros, hippopotamus, buffalo, lion, leopard, giraffe, zebra, quagga (an extinct South African zebra) and numerous species of antelope and smaller game. Rainfall varies considerably from region to region, with more rain falling on the east coast than the west due to oceanic influences, which is why there was traditionally more settlement towards the east.

South Africa was widely inhabited by San people during the Later Stone Age. They were small in stature, barely 1.5 metres, and led a nomadic existence as hunter-gatherers and sometimes fishermen, depending on the area. They were also painters and engravers of both real and abstract pictures. The ability to think in the abstract suggests a society far less one-dimensional than previously considered. They painted both the animals they hunted and the rituals associated with them. The eland was particularly important because the San believed that the eland gave up its strength to the hunter when it was killed. San medicine men, or shamans, would hallucinate and put themselves into a state of trance during their rituals. Some of the most beautiful examples of San art can be seen on rock faces and cave walls in the Soutpansberg and the Drakensberg Mountains. They give the impression that eland, elephant and other animals were once prolific in these areas.

When the Khoikhoi herders and later the crop farmers started to migrate into South Africa, the land was also able to support domesticated animals, although tsetse flies caused disease among livestock, especially in the subtropical north east. This limited where herders could settle.

The early immigrants to South Africa were all from within Africa; the country did not attract immigrants from beyond Africa until much later. This may have been because ocean currents impeded easy access by sea, and the coastline has few natural harbours. The Cape was subject to gale-force winds, and the coast in the area around what is now Durban was hindered by a shallow bar, which has only been dredged using modern technology.

As far as we know, it was not until the late 15th century that the Portuguese began their exploratory sea voyages down the west coast of Africa and around the Cape. The Dutch and then the French and the English followed suit in the following century. By the mid-17th century, some of these European explorers were starting to settle in the Cape. One effect of white immigration and subsequent migration into the interior of the country was that, by the end of the 19th century, much of the wildlife had been shot out by hunters who now used guns. Some species, like the quagga, were completely lost in the process.

When farmers started to arrive, the San lost access to a good deal of land, and the environment began to change. The San painted pictures about this too, and some 19th-century pictures of men on horseback with guns, and trains on railway tracks, can be described as South Africa's first protest art. Today only a few San remain in the Kalahari Desert in the Northern Cape province, and in arid regions of Botswana, northern Namibia and southern Angola. Two of these groups are the Gwi and the !Kung.

The guns and technology white settlers brought with them were previously unknown to the indigenous people, and they could offer little resistance to it. Some historians have gone so far as to see the arrival of white settlers as the start of a 'gun society' in South Africa,[6] although this suggests that most people owned guns, which was not the case. Nevertheless the arrival of guns and Western technology would change everything, and have important repercussions on economy, society and politics in the years to come.

CHAPTER 2

Early settlers from about 1000 BC to AD 1500

The Khoikhoi: herders and pastoralists

It was probably around the time of the birth of Christ, some two to three thousand years ago, that early hunter-gatherer societies began to make contact with pastoral Khoikhoi people. Like the San, the Khoikhoi are also believed to have come from the region of Botswana, through what is now western Zimbabwe, into southern Africa and then towards the Cape in search of good grazing lands for their animals. The Khoikhoi hunted and gathered as the need arose, but they also kept herds of domesticated animals, mainly sheep. It is thought that they only later acquired cattle, and that cattle then became their prime source of wealth. The fact that the Khoikhoi had domesticated animals was important: another stage in the evolutionary process. It was the Khoikhoi who gave the name 'San'[1] to the hunter-gatherers, although when the Dutch settlers arrived, they called them 'Bushmen' or 'men from the bush'.

It was also the Khoikhoi people that the first Dutch settlers met on the shores of Table Bay in the Cape in the mid-17th century. The Dutch called them 'Hottentots', a word that sounded like the way they spoke. The term is now considered derogatory, and 'Khoikhoi', which meant 'men of men' in the KhoiKhoi language, is preferred.

The Khoikhoi were genetically similar to the San, but taller. They lived in groups under chiefs, each with his own grazing territory, and their society was loosely knit. They had a fluid economy – it was based on stock wealth, which was easily lost both to cattle diseases and to trade with the Dutch, who often gave worthless trinkets, mirrors and alcohol in exchange for Khoikhoi cattle.

Khoikhoi groups who lost their cattle reverted to hunting and gathering, and the term 'Khoisan' refers to people whose identity became blurred. As Dutch expansion continued, the Khoikhoi and the San were gradually displaced and their societies began to break down. Loss of cattle to the Dutch was a major factor in the decline of the Khoikhoi. Allegiances between the Dutch and some groups of Khoikhoi at war with one another also shifted the balance of power and accelerated their decline. By the late 17th century, large numbers of Khoikhoi people had resorted to working for the Dutch, and through the 18th century, many would succumb to diseases such as smallpox, which had been introduced by the newcomers and to which the indigenous Khoikhoi had no resistance. In this respect the South African story is similar to those of the Americas and Australasia.

By the mid-18th century, despite Khoikhoi-instigated guerrilla resistance in the late 1730s and from the 1770s to about 1800, Khoikhoi society had virtually disintegrated. Today there are no survivors of this early herding people, although the Griqua and the coloured community are descended from them and other interracial relationships over a long period of time.

The Khoikhoi people were largely neglected in the histories written during the apartheid years, when most writing was from a Eurocentric point of view. In recent years, some of their stories have emerged thanks to the work of people like Mansell Upham, human rights lawyer and descendant of a Khoikhoi woman called Krotoa (Eva) – one of the first known 'black' characters in South African history.

In the mid-17th century, Eva learnt to speak both Dutch and Portuguese and was employed as an interpreter by Jan van Riebeeck, founder of the Dutch settlement at the Cape. She moved regularly between the Dutch and her own people, who lived a distance away, exchanging her Western clothes for Khoikhoi skins each time she went home. It was unusual for a woman of any race to work with men at that time, and Eva also had rare status among her own people because she was permitted to ride an ox. Perhaps because of the contradictions of her life, she developed a drinking problem and died in 1674 at the age of 32. In another apparent contradiction, she was given a proper burial (usually denied to black people at the time) at the Castle in Cape Town because she had become a Christian.

Another interesting character in our early history was a Khoikhoi man known as Doman. He was sent to Batavia to learn Dutch and must have played an important role as an interpreter for the Dutch at the Cape. He was scornful of Eva, whom he felt was allowing herself to become too much like the Dutch. In 1659, after a dispute over cattle, he led a Khoikhoi group against the Dutch in what became known as the First Khoikhoi-Dutch War. To protect themselves and keep the Khoikhoi out, the Dutch then built a series of fortified fences along the Liesbeeck River and an almond hedge in what is now Kirstenbosch National Botanical Gardens.[2] These fences and hedges restricted Khoikhoi movement and access to grazing land.

Another Khoikhoi woman, Sarah (Saartjie) Bartman, achieved fame in London and Paris – but for tragic reasons. In 1810, as a young woman, she was taken to England from the Cape by a ship's doctor, William Dunlop, who persuaded Sarah that she could make a fortune letting foreigners look at her body. To European eyes, her buttocks seemed unusually large and her exaggerated female form was the stuff of fetish. She subsequently went 'on show' in Piccadilly, where she was paraded around on a stage in scant clothing. In 1814 Sarah was sent to Paris, where she was given to a travelling circus featuring wild animals. During her lifetime her body was analysed by scientists, including Georges Cuvier, surgeon to Napoleon Bonaparte, and used as the basis for pseudo-scientific papers about the superiority of the white race.

After she died in 1815, parts of Sarah's body were preserved and displayed for more than 150 years at the Musée de l'Homme (Museum of Mankind) in Paris. Her remains were finally returned to South Africa, and on Women's Day, 9 August 2002, she was given an emotional re-burial in her homeland in a remote part of the Eastern Cape. Her grave has since been declared a national monument.

The Bantu-speaking people: cultivators and metal workers

Between AD 300 and 900, and possibly earlier, people who were crop farmers as well as herders had moved into South Africa. Their origin is uncertain, but it is thought they came from east and central Africa. They spoke languages that linguists have identified as related to the Bantu languages,[3] which are distinct from San and Khoikhoi languages, although some of the characteristic 'click' sounds of the San languages later found their way into both the Khoikhoi and the Bantu languages.[4] These farming people had a darker skin tone than the Khoikhoi and the San, and will henceforth simply be referred to as farmers.[5]

Cultivation was the next stage in the evolutionary process which South Africa has in common with the rest of the world. The farmers' knowledge of cultivation and herding meant that they lived in more settled communities and were not dependent on hunting and gathering. Interestingly, these farmers had little art compared to the San, although they did fire clay pots and decorate them with distinctive designs. Their political and social organisations were more complex than those of the San, and their economies more varied. Some people mined metals like iron, copper, tin and gold, and networks of trade developed, sometimes across considerable distances.

This time period is sometimes referred to as the South African Iron Age, and after approximately AD 1000 as the Late Iron Age, when more sophisticated states developed.

Mapungubwe and Thulamela: South Africa's first states

Several Late Iron Age settlements have been found, the two most important being Mapungubwe and Thulamela in northern Limpopo. Mapungubwe is older than Thulamela, but both were large, thriving communities with a range of activities.

Mapungubwe is situated just two kilometres south of the Limpopo River, which forms the border between South Africa and Zimbabwe. The site was discovered in 1933 and soon thereafter researched by archaeologists, who dated it at approximately AD 1000–1290. The area was archaeologically investigated between 1934 and 1940, but excavations were interrupted by World War II. Research continued sporadically in the 1950s, and then again from the 1960s to the late 1990s, when extensive excavations resumed.[6]

Mapungubwe is estimated to have supported a population of some 10 000 people over an area probably as large as modern-day Swaziland. It was South Africa's first major state.

Burial sites containing gold beads, bracelets and tiny carved wooden animals covered in thin gold foil were found at the top of a hill, together with a number of gold nails used to attach the gold foil to the carvings. The absence of soldering[7] – a process fairly well known in Europe at the time – suggests that this beautiful gold jewellery was made by local black people, and not people from other countries as was once suggested.

Coloured glass beads from India, Persia (modern-day Iran), Egypt and Arabia (now Saudi Arabia) were also found at the site, indicating widespread international trade. It is thought that the beads became a kind of currency.

There was activity at Mapungubwe for about 200 years[8] and then, sometime in the 13th century, probably because resources in the area had been exhausted, there was a political shift in power. The capital moved northwards across the Limpopo River to the site known today as Great Zimbabwe. About 200 years later the capital moved again: southwards, back across the Limpopo, to a third site we now know as Thulamela, although some people continued to live at Great Zimbabwe. It was only in the 1990s that Thulamela was discovered by archaeologists led by Sidney Miller.

Similar artefacts were found at Mapungubwe, Great Zimbabwe and Thulamela, suggesting it was descendants of the same people at all three sites: the ancestors of the present-day Venda in Limpopo and the Shona in Zimbabwe. This activity went on for over 600 years.

At Thulamela, found artefacts included Zimbabwe-type pottery, cowrie shells from the east coast, amulets[9] made of bone, a piece of Chinese porcelain from the Ming dynasty, an iron gong similar to those found in West Africa, and a ceramic crucible with drops of smelted gold[10] still attached to it. This is the only evidence of gold smelting in South Africa to date, and indicates advanced technological skill at least 500 years ago.

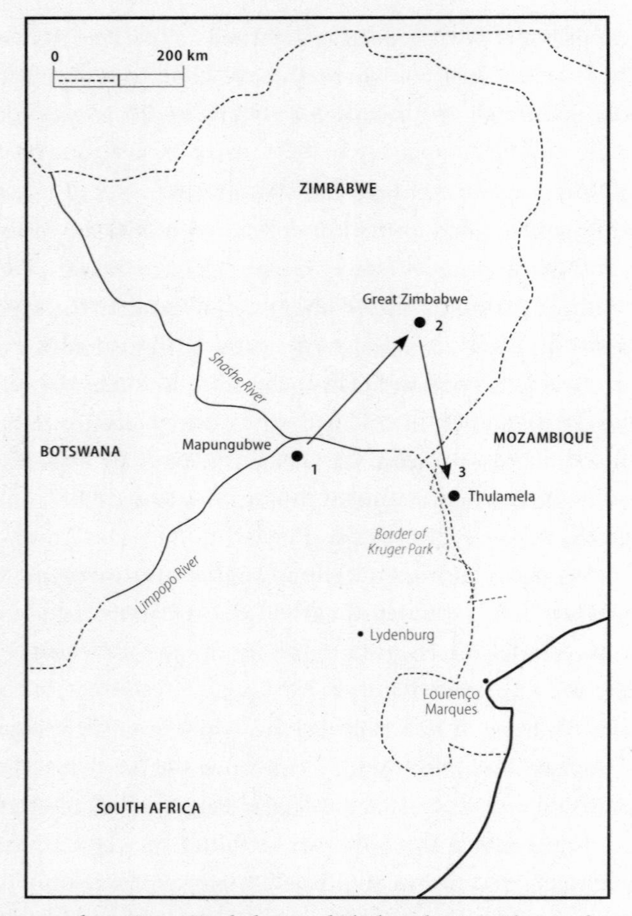

MAP 6 *The Mapungubwe, Great Zimbabwe and Thulamela sites. The numbers 1, 2 and 3 show how each place in turn became the capital over a period of 600 years. The map also shows the point where the Shashe and Limpopo rivers come together and form the boundaries of three countries, Zimbabwe, Botswana and South Africa.*

In July 1996, a particularly significant find was made at Thulamela when a grave thought to be that of a queen was found intact. She had been buried facing north an estimated 450 years before, and her age at death was about 40 years. Her teeth were in excellent condition, suggesting a good diet. The queen was wearing two gold bracelets, one of solid gold, the other a double strand of gold beads, some 291 small gold beads in all. When the dirt of centuries was scraped away, the gold gleamed as brightly as it would have done all those years before – whereas copper and iron artefacts rust and oxidise, gold is durable and retains its colour, which is why it has always been valuable.

The local Venda people named her Queen Losha because they said her posture, with hands folded under her cheek, resembled the *losha*, a gesture of respect, and that she was probably facing her husband's grave. They were correct: the king's grave was found about a month later. The king had been buried in a sitting position, also facing north, with his hands crossed over his chest, and various gold and other artefacts had been buried with him. The archaeologists named him King Ingwe, which means 'leopard king', because on the day they found his grave, a leopard had been waiting for them on their return to their vehicle, and more leopards were subsequently seen in the area.

The local Venda community were consulted and involved throughout the project. They asked that after carbon dating and DNA tests had been completed, the bodies be reburied at the site, and that no full photographs of the skeletons be published.

Traditional Shona and Venda still share similar beliefs about crocodiles and rulers. According to the Venda, 'the crocodile does not leave its pool' – this refers to the concept of sacred leadership. It is believed that the first man emerged from a sacred pool of water, much as a crocodile does from a river. The chief is believed to be directly linked to this person. It was also thought that crocodiles could communicate with ancestors from the spirit world, which was under the water. Traditional Venda chiefs swallowed pebbles taken from a crocodile's stomach to link with this spirit world. The crocodile motif is seen on wooden doors, drums and stone walls at sites in both Zimbabwe and Limpopo.

At both Great Zimbabwe and Thulamela there are oval-shaped, dry-stone walled[11] enclosures, which are thought to have been built to accommodate and protect the ruling family, who generally lived in a high place. The ruins of these enclosures can still be seen at both sites. Ordinary people lived in the surrounding hills and the valleys below, and rarely saw their chief. Archaeologist Sidney Miller says the layout at Thulamela suggests that the king's enclosure lay at the northernmost extremity of the site, above the cliffs. The enclosure would have protected him from public view.[12] In the 1500s, a Dominican priest called João dos Santos described people at Mutapa, in the north-eastern part of Zimbabwe, crawling up the hill on their stomachs to see their leader. They would address their chief in a prone position and crawl back down again, never appearing higher than him. It is thought that this probably also happened at Thulamela.

The ruins suggest that at one time about 2 000 people lived at Thulamela,[13] and it is evident that both economy and society were quite complex. There were different living and burial arrangements for different people, and there is evidence of an education system. At both Great Zimbabwe and Thulamela, platforms have been found that might have been used as stages. Dolls doing different types of work and in various positions of the sex act suggest that instruction was given to young people to prepare them for adulthood. Because similar dolls have been found at both Great Zimbabwe and Thulamela, it is possible that the two societies might even have exchanged their young people as a kind of 'finishing school'.

There are other sites similar to Thulamela in Limpopo. The discovery of the Machemma and Makahane ruins provides evidence that black people were living in large settled communities as early as the 11th century, and trading as far afield as West Africa, India and China. It dispels the myth perpetuated in past history books that white settlers in South Africa arrived in a land where nothing much had been happening. It is also clear that it was not just white people who connected South Africa with the rest of the world.

It is a mystery why this flourishing network suddenly came to an end. Arabs had operated as middlemen for traders from Asia, bringing to black people in the interior glass beads and other goods of interest. The decline of Thulamela corresponds with the rounding of the Cape by the Portuguese navigators Bartholomew Dias and Vasco da Gama in the late 15th century. The arrival of the Portuguese seems to have spelt doom for the existing trade: evidence of Portuguese forts along the east African coast suggests that the Arabs did not give in easily, but were ultimately usurped.

It also seems possible that the people of Thulamela did not much like the

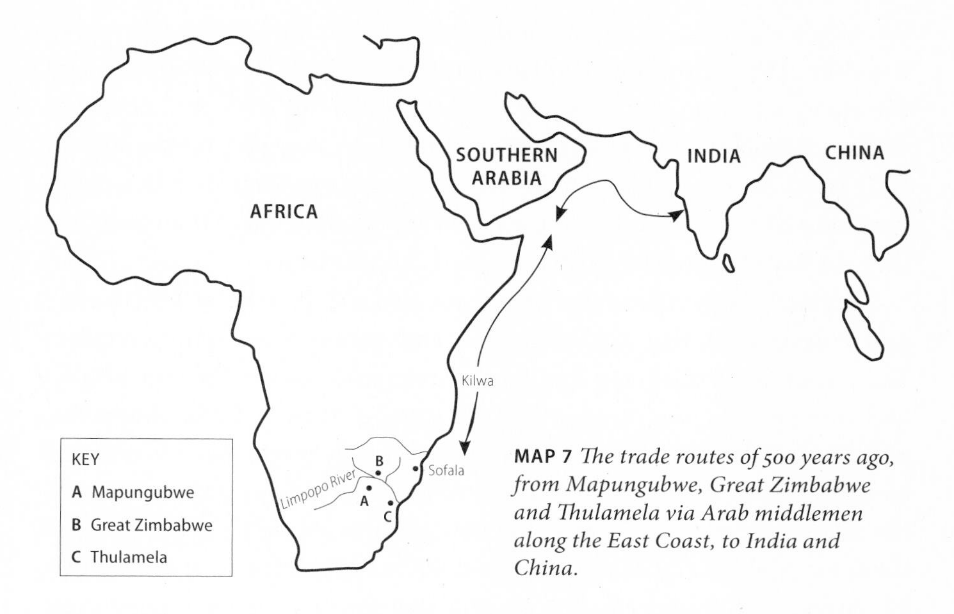

MAP 7 *The trade routes of 500 years ago, from Mapungubwe, Great Zimbabwe and Thulamela via Arab middlemen along the East Coast, to India and China.*

goods the Portuguese had to offer.[14] And once trade no longer flourished, the demise of places like Thulamela was inevitable.

There is similar mystery surrounding early mining sites that came to a sudden end. At about the same time as Thulamela (AD 1500), tin was mined and smelted in the area that in 1908 became the town of Rooiberg, about 60 kilometres west of the modern town of Bela-Bela (formerly Warmbaths) in the Waterberg district of Limpopo. There is also evidence that copper was mined at Musina (formerly Messina) in Limpopo possibly as early as the 8th century, as well as at Phalaborwa in the Mopani district of Limpopo a century or two later. One site at Phalaborwa yielded a series of dates ranging from AD 960 to AD 1130, and provided evidence of wide trading networks between some local communities and Zimbabwe further north. Copper was a much sought after trade item for jewellery, tools and other objects thought to be associated with ceremonial occasions. It was also sometimes combined with tin to make bronze tools that were superior to those made of iron.[15] Trade in these items appears to have taken place spasmodically however, and then, other than a few isolated examples, to have come to an abrupt end. It is not clear why.

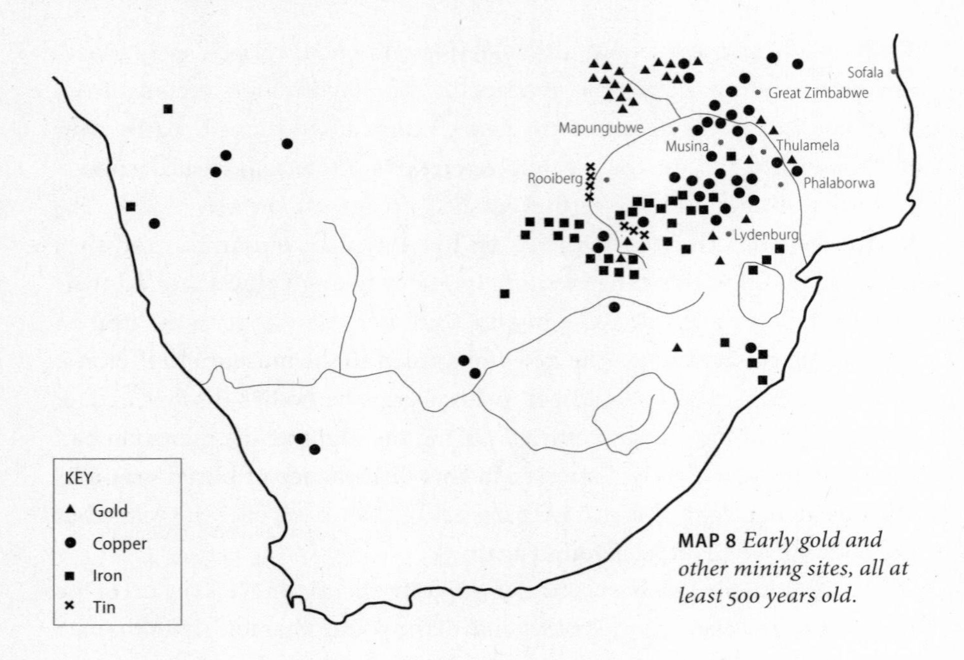

MAP 8 *Early gold and other mining sites, all at least 500 years old.*

At Rooiberg early mine shafts have been found which had been carefully filled in and covered over. In the 1820s and 1830s, early white travellers in the interior – including the missionary David Livingstone, the Voortrekker leader Louis Tregardt (Trichardt), and various officials of the Dutch East India Company trading at Lourenço Marques (today's Maputo) – referred in their journals to tin, or '*intoffe*' as the black people called it, but added that the 'natives' were secretive about where they obtained it. Louis Tregardt (Trichardt) recorded in 1838 that he had bought a 40-pound piece of tin in exchange for a sheep, and that he thought the tin would be useful for making bullets.[16] But in 1904, when geologists working in the area again found evidence of tin, the local black people seemed ignorant of its presence and neither, by then, did their oral traditions refer to it.

The metallurgy of tin extraction is regarded as particularly difficult, but early records indicate that not only were black people producing fairly pure tin, they were also smelting it with copper. Missionaries David Livingstone and Robert Moffat described Tswana men smelting copper and tin together in small crucibles to make bronze. Their travel records suggest they were in the Rooiberg area at the time, although this cannot be precisely ascertained.

An interesting story that appears in old handwritten records from Rooiberg is that in 1911, unusually heavy rains caused a small nearby river to burst its banks. In the cleanup operations afterwards, black workers from the mine found two bodies washed up against the river bank. The bodies were described as wrapped up like Egyptian mummies, and they had medallions with strange writing (possibly hieroglyphics) around their necks. Many people saw these bodies.[17] Runners were sent to the nearest town of Warmbaths to get the news forwarded to the museum in Pretoria. But before any experts could get to Rooiberg, the bodies disappeared. It is thought that they were re-buried during the night as the men who had found them were clearly distressed at this disturbance of burial grounds. Various archaeological digs have been held in Rooiberg over the years, but the bodies have never been found again.

The tin at Rooiberg has a particular impurity, nickel, which is typical of the tin in bronze artefacts found in the tomb of the young pharaoh Tutankhamen in Luxor, Egypt. This might have suggested that Rooiberg could have been the source, except that the time frame does not bear this out. Early tin mining at Rooiberg appears to have taken place in about AD 1500, which is 2 500 years too late for the pharaohs. Maybe more evidence will come to light.

Mining clearly has deep roots in this country. The mines at Rooiberg were re-opened in 1908 and then closed again when the price of tin collapsed in 1989. In April 2014, it was announced that the mines would possibly open again, or that the old mine dumps would be re-worked in an effort to recover more tin, but that negotiations would take some time.[18] Copper is also still mined in the some of the same areas as the early mines, and so is iron. The early miners did not however discover the Witwatersrand main gold reef or other main resources of modern times.

Settlement patterns after AD 1500

By the 1500s, black farmers had become the dominant occupants of the land, and by the 18th century, significant polities had begun to emerge.

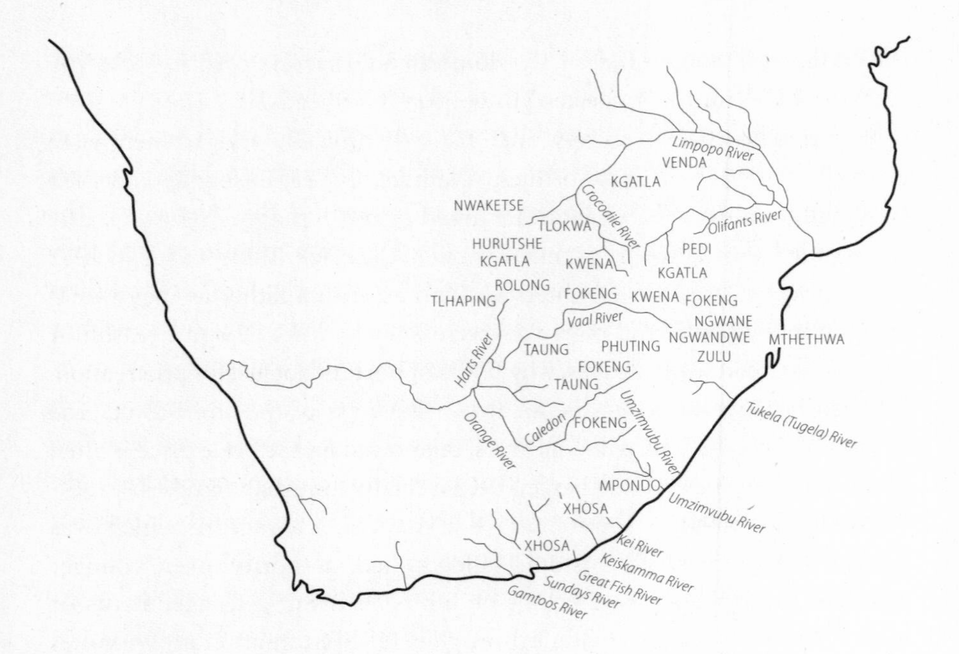

MAP 9 *The distribution of Bantu-speaking peoples by the early 1800s. Note how settlement favoured the east because of the better rainfall.*

In the interior of South Africa, most chiefdoms were Sotho-Tswana; further north they were Venda, and on the eastern side (between the Indian Ocean coast and the Drakensberg Mountains) they were Nguni: the Xhosa in the eastern Cape area and the Zulu in the area of KwaZulu-Natal. These were fairly fluid societies, with many divisions within them, and varying relationships with each other and the Khoikhoi and San communities.

A typical Nguni chiefdom was made up of several homesteads, an arrangement in which a man lived with his wives and children and other unmarried members of the family. A leader or chief would allocate the land – there was no individual ownership. This practice continues in some rural areas today.

Unlike the Khokhoi and the San, both of whom moved around, the houses of the farmers were permanent structures built from materials in the environment. In a typical homestead, men cleared the land and herded the cattle, and women did all the domestic and farming work, including carrying water for the homestead in pots on their heads.

Traditional African society was male-dominated, and women were generally under the control of men – fathers, uncles, husbands and then sons – all their lives. Marriage was marked by the exchange of gifts, usually cattle from the bridegroom's family to that of the bride. This is called lobola[19] (bride price). Attractive daughters were an asset to a father as they would bring in more lobola, and marriages were often arranged for this reason. A wealthy man had several wives, which was important not just for procreation, but also because women were an important part of the work force. The custom of paying lobola still continues, but nowadays the bride price is often calculated in money rather than cattle, especially for urban families.

Traditional African society was hierarchical, a structure which was maintained by various customs. Elders had authority over younger members, and people were senior or junior, according to age, status or wealth. Both boys and girls went through extensive initiation programmes when they reached puberty: for weeks or months at a time they were taken to a secluded place to attend separate-sex 'initiation schools', where they received instruction in adult behaviour and the traditions of the tribe. In a final ceremony, boys were circumcised and girls went through a procedure to stretch the hymen. These procedures often resulted in sepsis and even death, but this was regarded as one of the risks that had to be taken to fulfil the traditions of the tribe. These customs are still quite widely practised today, sometimes with qualified medical people present but often performed by elders in the traditional way.

Among the Venda people in Limpopo, girls performed the sacred *domba* dance during initiation. The Venda believed that a python god lived in Limpopo's sacred Lake Fundudzi. The *domba* dance paid homage to the python god, and was witnessed only by women. The girls formed a curving line like a python, each holding the elbow of the girl in front, and each year two young girls had to be thrown into the lake as a sacrifice to the python god. It is not certain when this practice ended and gifts instead of live girls were thrown into the lake. The *domba* dance is still practised by young Venda girls during puberty in some parts of Limpopo.

Ancestors also played an important role in African customs and religious beliefs. It was believed that ancestors had control over people's lives, and their spirits would thus be called upon in times of need. Sacrifices of sheep and cattle were made to them, and people did not like to live far from where their ancestors were buried. The Xhosa and Zulu chiefdoms were each named after an ancestral figure, while others, like the Sotho and the Tswana chiefdoms, were named after animals like the Kwena ('crocodile'), Taung ('lion'), Khatla ('monkey') and Tloung ('elephant'). Apart from belief in the ancestors, people also believed that certain living people had power over them, and could bewitch them and cause misfortune. This was often attributed to jealousy.

Belief in the ancestors and their powers of control are evident in many South African cultures today, and are often blended with Christianity. Animal sacrifices are also regularly made to appease the ancestors.

CHAPTER 3

Settlers from out of Africa

Early white visitors

South Africa's geography has played a significant role in its history: lying at the southernmost tip of Africa, it is also in a strategic position between East and West. Two oceans, the Atlantic and Indian Oceans, come together at its most southerly point, Cape Agulhas in the Western Cape.

White settlers only started arriving in South Africa in substantial numbers from the mid-17th century but people from Europe had been making exploratory voyages down the west coast of Africa for some 160 years before that. The first white explorers to reach the Cape were probably the Portuguese in the late 15th century. They were looking for an alternative sea route to India, as that through the Mediterranean and Arabian Peninsula had been blocked during the rise of the Ottoman Turkish Empire. The Portuguese stopped at the Cape for supplies – they did not try to colonise the area.

Key characters in this venture were sea captains Bartholomew Dias in 1488, and Vasco da Gama in 1497. Bartholomew Dias named the southernmost point of Africa 'The Cape of Storms' (*Cabo das Tormentas*), but it was later renamed 'The Cape of Good Hope' (*Cabo da Boa Esperança*) by King John of Portugal because it represented the promising opening of a new route to the east. Da Gama and his crew gave the name 'Natal' to the coast they were approaching on 16 December 1497, because the name carried the connotation of the birth of Christ in Portuguese.

In these days of sailing ships and rudimentary navigation, early explorers

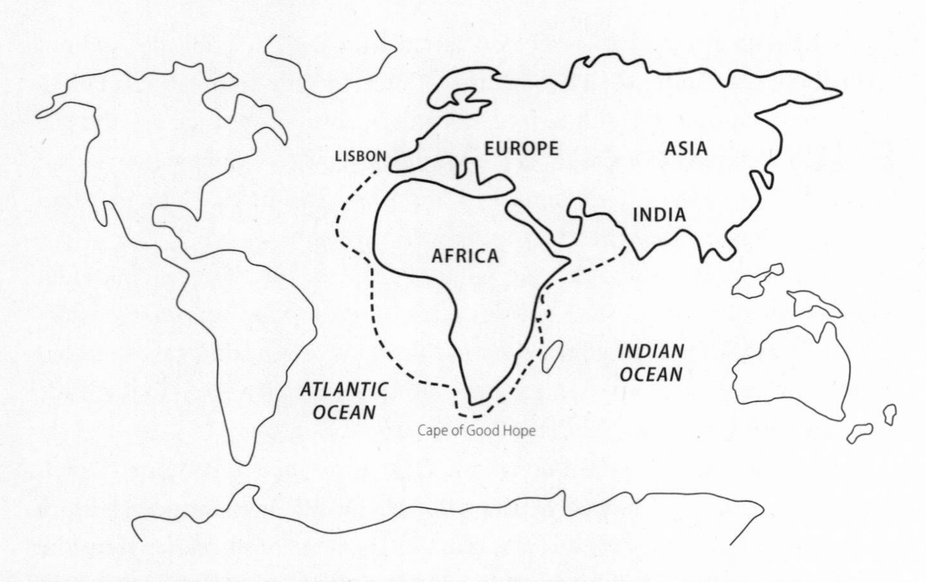

MAP 10 *Vasco da Gama's route. He hugged the coast-line for some of the way but in the approximate area of today's Sierra Leone he turned west across the Atlantic until almost the coast of Brazil when he caught the South Atlantic Westerlies to turn east again and sail past the Cape. He sailed a bit further out to sea as he approached the foot of Africa because of the notorious storms in that area.*

faced many difficulties. They were at the mercy of the wind, and the early sailing ships were small: each would probably have fitted into a modern tennis court, and the early seafarers spent weeks at a time in cramped conditions. Da Gama hugged the coastline for most of his journey down Africa, but in the approximate area of today's Sierra Leone he was blown off course in a westerly direction almost to the coast of Brazil before being able to turn eastwards again. He also sailed quite far out to sea as he rounded the Cape because of the notorious storms in that area.

The Portuguese left little evidence of their presence other than *padraos* (stone crosses), which they erected on beaches – possibly to show the Portuguese dominance of the sea at that time, or to serve as landmarks for those that followed, or even simply to demonstrate their Christian faith. The remnants of some of those *padraos* have been found, like those at Kwaaihoek, west of the mouth of the Bushman's River. One *padrao* has been reconstructed and is housed at the University of the Witwatersrand in Johannesburg.

The English also had an early association with the Cape but they did not settle there until more than two centuries later. In June 1580, Francis Drake sailed around the Cape on the return leg of his famous voyage around the world. They passed by on what was apparently a perfect Cape winter's day: the chronicler of the voyage remarked that it was the fairest Cape they had seen in the whole circumference of the world.

Further voyages followed, and in 1601 the first of the great national commercial companies, the English East India Company, was chartered by Queen Elizabeth I of England. Trading fleets were sent out, taking seven months to reach the Cape, which they rounded on their way to make trade contacts with Indonesia, Madras, Bombay and Calcutta.

A year later, in 1602, the Vereenigde Oost-Indische Compagnie (Dutch East India Trading Company), hereafter the VOC, was founded.[1] From then and for the next 50 years, the English and the Dutch rather than the Portuguese were the dominant traders in the route around the Cape.

Shipwrecks and their evidence

The numerous shipwrecks along the southern African coast bear testimony to the risks the early seafaring nations took. The coast is treacherous and the heavily laden wooden galleons of the 16th and 17th centuries often sank or ran aground on the rocks. There are at least 1 000 known shipwrecks along the coast of southern Africa, especially between the Eastern Cape and KwaZulu-Natal. The oldest wrecks are those of the Portuguese, but most of the wrecks known to have sunk in that area have never been found. Those that have been discovered are now protected historical sites, and special permits have to be granted for salvage work.

Artefacts both exotic and sinister have washed up from the shipwrecks, and occasionally beads and other small items are still found in rock pools along the coast. Indian cornelian beads; pieces of iron, tin and precious metals; Dutch, Spanish and even Spanish-American coins; shards of 16th-century Chinese porcelain; and muzzle loaders, parts of cannons and slave chains all testify to who was trading and what was being traded at the

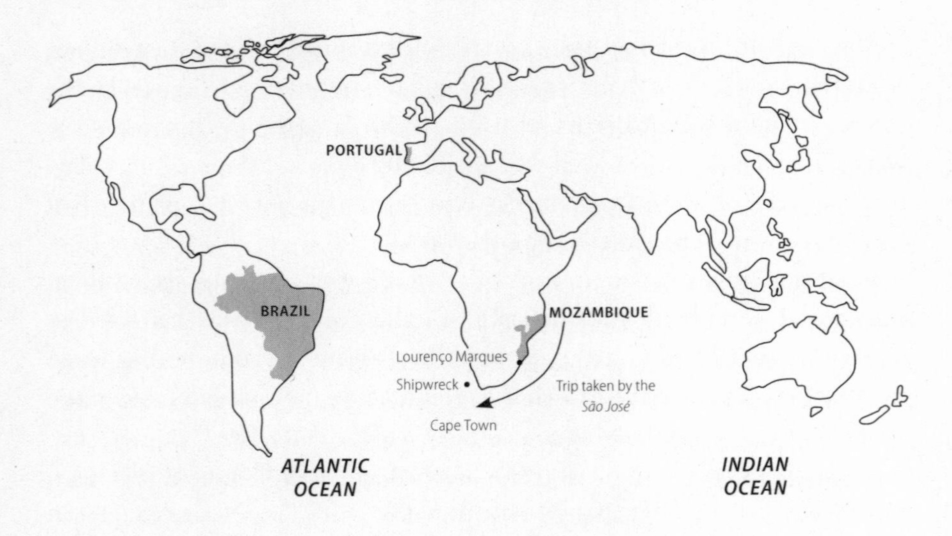

MAP 11 *The route taken by the* São José *from Portugal to Mozambique, then back around the foot of Africa, en route to Brazil.*

time. The spices and cloth for which the East was famous, and which must have formed part of the cargoes, did not survive in the sea.

It was evident from the slave chains that some of the wrecked ships had been carrying slaves, but until recently very little clear written documentation had been found. In May 2015, archaeologist Jaco Boshoff and anthropologist Stephen Lubkemann came across a captain's logbook among faded, dusty documents in the Cape Archives. This was the breakthrough they had been looking for: the logbook gave details of a stricken ship, the *São José-Paquete de Africa*, which had sunk on rocks near Clifton Beach, Cape Town, in 1794. It also gave the location of the wreck, which allowed Boshoff, Lubkemann and a team of divers to investigate further.

They discovered that the ship had come from Portugal to collect slaves from Mozambique. It was en route to Brazil carrying some 400 slaves, about half of whom drowned in the wreck, presumably still in their shackles. Those who survived were sold into slavery in Cape Town.

This documented evidence supplemented existing physical evidence that South Africa had been involved in the slave-trade network operating from East Africa to the Americas in the late 18th century. Sometimes black chiefs were party to this trade, and accepted bribes. Slave raids had been regularly carried out inland and the slaves taken to ports along the coast, especially Lourenço Marques – the most southerly port from which the interior slave trade was conducted.

The 2015 discovery of the slave ship *São José-Paquete de Africa* attracted worldwide attention and inspired further research, including that through the Slave Wrecks Project, which has grown into a multinational organisation.[2] The Smithsonian National Museum of African American History in Washington estimates that nearly half a million slaves were trafficked from East African ports to the Americas between 1800 and 1845.

Curious stories are told about people who survived the shipwrecks. Survivors of the Portuguese ship *São João*, which was wrecked in 1552 near Port Edward in KwaZulu-Natal, tried to walk all the way along the coast to the Portuguese base at Lourenço Marques, where people would be able to speak their language. Some survived the journey, with the help of black people whom they befriended along the way, and it is said that a few of them eventually even got back to Portugal.[3]

Other survivors of shipwrecks became assimilated with the people who helped them. In 1686, the Dutch ship *Stavenisse* was wrecked near what is now Port Shepstone in KwaZulu-Natal. In 1688, a ship sent in search of survivors rescued three men who had been living with the Mpondo (Pondo) people for the intervening two years, but they also met a man who did not want to be rescued. He was the survivor of another wreck, the Portuguese *Nossa Senhora da Atalaya* of 1647, and had been living with the Mpondo people in the eastern region of the Cape for more than 40 years. He had a wife and cattle and, according to a report at the time, spoke, 'Only the African language, having forgotten everything, his God included'.[4]

Members of an expedition to rescue survivors of the English ship the *Grosvenor*, which was wrecked off the coast of Pondoland in 1782, described seeing a clan of about 400 *abelungu* (the isiXhosa term for fair-skinned people, or people from the sea): these were possibly the descendants of European survivors of shipwrecks and the Mpondo people.[5] The light-skinned Mpondo chief Faku (1824–1867) was said to have been the mixed-race son of one of the survivors of the *Grosvenor* and a local person[6].

South African author Lawrence Green noted in the 1960s that many of the people in Pondoland were still 'curiously light-skinned', a characteristic he attributed to their 'strange ancestors'. [7] It would seem that the coastal parts of South Africa have been the meeting place of diverse people for at least 500 years.[8]

The Dutch

The first white people to settle in significant numbers in South Africa were the Dutch, who arrived in 1652. This was more or less the same time as other Dutch groups went to America and founded New Amsterdam, which was later renamed New York by the British.

In 1652, the Dutch East India Company (VOC) intended simply to establish a refreshment station at the Cape for ships passing en route to the East. By 1657, it was apparent that the Cape was becoming important not just for passing Dutch ships, but for the ships of other countries as well. The Dutch then changed their initial policy, and for the next 40 years encouraged large-scale settlement at the Cape.

The commander of the Dutch settlement in 1652 was Jan van Riebeeck, and he was to encounter problems similar to those of his counterpart in North America, Peter Stuyvesant. Van Riebeeck had been instructed to build a fort for protection and to lay out gardens to grow vegetables and fruit trees to supply passing ships. He was also told to acquire cattle, which he obtained from the Khoikhoi people, often with coercive methods.

The year 1652 has assumed exaggerated significance in the histories of South Africa written mainly from a Eurocentric point of view in the 20th century. For a long time it was suggested that this was when South African history began, because European people brought 'progress' and links with the outside world. Little recognition was given to the fact that the Mapungubwe state, with its international trading links, was active at least 600 years earlier than 1652, and that this was known about as early as the 1930s.

Although it was not the original intention, the arrival of Jan van Riebeeck in 1652 heralded the start of 150 years of Dutch rule in South Africa. In the years to come, the Afrikaans language – an adaption of Dutch together with Khoikhoi, Malay, isiXhosa, isiZulu, Portuguese and English words – was to take hold as an official language, and the descendants of the Dutch became known as Afrikaners.

During Van Riebeeck's administration, some employees of the VOC were allowed to become burghers (farmers) to increase farm production. The burghers started their farms in the area we now know as Rondebosch, clashing with the Khoikhoi over grazing land and cattle. The VOC encouraged burghers to acquire firearms and to serve in the militia, and with their guns, tools and generally superior technology, the burghers were able to take over Khoikhoi cattle and land. Raids and uneasy periods of truce were to mark VOC rule at the Cape (1652–1806), with only a brief break in between.

By the 18th and 19th centuries, the use of guns had become widespread, and much of South Africa's story would henceforth be shaped by armed conflict. Guns became a much sought after trade item for both hunting and war purposes, and were one of the reasons certain black chiefdoms came to dominate others. By the 1820s and 1830s, even small groups like the Griqua (mixed-race descendants of the Khoikhoi and Europeans) could wreak havoc because they had acquired guns and horses from the Cape Colony.

In 1657, the first slaves were imported into South Africa to work for the VOC. From then onwards, slaves were imported regularly from Madagascar, Indonesia, Ceylon (now Sri Lanka) and parts of India, as well as from Mozambique and parts of Africa, especially the east coast between Delagoa Bay and Zanzibar. The Khoikhoi were not slaves, although some worked for the Dutch and as a legally ambiguous group according to VOC law, they were often exploited for their labour.

The Castle at the Cape

In 1666, the Dutch started to build a castle to replace their original small fort. This was the Castle of the Cape of Good Hope, built at the entrance to Table Bay. Its purpose was to protect the settlement from possible attacks by British or other European rivals – although, in fact, the castle was never attacked. The castle took 13 years to build (1666–1679), and Van Riebeeck's rule was harsh: men from passing ships were detained against their will to help clear the site and quarry stone for the castle. Stories abound of men in leg irons doing this work.

The ground plan of the castle took the form of a five-point star, each point being a bastion of defence. The bastions were named after the main titles of Willem, the Prince of Orange: Leerdam, Buuren, Catzenellenbogen, Nassau and Orange. Overlooking the castle from a high position, the five-point star pattern is clearly discernible.

The Castle of the Cape of Good Hope is the oldest surviving colonial building in South Africa, and was declared a national monument in 1936. It now houses the headquarters of the army in the Western Cape, and the famous William Fehr collection of oil paintings, furniture and decorative arts.

By 1666 the Cape settlement was becoming known as Cape Town, and from then on it was administered from the castle. Cape Town's first four streets – Strand Street, Castle Street, Short Market Street and Long Market Street – still exist today. The castle also housed prisoners in the notorious dungeon, or 'dark hole'. According to the law of the time, a man could not be executed for a crime unless he confessed to it, and torture was regularly used. Prisoners were detained for long periods in the dark, damp dungeon, and suffered from ill health afterwards.

By 1688 the burgher population had risen to 600. The refreshment station had become a colony, and the borders were pushed slowly outwards to the north and east. In 1691, the office of 'Commander' of the settlement was replaced with 'Governor', and Simon van der Stel was promoted to the new position. Simon van der Stel encouraged immigration – even to the point of inducing people on their way to India (especially artisans and other skilled people) to settle at the Cape instead. He granted freehold farms to favoured people in the areas we now know as Stellenbosch (named after him), Drakenstein and Paarl, the future wine-growing areas of the Cape.

Stellenbosch is some 48 kilometres from Table Bay, and was the Cape's first country town. Simon's Town, some 36 kilometres south-east of Cape Town, was also named after Simon van der Stel, and was the VOC's official anchorage for ships bound for Asia. South Africa's largest naval base is still positioned there.

Groot Constantia and Vergelegen

The house that was built for Simon van der Stel was called Groot Constantia ('large' Constantia), and it remains a magnificent example of Cape Dutch architecture. Houses in this style have a distinctive design: they are H-shaped, with the front flanked by two perpendicular wings, and they have ornate rounded gables like those in the townhouses of Amsterdam. Simon van der Stel's son, Willem Adriaan van der Stel, who succeeded him as governor in 1699, owned Vergelegen, an equally beautiful home on vast grounds. Vergelegen means 'far away' – it is quite some distance from Cape Town, in what is now Somerset West. As the climate at Vergelegen varied on different sides of the farm, wine grapes and many other agricultural products were successfully farmed there.

Willem Adriaan van der Stel did much to improve farming at the Cape, but he was an unpopular man. He established a monopoly over contracts for produce that furthered his own interests but ruined many farmers. He also attempted to curry favour with the VOC directors in Holland. Two pictures that still hang on a wall at Vergelegen tell part of the story. One of them shows the Vergelegen estate plagued by lions and threatening black warriors, but leaves out the magnificent cultivated gardens in the front of the house. This was far from the truth, but Willem Adriaan van der Stel sent it to the VOC directors to persuade them of the everyday difficulties he dealt with at the Cape!

Willem Adriaan van der Stel's dubious activities led to petitions against him and he was eventually recalled to Holland and dismissed from the Company. By the time he left in 1708, there were some 1 700 white settler men, women and children living at the Cape, as well as a number of slaves.

It was during Willem Adriaan van der Stel's time as governor that permission was given for burghers to move beyond the original settlement at Table Bay. The first of these people were the trekboers,[9] who moved seasonally with their cattle and sheep and often returned to their original place. The trekboers' expansion into areas occupied by the Khoikhoi has been seen as the first stage of 'official' white takeover of land previously inhabited by people who had moved there thousands of years before.

By the 1770s the trekboers had spread eastwards as far as the rich grazing lands between the Gamtoos and Great Fish Rivers, which were occupied by Xhosa farmers.[10] Bloody clashes were inevitable and led to a series of what have subsequently been called the Cape Frontier Wars or Africa's Hundred Years' War (1781–1878). For the Xhosa, they involved terrible losses materially, politically and psychologically.

The last years of VOC rule

Burghers had no voice in decisions made throughout the period of VOC rule, but in 1778 a secret movement called the Cape Patriots began in Cape Town. Their aim was to improve burghers' rights, especially with regard to private trade. Petitions drawn up and presented to the Dutch government had little effect.

In 1786, the VOC formally extended the borders of the Cape colony to Graaff-Reinet and established a landdrost (magistracy) there to protect the white settlers. But raids and conflict continued. The last few years of VOC rule at the Cape had little to commend them: there were few periods of peace, and the government was financially weak. The decline of Dutch rule was also in part due to competition from the rise of British maritime power and the loss of some of its trade monopolies to the British Empire. The VOC was finally liquidated in January 1800.

The French

French immigrants arrived in South Africa in 1688. Although apparently not in significant numbers, the French had also been early visitors to the South African coast: there is evidence that French pirates plagued Portuguese ships, and that some French ships reached Mozambique and even Indonesia as early as the mid-16th century. Some of the shipwrecks along the Cape-to-KwaZulu-Natal coastline are of French ships.

In 1688, however, the French Huguenots (French Protestants) came to stay. There were probably only about 200 initial immigrants, but their influence is significant. The French king, Louis XIV, a Roman Catholic, had revoked an edict guaranteeing religious tolerance to Protestants, and

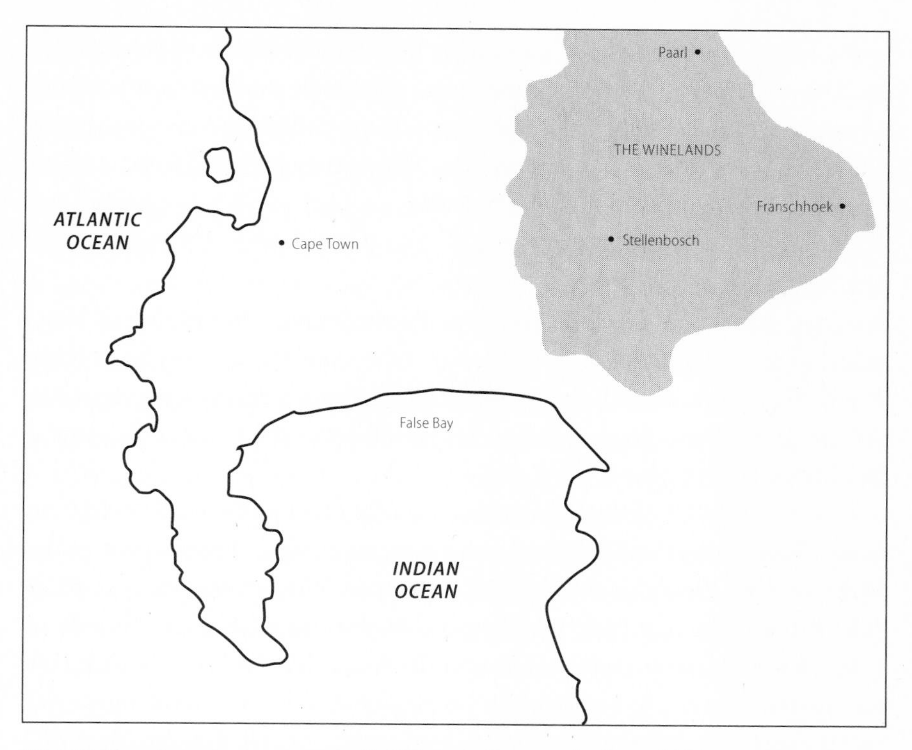

MAP 12 *The wine-growing areas in the Western Cape, at the foot of Africa. Adapted from a winelands brochure by Gail Nattrass*

the Huguenots came to the Dutch colony in the Cape to escape religious persecution in France. They were sponsored by the VOC, and granted farms at Drakenstein, Paarl and Franschhoek (which means 'French corner') on the same terms as the Dutch burghers.

The Cape wine industry owes much to these early French settlers. The French were not the first to plant vines (both Simon and Willem Adriaan van der Stel had planted vines and exported good-quality wine to Holland and the East Indies), but they were the most successful. In 1713, the VOC gave a beautiful estate to the French Huguenot Jean le Long. He named it Bossendaal (now Boschendal), which means 'wood and vale'. In 1716, the De Villiers family bought Boschendal and held it for the next 160 years. They developed vineyards and built the beautiful manor house in the distinct Cape Dutch style, with gables and white lime-washed walls.

The three De Villiers brothers – Pierre, Abraham and Jacques – owned just one horse between them, and took turns to ride the 20 kilometres to church every Sunday. Religious people, they apparently saw nothing incongruous in the fact that each owned several slaves. Chardonnay, Pinot Noir, Sauvignon Blanc and Merlot grapes are still planted at Boschendal, just as they were 300 years ago. While he was governor at the Cape, Simon van der Stel encouraged all the colonists to plant new trees, especially oaks. Avenues of oaks are still part of the setting at Boschendal and many other old Cape wine farms.

Boschendal also owns one of the world's finest collections of Chinese porcelain from the Ming dynasty. In Dutch it is called *kraakporselein*, a distinctive type of porcelain that is nearly always blue and white, and which was first developed for export during the reign of Emperor Wan Li (1573–1619). The VOC ships later brought pieces to the Cape and to Europe, where *kraakporselein* influenced the production of Delft and Wedgewood china. The colours blue and white dominated in both, whereas they had not been popular in porcelain or china before.

The assimilation of the French

The French immigrants were generally from a more sophisticated class than the VOC burghers and relations between the two European groups were sometimes strained. Although French-owned farms were interspersed with those of the Dutch, the French language was not encouraged because Simon van der Stel wanted the new immigrants to become assimilated as soon as possible. Intermarrying was inevitable, and within about three generations the French language had died out at the Cape. South African surnames like Cronje (previously Cronier), De Lange (previously Le Long), De Villiers, Du Buys (previously De Buis), Du Plessis, Du Toit, Joubert, Le Roux, Lombard, Malherbe and Marais are all French in origin. Many South Africans can trace their roots back to the French Huguenots, including former president FW de Klerk – his surname derived from the Huguenot 'le Clercq', which over time became 'de Clercq' and then 'de Klerk'.

The slaves

The first slaves were brought to the Cape in 1658. In 1713, the decision was made to import more slaves to relieve labour shortages, and slaves gradually became a feature of business and domestic life at the Cape. Slaves owned by the VOC were housed at a slave lodge, and there were also 'house' slaves and 'field' slaves who were owned by businessmen and burghers. The field slaves worked mainly on the wine farms, where slave bells (used to call them to work) can sometimes still be seen. At Vergelegen, a museum has been built over the old slave lodge.

Slaves were the property of their owners and they had no rights. There were some statutes in place that were meant to give some protection, but these measures were often ignored. When complaints were taken to the landdrost, decisions generally favoured slave owners.

In 1793, two years before the British first took over from the Dutch, there were more slaves than free burghers at the Cape – an official statistic states that there were 14 747 slaves (including 9 046 men, 3 590 women and 2 111 children), compared with 13 830 free burghers (white farmers and their families).[11] Within Cape households, there were often close relationships between slave owners and slaves, but this tended to be paternalistic – incorporating slaves into family structures made it less likely that they would rebel.

Slave characters

Against the odds, some slave characters did emerge, three of whom were known as Katie, Lodewyk and Galant (names presumably given to them by their owners).

In 1910, when she was 96 years old, Katie was interviewed at her humble home in Hanover Street, District Six on the east side of Cape Town.[12] She was one of the few surviving ex-slaves at that time. She said she had been born on a Mr Mostert's farm, near Kalabas (Kalbas) Kraal in the Swartland area of the Western Cape. She did not know the exact day but recalled that she was about 19 or 20 years old when slaves were emancipated in 1834, which suggests she was born in 1814 or 1815. Her father was a Malagasy, and her mother a Cape woman. When Mr Mostert decided he was too old to continue farming, he divided his possessions (cattle, horses and slaves) among his sons, whom he had set up as farmers in the neighbourhood. Katie was given to one son and her mother to another – Katie never saw her mother again and did not know what happened to her.

Katie began to work when she was still very young, first in the fields as a herder, and later as a wet nurse to her owner's child, during which time she was allowed to sleep in the owner's house – on the floor of the dining room. Although there was no legal marriage facility for slaves until 1823, she had a partner, Jacob, who lived on another farm; they had children together, which was unusual because slave women were often infertile due to hard work and a poor diet. Katie confirmed that she was quite well treated on the farm, but that her partner had suffered much abuse. One morning in 1834, the slaves were ordered to dress in their best clothes and meet in the dining room, where a magistrate told them that in four years' time, they would be free. There was to be a period of 'apprenticeship' in between. Her father did not live to see that day: he died in slavery.

On the day of emancipation, Jacob's master drove his slaves off his farm with a gun. Katie's master offered to employ both of them. Jacob wanted to leave the area altogether but was persuaded to stay when Katie's 'missus' (her master's wife) wept at the idea of Katie leaving her. 'No; you must stay!' she had cried. 'Think of my son, whom you have suckled and nursed, and who has now grown so fond of you. What will become of him? No; you must stay; you cannot go!' [13]

Katie and Jacob remained on the farm for another three or four years before moving on to Durbanville, where they were baptised and married. After several more moves, they settled in District Six. 'There was more love in the old slave days,' continued Katie. 'It was more peaceful. Now the electric trams pass my door from early morning till late at night, and the whole day long people shout at one another.'[14]

Lodewyk was a slave who was bought and sold a few times and, unusually, was recognised as a skilled tailor in the Cape community, and Galant, another slave, organised a slave rebellion – even though farms were far apart and communication difficult. Galant was unusual in that he refused to call his owner 'baas' (master), and was allowed to drive his owner's wagon to market. Although this gave him a measure of freedom and enabled him to hear news about the colony, he was also regularly beaten.

These three known slaves were exceptions in the abhorrent system; by and large, few slaves escaped submission.[15] A community of runaway slaves did, however, exist for almost 50 years at Cape Hangklip, on False Bay near Cape Town. After running away from his employer in 1725, a slave named Reijnier van Madagascar survived some 22 years on his own, living on fish and dassies (rock rabbits) in the mountains behind the Berg River. Reijnier van Madagascar's name indicates where he originally came from, as does that of a woman with whom he had children, Manika van Bengal.

In 1807, a year after the second British occupation of the Cape, the slave trade was abolished throughout the British Empire. Although slave ownership continued at the Cape, it became difficult to obtain new slaves. By the 1820s there was some lessening of the punishments which could be inflicted on slaves, and there was talk of emancipation. After 176 years of practice at the Cape, slavery only ended in 1834, when it was officially abolished throughout the British Empire. There were some 36 000 slaves in the Cape colony at the time of emancipation.

It is not entirely clear whether the elimination of slavery was influenced by humanitarian movements back in Britain, or if they simply reflected the British preference for developing a capitalist economy, in which slave labour was counterproductive. Other forms of slavery – like the trade in 'black ivory'[16] and indentured labour[17] – were to continue, especially in the more remote regions of the interior.

The Bo-Kaap Museum

After slaves were freed in 1834, many moved to the Bo-Kaap area in Cape Town. There, along with other Muslim immigrants, they gradually established themselves as a distinctive though ethnically mixed community. They came to be known as Cape Malays, although this name was not entirely accurate: while some freed slaves had their roots in Malaysia, most were originally from India and Indonesia. Still today the Bo-Kaap stretches from Buitengracht Street up Signal Hill, above Cape Town's city centre.

Although the languages the slaves spoke have now died out, some of their words crept into Afrikaans – examples are 'piesang' (banana), 'blatjang' (chutney), 'baadjie' (jacket) and 'baie' (many). Afrikaans is the language spoken by most coloured people in the Cape today – a people descended from the relationships that took place between slaves, slave owners, Khoikhoi, San and other black and white groups.

Evidence of slaves has been found in the Bo-Kaap and on some wine farms. The skeletal remains of slaves have also been found in Cape Town itself – for example, at Cobern Street in Green Point, when foundations were being dug for a housing complex in 1994. Modern technology has made it possible to trace the slaves' origins from dental modifications and the enamel on their teeth. That and the number of graves found has led researchers to conclude not only that the number of slaves brought to South Africa has been grossly underestimated, but also that the slave network was not a simple route from birthplace to place of enslavement. Slaves buried in the same grave did not necessarily come from the same place, and it is likely that slaves from various origins were taken to central slave markets far from home. The Indian Ocean slave trade, it seems, was complex and multidirectional, and there is no doubt that the ignominious trade in human beings contributed to the distribution of different cultures and beliefs around the world.[18]

The English

After the Dutch and the French, the English were the next group of white settlers at the Cape. Interestingly it was the English and not the Dutch who were the first to think of permanent settlement at the Cape: in 1620, however, the idea had not been supported by King James I. The English only established their authority at the Cape some 186 years later in 1806, although this had been preceded by a brief period of British occupation (1795–1803), followed by a brief three years of Dutch (Batavian Republic) rule (1803–1806).

British rule was destined to dramatically transform South Africa's economy, polity and society. Having been through an industrial revolution, the British were the most powerful industrial economy at the time, and their occupation meant that South Africa became linked to the British economy and markets, their political system and to some extent a different style of thinking. In the 1800s, a wave of humanitarianism was sweeping through England as a result of the work of politicians like William Wilberforce,[19] although it was a qualified, almost paternalistic humanitarianism. It was the British who eventually ended the slave trade and encouraged free labour and free trade, and it was also the British who were instrumental in bringing Christian ideas to the indigenous people, mainly through their missionaries.[20] Christianity and the desire to spread Christian ideas was associated with this wave of humanitarianism, although there is little to suggest that white people at the time regarded black people as social equals.[21] The new British colonies in the Cape and Natal nevertheless had a more liberal spirit than the Boer republics in the interior.

The first period of British administration introduced a much celebrated figure in early Cape history: Lady Anne Barnard, the daughter of an English earl and wife of colonial secretary Andrew Barnard, who was 12 years her junior. She became the official hostess of the governor, Lord Macartney, because his wife had not accompanied him to the Cape. Lady Anne Barnard hosted balls and other functions, and promoted the use of local wines; she was openly scornful of people who thought good wine had to be imported. Her presence did much to foster good relations between the English and the Dutch, and her diaries have provided much insight into life at the Cape at the time.

From their second occupation of the Cape colony, the British were to remain in charge until the Cape became part of the Union of South Africa in 1910. In 1806, the population at the Cape was roughly 20 000 white colonists, 25 754 slaves and approximately 1 700 free blacks.[22] The number of Xhosa living towards the Great Fish River in the eastern Cape and beyond were not recorded.

The Great Fish River was meant to be the colony's eastern border, with the trekboers and Boers on the one side and the Xhosa on the other. By then, farmers of Dutch descent (the former burghers) who had settled on farms, and were not moving around like the trekboers, were referred to simply

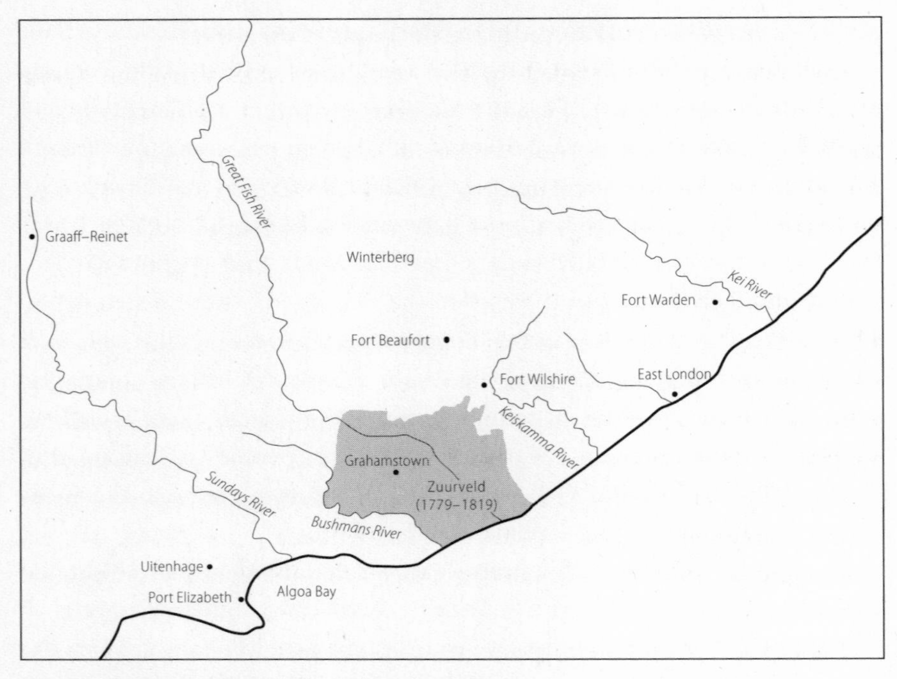

MAP 13 *The eastern Cape in the early 19th century.*

as 'Boers' (which means 'farmers' in Afrikaans). The Great Fish River was not particularly wide or filled with fish, and neither was it an effective barrier – it was the scene of eight frontier wars between 1799 and 1853, and more blood was shed there than anywhere else in South Africa. The Boers and the Xhosa were both cattle-keeping societies, and both wanted access to the fertile land (the Zuurveld – literally 'sour grass') favoured by cattle around the Great Fish River.

In 1812, the new British governor at the Cape, Sir John Cradock, sent a force of British, Dutch and Khoikhoi troops commanded by Colonel John Graham to the eastern border. Some 20 000 Xhosa were driven out of the Zuurveld and their cattle taken. Cradock's comment was that this was necessary to impress on 'the minds of these savages' a proper degree of respect. Military outposts were constructed, one of which was Graham's Town (now Grahamstown), named after Colonel John Graham. The force of mixed white and coloured troops that drove away the Xhosa is an example of the alliances that were made according to the needs of the time.

An uneasy peace prevailed for five years until 1817, when the Xhosa attacked Grahamstown, followed by two years of conflict. The eastern border was some 900 kilometres from the seat of administration at Cape Town – European people were not used to such distances and communication across the colony was difficult, especially as tensions rose.

The 1820 British Settlers

In the 1820s, the British Parliament voted to spend money promoting British settlement at the Cape. Their reasons were twofold: to relieve population pressure and poverty in Britain after the Napoleonic wars, and to swell the number of white settlers in the eastern districts of the Cape, as a kind of buffer against the Xhosa. The new settlers were to be given 100-acre farms in the Zuurveld west of the Great Fish River. Some 4 000 British settlers came initially, with approximately another 1 000 following, in groups led by retired naval captains.

The new settlers had been given unrealistic expectations about life in the new colony. They did not understand the conditions in the eastern Cape, and most of the early farming ventures, especially in the area of Albany where they were first settled, were a disaster. Those who had other trades to fall back on moved to the burgeoning towns[23]. But some settlers gradually began to farm successfully, especially as pastoralists; many had brought with them the knowledge of stock farming for which 18th-century Britain was renowned, and they were not afraid to experiment with Merino sheep which had originally come from Spain, whereas the Dutch farmers were reluctant to switch from fat-tailed sheep. Large numbers of Merino sheep were imported and the production of wool became an important trade commodity.[24] Merino sheep did well in the dry Karoo regions around towns like Cradock and Graaff-Reinet, and they still thrive in these areas today.

The British settlers had thus also started to enter trade and commerce. Many of them moved into towns like Grahamstown, which had started as a military post but became an active trading centre. The Grahamstown settlers also persuaded the Cape government to allow the Xhosa to come into the colony to trade: in 1828, trading between the two groups became legal. Ivory, ostrich feathers, wool, cattle hides, knives, buttons and beads were some of the items traded there. Some of the Xhosa groups had by then acquired firearms to facilitate hunting, and it seems likely that this was a fairly prosperous time for them.

Grahamstown also became a base for disseminating information about the lands beyond the colony. It was a place where British and Boers established friendships, even though their languages were different. The first settler newspaper, *The Grahamstown Journal*, also had its beginnings in Grahamstown. One of the 1820 settlers, Thomas Pringle, is credited with starting the long struggle to achieve freedom of the press in South Africa – a freedom which has not always been easy to maintain.

The Grahamstown Journal put the Cape in touch with news from the outside world, establishing the international links we take for granted today. There were also regular articles about local matters: the good times that were had when the Boers came into town to attend church services (nagmaal) and to buy supplies for their farms. This suggests that the grievances which made thousands of Boers leave the eastern Cape on their Great Trek into the interior in the 1830s had more to do with the British government than the British settlers. Left to the people, relations were generally cordial.

The British, however, remained a distinct culture in the Cape, unlike the French who were quite quickly assimilated by the Dutch.[25] Still today, Grahamstown is associated with the British settlers, which is evidenced by the town's style of architecture. Grahamstown is also associated these days with an arts festival held annually in July. This started as an event to promote and celebrate the English language, but has now become a cross-cultural festival. The other colony established by the British was Port Natal (today's Durban) in 1824 – a city which has also retained a distinct British influence.

Surnames in South Africa that recall the 1820 English settlers include: Hobson, King, Pringle, Rennie, Trollip, White and Wilmot. The English legacy is also evident in place names such as Port Alfred (named after the second son of Queen Victoria), Bathurst (named after Lord Bathurst, Secretary of State for the Colonies, 1812–1827), Somerset West (named after Lord Charles Somerset, governor of the Cape Colony, 1814–1826), Port

Elizabeth (named after the late wife of the acting governor, Sir Rufane Donkin, 1820–1821 – she died of fever in India) and Grahamstown (named after Colonel Graham, whose forces defeated the Xhosa in the Zuurveld in 1812).

The overlay of British law

When the British took over the Cape in 1806, a legal system based on Roman Dutch was in place at the Cape. The British gradually added their own overlay of British law, with the result that South African law is now rather hybrid.

Between 1827 and 1834, the British introduced measures that separated the powers of state, making it impossible for any one person or section to dominate. The first of the changes was the establishment of a separate, independent judiciary. The British also brought in an updated version of the Rule of Law, which states that no man is above the law, no matter what his status is. This concept has its origins in Greek and Roman times, and Roman Dutch law had accorded with this principle.[26] The British also brought in the *stare decisis* (Latin for 'to stand by things decided'). Whereas under the Dutch, past decisions in the courts were merely a guide, under the British Rule of Law, the courts had to follow precedents. *Stare decisis* stands in the way of courts being able to make drastic innovations. These British additions are still part of South African law today.

A representative government

In 1854, Britain granted the Cape Colony a system of representative government and a new constitution was granted at the Cape. This made provision for a parliament with two chambers, and the franchise (the right to vote) was extended to all males, irrespective of race. The qualification requirement for the franchise was property ownership of £25 or a wage of £50 per annum. The constitution thus ensured that poorer whites and most black and coloured people were excluded, but was nevertheless the most liberal anywhere in the world at that time – better even than the one in Britain. For the best part of a century, men of all races participated in the Cape elections and there was a similar arrangement in Port Natal. While very few people of colour qualified to use that franchise, it nevertheless did exist – which puts paid to the widely held belief that all races were enfranchised for the first time only in 1994. The British colonies of the Cape and Natal always had a slightly more liberal tradition than the Boer republics of the Transvaal and Orange Free State that were established in the interior.

The British system of representative government was the British Westminster system, and it has been the foundation of South Africa's system of government ever since. Parliament makes the laws and the judiciary ensures the laws are carried out. The British also developed a system of mercantile law to deal with increased trade and commerce.

The Cape colony was encouraged to assume some of the responsibility for its own defence, and colonial forces were established. These forces were deployed in six of the nine wars and campaigns that were fought in South Africa between 1877 and 1881.

English sports

South Africa's English heritage is evident in the sports its people still enjoy – cricket, rugby, football and horse racing. In Green Point, Cape Town, as early as the 1820s, 'Malays and Negroes mingled with whites, all crowding and elbowing to get a sight of the momentous event' (a horse race).[27]

Football

Football was first documented in the Cape in 1862, when matches between British civil servants and soldiers were played in Cape Town and Port Elizabeth. Between the 1880s and 1910s, football was also played at mission schools that had been established for black children; and African, Indian, and Coloured football leagues were developed in Cape Town, Kimberley, Durban and Johannesburg. The British style of football was gradually adapted to suit local customs and traditions, and religious and traditional rituals became part of the local game. Football was relatively cheap to play and caught on quickly in poorer areas.

Two of South Africa's biggest soccer clubs, Orlando Pirates and Moroka Swallows, date back to 1937 and 1947 respectively. By then there had been a dramatic increase in the number of black people living in the cities, and the games were well attended. Another well-known club, Kaiser Chiefs, was founded in January 1970.

Rugby

Former Springbok fly half and well-known rugby commentator Naas Botha once remarked that rugby in South Africa was to a great extent the 'Afrikaners' game'.[28] Nevertheless, the game has its origins in England, and it was the English who first brought it here. Tradition has it that the game originated at Rugby, a public school in Warwickshire, England, in 1823 as the result of the unorthodox actions of a schoolboy named William Webb Ellis, who picked up a football and ran with it.

A version of rugby played at Winchester was introduced to the Cape in 1861 by the Reverend George Ogilvie, headmaster of Diocesan College (now Bishops High School) in Rondebosch. Bishops subsequently played a leading role in establishing the game of rugby in South Africa. The first report of a rugby-football game played in South Africa appeared in the *Cape Argus* newspaper on 23 August 1862 after a team of British officers from the 11th Regiment played a Civil Service XV at Green Point. The green jerseys that have become South Africa's national colours were the colours of the old Diocesan Rugby Football Club. They were worn for the first time by a South African side in 1903.

Afrikaners were first introduced to the game of rugby on St Helena Island. Many were sent there as prisoners of war during the South African (Second Anglo-Boer) War (1899–1902). St Helena Island was held by the British and it is said that the officers in charge of the prisoners taught rugby to give the prisoners something to relieve their boredom.[29] The Afrikaners on the island had never played rugby before but within the next 50 years or so, they would claim it as their national game.

Black South Africans also have a long history with rugby. The Western Province Coloured Rugby Union (WPCRU) was formed in Cape Town in 1886, only three years after white rugby players had formed the exclusive Western Province Rugby Union. The WPCRU included clubs from District Six (Roslyns) and the Bo-Kaap (Arabian College), and members of Arabian

College were drawn from the Muslim community. By the turn of the century, rugby had spread beyond Cape Town to Stellenbosch, Paarl and other surrounding areas, and by 1930 there were more than 200 black rugby clubs.

Cricket

Cricket was also brought to the Cape by the British; it is recorded that a match between two groups of (white) officers was played in 1808. In 1876, the city of Port Elizabeth presented a 'Champion Bat' for a competition between South African towns, and on 12 and 13 March 1889 the first test match between South Africa and England was played at St George's Park in Port Elizabeth. This was the start of cricket in South Africa at both test and first-class level.

In 1857, the British governor George Grey was instrumental in introducing cricket to the sons of black chiefs in rural areas of the Cape. He also set up a college, Zonnebloem, in District Six, Cape Town, and invited Xhosa chiefs to send their sons there. But his reasons were questionable: the education the young men received would include cricket in order to demonstrate 'the most striking proof of British power' and provide 'a perfect system of ethics and morals'.[30] It would also break down the social structure of the Xhosa, as Grey believed that once educated in the Western way, the boys would be reluctant to return to their tribal origins. Sandile and Maqoma were among the chiefs who agreed to send their sons there, but they insisted it be their second eldest – their eldest sons had the responsibility of taking over from their fathers.

The game of cricket was seen as preferable to the amusements of tribal Africans, which were 'incompatible with the Christian purity of life'.[31] In the eastern Cape, Lovedale, a Presbyterian college established in 1841 near Alice, and Healdtown, a Methodist school near Fort Beaufort, were known for their cricket. Inter-college matches were sometimes played against white colleges – it is recorded that in 1891, Lovedale beat Dale College in King William's Town by 15 runs.[32]

Former president Nelson Mandela has said of Healdtown a generation later: 'The English gentleman was what we aspired to be. We were taught and we believed the best ideas were English ideas and the best government was the English government'.[33]

Missionaries

The Protestant Moravians were the first missionaries to arrive at the Cape, and by the 19th century there would be several different practising missionary societies. In 1737, Georg Schmidt established a mission station, the Moravian Brethren at Baviaanskloof (later renamed Genadendal, Valley of Grace) in what is now the Western Cape province. It was short-lived because of tensions with the Dutch Reformed Church, but the Moravians returned in 1792 and their mission spread from Genadendal throughout the Cape. Today there is a historic village and museum at Genadendal, about 6 kilometres from Greyton.

In 1801, two missionaries from the London Missionary Society (hereafter LMS), James Read and Johannes van der Kemp (who was Dutch), founded a mission station at Bethelsdorp, near modern-day Port Elizabeth. They worked among the Khoikhoi people and the Xhosa, and, like other missionaries, established schools for black and coloured children. The missionaries made few conversions to the Christian faith, except among the Khoikhoi – Van der Kemp baptised over 100 Khoisan people before he died in 1811. The missionaries' strong views about equality between whites and blacks often caused tension with the white colonists.

The British missionaries saw it as their duty to 'civilise' black people according to British norms. They established schools for black and coloured children, which also played a part in extending British control, even if that was not their main intention. In 1828, the LMS missionary John Philip said that the missionaries of his society were 'scattering the seeds of civilization and extending British influence, creating new wants among the African people and making them more dependent on the colony'.[34] Philip believed in human rights, however, and encouraged Khoikhoi servants to report instances of maltreatment by their 'masters' to the courts. This did not sit well with the Boers and was a contributing factor to the decision of thousands of them to leave the eastern Cape in the 1830s.[35]

Another of the LMS missionaries, Robert Moffat, started his work among the Tswana people at Kuruman in the northern Cape in 1821. He taught them about ploughing, irrigation and other improved farming methods, and Kuruman became a haven in times of drought. Moffat learnt the Tswana language and translated the Bible into Tswana. He regarded this time in his life as an 'apprenticeship'[36] for the more serious work he was to do among the Ndebele under Mzilikazi in subsequent years.

Some African communities encouraged the presence of missionaries because of their knowledge of technology and Western products, for it was known that trade followed the cross. The Sotho king Moshweshwe, for example, wanted missionaries to join him because he knew that traders would follow to his kingdom. The missionaries also generally carried guns for security and for hunting. The Zulu king Dingane wanted the missionary Francis Owen to give him a gun and teach him how to use it, and there were problems when Owen refused.[37] Dingane also wanted Owen to teach him to read, which Owen was prepared to do, but he records in his diary that most appointments made with the king were not kept – Owen often arrived to find the king asleep and no one prepared to wake him.

As a source of information, the records the missionaries were obliged to keep have been invaluable. Apart from the Moravians and missionaries from the LMS, there were also Swiss missionaries and missionaries from Berlin who worked among the Venda; American missionaries who worked among the Zulu; Wesleyan missionaries who worked with the Tswana; French missionaries who worked with the Sotho, and others.

CHAPTER 4

Migrations within South Africa

The rise of powerful black kingdoms

Thus far in this history, much attention has been given to activities in the Cape, but other parts of southern Africa were also undergoing change. In the 1820s, upheavals were taking place in the northern parts of what is now KwaZulu-Natal. It was a time of transformation that has become known as the Mfecane. The term is derived from the root '*feca*', which means 'to crush'. During the Mfecane, wars and raids took place across wide areas of the country, especially in the eastern half of southern Africa – they started in present-day KwaZulu-Natal and spread to the Highveld,[1] where the Sotho people called them the Difaqane.

The effect of the warfare and migration during the Mfecane was the deaths of thousands of black people and the depopulation of large areas of southern Africa. Missionaries reported coming across people so demoralised and worn down by years of warfare that they had taken to living in trees out of fear of wild animals, and were surviving by cooking the human flesh of deceased people.[2] The missionary Robert Moffat commented in his journals that he travelled through areas in the interior which were completely depopulated, and he was told that the ruined towns had once been 'populous like locusts'; one particularly large ruined settlement had belonged to 'the great chief of the blue cattle', who had once lived with thousands of people and 'cattle like a dense mist'.[3]

Many groups were driven out of their traditional lands, which might have given white settlers the impression that they could settle there. Indeed, in the 1970s, the architects of the apartheid policy would also use this theory – that their ancestors had moved into land that had been abandoned, and were therefore justified in taking it. Nevertheless, French hunter and naturalist Adulphe Delegorgue, travelling between KwaZulu-Natal and the Magaliesberg in 1843, 'was surprised to find Sotho-speaking people everywhere',[4] which suggests that not all areas were as depopulated as was believed. In fact, many black people were simply displaced and, not wanting to live far from the graves of their ancestors, many intended to return home when the wars were over.

Some tribal groups ended up long distances from their original homes, which explains why societies living in the far north of South Africa and even beyond its borders can trace their roots back to what is now KwaZulu-Natal. The Ndebele leader Mzilikazi, for example, had come from the Natal region. He had been in the Zulu king Shaka's army but had quarrelled with Shaka and had left with a group of supporters to forge his own nation. They settled in several places in the interior before ending up across the Limpopo River, in what is now Zimbabwe. Mzilikazi also incorporated the people he conquered along the way. Robert Moffat, who knew him for 30 years, commented that the physical features of Mzilikazi's people had changed noticeably during this time.

Some tribes became fragmented and disappeared as separate entities – some weaker and smaller tribes joined with stronger groups. The Sotho leader Moshweshwe encouraged refugees into his kingdom, and consolidated his nation in what is now Lesotho.

Many myths and distortions have arisen about those troubled years and debates continue. But the fact remains that the 1820s and 1830s were a time of warfare, migration, consolidation and change, and that some powerful black kingdoms emerged – notably the Zulu, Sotho and Ndebele. The Mfecane and Difaqane produced some of our most famous historic leaders: Shaka (Zulu), Manthatisi (Tlokwa), Mzilikazi (Ndebele), Moshoeshoe (Sotho), Moletsane (Taung), Sekwati (Pedi) and Montshiwa (Rolong), all of them leaders who gathered together what was left of their tribes and rebuilt consolidated communities.

The emergence and decline of chiefdoms had been going on for centuries, but the Mfecane and the Difaqane accelerated the process, as the following case studies illustrate.

Shaka and the rise of the Zulu

The man most associated with these upheavals is the Zulu king Shaka. There is still an aura around the name Shaka, and he is remembered as a fearless and ruthless leader who destroyed other tribes and built the Zulu chiefdom into the most important power of the time.

Shaka came from the then small Zulu clan.[5] He was born circa 1787, the illegitimate son of Senzangakona, king of the Zulus. Shaka and his mother, Nandi, were exiled and found refuge in the Mthethwa kingdom, whose ruler was Dingiswayo. The Mthethwa under Dingiswayo and the Ndwandwe under Zwide were the two most important kingdoms at the time.

Under Dingiswayo, Shaka rose through the ranks of the military. He was skilled in battle strategy and became one of Dingiswayo's foremost commanders. When Shaka's father, Senzangakona, died, Dingiswayo helped Shaka usurp the Zulu throne from his older brother, and in 1816 Shaka became king of the Zulus. Two years later, Dingiswayo was murdered by Zwide, and Shaka saw the opportunity to take over much of Dingiswayo's chiefdom as well.

Shaka had worked with age regiments[6] under Dingiswayo and continued to use them as an effective military force. His men used short stabbing spears, which were more effective than the old long spears that had to be thrown at the enemy. Once in power, Shaka proceeded to set about eliminating his rivals: the rise of the Zulu kingdom is traced to this time. Environmental factors must also have played a part: there was natural population growth in the fertile Tugela Valley, and need for resources.

The term 'Zulu' has been translated as 'people of the sky', or 'as the heavens, thunder and lightning'. A praise name for the king was '*izulu eliphezulu*' (he who is in the heavens). According to some Zulu oral traditions, in battle the Zulu would generally start by burning houses and making a great noise, and this is how they acquired their name. This opinion is not shared by all: a more likely explanation is that Zulu was simply the name of the ancestor who founded the Zulu royal line in about 1670.

Shaka is also described in Zulu oral traditions as a 'lion', 'a man as big as the great mountains' and one 'who beats but is not beaten'. Of the white people who met him, traders Henry Francis Fynn and Nathaniel Isaacs referred to him as a 'savage' and 'ferocious despot', and missionary Arthur Bryant referred to him as a man who had 'no feelings for other people'.[7] The journals of a few of the Voortekkers (Boers) moving into the interior refer to a feeling of fear towards the Zulus; their servants ran away during the night if they heard rumours that the Zulus were coming.[8]

While these perceptions must have been grounded in some fact, it must be remembered that evidence often reveals more about the people who give it than of the event itself, and the comments of witnesses must be seen within the context of the time. Fynn and Isaacs wanted Britain to annex Zululand to secure land for themselves and to facilitate their trading activities, so it was in their interests to portray him badly and to suggest that he needed to be controlled. Others who came into contact with Shaka spoke well of him, and there is no evidence he ever hurt white people; Shaka's wars were against other black tribes.

The powerful image of Shaka has been perpetuated in modern times by popular television series such as *Shaka Zulu* in 1986, when Shaka was portrayed by the muscular and impressive actor, Henry Cele. The movie *Zulu Dawn*, which is not about Shaka, shows Zulu men with fine physiques dancing up a storm without signs of fatigue. Much of this imagery is fuelled by the need in all of us to find heroes in history.

Shaka remains an enigma. What we do know is that he had an aura of statesmanship and was a military genius. He conducted national ceremonies that promoted a sense of Zulu identity. It has been suggested that it was Shaka who first started using dance forms when his warriors were gathered together because he wanted them to think alike.[9]

He could also go to pieces when things did not go his way. According to some Zulu oral traditions, when his mother, Nandi, died, his grief was uncontrollable and he wanted others to suffer too. Terrible acts of cruelty towards people and animals followed. People were instructed to cry audibly and were punished if they did not. Oxen were slaughtered to appease the spirits but their meat was not allowed to be eaten; cows were also slaughtered so that calves would know what it was like to lose a mother. This continued with little relief for three months until his own grief began to pall and one of the elders managed to convince Shaka of the damage he was doing to the nation.

Shaka was assassinated in 1828 on the orders of his half-brother, Dingane. He left no heirs and Dingane succeeded him. Over time, Shaka has become a Zulu icon evoking the qualities of courage, military might and political skill. In 1975, when Inkatha (meaning 'crown'), a cultural liberation movement for Zulus, was founded by Mangosuthu Gatsha Buthelezi, it drew heavily on the image of Shaka. His name has also been used to promote business leadership and to make money. On the Durban beachfront, uShaka Marine World is a theme park comprising shops, restaurants, aquarium attractions, water rides and other entertainment venues.

Since the 1980s there has been debate about whether Shaka was as great a leader as has been made out, and whether he was the main cause of the disruptions in the 1820s and 1830s. Historian Julian Cobbing raised hackles by suggesting that the concept of a Mfecane started by Shaka was a myth created by white settlers and traders to cover up their own slaving activities. He blamed white (mainly Portuguese) slave traders who had been operating in the interior around Delagoa Bay (Lourenço Marques) for the conflicts, and said mounted Griqua to the north had also been involved. As mentioned earlier, the Griqua (descendants of the Khoikhoi and other mixed-race people) had acquired guns and horses from the colony and could wreak havoc in small groups. Cobbing argued that the activities of other chiefdoms, such as the Ndwandwe and Mthethwa, also needed to be taken into account. His opinions stimulated debate and the term 'Mfecane' began to be questioned as perhaps being too Zulucentric.

Historian John Wright added to the debate by suggesting that the activities of the Tswana chiefdoms also needed to be considered, especially the Ngwaketse, Hurutshe, Kwena, Kgatla, Rolong and Tlhaping. Some very large Tswana towns had emerged in Shaka's time and there had been much rivalry and conflict over trade between Tswana and Basotho[10] chiefdoms.

Indeed there was a lot of activity in the region at the time. The Taung and Tlokwa chiefdoms had been asserting themselves, as had the Hlubi and

Ngwane, who had moved onto the highveld south of the Vaal River. The Ndebele under Mzilikazi, who had left Zululand, established themselves near the upper Vaal River, and then moved again, leaving disruptions in their wake.

On the colony's eastern frontier, small groups of Xhosa were leaving the region and settling along the middle Orange River, where they clashed with the groups already living there. The Maroteng (or Pedi), who had been settled near the Olifants River, also moved around at this time, and the Dlamini moved from the area south of Lourenço Marques into what is now Swaziland, where they formed the nucleus of the Swazi nation. The Gaza kingdom under Soshangane between Mpumalanga and Mozambique was also emerging, and there was competition for land and resources. All these activities contributed to the disruptions of the 1820s and 1830s – a complex set of events, not only caused by the Zulu.

There is also debate about whether Shaka really did control the whole of what is now KwaZulu-Natal and beyond, as has been claimed. As he died in 1828, it seems unlikely he could have accomplished so much in 12 years. Nevertheless, as John Wright points out, the term 'Mfecane' persists because it satisfies a deep-seated need to give a name to a particular series of events. And there is no doubt that a powerful Zulu kingdom emerged at this time.

A kingdom ruled by a woman: the Tlokwa under Manthatisi

There were other powerful black leaders. In the area near present-day Harrismith in the Free State, the Tlokwa people were ruled by a woman, Manthatisi, on behalf of her son, Sekonyela, who was too young to become chief when his father died in 1815. Her people called her 'Mosayane' (the little one) because of her small size. She became an effective ruler, and her subjects began to call themselves Manthatisis instead of Tlokwa.

The missionaries referred to her people as 'Mantatees' and they were generally feared, although other marauding people were often mistaken for Mantatees.[11] Manthatatisi was subjected to Griqua raids and attacks from other displaced Nguni groups and slave traders, and sometimes forced to flee. In such circumstances, the old, very young and the sick were simply abandoned. Despite the turmoil of the time, Manthatisi managed to secure a place for her people in the Caledon valley and then survived a three-year drought. In about 1817, she launched expeditions into the lowlands, probably against the Hlubi, scored a major victory and secured vast herds of cattle.

Manthatisi is thought to have ruled 40 000 people during her regency and was a considerable presence on the land. She was a diplomat and an opportunist. She arranged marriages for Sekonyela with daughters of the powerful Sotho chief Moshoeshoe, as well as with women from neighbouring communities as a way of keeping peace. But Sekonyela was not as able a ruler as his mother. In 1852, he provoked conflict with Moshoeshoe by raiding his cattle, and was soundly defeated. The Tlokwa lost their independence, and were incorporated within Moshoeshoe's kingdom.

Mzilikazi (c. 1795–1868) and the Ndebele: a migratory kingdom

Mzilikazi (also spelled Moselekatse) was another of the great leaders. He had broken away from Shaka in 1821 and taken a small band of 200–300 men with their wives and children into the interior, migrating westwards and northwards, raiding and conquering smaller chiefdoms and incorporating many of them as soldiers or clients.[12] His following grew, and at different times he had military outposts in the provinces we now know as Mpumalanga, Gauteng, the Free State and the North West, and in the Magaliesberg Mountains. Mzilikazi's migrant kingdom was unusual in that he and his followers had no attachment to place and apparently showed no inclination to stay where their ancestors were buried. At one time his base was on the Apies River, not far from present-day Tshwane (Pretoria), and it was there that the missionary Robert Moffat first visited him in 1829. This visit was the start of a remarkable friendship, which was to last some 30 years. Much of our knowledge of Mzilikazi comes from Moffat's recollections of their meetings.

Mzilikazi was probably the most disruptive force in the interior during the Difaqane. His troops attacked at night or early dawn, causing havoc with their firebrands and spears, and leaving devastation in their wake. He had thousands of his own people put to death for disobeying him, but he also had loyal warriors who followed him everywhere, and he appeared to win the allegiance of the people he conquered. By 1829 he had a kingdom estimated to be about 60 000 people.[13] In the various places where he settled he was attacked by armed Griqua and Korana people, the Zulu and armies made up of *Bergenaars*,[14] Korana, Rolong (Tswana) and Griqua from the mission station at Philippolis[15] – evidence of the unexpected and often rather unlikely liaisons that arose out of the needs of the time.

When Mzilikazi was away on one occasion, thousands of his cattle were taken. Mzilikazi's men found the raiders while they were sleeping not far from today's Sun City.[16] They recaptured the cattle and inflicted heavy casualties.

In October 1836, one of Mzilikazi's generals attacked the Voortrekkers at Vegkop[17] and took all their stock. This was the first major conflict between the Voortrekkers and black people in the interior. In January 1837 and again in November 1837, combined Voortrekker, Griqua and Rolong forces with guns and firearms defeated Mzilikazi at Mosega (in the now North West) and at a site further north respectively. It was this set of events that finally drove Mzilikazi over the Limpopo River into present-day Zimbabwe. It was to be his last move.

Mzilikazi's life had been one of almost continuous warfare, but he survived to die peacefully of old age in Zimbabwe, where he left behind a 'new' people, the Ndebele or Matabele, made up of all the people he had conquered or assimilated into his tribe over the years; probably only about two-thirds of his people were still of Nguni descent.[18] Mzilikazi's new kingdom became known as Matabeleland. He built his new capital in the Matopo Hills and called it Bulawayo. His kingdom survived until 1893, when it was destroyed by British South African forces looking for gold. By then, Mzilikazi had been succeeded by his son, Lobengula.

Mzilikazi was much maligned in history books of the past. From a Eurocentric point of view, he was seen as a tyrant and destroyer of human life, and the man who resisted the Voortrekkers when they tried to move into the interior. Robert Moffat, however, testified to 'the discipline and superior morale' of the people under his rule, and to their 'strict courtesy', 'manners' and 'happy spirit', which was unlike the climate of intimidation and fear with which the Zulu lived under Dingane (Shaka's successor).

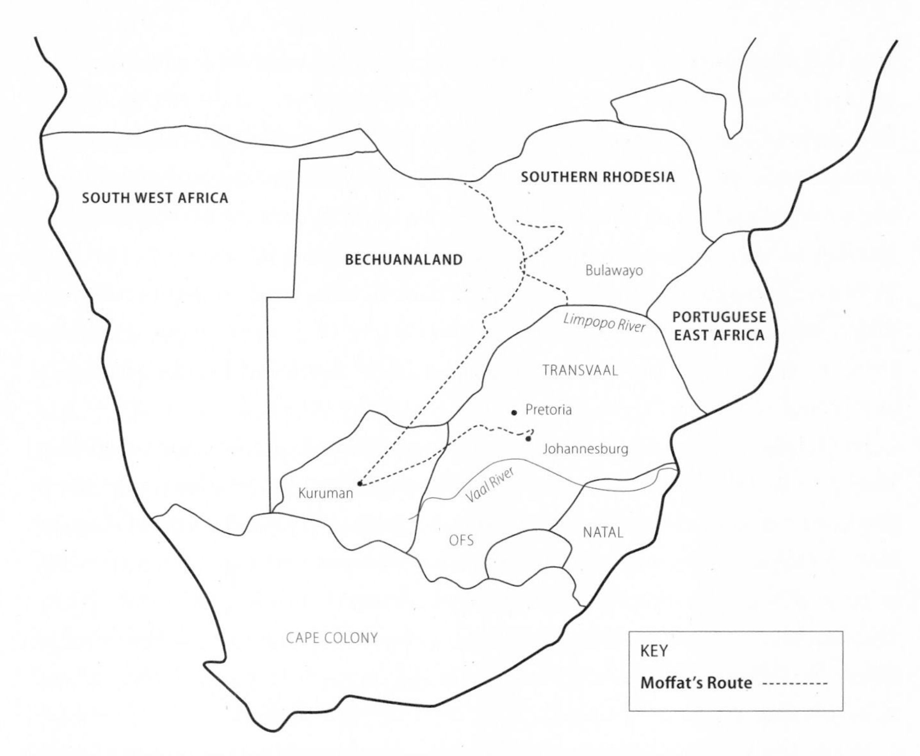

MAP 14 *Mzilikazi and his Ndebele traversed much of southern Africa in the period 1821–1837. The dotted lines on the map show the long journeys the missionary Robert Moffat undertook from his base at Kuruman, to find him over 30 years.*

Mzilikazi said he wanted to 'increase the number of his people rather than diminish them'. Moffat also refers, however, to extreme cruelty and punishment to wrongdoers, and to how Mzilikazi was evasive when asked about the people he had ordered to be put to death.[19]

Mzilikazi's extraordinary friendship with the missionary Robert Moffat started in 1829 and lasted until the latter was recalled to England some 30 years later. Moffat made many arduous journeys to find Mzilikazi in the various places where he re-established his kingdom. Mzilikazi always eagerly awaited his arrival – his runners were usually sent out days before, once they got wind of the fact that Moffat was on his way. Mzilikazi could not wait to see the gifts Moffat had brought him, and was fascinated by objects like the canister with a lid and a handkerchief sent to him by Moffat's wife, Mary.

Despite the bond between them, at no point did Mzilikazi contemplate becoming a Christian and he often commented on the fact that Moffat had only one wife, which he found disappointing. Many a night the two men lay side by side under the stars, covered by a kaross (a blanket made of animal skins), exchanging stories. Mzilikazi liked to hear about Moffat's queen (Victoria) across the sea.

Their final meeting is described in some of the most beautiful writing in Moffat's journals. They were both old men by that time, and Moffat had been recalled to England. When he arrived at Mzilikazi's kraal, Mzilikazi did not get up to greet him as he usually did. He was huddled in a corner of his hut and his kaross was drawn across his face. When he eventually got up, the kaross fell away and Moffat saw to his surprise that the old chief, perpetrator of thousands of deaths, was crying.[20] The story of their friendship is one of great psychological interest, the significance of which has never been fully understood.

Apart from Robert Moffat, Mzilikazi also befriended some of the white hunters, traders, scientists and others who came into his country,[21] although they first had to go via Kuruman to be vetted by his trusted friend Robert Moffat. Mzilikazi never trusted the Voortrekkers, nor other missionaries, especially the French, who also tried to work with him.

Soshangane and the Gaza Empire, 1824–1895

To some extent, Soshangane was also a migratory leader. He and Mzilikazi both initially lost out to Shaka, but moved out of his orbit and successfully established kingdoms of their own.

Originally a general in the Ndwandwe army under Zwide, Soshangane had broken away with a group of followers after the Ndwandwe were defeated by Shaka in 1820. Soshangane led his followers northwards, away from Shaka's control. He headed towards the Lebombo Mountains in Mozambique, forming alliances with some chiefdoms, defeating others and gradually carving out an empire of conquest known as the Gaza (or Gasa) Empire, named after his grandfather, Gasa KaLanga. The Gaza kingdom eventually extended over parts of present-day Mozambique, Mpumalanga and Limpopo.

Soshangane died in 1856. Two of his sons disputed the succession, and a grandson, Gungunyana, eventually took over. In 1895, Gungunyana was defeated by the Portuguese, who had once been allies, and the Gaza kingdom went into decline.

Moshoeshoe (or Moshweshwe) c. 1786–1870: a kingdom based on accommodation and survival

Another of the great leaders was Moshoeshoe. He was the first paramount chief of the Sotho in the Caledon River area (today's independent kingdom of Lesotho). Moshoeshoe united various small Sotho groups, many of them refugees from the Difaqane, and incorporated them into his tribe. In this way, he built the southern Sotho (or Basotho) into a large and important nation. He and Mzilikazi are two of the few leaders to rival Shaka's fame.

Moshoeshoe acquired the nickname 'Moshweshwe' because it was said that in his younger days he could steal cattle as neatly and silently as a razor shaves hair – the sound of 'Moshweshwe' is similar to that of a razor shaving hair. Moshoeshoe, however, is the correct spelling in Lesotho orthography.

In about 1821, Moshoeshoe established his village on the slopes of the Butha-Buthe Mountain, from where he managed to withstand the first invasions of the Difaqane. He was attacked by the Ngwane under Matiwane and the Tlokwa under Manthatisi, but on both occasions his men rolled boulders down the steep slopes of the mountain, driving the invaders away.

In 1824, he moved his capital to the mountain Thaba Bosiu, which means 'mountain of night' because it was believed the mountain increased in size at night. Moshoeshoe encouraged this belief, and enemies seldom came there after dark. Thaba Bosiu was an ideal place. Its height made it easy to see approaching enemies. It was also well watered and fertile. Maize and sorghum[22] could be grown on the summit, and Moshoeshoe could thus withstand a siege for indefinite periods of time. In about 1828, Matiwane attacked Thaba Bosiu but the assault failed and Moshoeshoe became the undisputed ruler of the land stretching from the Caledon River westwards to the soon-to-be-established mission station of Thaba Nchu.

Despite his reputation as a raider in his early years, Moshoeshoe never participated directly in a Difaqane raid, nor left his home base. He was attacked intermittently by all the main Difaqane marauders, but he used a combination of force and diplomacy to withstand the onslaughts. He sent cattle to feed departing enemies with the message that he knew they were far from home and therefore hungry. He did this when Mzilikazi tried to attack him, after which Mzilikazi left him alone. Moshoeshoe also sent his enemies gifts of cattle during times of drought and while Shaka was alive, he sent gifts of crane feathers, which were used in Zulu regalia.

Moshoeshoe welcomed former enemies into his fold and lent cows to impoverished newcomers who wanted to join him. He also lent cows to some of his own people who had fallen on hard times, and in return some of the calves that were born were ceded to him in what was known as the *mafiso* system. This enabled struggling men to rebuild their herds, and at the same time increased Moshoeshoe's influence and popularity.

In another diplomatic move, Moshoeshoe married the daughters of his rivals, and he was estimated to have had about 100 wives. In 1848, the Sotho state numbered about 80 000 people; by 1865, about 150 000. He said he had united 23 population units in forming the BaSotho (Basuto) nation.[23]

Moshoeshoe was aware of the new influences entering the country and initially he embraced them. In 1833 he invited missionaries from the Paris Evangelical Missionary Society to visit him. One of them, Eugène Casalis, became an adviser in his dealings with the whites. Moshoeshoe was also very interested in the settler products the traders brought. He bought European clothes, which he wore to receive white visitors. He bought household utensils and wagons, and was particularly anxious to acquire firearms and horses. He also planted European vegetables, wheat and fruit trees, and developed a taste for sugar.

By about the 1840s, however, Moshoeshoe had started to revive traditional practices of raids and warfare, and he was disturbed when the missionaries preached against this. He tried to keep his people away from them, and his relations with the British government also began to deteriorate. In January 1846, an official from the Cape, Major Warden, was sent to the Free State to define boundaries. Moshoeshoe's land bordered on that occupied by Boers (former Voortrekkers), although they had no official status there yet. It was the start of years of disputes over boundaries.

When Harry Smith became governor at the Cape, he was anxious to expand British influence beyond the Cape and to persuade the Boers to accept it. He did this by allowing them to buy farms more or less wherever they wished, and by recognising their independence. It was the start of official white appropriation of land in the interior. Many Boers then secured farms in inland parts of present-day KwaZulu-Natal, Griqualand and the Free State, which restricted black people's access to land. Moshoeshoe was one of the chiefs affected. When he objected and was asked to define his boundaries, his answer was always simple: 'My lands are where my people are.'

By 1850, the British had resorted to force. Moshoeshoe's stronghold at Thaba Bosiu was never breached and the British were forced back, but thousands of cattle were seized by the British in the process. In 1852, Moshoeshoe raised troops of some 6 000 mounted men to turn back the British, which he succeeded in doing. No one before him, nor Mzilikazi, Dingane or any of the Xhosa leaders, had marshalled, armed and mounted forces on such a large scale on an open battlefield and carried the day.[24]

It was a year later, however, in October 1853, that the British and the Boers signed the Bloemfontein Convention, giving the Boers sovereignty over the area. The new independent republic of the Orange Free State, proclaimed in 1854, included some of Moshoeshoe's former lands. Although Moshoeshoe retained some good land, and chiefdoms elsewhere (the Xhosa, Zulu, Hurutshe, Rolong and Fokeng) were relatively unaffected, the movements of many other chiefs were now limited. It was also a sign of things to come that from about 1860, Moshoeshoe started sending young men to work for wages in places like the distant Cape Colony and Natal, and in 1867 some of his men went to Kimberley after the discovery of diamonds. With the money they earned, they could buy the cattle they had once captured in raids.

By 1866 Moshoeshoe was under pressure again from the Boers in the Orange Free State. Under their president, Johannes Brand, the Boers were out for war. In 1868, Moshoeshoe asked for British protection, having decided that British sovereignty was a better option than control by the Orange

Free State. The outcome was that his country was annexed by the British, and became the British colony of Basutoland. In 1869 the British signed a treaty with the Boers at the town of Aliwal North, defining the boundaries of Basutoland. The new boundaries effectively reduced Moshoeshoe's kingdom to half its previous size. The boundaries of Moshoeshoe's kingdom were regularly revised, and disputes are ongoing to this day.

Moshoeshoe died in 1870, having led the Sotho people for over 40 years. He was buried on Thaba Bosiu, his mountain home that was never conquered. It remains a hallowed place. In 1966, after nearly a century of British rule, Basutoland became independent again, as Lesotho. The Kingdom of Lesotho still claims part of today's Free State.

Moshoeshoe fared the best and lasted the longest of the leaders at the time. He had the ability to wear different hats: he could be both tribesman and statesman, was able to deal with his own people and his rivals, including the British and the Boers. It is appropriate that one of the biographies of him, written by Leonard Thompson in 1975, is entitled *Survival in Two Worlds*.

Interactions in the eastern Cape and the Xhosa cattle-killing

In 1835 and 1857 some particularly horrific incidents occurred which indicated the pressures of the time, and the very different cultures and beliefs at play. The eastern Cape had already seen a century of conflict between white and black farmers, especially in the Zuurveld, and in the years to follow, some Xhosa chiefs were to suffer great humiliation.

In 1835, the Gcaleka chief Hintsa was tricked into captivity by the British and then shot when he tried to escape. The British governor Sir Harry Smith claimed in his memoirs to have shot Hintsa himself, after a heroic chase on horseback. Hintsa's body was mutilated, both his ears cut off as souvenirs, and his body left for his people to find.

The next governor, Sir George Grey, embarked on a programme inspired by his recent dealings with the Maori in New Zealand. Xhosa chiefs were to become salaried officials responsible to white magistrates. They were to undertake public works, like road building, to 'civilise' the Xhosa and teach them the dignity of wage labour.[25] It was Sir Grey who started the school at Zonnebloem, where the sons of chiefs learnt to play cricket. For a while there was relative peace, but then a terrible lung sickness spread among Xhosa cattle, killing an estimated eighty per cent of their herds.

What followed was a curious combination of traditional belief in sacrifice and Christian belief in resurrection. A 16-year-old Xhosa prophetess, Nongqawuse, claimed she had been told by the ancestors that if the remaining cattle were slaughtered and all crops and stores of grain destroyed, the dead cattle would come alive again and the ancestors would rise from the dead to help the Xhosa drive the British into the sea, from whence they had come.

Some mystery surrounds how and why people believed her, but it is known that Nongqawuse had the support of her uncle, a trusted councillor of the chief Sarhili (or Sarili), the son and successor of Hintsa. The uncle, Mhlakaza, who had converted to Christianity, was initially against the story, but his mother urged him to support Nongqawuse because she longed for her dead husband, who she hoped would rise again.

The community became split into believers and non-believers. On an appointed day, the new moon on 18 February 1857, an estimated 400 000 head of cattle were slaughtered and stores of grain destroyed. The Xhosa waited all day for the sun to turn its course as Nongqawuse had prophesied – but in vain. It is estimated that at least 40 000 people (about one third of the Xhosa nation) died of starvation in the famine that followed. Nongqawuse and her supporters apparently placed the blame on those people who had not killed their cattle.[26]

The event weakened the Xhosa people, thousands of whom drifted into the Cape Colony in search of work. In 1866, all the land west of the Kei River between the mountain escarpment and the Indian Ocean was incorporated into the Cape Colony, despite evidence that this had long been the land of the Xhosa (Gcaleka, Ngqika and other chiefdoms). The remaining Xhosa people and the Mfengu, who were more recent arrivals, were confined to small land holdings in the newly annexed territory.

A white migration: The 'Great Trek'

In the 1830s, the later years of the Mfecane and Difaqane coincided with the migration of the Boers (the white Dutch/Afrikaans-speaking farmers). The Boers, especially those who had moved out to the eastern borders of the Cape colony, felt that the British government was not doing enough to protect them from raids, especially from the Mfengu, who were moving southwards away from the Shaka's wars. There was also concern about the promise of slave emancipation, and resentment towards the missionaries' humanitarian ideas about servants.

Over a period of about 20 years, thousands of Boers crossed the Orange River, leaving the colony and heading northwards into the interior, and eastwards towards Natal. These people became known as the Voortrekkers or trekkers, and they had very different intent from the trekboers, who had moved around seasonally. The Voortrekkers packed all their worldly goods into wagons, and trekked with their animals as well. Their intention was to forge new settlements and create governments of their own.

Much has been made of the courage and determination of the Voortrekkers. One woman, Anna Steenkamp, described in her memoirs how her husband had died shortly before they left, and so it was she who drove the wagons out of the colony. She was in her forties at the time, and she must have been pregnant because she also described how her youngest child was born in mid-winter in a wagon on the windswept plains of what would later be the Orange Free State. By and large the trekkers appeared to be a robust people, and their traditional love of coffee may have saved them from many a stomach upset because it meant that they boiled their water.

This migration in the 1830s and 1840s became known as the 'Great Trek', although not all Afrikaners took part in it, and the grandiose name was only given by Afrikaner nationalist historians later. It is interesting to note that the Great Trek probably involved about 15 000 people; by comparison, the westerly migration of white settlers in North America involved hundreds of thousands of people and was probably the largest migration of humans in history. The trekkers numbered about one tenth of the white population in the Cape at the time,[27] and the participants were mainly from the eastern

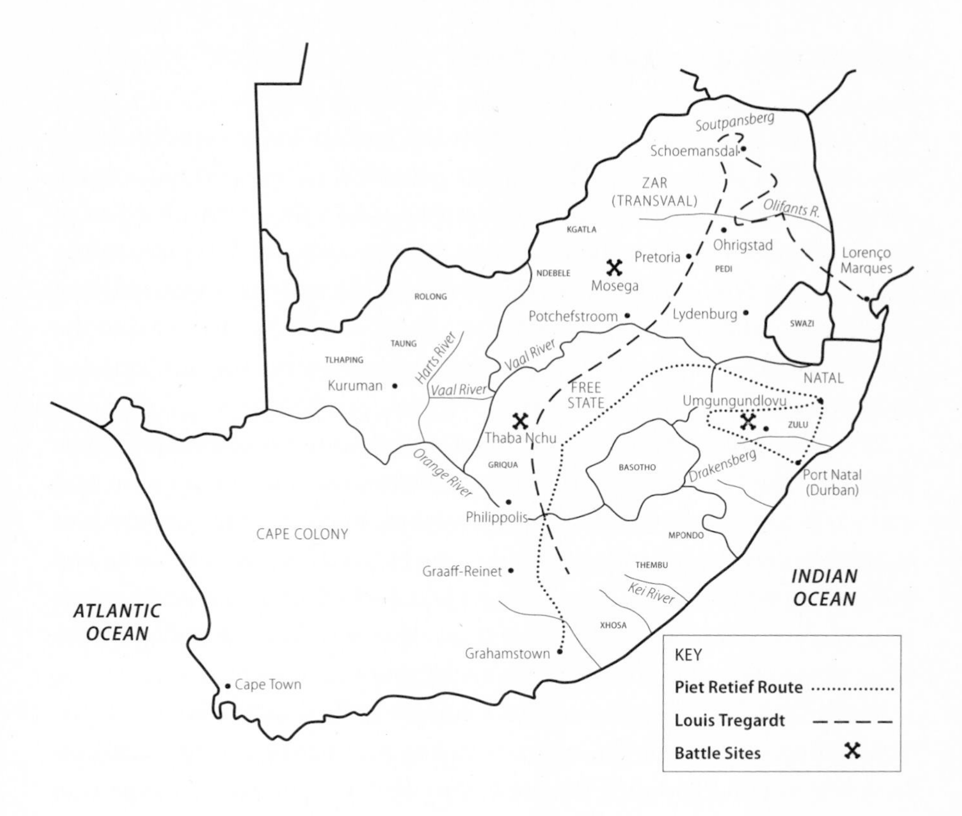

MAP 15 *Incidents of the Great Trek, and some of the towns established by the trekkers, notably Lydenburg, Potchefstroom and Schoemansdal. The map also shows two of the different routes taken by trek leaders: Louis Tregardt (Trichardt) who, like Hendrik Potgieter, headed north; and Piet Retief, who headed east. This is evidence that despite what some Afrikaner nationalist historians have said, the trekkers were not a united group.*

side of the colony – the Dutch settlers living in and around Cape Town generally did not join the movement. Neither did the British farmers in the eastern Cape, who would have had the same grievances.

British authority extended to the Tropic of Capricorn and some of the trekkers headed as far north as today's Limpopo to be beyond British jurisdiction. The response of black people to the Voortrekker settlers in the interior often led to strife. In the decades to come, many wars would be fought over land.

Thaba Nchu, 1835–1836

When the trekkers left the colony, they headed towards a mission station west of the Caledon River called Thaba Nchu, which means 'black mountain'. This mission station had been started by James Archbell and some Wesleyan missionaries in 1833 for groups of Rolong (Tswana) people who had been hard hit by the Difaqane. It was here, about 75 kilometres from what is now Bloemfontein in the Free State, that the trekkers rested after the arduous initial stages of their journey.

One of the first trekker groups, one led by Hendrik Potgieter, stayed at Thaba Nchu for a few months around December 1835 before heading north. In October 1836 at Vegkop, near present-day Heilbron in the Free State, they were attacked by the migrant Ndebele chief Mzilikazi and an estimated 5 000 warriors. The trekkers had guns and were able to repulse the Ndebele, but they lost all their cattle and supplies, and were left stranded in the highveld. Word reached the Rolong at Thaba Nchu, and one of the nearby chiefs, Moroka, sent men to rescue the trekkers, give them food and bring them back to his place, Morokashoek. There they were given gifts of cattle and helped to recover before setting off again.

In 1931, the renowned Rolong journalist and writer Solomon (Sol) Plaatje wrote: 'If South Africans were as romantic as white people in Europe and America, Morokashoek would be a hallowed spot among Voortrekker descendants, and efforts would surely be made to keep the memory of the benefactors of their ancestors. Instead there is nothing there to commemorate this act of kindness.'[28]

Blood River, 16 December 1838

Another group of trekkers, one led by Piet Retief, headed towards what is now KwaZulu-Natal, into the territory of Dingane, Shaka's successor. In 1837, Retief and a small group of his followers went to Dingane's capital at Umgungundhlovu to open negotiations. Dingane was cautious about the trekkers because he knew they had just defeated Mzilikazi and his Ndebele. The trekkers had guns, whereas Dingane's efforts to obtain guns had failed.

Negotiations went on for weeks and at first seemed to be going well, but in February 1838, while Retief and some of his men were watching the

Zulus dance in an Umgungundhlovu arena, there was the command from Dingane to 'kill the wizards'. Retief and his men were dragged out and murdered nearby on what became known as the 'hill of execution'.

Boer and Zulu oral traditions vary about the use of the word 'wizard', or *abathakathi*. The trekkers had circled the arena before coming in. They were in fact looking for the entrance, but according to Zulu superstition this behaviour is synonymous with witches or wizards, and there was reason for mistrust.[29]

The murder was later seen by Afrikaner nationalist historians as an outrageous act of treachery on the part of Dingane, and Retief became an instant martyr. Little attempt was made to understand why Dingane might have acted this way after the white people had entered his territory and asked for land, offering nothing in return. The trekkers had had firearms and tricks like handcuffs, which they had demonstrated to Dingane. Dingane had probably also been aware that the rest of Retief's party were already coming down the Drakensberg into his land before the negotiations had been completed, which was disrespectful to him as king of that land.

Some years before, a man named Jacob Hlambamanzi,[30] who had spent some time with white people in the Cape and Natal, had told Dingane that white people would start coming into his country in twos and threes (like, presumably, the missionaries and other travellers) but that others would then come in big numbers in houses that moved (wagons), and that these people would want to stay. This prophecy must have seemed to Dingane to be coming true.

The trekkers in Natal were leaderless until November 1838, when a new leader, Andries Pretorius, arrived in Natal with a mixed commando of 468 trekkers, 3 British men, 60 black soldiers and an unknown number of servants. A revenge battle was to take place and the site was selected with care: it was to be the Ncome River (later renamed Blood River because of the blood spilt in battle there). The trekkers set up camp and waited for the Zulu to come to them. They positioned their wagons in a laager[31] beside a deep donga that formed a natural barrier on one side. Some 300 metres to the east, the river formed a deep pool.

At first light the next morning the Zulu army was seen approaching, and the battle began well before sunrise. It is said that the Zulu liked to attack at dawn as that is when men's spirits are at their lowest. An estimated 10 000 Zulu warriors took part in the battle, and at least 3 000 died, many meeting their deaths by being cornered in the donga and the pool, pursued by Pretorius and 150 mounted-and-armed men. There was no loss of life on the trekker side, and only three were wounded.[32]

In the decades to come, some Afrikaner nationalist historians saw much significance in this trekker victory, believing it to be ordained by God: a few days before the battle, some members of Pretorius's group had taken a vow that if God gave them a victory against the Zulu, the day of the battle (16 December), would always be celebrated in his name. It would be known as the Day of the Covenant (and after 1982, the Day of the Vow). A small church was built in commemoration and still stands in Pietermaritzburg, and 16 December was subsequently celebrated as an annual public holiday. Since 1994 is has been referred to as the Day of Reconciliation.

Some historians have disputed this incident's significance. In 1988, Ben Liebenberg questioned whether a vow taken by a small number of people could be seen as binding for all Afrikaners when most Afrikaners did not even know that the battle was taking place. He contended that the victory at Blood River was simply the inevitable outcome of superior military strategy and firearms over assegais. The concept of divine intervention, in his opinion, was a myth created to underpin Afrikaner nationalism.[33]

Schoemansdal – a Voortrekker settlement, 1848–1867

Schoemansdal was the trekkers' northernmost settlement. It is situated at the foot of the Soutpansberg ('salt pan') Mountains in the far north of Limpopo, close to the border of Zimbabwe.

The trekkers who arrived there under the leadership of Hendrik Potgieter and later Stephanus Schoeman were mostly rebels who had quarrelled with other trekker leaders and decided to go their own way. By the time they reached Schoemansdal, they had travelled some 1 600 kilometres in wagons from the eastern Cape. In travelling so far north, this rebel group of trekkers had crossed the Tropic of Capricorn, which meant they were beyond British jurisdiction.

Venda[34] people lived in the area of Schoemansdal, and had done so since about the 13th century. There they mined copper (near what is now Musina) and iron, and traded with the Shona in the north. One of their trade routes through the mountains into Zimbabwe can still be seen from the air. They rarely ventured south. The Soutpansberg had also been home to San hunter-gatherers, and examples of their art can still be seen in high places.

The Venda had an interesting interpretation of this San art: they did not believe it was the work of people. Instead, they believed that the paintings were representations of their own ancestral spirits, and that if they did not bring them gifts, the pictures would disappear as a sign that the gods were angry. At a place known as Tombo-la-ndou ('rock of the elephant'), in front of paintings of red elephants very high up, sticks can still be found driven into the ground adorned with the remnants of copper-wire bangles, cloth, buttons and other gifts.

Guns feature prominently in the story of Schoemansdal, especially with regard to hunting. In coming so far north, the Boers were probably following elephant, which had been largely shot out in the Ohrigstad area where they had previously been living. At the time, ivory was a much sought-after commodity by European (especially Portuguese) traders from Delagoa Bay (Maputo).

Relations between the trekkers (henceforth the Boers) and the Venda were initially fairly cordial. Although Boers who crossed colonial boundaries into the African interior were forbidden to sell guns to black people, these regulations were ineffectual so far north. The Boers gave the Venda guns, and they became hunting and trading partners, especially for ivory. The Soutpansberg area was a hunter's paradise because animals were attracted by the salt in the pan at its western base. After the Boers arrived, Schoemansdal became an important trading centre for ivory, game skins, horns, wood and salt, with the Boers gradually gaining control. The amounts that were traded can never be accurately estimated, but there are reports that enormous amounts of gunpowder and lead were sent there, and former curator of the Schoemansdal museum, Dirk de Witt, estimated over a century later that in 1856 alone, 10 000 elephant were shot, equalling 80 000 tons of ivory.[35]

One of the traders was João Albasini, a Portuguese man from Mozambique. He came to the area regularly with goods carried by donkeys and porters to trade for ivory. In 1853 he settled in the Schoemansdal area and lived there until his death in 1888; a dam in the area is named after him. Albasini had a large following of Tsonga-Shangaan people who had come with him from Mozambique, and whom he taught to use muzzle loaders and to treat ivory and animal skins for the export market. His Tsonga hunters operated especially in the eastern tsetse[36] country, where the Boers would not risk taking their horses. Albasini's men used donkeys for transport because they resisted the sleeping-sickness disease better. He became superintendent of the Soutpansberg in 1869; and in another twist in the tale, he and his Tsonga-Shangaan vigilantes became tax collectors for the Boer 'government'.

The taxes levied on the Venda were 5 beasts, 5 pieces of ivory, 35 pieces of copper or 20 hides of leopard.[37] Every hut had to pay a goat and a sheep. The introduction of taxation was foreign to the Venda, and evidence of forts at Schoemansdal and on Albasini's farm suggest that there was much resistance.

Close to Schoemansdal was a mixed-race community headed by a white man, Coenraad de Buys, who had come to the area from the Zuurveld area in the Cape in 1821. He was probably the first white man in the area, ahead of Albasini and the Boers, having travelled north after being wanted for illegal activities in the Cape. He and his entourage settled in the Mara area about 50 kilometres west of Makhado (Louis Trichardt). Coenraad de Buys was nearly seven foot tall. He had several wives (a coloured woman of Cape Malay decent and several black women) and numerous children. Three of his sons married Venda women, and their mixed-race descendants still own the land in a small town called Buysdorp in Limpopo's Mara area.

The remote far north attracted hunters and adventurers and became quite a cosmopolitan community. Schoemansdal was a flourishing town before the trekkers established the more well-known towns of Pretoria (now Tshwane) or Pietersburg (now Polokwane). It is the only town established by the Voortrekkers that no longer exists.[38]

In 1864, the Venda chief Ramabulana died without appointing a successor, and his son Makhado became the ruling chief. The Boers had supported Davanha, Makhado's brother, and relations between the Venda and the Boers subsequently became tense. In 1867, the Commandant-General of the Transvaal, Paul Kruger,[39] visited Schoemansdal and ordered the Boers to abandon the town, saying he could not protect them so far north. The Boers broke down their houses and took what they could to settlements further south. Some Venda came to the site after they had gone and burned down what was left, suggesting that there was terrible conflict by that time.

Dirk de Witt believes that the trekkers' prime reason for leaving Schoemansdal after only 19 years was because there were no more elephants, although the usual explanation is that the Venda drove them out.[40] After the Boers left Schoemansdal in 1867, the Venda and the Tsonga took control of the ivory trade, but by the 1880s the Boers had established much firmer control over the whole area that later became known as the Transvaal, and which included land right up to the border of what is now Zimbabwe.

The town of Schoemansdal was never rebuilt and was eventually reclaimed by bush. It remained that way for 120 years, until archaeological excavations revealed the site, and the decision was made to try to recreate Schoemansdal as a living museum. Replicas of the original houses were built using materials from the environment, as the trekkers would have done, but the project was never completed. In 2008, a runaway winter veld fire destroyed the museum. Schoemansdal had existed for the brief period of 19 years, but provides a microcosm of pioneering life.

'Black Ivory'

Slavery was officially abolished in the Cape Colony in 1834, but there is evidence that a kind of slavery persisted right into the 1860s in some northern parts of the country, including in the Soutpansberg area. It involved black children who were stolen away from weaker or unsuspecting tribes and sold to the Boer farmers. Boer Republican law forbade slavery but permitted the sale of children for labour, a loophole which led to widespread abuse. German scientist and explorer Karl Mauch described the baskets, carpets and boxes used to hide children on wagons in the Soutpansberg, and noted that the practice usually took place under the cover of night.[41] Similarly, missionaries Heinrich Grützner and Alexander Merensky recorded in 1866 that up to a thousand children were entered into a contract book at the Soutpansberg landdrost's office each year,[42] and were sold or exchanged for items such as blankets, guns and hunting dogs. The children became *inboekselinge*, children literally 'booked in' for a period of labour (usually several years) on Boer farms. They were also referred to as 'black ivory'.

The significance of the Great Trek

The trekker migration resulted in the establishment of two Boer republics: the Zuid-Afrikaansche Republiek (ZAR or South African Republic, later simply called the Transvaal) in 1852, and the Orange Free State (OFS) in 1854. This meant that in the mid-19th century, 'South Africa' consisted of an independent republican north (the Transvaal and the OFS) and a colonial south (the Cape and Natal, which were still under British government), as well as a series of black kingdoms of varying size and strength.

Not long afterwards, when mineral wealth was discovered in the interior, the British government regretted their decision to allow the Boers to establish their two republics. In 1877, the British Colonial Secretary, Lord Carnarvon, proposed a federation of the republics and colonies, but this met with resistance from the Boers. The First Anglo-Boer War (1880–1881) was fought over this issue, and the Boers retained their independence. In 1899, a Second Anglo-Boer War (the South African War) broke out. This time, the Boers were defeated and the republics were annexed to Britain. By then, Afrikaner republican ideals had taken root in the former Boer republics, and would grow and develop in the years that followed.

The ascendancy of the Afrikaners in the 1930s and 1940s can be attributed in no small measure to the Great Trek. Easily recognisable symbols of wagons and laagers, as well as stories of bloodshed and martyrdom – especially the murder of Piet Retief and the battle at Blood River – served to inspire and unite Afrikaners, irrespective of age or class, and paved the way for the more extreme forms of Afrikaner nationalism that took hold in the years to come.

CHAPTER 5

The mineral discoveries

In 1867, transformation of a different kind began in South Africa. This was when diamonds were discovered in the areas now known as Hopetown and Kimberley in the northern Cape, followed 19 years later in 1886 by the discovery of the main Witwatersrand gold reef running through Johannesburg in what is now Gauteng – the name 'Gauteng' means 'place of gold' in the Sotho language. In the early 1900s, base metals (copper, tin, iron and others) were discovered in what is now Limpopo, and it became clear that South Africa had deposits of almost every important metal and mineral known to man.

These mineral discoveries changed South Africa from an essentially agricultural and rural country to one that was increasingly industrial and urbanised. The change took place quickly, and is referred to as South Africa's 'mineral revolution'. Although black people had mined gold, copper, iron and tin for centuries, the new discoveries were on a scale unprecedented until that time. Diamonds and gold attracted people from the rest of South Africa and all over the world. A second great trek, much larger than the first, began to Kimberley and Johannesburg, swelling the number of white people in the country and bringing in more skilled workers (miners, engineers, geologists, artisans and others). This was to have significant implications for the lives of black people and Afrikaners, the majority of whom were farmers.

For over three decades, from approximately 1970 until 2007, South Africa would be the world's leading producer of gold. The richest gold mine in the world for much of that time was West Driefontein gold mine,[1] approximately 10 kilometres from the town of Carletonville in western Gauteng (about 67 kilometres west of Johannesburg). By the time the mine had come into full production in 1970, South Africa produced 79 per cent of the 'free world' gold (or 62 per cent of total production including gold produced in Communist Bloc countries). In more recent years, other countries have risen to the fore: in 2007, South Africa's production of 220 metric tonnes was overtaken by China, which produced 276 metric tonnes, and the following year the United States, Australia and China all posted higher production figures than South Africa. The total amount of gold mined in the world since the beginning of measured time still remains surprisingly small: an estimated 174 100 tonnes, an amount that would constitute a cube some 21 metres each side – which could be carried by any modern large transport tanker.[2] South Africa still ranks within the top five producers of gold and diamonds in the world.[3]

Neighbouring Botswana is now the world's leading producer of diamonds. Within South Africa, the diamond fields at Kimberley, Cullinan (north of Pretoria) and the Venetia site in Limpopo are famous worldwide, as are the deposits in the seabed off the northern coast of the Western Cape. Some of the largest diamonds in the world have been found at Cullinan, the most famous being the Cullinan Diamond, named after the owner of the mine, Thomas Cullinan, and discovered in 1905. In its uncut state, it measured roughly 98 millimetres long, 57 millimetres wide and 67 millimetres high, and weighed 3 106 carats (621 grams).[4]

Gold has had value since time immemorial – for centuries, it has been an internationally trusted store of wealth. Banks kept gold in their vaults and issued bank notes representative of that value. Gold never loses its lustre: the gold jewellery at Mapungubwe and Thulamela gleamed as brightly on the day it was rediscovered as when it had been buried hundreds of years before. The highest demand for gold is still from the jewellery industry, nowadays mainly from India and other countries in Asia whereas the biggest markets used to be Europe and North America.[5] But in recent times, the gold mining industry in South Africa has fallen into what some financial advisers call a 'twilight zone', one of the reasons being the prohibitive cost and time involved in starting a new mine – it can sometimes take as much as 15 years before full production is reached. The industry is no longer attracting overseas investment as it did before; gold has lost some of its 'shine' and is not seen as much of a 'hedge' against inflation any more. Most nations abandoned the gold standard as the basis of their monetary systems in the 20th century, although many still hold substantial gold reserves; the trend is now towards industrials.[6]

In 1886, when the main Witwatersrand gold reef was discovered, there was great excitement; it was probably the largest single capitalist development to occur outside Europe and North America in the last two decades of the 19th century. The discovery had global implications and caused much frenzied (and often unwise) speculation on the stock exchanges of the world, especially in London.[7]

The gold-bearing reef turned out to be 300 kilometres in extent and has produced the richest and deepest gold mines in the world. The production records set at the Driefontein mines have never been surpassed, nor have the deep levels set by Western Deep Levels mine and more recently AngloGold Ashanti's TauTona mine, both near Carletonville. In 2008, TauTona reached a depth of 3.9 kilometres. It can take an hour for workers to reach the rock face in lift cages travelling at 58 kilometres per hour, and sophisticated air conditioning is needed because temperatures can reach 55 degrees centigrade.

South Africa is also rich in semi-precious stones and base metals. The Bushveld Complex in Limpopo is regarded as one of the geological wonders of the world for the variety of base metals it contains. It extends some 66 000 square kilometres (the size of Ireland) and has the world's largest reserves of the platinum-group metals, as well as large quantities of iron, tin (rare in other parts of the world), copper and other base metals. There are also rich deposits of silver and base metals, especially lead, zinc and copper in the area around Aggeneys in the Northern Cape. Remarkably, geologists say there is still huge potential for the discovery of more deposits in areas yet to be exhaustively explored.

A former prime minister of South Africa, Jan Smuts, when referring to South Africa's mineral wealth, once said simply: 'God emptied his pockets over this southern continent, and scattered on our land not just gold and other mineral wealth but beauty and something to appeal to the human spirit.'[8]

Two of the world's biggest, diversified mining companies also originated in South Africa: BHP Billiton, which arose from a merger between the South African company Billiton and the Australian company BHP; and Anglo American plc, which owned many major subsidiaries such as Anglo American Platinum, Anglo Coal, Impala Platinum and Kumba Iron Ore. In 2016, Anglo American went through major restructuring of its divisions, disposed of some of its assets and trimmed its investments to focus on platinum, diamonds and copper.[9] In May 2015 it was reported that the government had set up a team to investigate and assess the possibility of shale-gas development in South Africa, an indication that fracking will also be part of South Africa's future.

It was the mineral revolution that led to the development of South Africa's infrastructure, its railways and harbours, and a more capital-intensive agriculture to meet growing markets and the needs of a growing population.

Diamonds

Kimberley

The story of diamonds starts in 1867 when a farmer's son picked up an interesting stone near the confluence of the Harts and Vaal Rivers in the area of Hopetown. He put it in his pocket and later used it in a game of five stones. His mother noticed its unusual appearance and asked a neighbour to look at it. It turned out to be a 21.25-carat diamond, later cut to a 10.73-carat brilliant and named the Eureka Diamond, meaning 'I found it!' The diamond had probably been spewed from a diamond-bearing volcanic pipe in the area of Kimberley, 126 kilometres away, and washed down by one of the rivers.

It is said that the local Tswana people had known about these stones for years and that after it rained, they would join hands and walk in a human chain, eyes downcast, looking for them. Diamonds do not sparkle until they are cut into facets (faces or sides), but when wet, their opaque colour reflects sunlight. The Tswana collected the stones for their traditional healers, who used them in rituals. It is possible that many diamonds still lie buried in the area around Hopetown and Kimberley.

The rich diamond-bearing volcanic pipe at Kimberley was discovered in 1869 and subsequent excavations there resulted in the Kimberley 'Big Hole'. A further six diamond-bearing volcanic pipes were to be discovered in the area. The Big Hole was on a farm owned by the De Beer brothers, who had bought it for £50 in 1860. In 1867, they sold the farm for £6 000, believing they had made a fortune. Within 50 years, diamonds to the value of £95 million had been mined on that farm. One of the first mining companies established there by Cecil John Rhodes kept the name 'De Beers', even though the brothers were no longer the owners, and the name has become synonymous with South African diamonds.

In its heyday, the Big Hole was excavated to a depth of 240 metres. It was dug by pick and shovel, and was the largest manmade hole in the world at that time. Over the years, it has filled with debris and water, with the result that only about 175 metres of the hole is visible now. The mine ceased production in 1914. Experts say that there are probably more diamonds remaining in the volcanic pipe than have ever been removed, but they are too deep to recover.

Mining the Big Hole was hazardous, and Kimberley was a dangerous place – many lives were lost. Men had their stomachs slit open and searched if it was suspected they had found diamonds and swallowed them until they could get safely away.[10] Cocopans are small carts about 2 metres high that run on rails, and they were used to transport ore underground. Next to the Big Hole is a cocopan with a sign that reads: 'If all the diamonds recovered from the mines could be gathered together they would fill three cocopans such as these.' It is a poignant reminder of the value people have attached to certain objects and the risks they have taken to attain them.

When the diamond-bearing volcanic pipes were discovered in the Kimberley area, there was controversy over who owned the land since many boundaries came together almost at that point. The De Beer brothers' farm lay between the rivers that formed the natural boundaries of the Orange Free State, a Boer republic. The Boers in the OFS believed they had the right to the land, but it was also claimed by the Boers in the South African

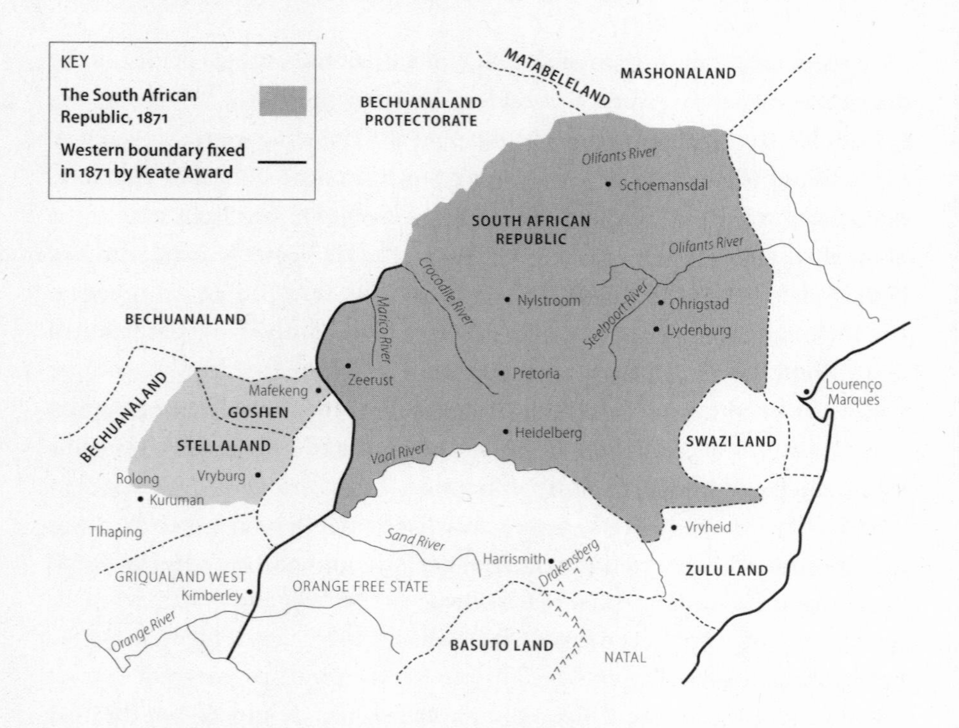

MAP 16 *Diamond areas, and areas of land dispute, 1870–1890.*

Republic (Transvaal), the Tlhaping (Tswana) chief, Mahura, and the Griqua leader, Nikolaas Waterboer.

The Griqua people had been forced into a semi-nomadic existence beyond the Cape borders, but with missionary assistance they had established two settlements: Griquatown under the leadership of the Waterboer family, and Philippolis in the southern Transorangia under the leadership of Adam Kok II. In the diamond-areas dispute, the British supported the claims of Nikolaas Waterboer, although their motives were dubious. In October 1871, the British administrator of Natal, Lieutenant Robert Keate, was called in to arbitrate and the decision was made to annex[11] the area, ostensibly in support of the Griqua, under the name the Crown Colony of Griqualand West. In 1880, however, Griqualand West was incorporated within the boundaries of the Cape Colony.

The OFS contingent were offered £90 000 in compensation to withdraw their application for the diamond areas. The British had effectively taken over the area at the expense of the Griqua and all other contenders. The area came to be called Kimberley after Lord Kimberley, the British Secretary of State for the Colonies. It quickly became the second-largest town in South Africa: only Cape Town was larger, and Johannesburg had not been developed yet.

By 1871, some 13 000 whites and 15 000 blacks had descended upon Kimberley, and by the 1880s there were some 50 000 people living there. The town was laid out quickly to meet the demand for houses, and it is still easy to get lost in Kimberley's higgledy-piggledy streets.

Kimberley is a city of firsts in many respects. The first professional nurses were trained in Kimberley, the first aerodrome in Africa was established there and the first South African pilots were trained to fly Paterson Biplanes[12] at the Kimberley aerodrome. Kimberley was also the first city in the southern hemisphere to have electric street lighting – the lights of Kimberley came on in September 1882.

Cecil John Rhodes

Cecil John Rhodes was key in the developments at Kimberley. He had come to South Africa from England as a young man, sickly and virtually penniless, and had worked initially as a labourer hauling buckets on a cotton farm in Natal, and then as a speculative digger in Kimberley. He said later that these experiences taught him the dignity of labour, something he intended to impart to others. In 1888, Rhodes raised £1 million from the Rothschild family in London, which enabled him to buy out all his rivals in Kimberley and establish De Beers Consolidated Mines. This gave him and his partner, Charles Rudd, effective control of the diamond industry. Cecil Rhodes, Barnett Isaacs (better known as Barney Barnato), Lionel Phillips, Dale Lace and others like them would lay the foundations for modern capitalist development in South Africa, but it came at a cost as the old ways of life were destroyed.

Rhodes made money in diamonds and then moved on to gold in Johannesburg, where in 1887 he established the company Gold Fields of South Africa Ltd, a company that was to last over a hundred years until its merger with another mining house, Gencor, in 1998.

Rhodes died in 1902 at the age of 49. By then he was a millionaire many times over, but the story is told that he could have made even more: during 1886, in the initial rush to stake gold claims, Rhodes was in Johannesburg but left in a hurry when he heard that Neville Pickering, his secretary (believed to be his partner) was dying back in Kimberley. As there was no room in the horse-drawn coach, Rhodes travelled on the roof of the coach in his haste to get to him.

As a young man, Pickering had come to Kimberley from Bulawayo in Rhodesia (now Zimbabwe) to make his fortune, leaving a young fiancée back home. Both were the children of missionaries. After he began working for Rhodes, Pickering's return visits to Bulawayo dwindled, and it was rumoured that he was in a homosexual relationship with the much older Rhodes. When she heard the news, his fiancée committed suicide. A plaque on a small house in Bulawayo commemorates the life of this young woman, who is also believed to have been the first white child born in Rhodesia.[13]

Rhodes died gasping for breath at his home in Cape Town, saying, 'So much to do, so little time.' It had been his intention to spread British control from the Cape to Cairo and had got as far as the two Rhodesias (today's Zambia and Zimbabwe), which for years bore his name. It was always thought he had suffered from lung problems, but modern medical knowledge suggests his symptoms were synonymous with what is commonly called a hole in the heart,[14] which is easily corrected nowadays, usually in infancy. Part of Rhodes' vast fortune was left for scholarships for young men to study at Oxford[15] because he believed that British education was the best in the world.

In the 1920s, Sir Ernest Oppenheimer, who had come to South Africa in 1902 as a representative for a London-based diamond company, bought the controlling interest in De Beers, and it was no longer associated with Rhodes. The two men never met. In 2006, De Beers sponsored renovations of the Big Hole and the surrounding historic village at Kimberley. An open-air museum and miniature diamond-rush town complete with shops, houses, banks, a church, taverns and a boxing academy recall the frenzied early years. The Eureka Diamond – the first diamond in South Africa, discovered by a farmer's son – is also on display there.

On 2 December 2015 it was announced that De Beers had sold its Kimberley mines to a consortium controlled by Ekapa Mining and Petra Diamonds, thus bringing to an end 127 years of De Beers mining at Kimberley.[16] In 2014, 722 000 carats of diamonds were recovered from tailings (waste rock) from the Kimberley mines, but there have been no new major discoveries in the area since the 1990s. Large diamonds are still discovered elsewhere, however: in January 2014, a 12-carat diamond described as being of unique colour, clarity and size was discovered at the Cullinan mine near Pretoria and named 'Blue Moon'. After a period on exhibition, it was sold for the world-record price of $48.4 million: the Hong Kong buyer bought it for his seven-year-old daughter and renamed it 'The Blue Moon of Josephine'.

For many people, Cecil John Rhodes is associated with much that went wrong in South Africa, especially the exploitation of black labour and the reduction of franchise opportunities for black people. The British had instituted a system which allowed for a limited franchise based on property ownership, but when Rhodes became prime minister of the Cape in 1891, he raised the property qualifications for the franchise from £25 to £75, which effectively disenfranchised most black and coloured people. In April 2015, human excrement was thrown over a statue of Rhodes at the University of Cape Town, and the statue was eventually removed.

Gold

Pilgrim's Rest

In the 1860s and 1870s, 'gold fever' was also in the air, with large numbers of prospectors looking for alluvial gold in the sand and gravel of river beds and streams in the area of what is now Sabie in Mpumalanga. The story goes that a prospector, Alec Patterson, nicknamed 'Wheelbarrow Patterson' because he carried all his meagre belongings in a wheelbarrow, moved away from Sabie because it was too crowded, and found gold in a stream about 5 kilometres away in the area that became known as Pilgrim's Rest. He tried to keep his find a secret, but a rush of prospectors followed and further

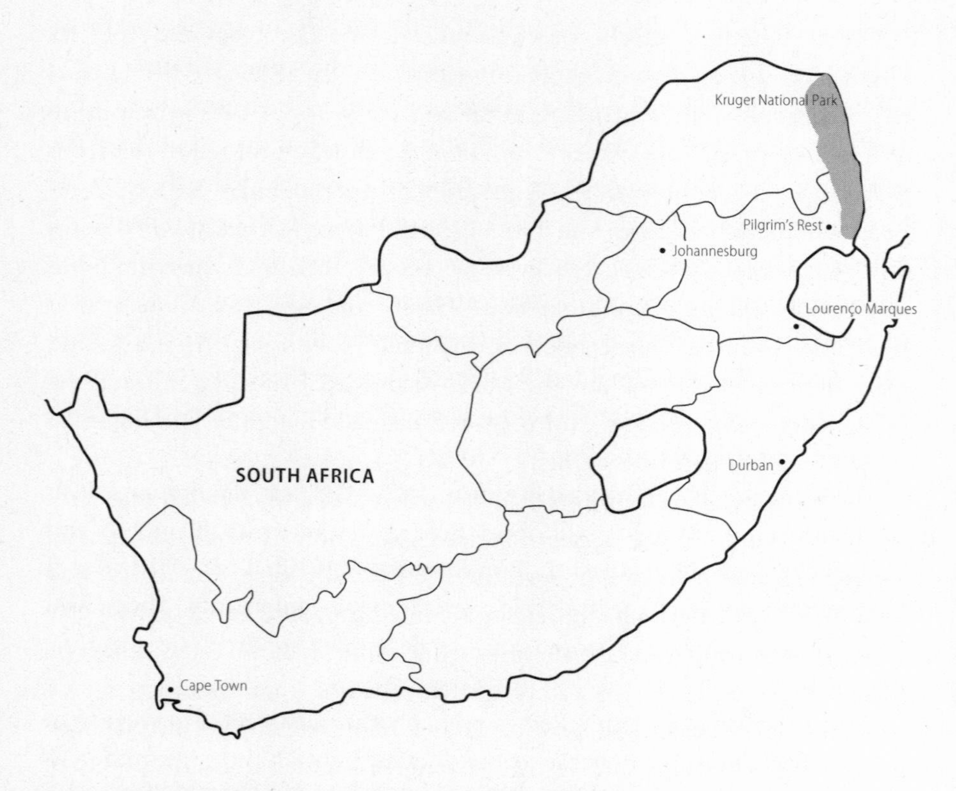

MAP 17 *Pilgrim's Rest, South Africa's first payable gold mining centre.*

deposits were found in the hills nearby. On 22 September 1873, Pilgrim's Rest was officially proclaimed a gold field, and in less than a year, 1 500 diggers were working 4 000 claims there. Pilgrim's Rest became the most payable gold-mining venture of the time.

Transport riders bringing equipment and supplies from Lourenço Marques (now Maputo) to Pilgrim's Rest had to pass through lion country in what is now the Skukuza area of the Kruger National Park. Many of them never made it out: game wardens doing excavations in the Kruger Park still come across the bones of some of those early transport riders and their oxen, some still with rusted harnesses around their necks.

One of the transport riders was Percy FitzPatrick (1862–1931), the celebrated author of *Jock of the Bushveld*, a book about his adventures as a transport rider to Pilgrim's Rest with his faithful dog, Jock, a Staffordshire bull terrier. The book was published in 1907 and became a children's classic that is still read today.[17] FitzPatrick was born to Irish parents in King William's Town in what is now the Eastern Cape, but moved all over the country during his varied career. He brought back wild animals from his hunting trips to start what is now the Johannesburg Zoo, and helped to establish citrus farming in South Africa. He also became a leading mining financier and politician in Johannesburg and Pretoria, supporting British interests in South Africa, especially around the time of the Anglo-Boer War. FitzPatrick was knighted for his services to the Crown, becoming Sir Percy FitzPatrick in 1902, before writing his famous story. His name remains synonymous with Pilgrim's Rest.

The whole town of Pilgrim's Rest was declared a national monument in 1986, and some mining is still done there. A stream runs through it and visitors can walk along it past the boulders that were lifted out of the stream long ago, to see if nuggets of gold were trapped underneath. Shops and places to stay have been restored, and the little town captures the spirit of a bygone era.

The graveyard at Pilgrim's Rest is probably the most visited graveyard in South Africa, most likely because it is situated right on the edge of the village and people can easily walk to it. Many of the graves are of young men who died of fever. The graves are above the ground because the ground was too rocky to dig down, and they all face the same way, except for one: the 'Robber's Grave'. It is said that he was buried perpendicular to the others so that he could not see the rising sun.

Barberton and the Witwatersrand

In 1884 quartz gold was discovered at Barberton in Mpumalanga, and in 1886 an Australian maverick called George Harrison stumbled across a rocky outcrop of conglomerate gold on a farm, Langlaagte, which is now a suburb of Johannesburg. Harrison recognised the potential of this outcrop as he had seen something similar in Australia. He had, in fact, stumbled across the main Witwatersrand gold reef. When he sent rock samples for testing, he apparently said, 'I think I have found a payable gold field'. He was

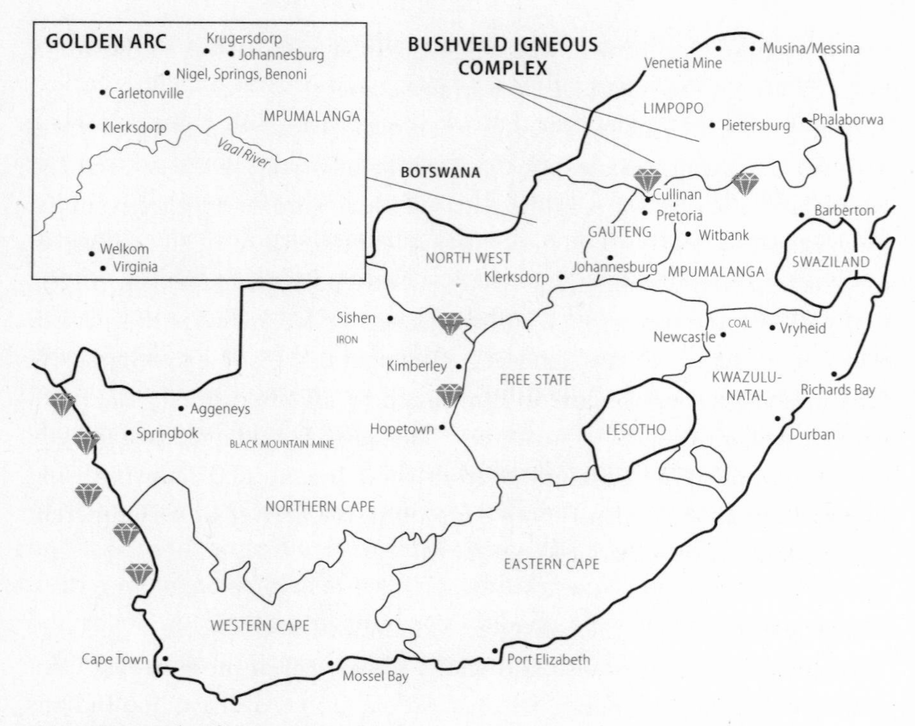

MAP 18 *Mineral-rich areas in South Africa.*

KEY

Bushveld Igneous Complex: This area is rich in the platinum-group metals – platinum, palladium, osmium, indium, rhodium and ruthenium – as well as iron, tin, chromium, titanium and vanadium.

Springbok, Aggeneys, Pofadder and surrounds: These areas have rich deposits of copper, zinc, lead and silver. They are also close to the famous Namaqualand wild flowers reserves that attract visitors in their spring season, August to September.

not wrong: his was the discovery that launched the gold-mining industry in the Transvaal in earnest. Not long afterwards, George Harrison sold his discoverer's claim for a small fee rumoured to be about £10, and disappeared from history. Nothing further is known about him.

In 1886, there were probably about 3 000 people living in and around Johannesburg. The area had not previously attracted much settlement because it was not considered good farming land. Within ten years, when an official census was taken in 1896, there were 100 000 people living there.[18] In the space of a century, Johannesburg was rebuilt four times. First it was a tented camp, then a town of tin shanties, then of four-storey Edwardian brick buildings, then a city of modern skyscrapers.[19]

People came to Johannesburg from all over: Britain, Germany, France, Australia, the United States, Russia, Lithuania, Poland, Hungary and the Netherlands, as well as from other parts of South Africa. The biggest immigrant group was the English. Between 1895 and 1898 a total of 86 000 British citizens arrived in South Africa, making South Africa the second most popular port of emigration from Britain (after the United States) in this period. Historian Charles van Onselen has commented that his research into early Johannesburg brought home to him just how mobile ordinary men and women were in the late 19th century, and how they adapted to radically different worlds. The immigrants from rural Ireland and industrialising England are an example of those who found themselves in very different circumstances at the foot of Africa.[20]

The arrival of Asian immigrants and Mohandas Gandhi

The mineral discoveries also stimulated the arrival of more people from Asia. Over the 50-year period between 1860 and 1911, over 150 000 Indians were brought to South Africa to work as indentured labourers on the sugar plantations in Natal.[21] Indians had first been brought to South Africa by the VOC as slaves in the 17th century. After 1849, small numbers had been brought in as indentured workers to work on the Natal sugar farms, in accordance with a belief that Indians were more suited to plantation work than black people. The practice of bringing in Indians as indentured workers accelerated after the mineral discoveries, and Indian labour stimulated the production of sugar to such an extent that it became the main item in the Natal economy. Indians were given five-year contracts at the end of which they could return to India, but at least 50% chose to stay, despite the harsh conditions. Many also became informal traders, seizing the opportunities afforded by the mineral discoveries and the growing population.

In 1904, just after the South African (Anglo-Boer) War (1899–1902), 60 000 Chinese men arrived in South Africa. The gold mines had closed during the war, during which time many black workers had returned to their rural homes. They were reluctant to come back in case the fighting started again. The Transvaal government negotiated with the Chinese government for workers, who were drawn from the poorer northern regions of China. The workers helped the mining industry recover. Although most were sent back in 1908 because of pressure from white mine workers' unions, some did stay on.

Indian and Chinese people had to live separately from whites and they faced the same kind of discrimination as did black people. So too did the famous Indian lawyer, Mohandas Gandhi, when he came to South Africa aged 24 in 1893 to work as a legal representative for Indian traders based in Pretoria. Gandhi was thrown off a train in Pietermaritzburg for refusing to move from a first-class carriage reserved for whites; he was also barred from several hotels and even ordered by a magistrate in a Durban court to remove his turban, which he refused to do.

These events were a turning point in Gandhi's life, and made him aware of social injustice, a cause which he would resist by nonviolent means for the rest of his life. His strategy of nonviolent resistance became known as satyagraha, and it has inspired popular struggles all over the world.[22] His own efforts became focused on both improving the rights of Indians in South Africa and on leading the independence movement (from Britain) in India. Interestingly, although he deplored the policy of discrimination in South Africa, he nevertheless encouraged more Indians to come here.

Gandhi's experiences in South Africa also shaped his religious views. Gandhi's religious background was mixed: his father was a Hindu and his mother from a Pranami Vaishnava (both Hindi sects) tradition. During the 21 years he spent in South Africa, his clients included both wealthy Muslim businessmen and impoverished Hindu indentured labourers. He regarded them all as Indians, irrespective of caste, and said later that his experiences in South Africa had helped him to understand the social complexities of India.

Early Johannesburg's inhabitants

Johannesburg attracted a cosmopolitan mix of adventurers and risk-takers, people prepared to work for and invest in the mining industry despite the problems. The people who came to Johannesburg were quite different from those in Pretoria, the more conservative seat of government only some 50 kilometres away – Johannesburg probably had (and possibly still has) more than its share of what sociologists call the 'A-type' personality.[23]

Historians have commented on the 'Jewishness' of the early mining industry, especially among its successful names: Alfred Beit, George Albu, Lionel Phillips, Barney Barnato, Solly Joel and Sir Ernest Oppenheimer were all Jewish. There were also a number of Jewish East Europeans who became gold-mining entrepreneurs. The Hungarian Alois Nellmapius, for example, befriended President Paul Kruger and won a concession to run a horse-drawn tramway in and around Johannesburg, and Sammy Marks was given a concession to set up a factory near Pretoria to make liquor from Boer farmers' excess grain.[24] Van Onselen estimates that there were some 7 000 Jews from Lithuania, Russia and Poland in Johannesburg in 1898,[25] many of whom became wealthy in their own right.

When the city of Johannesburg was laid out, suburbs for the rich (Doornfontein and Parktown) were zoned on the east and those for the poorer whites (Fordsburg and Vrededorp) on the west. This was a deliberate reversal of the situation in London, where the rich lived in the famous West End and poorer people came from the East End, and was done to avoid the stigma apparently attached to people like mine owner Barney Barnato, who came from London's east side.

The mine owners were dubbed the 'Randlords' as they tried to dress and live the lifestyle of the wealthy back in Britain. The Randlords and their wives lived originally in Doornfontein, on the east side of downtown Johannesburg, but gradually began to move out towards what is now Parktown, away from the dust of the mine dumps. They built stately homes, a few of which still stand today. The houses, complete with rolling lawns and stables for the horses, were modelled on similar stately homes back in England and other parts of Europe, even to the extent of facing south instead of north, which would have been more appropriate to the local climate. Notable among these mansions are Northwards, Villa Arcadia and The View. The first of them, Hohenheim (meaning 'home on the hill' in German), built for Lionel Phillips and his wife, Florence, between 1892 and 1894, was demolished in 1972 to make way for the Johannesburg General

Hospital. Interestingly, when Phillips returned to England, his house was bought by Percy Fitzpatrick of *Jock of the Bushveld* fame.

While most black people came as migrant workers for the mines, some came to do domestic work or to provide laundry services at the Braamfontein Spruit. On the East Rand (east of Johannesburg), some previously rural black women who had followed their men to the mines set up lucrative but illegal beer-brewing businesses to supplement their income. Because women were not allowed to live with their men in the single-sex compounds on the mines, they lived wherever they could – including in slum conditions in backyards or on the outskirts of town.

During Lord Milner's administration of the Transvaal in 1902 it was decided to import white girls for domestic work, to free up black male 'houseboys' for work on the mines. Irish girls were particularly requested because they were deemed to be 'generally stronger and less liable to illness than the Scotch or English girls'.[26] In one instance, a boatload of young white women from Ireland arrived to work as maids for the wives of the Randlords. Being attracted to people of the same class, some of the Irish women began relationships with the black men employed to work in the mansions' stables – an unexpected turn of events in South Africa at the time.

A number of Afrikaner farmers had also seen opportunities in early Johannesburg and came to set up transport businesses carrying men and equipment around the mines in their oxen- or horse-drawn cabs, and making bricks that they baked in the sun. They did not have the technological skills the mines needed, but they could use their rural skills in the urban setting. They lived in the suburbs of Vrededorp and Fordsburg.

Inevitably in a mining setting where most of the population was male, there were also the prostitutes. Between 1892 and 1894, Johannesburg's prostitutes came mainly from the Cape Colony but after a rail link was established from Lourenço Marques to Johannesburg in 1895, women from other countries, notably France, Germany, Belgium, the United States and Russia, came to Johannesburg as well. The number of French-speaking women engaged in prostitution was substantial enough that newspaper reporters began to refer to a block in downtown early Johannesburg as

'Frenchfontein'. Some of these French-speaking women had worked on the vineyards in France until crop failures had forced them to seek new job opportunities. They'd come by boat along the east coast of Africa, disembarked at Lourenço Marques, then travelled by train to Johannesburg. Van Onselen describes how 'from the doors, windows and verandahs of brightly painted houses in Frenchfontein, women – in various stages of undress – called out endearments and invitations to passing men'.[27]

The Gold Reef City entertainment venue south of Johannesburg, built on the site of the old Crown Mines, has tried to recreate early Johannesburg with models dressed in the style of Victorian England: stylish men in formal suits, and elegant women with long dresses and hats with ostrich feathers. Van Onselen has shown that while this might have been true for the rich, it was hardly the case for the majority. Putting 'a collar and tie' on early Johannesburg to make it respectable was nigh impossible.[28] Men of all colours and cultures outnumbered women ten to one,[29] and it was a rough place.

In a letter dated 13 November 1898, the author Olive Schreiner described Johannesburg as 'a great fiendish hell of a city sprung up in ten years ... a city of glitter and gold and wickedness, palaces, brothels, and gambling halls'.[30] Schreiner was 'astounded' by what was happening there. Indeed, early Johannesburg had an inevitable underworld of gangsters and criminals. One of the worst was the notorious racketeer and psychopath Joseph Silver (although he used several names) – a man who had operated all over the world and who might even have been the serial killer Jack the Ripper.[31]

Economic considerations: the migrant labour system

By the end of the 19th century, the Witwatersrand was the world's largest single producer of gold,[32] with mines that were producing a quarter of the world's newly mined gold. As far back as 1820, the British Government had adopted the gold standard, which meant British currency was backed by reserves of gold. Other trading countries, including South Africa, gradually followed suit, and by the late 19th century, the gold standard was almost but not entirely universal.[33] This meant that the price of gold was fixed internationally, and this is still the case[34] – unlike the price of diamonds, which fluctuates according to supply and demand. The fixed price of gold had important implications for the mining industry: if the ore was low grade or a mine experienced problems, the price of gold could not compensate. Mine owners thus resorted to cost-cutting methods, which led to the exploitation of labour – especially vulnerable black labour.

At mines in both Kimberley and Johannesburg there were problems of recovery. At Kimberley, in the days before X-ray sorters, recovery was erratic, and mining the Big Hole was dangerous because only primitive ropes and hauling equipment were used. In the case of gold, the mines were rich in terms of extent, but poor in terms of yield: the actual seam of gold is thin, and an enormous amount of ore has to be mined in order to yield a small amount of gold (sometimes about 2 tons of ore for just 21 grams of gold). The gold-bearing ore is also deep, which raises the problem of ventilation. In the Witwatersrand the ore is embedded in pyritic rock, which is hard and does not yield easily.

The mines were thus capital intensive. Small-claim holders quickly lost out and companies with large amounts of capital took over. Shares in these companies were floated on the stock exchanges of the world, and attracted French, German, British and American investment capital. The company Wernher-Beit, for example, was started by Germans Julius Wernher and Alfred Beit, but most of its shareholders were French. In 1893, the Robinson Deep Mine south of Johannesburg had 2 055 shareholders, 913 of whom were French.[35] While overseas investment certainly accelerated the mining industry's financial success, company directors were constantly under pressure to make profits and keep their shareholders happy.

Equipment and skilled labour had to be imported and wages for skilled workers had to be high enough to attract skilled people, so some costs could not be avoided. The early, low-technology mines also needed large numbers of manual labourers, and so it was there that mine owners cut costs. On an average gold mine in 1897, a black worker categorised as 'unskilled' was paid £2 to £3 a month as opposed to the £18 to £22 paid to the 'skilled' white worker.[36]

Single black men from the rural areas could come to the mines as migrant workers, and could be housed cheaply in compounds without the mines having to provide for whole families. Compounds also provided an effective means of control over the workforce: compounds could be easily surrounded if there was trouble. There were usually separate compounds for different tribal groups, which meant that ethnic differences could be maintained and workers were unlikely to form a united opposition against management. This system began in Kimberley and soon spread to the Witwatersrand.

Conditions in compounds varied but were generally appalling. With men living in close proximity to each other, influenza, pneumonia, tuberculosis and other respiratory and contagious diseases spread. The most dreaded miners' disease was silicosis, or phthysis, which is when a miner's lungs become clogged with dust from underground. It was generally referred to as 'the white death' because it seemed at the time to affect mainly whites. The historian Elaine Katz has shown that black miners did get it, however, but sometimes fared better because after each contract they returned to their rural homes, where they breathed clean air. It is not known how many black men did, in fact, die of silicosis as proper records for black people were not kept in the early years of the mining industry;[37] it was also never investigated why some men did not return for second contracts. This may well have been because they were too ill, or had succumbed to the disease.

Many mine owners had the ear of the politicians in the Cape or were in politics themselves, and thus had the means to influence policy towards specific interests: Cecil Rhodes, for example, became prime minister of the Cape in 1891, and Lionel Phillips became a Member of Parliament and president of the Chamber of Mines in 1892. They were influential in having laws passed that imposed taxes on black people living in homesteads in the rural areas, forcing them to go to the mines to earn the money to pay them. This ensured a consistent and regular supply of labour. In a sinister foreshadow of apartheid policy, black people's movement also became controlled with the use of passes that forced them to go to the areas where their labour was needed.

Most migrant workers went to the mines out of economic necessity. According to one man who gave evidence to a commission: 'I ran away from school during the East Coast (red water) fever[38] and am illiterate. I was married before I went to the mines. My father's eldest brother paid the first bride wealth, seven heads of cattle. That was not the end. I had to pay nine more. Things were hard so I went to the mines 12 times and finished before I was old. I had a second wife when I finished. I bought cattle and clothes.'[39]

Young men sometimes went to the mines because the money earned in '*Egoli*' (Johannesburg, the 'City of Gold') and Kimberley gave them status back home. For others, mine work provided a chance to earn cash for specific ends. The Pedi (northern Sotho) king Sekhukhune, who ruled in the area of today's Mpumalanga between 1861 and 1882, sent whole regiments of men to Kimberley in the early 1870s to earn money to buy guns. For security, the men travelled in regiments of about 200 at a time. A contract of four to eight months was generally sufficient to buy a gun, which the men then bought from traders on their way home. The Hlubi chief Langalibalele (in what is now KwaZulu-Natal) did the same. It was the demand of the local magistrate that he surrender his guns that sparked off the Langalibalele Rebellion in 1873.

It was usually the fit young men who went to work in Kimberley and Johannesburg, and so the rural areas declined.[40] Women and old men had to farm as best they could, and children grew up without fathers. Unlike in other industrialising societies where labour migration is a temporary transition from rural to urban life, the migrant labour system still continues in South Africa today, with many men still living in compounds or hostels.

Trade unions

In the early years of the mining industry, black and coloured workers were not allowed to form unions to negotiate for better conditions. It was only in 1982 that the National Union of Mine Workers (NUM) for black mine workers was founded under the leadership of Cyril Ramaphosa, and other unions followed suit.

In the days of the early mines, however, artisans from Britain had brought ideas of unions with them, and white workers quickly established unions to protect their privileged positions from undercutting. Militant unionism added to the problems of the early mine owners, because whites insisted on a policy of job reservation and resisted attempts to 'de-skill' jobs to enable parts of them to be done more cheaply by blacks. As a result of pressure and threats of strikes from the unions, 'job reservation' or the 'job colour bar', which reserved certain jobs for whites, was in place as early as 1893 and continued long after it would have been in the interests of the mine owners to do away with it.[41] The state also aided in job restrictions. The state mining engineer AJ Klimke reserved two major job categories for whites: hauling and blasting. The latter required the use of dynamite, and Klimke maintained that the restriction was for purposes of safety – the implication being that blacks could not be trusted with jobs where safety was at stake.[42]

The Kruger government

The diamond fields were in the British colony of the Cape, but gold was in the Transvaal, a Boer republic, which was headed at the time by President Paul Kruger. Paul Kruger's government was conservatively run with Boer interests at heart. As president, Kruger was concerned about the pace of developments and the increasing demands of the predominantly British mine owners once gold had been discovered in his country. He was determined that his Boers would not lose out, but the measures he took frustrated the mine owners, who felt his essentially agricultural government was out of touch with the demands of a developing gold mining industry and a hindrance to its success.

Kruger's tactics were quite wily: he resisted implementing electric trams, which would have facilitated transport in Johannesburg, because his Boers provided transport services with horse- and oxen-driven wagons. He also gave concessions to favoured people and imposed protective tariffs to stop mine owners from importing goods that could be made locally: a major grievance was dynamite, essential for blasting, which could have been imported more cheaply. Kruger was also criticised for failing to provide the infrastructure to police the migrant labour system and prevent desertion from the mines. The mine owners' grievances, especially with regard to Kruger's governance, contributed in part to the outbreak of the South African (Second Anglo-Boer) War in 1899.

British imperialist ambitions

The last three decades of the 19th century were a time of unprecedented change in South Africa. Few leaders of the time understood the diverse needs of a rapidly industrialising society, or could offer satisfactory solutions. Local problems escalated against the very real backdrop of British imperialist ambition. Following the precedent of the Canadian Confederation in 1867, Britain began to have similar ideas of a confederation or federation in South Africa. This would entail bringing together the British colonies of the Cape and Natal, the Boer republics of the Transvaal and the Orange Free State, and the various African chiefdoms in a union under the British crown.

Before the discovery of diamonds and gold, South Africa had not been regarded as much of an asset, but from the mid-1870s, after diamonds had been discovered, Britain's attitude towards South Africa began to change. Although the main Witwatersrand gold reef would only be discovered in the mid-1880s, gold fever had been fuelled a decade earlier by sporadic finds of gold recorded in the eastern Transvaal, which was administered by the Boers. As it became evident that there was mineral wealth in South Africa, the British began to envisage a closer union – one that would be easier to administer and which would have important strategic and economic implications for empire.

The Boers needed to be persuaded to become part of such a union; Boers living in the Cape as well as in the Boer republics had to be convinced of the advantages of a confederation so that they didn't form an alternative focus of loyalty. Black people had been acquiring firearms for some time and this was seen as a threat both to the Boer republics in the interior, and to the security of the proposed confederation. To remove this threat, the independent African kingdoms were to be disarmed or absorbed. In return for the Boers' cooperation, the British undertook to reduce the power of the independent African kingdoms, especially the Pedi and the Zulu, who were located on the borders of the Transvaal. This guarantee of security would also encourage British investors to increase their purchases of shares in South African companies.

In fact, these early British federation plans ended in failure, but one has to keep them in mind when considering the next section: the decline of the African chiefdoms.

CHAPTER 6

The decline of the African chiefdoms and the rural areas

The Xhosa and the southern Sotho

For a while, some of the African kingdoms were affected positively by the mineral discoveries, especially those living close enough to supply food and other services. For some, it was a golden age of farming.

Historian Colin Bundy refers to trade in Fingoland[1] (Xhosa country) in the eastern Cape worth £150 000 in 1875, and to a firm in Port Elizabeth that had an annual turnover of £200 000 from the African trade. Moshoeshoe's people (the southern Sotho) also prospered, and Basutoland was regarded as the 'grain basket' of the interior at one time. It was also recorded that some poorer Boers did transport riding for the wealthier Sotho farmers. All of this came to an end when black farmers lost access to much of their land.[2]

The Xhosa were the first to be affected. In 1865, the Cape Colony incorporated the area later known as the Ciskei (in the eastern Cape). In 1875 it annexed Fingoland, followed by Gcalekaland and Thembuland in 1885, and Mpondoland in 1894 – the areas later known collectively as the Transkei. Colonial forces had clashed with different Xhosa groups in nine frontier wars, the last of them in 1877 and 1878, when colonial forces together with burgher and volunteer units had fought the Xhosa in the Ciskei and the Transkei, effectively ending Xhosa independence.

In 1878, in what became known as the Northern Border Rebellion, colonial forces were also deployed against the Korana[3] in the districts along the

Orange River. Two years later, they were employed against the Sotho, but in the case of the latter, the outcome was different.

The southern Sotho kingdom of Basutoland had been annexed by Britain in 1868, at the request of Moshoeshoe. He had asked for British protection after years of conflict with the Orange Free State Boers on his borders. From 1868 to 1871, Basutoland was a British Protectorate, but in 1871 it was placed under the nominal control of the Cape authorities. Traditional Basotho leaders still wielded some power until the late 1870s, when Cape authorities made moves to exercise more control over Basutoland. It was proposed that part of Basutoland be released for white settlement, and that the Sotho people surrender their guns to the Cape authorities in terms of the Peace Protection Act. These guns had generally been hard earned on the diamond fields at Kimberley, and most Sotho were not prepared to do this. They were not offered compensation, either.

In the chaos and civil conflict between rival chiefs that followed, Moshoeshoe's successor, Letsie, was prepared to comply with the legislation about guns, but his son, his brother and some other chiefs were not. The Cape prime minister, John Sprigg, made a fruitless visit to Basutoland to negotiate, and Cape colonial forces were then sent to Basutoland to quell the rebellion. What ensued between Sotho rebels and Cape forces became known as the Gun War (1880–1881).

The Sotho rebels resorted to guerrilla warfare, and they had the advantage that they knew the mountainous terrain of their country well. The neighbouring Mpondomise joined in the conflict in support of the Sotho, and the Cape forces suffered heavy casualties. In October, a mounted column of British Army Lancers (1st Regiment, Cape Mounted Yeomanry) was ambushed at Qalabane Mountain near Mafeteng, killing 39 people.

This defeat and the already high cost of the war discouraged the Cape authorities. A peace treaty was signed with Sotho chiefs in 1881, which conceded to them most of the points in dispute. The land remained in Sotho hands, and it was agreed that the Sotho register their guns rather than hand them in. Some Sotho were not satisfied, however, and the unrest continued.

It had become increasingly clear that the Cape government could not control Basutoland, and they asked the British Crown to take over, which it did in 1884. Basutoland was brought under the direct authority of the British monarch (Queen Victoria at the time), with legislative and executive powers vested in the High Commissioner. Basutoland was the first of the British High Commission territories.[4] British rather than Cape control of Basutoland meant that Basutoland would be independent from the future political developments in South Africa, and it still exercised some internal autonomy. In 1966 it became independent as the Kingdom of Lesotho.

The Griqua

The Griqua were also to lose their independence. They were pastoral or cattle-keeping people of Khoikhoi and other mixed-race origin,[5] and had settled in the northern Cape Colony before being forced into a semi-nomadic existence beyond the borders. Their various treks had assumed similar proportions to those of the more well-known Afrikaner Voortrekkers, but with the help of missionaries they had established two small kingdoms north of the Orange River[6]: Griquatown in 1804, under the leadership of Nikolaas Waterboer, and Philippolis in 1826, under the leadership of Adam Kok. Philippolis was named after the London Missionary Society member John Phillip, and is the oldest settlement in what is now the Free State.

In the 1830s, Griqua who had acquired horses and guns from the Cape Colony were a dominant force along the middle Orange River. After diamonds were discovered near Griquatown in 1867 however, the writing was on the wall for the Griqua living there: the land was annexed as Griqualand West in 1871, and then incorporated into the Cape Colony in 1880. Griqua who sold their farms to white settlers became poverty-stricken.

Adam Kok's Griqua suffered a similar fate. Adam Kok was succeeded by Adam Kok II and then Adam Kok III, who in 1861 became the victim of a secret agreement between the British and the Free State Boers to make the Griqua give up some of their lands. After Griqualand West was annexed in 1871, about 2 000 Griqua, led by Adam Kok III, embarked on a two-year trek across the Drakensberg Mountains to find a new place to settle.

In 1872 the town of Kokstad was founded, but in 1875 Adam Kok III was killed in a road accident: he fell off a cart in the mountains of Mzimkulu. At about the same time, the Cape government lifted its ban on the sale of alcohol and by 1878 Griqua society had virtually disintegrated. In 1879 Griqualand East was also formally annexed to the Cape Colony.

The Tswana (or Western Sotho)

The Tswana chiefdoms suffered a similar fate. The Tswana were a populous but disunited people who had been badly affected by the Difaqane[7] of the 1820s and 1830s. For a few years in the late 1860s and early 1870s, some southern Tswana people, especially the Tlhaping, made a good living supplying food and fuel to the people in Kimberley. For a time, the area between Hopetown and Kimberley abounded with antelope, and abundant trees provided fuel for the mines. But the antelope were eventually shot out and trees were cut down faster than they could reproduce. By the early 1890s, there had been a rapid decline in the Tlhaping's fortunes.

The Tswana also became pawns in a conflict over land between the British and the Boers. Both the British and the Boers took advantage of divisions between the different Tswana groups and formed alliances with them. The Boers temporarily won a round in the disputes and carved out two new small republics: Stellaland and Goshen[8] in the areas which are now Vryburg and Mahikeng (formerly Mafikeng and historically Mafeking), both created on Tswana land. But the republics were short-lived, and in 1885 the British annexed most of the land in the area as British Bechuanaland. Of that land, only 8% was reserved for African occupation.[9] In 1895, the northern parts of Tswana land were annexed to Britain as the Bechuanaland Protectorate. Part of that land now falls under North West, but the rest is part of the independent republic of Botswana, established in 1966.

For years after the Union was established in South Africa in 1910, there were attempts to bring Bechuanaland into the South African fold, but Britain had always resisted.

For some years there was an independence movement in Bechuanaland led by Seretse Khama, the legitimate heir to the Ngwato chieftainship.

Khama had studied at Oxford, where he married a British woman, Ruth Williams, in 1950. This caused consternation in South Africa, because by then Afrikaner nationalist policies were in place and there was a ban on interracial marriages. Pressure from South Africa contributed to the British decision to ban Seretse Khama and his wife from returning to Bechuanaland. It was six years before he was allowed to return, but as a private citizen he was banned from inheriting the tribal kingship.

Botswana's independence came about in the spirit of the 1960s, when Britain was letting go of most of her colonies. In June 1964, Britain finally accepted proposals for a democratic self-government in Bechuanaland, and in 1965 the seat of government of Bechuanaland was moved from Mahikeng in South Africa to the newly established city of Gaborone, near the South African border. A new constitution was drawn up, and the country became independent on 30 September 1966. In the first general elections, Seretse Khama was elected as the first president, and was subsequently re-elected twice.

The Zulu

The powerful Zulu were also victims of British imperialist ambitions, but the outcome for them was different to that of the Tswana. They would lose their independence, but not before a war was fought that captured the imagination of the world and became one of the most notorious wars in Africa: the Anglo-Zulu War of 1879.

After Shaka, the Zulu leaders were Shaka's half-brother, Dingane (1828–1840); Dingane's half-brother, Mpande (1840–1872); Mpande's son, Cetshwayo (1873–1884); and Cetshwayo's son, Dinuzulu[10] (1884–1913). Mpande had a long reign of 32 years and there was relative peace during this time. He was not militaristic, although he did embark on campaigns against the Swazi. In 1853, during Mpande's reign, Theophilus Shepstone[11] became the Secretary for Native Affairs in Natal. The Zulu called him *Somstewu*, 'Father of whiteness'. Shepstone pretended to be friendly, but in fact instituted a system in Natal that contributed to their decline: he said that black people 'could not expect to live as before', and created a system of reserves administered by white officials. Many historians have seen this as the forerunner of South Africa's racial segregation and apartheid.

In 1873, Shepstone went to Zululand to attend the coronation of Cetshwayo, taking with him a tinsel crown, a scarlet-and-gold cloak and other tawdry coronation gear, hoping to impress the new king and make him accept a form of indirect British rule. The Zulus, however, had already proclaimed Cetshwayo as their king, and Cetshwayo delighted in making the British delegation wait several days before another ceremony took place. During the second ceremony, Shepstone gave a lengthy speech warning against unnecessary shedding of blood and other issues that were not of British concern in Cetshwayo's Zulu kingdom.

Shepstone was aware that Cetshwayo had restored Zulu militancy (after Mpande's relatively peaceful reign), and that he could call on some 15–20 000 men from his age regiments if the need arose.[12] Cetshwayo had done this partly as a show of independence against growing British interference, but ultimately this tactic was used against him. Shepstone made it sound like a threat to peace and prosperity in South Africa, and advocated that Zulu power be broken.

This was also in keeping with the federation plans that were underway. In 1874, Henry Bartle Frere was sent to South Africa as High Commissioner to try to bring about a federation similar to that which had been achieved seven years earlier in Canada. Shepstone supported this, and he and Frere were in collaboration. The stumbling blocks were the two Boer republics and the Zulu and Pedi kingdoms on their borders.

Shepstone set about persuading the Boers in the South African Republic (Transvaal) that annexation by the British and joining a federation with the British colonies of Natal and the Cape would be in their best interests. In return, black kingdoms that posed a threat – especially the Zulu and the Pedi – would be suppressed. His efforts bore fruit, and on 12 April 1877, Shepstone annexed the Transvaal to the Crown, hoisted the Union Jack, and stayed on as its administrator. In 1878, the Cape passed legislation allowing the governor to disarm entire districts. The Zulu in colonial Natal would also be affected by this legislation.

The Anglo-Zulu War of 1879

The Battle of Isandlwana

In fulfilment of his deal with the Boers, Shepstone's next step was to suppress the Zulu. In 1878 a quarrel was provoked with Cetshwayo. Frere, acting on his own initiative and without waiting for permission from Whitehall[13], sent Cetshwayo an ultimatum the terms of which he could not accept. One of the terms was that Cetshwayo's military system be discontinued and other military regulations adopted – on consultation with British representatives. This was, in effect, asking him to disband his army.

Other terms reflected British interference in Zulu customs and laws. Cetshwayo was told his men should be free to marry, not be forced to wait until they had served in an age regiment and washed their spears in blood. He was also ordered to send back two of his men who had entered Natal looking for the wives of one of his chiefs, Sihayo. The wives had been accused of adultery and had sought refuge in Natal. The men had found the wives and taken them back to Zululand, where they were executed. Cetshwayo was told to send the men back to Natal, where they would be tried for murder. He was also ordered to pay a fine of 500 cattle for this outrage, and told that a British agent would be stationed in Zululand to make sure these provisions were carried out. When Cetshwayo refused to agree to the terms of the ultimatum, he was made to look the aggressor. Cetshwayo had not sought or wanted conflict, but the British now had an excuse for war.

Not all British officials were in favour. Sir Michael Hicks Beach, Secretary of State for the Colonies, wanted a peaceful settlement with the Zulu people, but Frere took advantage of the time delay in communication with London, and issued the ultimatum before Hicks Beach's reply had been received.[14] In January 1879, Frere ordered British troops, including men of the 2/24 regiment led by Lord Chelmsford accompanied by volunteer Natal military units and members of the Natal African Contingent (some 1 700 men altogether), to invade Zululand and head towards Cetshwayo's capital at Ulundi.[15]

The month of January in KwaZulu-Natal is hot and wet, and the rivers are often in full flood. The British soldiers and their allies crossed the border of Natal into Zululand on 11 January 1878 and moved slowly, often through pouring rain, with oxen pulling heavy wagons. The soldiers were inappropriately dressed in heavy red uniforms and boots, and they carried cumbersome Martini-Henry rifles,[16] which had to be reloaded after every shot. By 20 January, after nine days, they had only marched some 16 kilometres, and set up camp at Isandlwana, east of the Tugela River. Isandlwana is a strange-shaped mountain said by the Zulu to resemble the stomach of an ox.

By contrast, the Zulu knew the terrain and moved quickly, covering around 80 kilometres in five days. Zulu women and adolescent boys accompanied the army for the first few days, shouting and ululating, and carrying pots of porridge on their heads to supplement the food the Zulu soldiers had with them. The Zulu wore protective charms around their necks and smoked horns of cannabis to give them courage. They were equipped with assegais (thrusting spears), throwing spears, clubs, shields made of cowhide and guns. The Zulu had acquired hundreds of guns by this time, but they were generally of poor quality. Many of the British troops who died at Isandlwana nevertheless had gunshot wounds.

Isandlwana was only meant to be a temporary camp and Chelmsford did not take the necessary precautions to secure it, something for which he was heavily criticised later. He had also boasted beforehand that such unsophisticated people as the Zulu would be easy to beat, despite their superior numbers. He was wrong on that account as well.

There are many Zulu oral traditions about what happened next. One of them is that in the British camp that first night, the soldiers could see the flare of camp fires a distance away to the east, and believed that was where the Zulu were. It was, in fact, a trick: a few men had lit the fires as a decoy, but the army of some 20 000 men was hiding in the opposite hills.[17] This may be the reason why Chelmsford headed off eastwards the next day, believing the Zulu army, or part of it, to be there. In fact, no one knew for sure where the Zulu army was, or how many warriors there were.

The first inkling of danger was early the next morning, when thousands of Zulu were seen on the ridge above Isandlwana, sitting on their shields in utter silence, waiting for the war cry, '*Usuthu*', to attack. Then, as they approached the British camp, they made their distinctive war hiss like a swarm of bees.[18]

Chelmsford had incorrectly thought the Zulu would fight like the Xhosa, in small guerrilla groups, and he had divided the British troops into five sections. He had moved out eastwards, to support a reconnoitering party, leaving the camp in charge of Colonel Pulleine. But the main Zulu army attacked the camp in Chelmsford's absence, and was led by chiefs Ntshingwayo kaMahole and Mavumengwana kaMdlela Ntuli. They used their famous encircling tactics, like the horns of a buffalo: they sent the main part of their army (the 'head' and 'chest') forward, and then the 'horns' of additional soldiers, about five kilometres apart, encircled the enemy.

The Zulu defeated the British at Isandlwana on 22 January 1879 in what was one of the bloodiest battles in Victorian times. At noon, in the heat of battle, there was an eclipse of the sun and the sky went dark, adding to the battle's mystical aura, and evidence suggests that both sides were very frightened. According to one Zulu warrior, 'Our eyes were dark and we stabbed everything we came across.' It was indeed a 'slaughter so savage that even God closed his eyes'.[19]

Chelmsford's force was unaware of the disaster that had overwhelmed Pulleine's troops back at Isandlwana until the news filtered through that the camp had been taken. Chelmsford was staggered, saying, 'But I left 1 000 men to guard the camp.'[20] One reason given for the British defeat is lack of sufficient ammunition and problems of resupply, especially as the British army had been divided into sections. Lieutenant Colonel Durnford's column on the east flank, for example, ran out of ammunition and had to ride back into Isandlwana, leaving the right side of the camp open to attack. The 2/24 based at the camp was however well-equipped.[21]

Fifty-two British officers, an estimated 800 British troops and 500 of their allies were killed at Isandlwana. Some 471 of those allies were members of the African Contingent, who died fighting for the British. An estimated 1 000 to 2 000 Zulu soldiers died fighting against them, either on the field or afterwards, from wounds sustained in battle. Surviving Zulus captured 1 000 rifles and much of the reserve columns' supply ammunition. Only about 50 British soldiers managed to escape, fleeing down what came to be called Fugitive's Drift. The fugitives on horseback struggled with the steep terrain and the swollen Buffalo River that they had to cross. The Zulu, running barefoot, kept up despite having already marched 100 kilometres or more from their homes near Ulundi to the battlefield.[22] It is thought that many of these fugitives were killed by Zulu soldiers and local Zulu, who had come down to the river to help.[23]

Despite the victory, as news of battle reached him at Ulundi, Cetshwayo sensed it was the beginning of the end for the Zulu as an independent nation. He is said to have uttered the words: 'First the trader, then the missionary and then the red soldier … It is as if an assegai has been thrust into our belly.'[24] The 'red soldier' referred to the British soldiers' distinctive red uniforms.

The Battle of Rorke's Drift

Rorke's Drift was a Swedish mission station that had been turned into a supply depot and temporary hospital for the British soldiers. Against Cetshwayo's wishes, the day after Isandlwana, about 3 000 to 4 000 Zulu men who were in the reserve force and who had not yet washed their spears in blood, attacked Rorke's Drift. What followed was a 10-hour-long defence by approximately 150 British soldiers, 30 of whom were sick or wounded. The men reinforced their station with mealie sacks and biscuit tins, and cut slits in the walls to fire through. The Zulu suffered heavy casualties in this incident. Eleven VCs (the British military honour known as the Victoria Cross) were awarded that day, more than on any other day in British military history.

The Battle of Ulundi and the aftermath of the Anglo-Zulu War

After Isandlwana and Rorke's Drift, reinforcements from Britain arrived and the tide turned in the battles that followed. In July 1879, at the Battle of Ulundi, more than 1 000 Zulu were killed. Cetshwayo was captured and exiled to the Cape. In the post-war settlement, the Zulu kingdom was divided into 13 chiefdoms, breaking its power. Britain began to exercise indirect rule over Zululand after this, and the Zulu economy took strain.

Supported by the Bishop of Natal, John William Colenso,[25] Cetshwayo

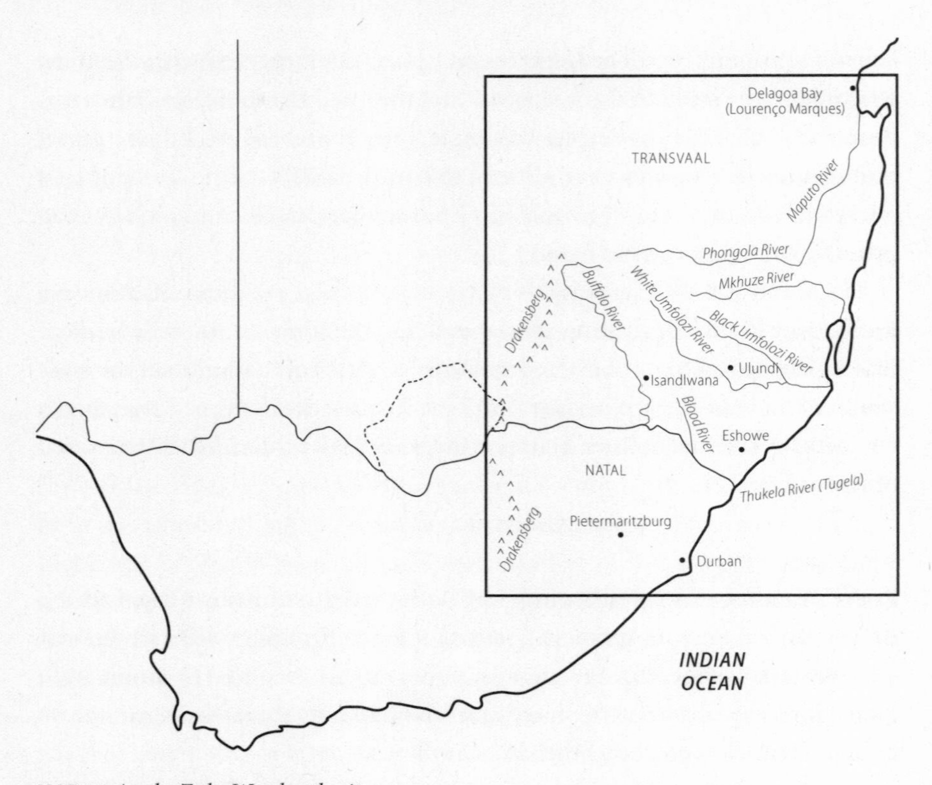

MAP 19 *Anglo-Zulu War battle sites.*

visited England to plead his case. The bishop also exposed Frere's deceits, which had led to the war. Cetshwayo evoked sympathy when he appeared in public and even received proposals of marriage from young English girls. In 1883 he was reinstated as king of the Zulu, but his powers had been curtailed, his kingdom had been reduced to about a third of its previous size, and the Zulu army had to be disbanded. In a letter to the Colonial Secretary, Earl Kimberley, Cetshwayo said: 'I fought when I was attacked, even as any other person would. No European king would have been treated this way.'[26]

Cetshwayo's main rival for status under the new arrangements was Zibhebhu, who tended to side with the colonial authorities; Cetshwayo was supported by Usuthu[27] loyalists. In 1883, the same year that he was reinstated, a battle between these two rival Zulu factions broke out at Ulundi. Historians believe this battle also contributed to the decline of the Zulu because thousands of Zulu lost their lives there, and the men killed included a number of the Zulu elite. Cetshwayo and his followers were severely beaten and shortly afterwards, in 1884, Cetshwayo died under mysterious circumstances. One of his sons, Dinuzulu, succeeded him but in the role of a relatively minor chief. The balance of power had shifted in favour of the colonial authorities in Zululand.

The Usuthu transferred their loyalty to Dinuzulu after Cetshwayo's death. In 1886, Dinuzulu entered a military alliance with the Transvaal Boers, which he did to secure a measure of protection against Zibhebhu. This was successful to the extent that Zibhebhu was forced out of Dinuzulu's territory, but it came at a cost: the Transvaal Boers proceeded to take some of Dinuzulu's land.[28]

The situation in Zululand had now become a competition between rival Zulu factions supported by opposing white authorities. When the Transvaal Boers demanded more land and the Usuthu refused, tension grew and the British were forced to intervene to avoid more bloodshed. Dinuzulu was allowed to keep most of his land in central Zululand, but the Boers were given land around what later became Vryheid, and a reserve area was set aside for the followers of Zibhebhu.

In 1887 and 1888 there was a brief period of rebellion after the Usuthu followers of Dinuzulu attacked the settlement of a new white magistrate stationed on the Okulu River. This had been successful at first but was then quite easily suppressed. Dinuzulu and his main supporters were tried for treason, sentenced and sent to prison on St Helena Island. In 1894 Dinuzulu was allowed to return to Zululand but as an induna[29] with no chiefly powers. On 19 May 1887, the British annexed what was left of Zululand, and in 1888 a hut tax was imposed on the Zulu to finance the British administration.

In 1897, ten years after being annexed, Zululand was incorporated into Natal and the region was opened to white settlement. By the turn of the century, the Zulu, like other black chiefdoms by that time, had lost much of their land and had to seek work to earn wages. In 1906, there was a brief fight back when Chief Bambatha kaMancinza of the Zondi, a Zulu clan that lived near present-day Greytown, refused to accept a new poll tax that was being implemented by the Natal colonial administration. Supported by other chiefs in the area, he launched a series of attacks against the colonial forces, using the Nkandla Forest as a base. These attacks became known as the Bambatha Rebellion, but they ended in defeat for Bambatha and his supporters. The independence of the Zulu was over.

Images of the Anglo-Zulu War

The Zulu victory at Isandlwana made headlines in Britain and spread to the rest of the world, adding to the fame of the Zulu and making them better known than any other tribe in southern Africa. Imaginations were captured both by the Zulu defence of their land and of the Welshmen of the 2/24 Regiment defending 'Queen and colour' (also known as the Queen's colour, the flag of their regiment) in far-off Africa.[30] Towards the end of the battle, Lieutenant Teignmouth Melvill is thought to have collected his regiment's flag and ridden off with it towards the Tugela River, pursued by Zulu warriors. The river was flooded and halfway across he came off his horse, still holding the flag, which was swept away. His comrade, Nevill Coghill, then plunged in to save both him and the flag. Lining the banks, the Zulu fired at them, and Coghill's horse was killed. The two men struggled to the bank but were subsequently killed, as well. Two weeks after the battle, their bodies were found by a search party and both are buried at Fugitive's Drift.[31]

In stories written about Isandlwana, both sides attested to the bravery of the other. In letters written home, British soldiers described how the Zulu 'came at them like bees, fighting like lions, unafraid of death, and as one man fell, another took his place'. Mehlokazulu, one of the Zulu leaders, said of the British, 'We were astonished at the way they fought.'[32]

At the time, parallels were drawn between the 'sexually frustrated' Zulu men, who could not marry until they had 'washed their spears in blood', and the equally frustrated young British soldiers who had been at boys-only public schools – aggressive warfare was seen as an outlet for frustration on both sides.

The fighting was also likened to sport, and described in the exhilarating language of the chase: 'We had a glorious go in, old boy, pig-sticking was a fool to it … With a tremendous shout of Death, Death! we were on them.'[33] This referred to wild-pig hunting and to a ritual called 'pig'[34] in India, where some of the British troops had already seen service. An analogy to cricket also came into it. When Chelmsford – who had misjudged the situation at Isandlwana – came in for criticism in some quarters, others defended him on the basis that he was a cricketer who knew both how to win and lose; his critics, therefore, were 'clearly not cricketers'.[35] In truth, the careers of both Chelmsford and Frere had been blighted by Isandlwana, and Chelmsford was never again allowed to command troops.

The death of Eugene Bonaparte, the only son of Napoleon III, added to the aura: the young prince had come out to South Africa at the age of 22, and was killed while serving as a member of a scouting party. His father had abdicated some years before, in 1871, after defeat in the Franco-Prussian War, and France had become a republic again, but there were nevertheless Bonapartists[36] who saw him as the heir apparent. With his death, the Bonaparte family lost much of its political appeal, but there have nevertheless been a series of pretenders to the throne ever since.[37]

The Pedi (North Sotho)

The British used similar tactics as those used on the Zulu to defeat the Pedi, making them appear to be the aggressors. In the 1860s, the Pedi was still a relatively powerful kingdom, but by the 1870s there were serious challenges. The Boers and the Swazis had been working together to launch attacks on the Pedi and stealing Pedi children to become *inboekselinge* on Boer farms,[38] and British federation plans were also underway.

In 1877, when the Republic of the Transvaal was annexed by the British, the Pedi chief, Sekhukhune, was advised to submit to their authority. The British also imposed a fine of 2 000 cattle on him, supposedly for inflicting suffering on the Boers when combined Boer and Swazi forces had attacked him in 1876. Sekhukhune had been hard hit by a drought and could not meet these demands. These and other incidents were used as an excuse to provoke war against him.

There were three Pedi wars altogether: the Boer/Swazi-Pedi War of 1876, the First Anglo-Pedi War of 1877 and the second Anglo-Pedi War of 1878.

The Pedi were finally defeated in the last one, and suffered heavy losses. At least 1 000 men lost their lives, and Sekhukhune was captured and taken as a prisoner to Pretoria.

Ecological factors also played a role in the decline of the Zulu and Pedi at a time when they were politically vulnerable. They were hard hit by drought, especially during 1876, 1877, 1885 and 1894–1897, and by outbreaks of cattle diseases such as Bovine Babesiosis (redwater and tick fever[39]) and lung sickness. In 1894 and 1895, plagues of locusts destroyed grain crops in Zululand, and in 1896 and 1897 outbreaks of the highly contagious cattle disease rinderpest[40] wiped out an estimated 90–95% of cattle throughout southern Africa, affecting black and white farmers.

After these disasters, many more African men – including the Zulu, who had held out the longest – joined the migrant labour system on the mines.

CHAPTER 7

The Two Anglo-Boer Wars, 1880–1881 and 1899–1902

The First Anglo-Boer War 1880–1881

Sir Theophilus Shepstone's annexation of the Transvaal in 1877 set off a chain of events that culminated in the First and Second Anglo-Boer Wars, from 1880–1881 and 1899–1902 respectively.

As part of British confederation plans, the Transvaal Boers had accepted annexation by the British in 1877, but then regretted it and announced that the former Boer republic was to be restored. This prompted the First Anglo-Boer War, or Transvaal War of Independence (1880–1881). The reasons for this war were similar to those which prompted the American War of Independence a century before (1775–1776). In both wars, the British lost out in ways they did not anticipate. In the Transvaal War, British troops sustained heavy losses in battles at Bronkhorstspruit, Laing's Neck, Schuinshoogte and Majuba. The Battle of Majuba Hill (in today's northern KwaZulu-Natal) is the one that is most remembered. It was also the last time the British wore their distinctive red coats: they were too easily seen by their opponents who, by contrast, did not even have uniforms.

In February 1881, colonial forces from Natal led by Colonel George Colley occupied Majuba Hill in an attempt to march into the Transvaal. Boer volunteers responded by storming the hill while British troops were asleep. The battle was over quite quickly – a victory for the Boers. Colonel Colley was among the approximately 200 British soldiers killed, while only two Boers suffered injuries. Back in England, the Liberal government under Prime

Minister William Gladstone decided to abandon federation schemes for the moment, and to restore Boer independence in the Transvaal.

The British in South Africa had underestimated the Boers, who knew the countryside well and were good shots. Nevertheless, they tended to regard Majuba as an undeserved victory and aimed to seek retribution. Some historians have seen the First Anglo-Boer War as a curtain-raiser for the more prolonged and ruthless Second Anglo-Boer War that was to follow some eighteen years later. 'Remember Majuba!' became a battle-cry for the British during the Second Anglo-Boer War.[1]

The Second Anglo-Boer (South African) War 1899–1902

The Second Anglo-Boer War was the more significant one, both in terms of international participation and in terms of results. It was also the most costly war fought by Britain in the period 1815–1914, and is the most destructive modern armed conflict in South African history.[2] It can be argued that between the mineral discoveries of the late nineteenth century and the first democratic elections of 1994, nothing in South African history attracted more global interest than the Second Anglo-Boer War.

Three months before war broke out, a convention of world leaders at The Hague in the Netherlands had decided that the unnecessary suffering of combatants and civilians during warfare had to be eliminated.[3] There were no South African signatories at the Convention, but the principles should nevertheless have applied. In fact, the very next war to follow the Convention, the Second Anglo-Boer War, led to thousands of deaths on the battlefields as well as those of civilians of all races, including women and children. Farms were looted and burnt, and the rules of 'civilised' warfare were not followed.

In recent years, the Second Anglo-Boer War has been re-named the South African War because although it was intended to be a 'gentleman's war' between the British and the Boers, it was inevitable that many other South Africans would become involved, but it continues to be recognised by its original name, the Anglo-Boer or simply the Boer War.

Causes of the Anglo-Boer (South African) War

The causes of the war are still disputed. It has been seen as a war to secure British imperialism and economic supremacy, and also to benefit the mining capitalists, many of whom were British. Both causes are true to some extent, and there are links between them: some of the mine owners – for example, Cecil John Rhodes, Lionel Phillips and Percy FitzPatrick – were also politicians in the Cape Colony, and could influence laws being passed to direct labour to the mines.

A new kind of British imperialism had arisen in South Africa after the mineral discoveries. As historian Bill Nasson has pointed out, the kind of aggressive British imperialism that followed the discovery of gold in the Transvaal would hardly have happened if South Africa had only been producing potatoes and peas.[4]

By the 1870s, there was a worldwide depression, and Britain had begun to lose her position as the dominant global manufacturing and trading power, while the United States and Germany were catching up. A global monetary system based on gold was in place, and the British currency was backed by gold, but the Baring Brothers Bank[5] was under threat of collapse. Britain needed to secure her position at the centre of the world's money market, and she needed her colonies, especially South Africa, which had rich resources and where exports were booming.

After the discovery of gold, the economic hub of southern Africa shifted from the Cape Colony to the independent Boer republic of the Transvaal. President Paul Kruger was seen by many of the mine owners as a hindrance to profit-making: while Kruger appreciated the tax revenue from the mines that was benefiting his republic, he also resisted changes, which meant fewer work opportunities for his Boers.[6] Not wanting his Boers to be outnumbered by the large numbers of immigrants that were coming into his country, he had been stubborn about giving 'uitlanders'[7] citizenship rights and the franchise (the right to vote) in his republic, and had imposed requirements that meant it took years for people to qualify. Not all mine owners were against him, however. The German George Albu,[8] for example, thought the Kruger government was doing a fair job, because Kruger had allowed foreign capital to be invested in South Africa with few restrictions, and had imposed a tax of only 5 per cent on declared profits.

It has also been contended that rather than trying to fight Kruger to reduce costs and make the mining industry more profitable, the Randlords and their associates were using the stock market as the prime vehicle to amass their fortunes. As mine owners they had inside information about deep levels and their prospects, and because the mines were not required to provide stringent reporting, they could use this information for speculative activity.[9]

In 1895, the Jameson Raid (a preliminary to the war) took place. This was a British attempt to topple the Boer government in the Transvaal, but it did not have the support of all the mine owners or uitlanders. The idea was to stage an uitlander rebellion as a protest against alleged injustices against them: there would then be an excuse for Britain to intervene, and a small, armed colonial force would move into the Transvaal. The British colonial secretary Joseph Chamberlain was said to have been deeply involved, although this was kept secret at the time the Raid was planned. Mine owner and politician Cecil John Rhodes sponsored the Raid, and it was planned in the offices of his company, Gold Fields. Rhodes's chief engineer, the American John Hays Hammond, was also involved; it was largely due to his influence that the Raid was conducted in a way reminiscent of the Wild West, with men on horseback similar to the cowboys of the American frontier.[10] The Raid was led by the medical doctor and politician Leander Starr Jameson,[11] who was also the confidant of Rhodes.

Jameson and some armed forces were meant to invade the Transvaal from British Bechuanaland (now Botswana), and then to link up with more armed forces on the Witwatersrand. However, communications broke down: telegraph lines were not cut as planned, and the Boers got wind of what was happening. There were also arguments among the uitlanders who were meant to stage the rebellion, because not all of them wanted to take part. The planned uprising did not take place on time; Jameson's forces were left stranded and forced to surrender on 2 January 1896 at Doornkop, approximately 20 kilometres west of Johannesburg.

The Raid failed dismally. Uitlander leaders who had been part of the plot were put on trial in Johannesburg. Some of them were condemned to death, but the sentences were later reduced to large fines. Rhodes was forced to resign as prime minister of the Cape, and he never quite regained the same power he had before. For its involvement in a conspiracy against another country, Britain's reputation was muddied.

In 1897, Alfred Milner arrived in South Africa as British High Commissioner.[12] He was an arch imperialist, arrogant and disdainful of the Boers, and he wanted war. Kruger, who did not want war, offered some reforms to help the mining industry and was prepared to allow leniency regarding the time to qualify for the franchise. In fact, in the words of mine owner Lionel Phillips, 'few of us cared a fig about [the franchise]'. Milner nevertheless made a big issue of it and turned down Kruger's offers, saying the franchise qualifications had to be removed altogether. This prompted Kruger's comment: 'It is not the franchise but my country they want.'[13]

In September 1899, acting on Milner's advice, the British War Office dispatched 10 000 troops to the Cape and Natal. The Boer republics had entered into an agreement in 1897 that they would support each other if their independence was threatened, so when the British troops arrived, they reacted. Their presidents, Kruger in the Transvaal and Marthinus Steyn in the Orange Free State, sent an ultimatum to London demanding that Britain back off. When this was not accepted, the Boer republics declared war, making them seem like the aggressors.

Some incidents in the war

The first offensives went the way of the Boers, and it became clear that the British soldiers would not be home by Christmas, as many had previously thought. The Boers inflicted some humiliating defeats at places like Colenso and Magersfontein (near Kimberley) and laid siege to strategic places like Mafeking,[14] Kimberley and Ladysmith.

For most of the seven months of the Mafeking siege (mid-October to 17 May 1900), a Lady Sarah Wilson was holed up with her husband, Captain Gordon Wilson. Lady Sarah was the daughter of the British Duke of Marlborough and a member of the prestigious Spencer-Churchill family. She and others like her had accompanied their husbands to South Africa, thinking it would be an adventure playground and that the war would be

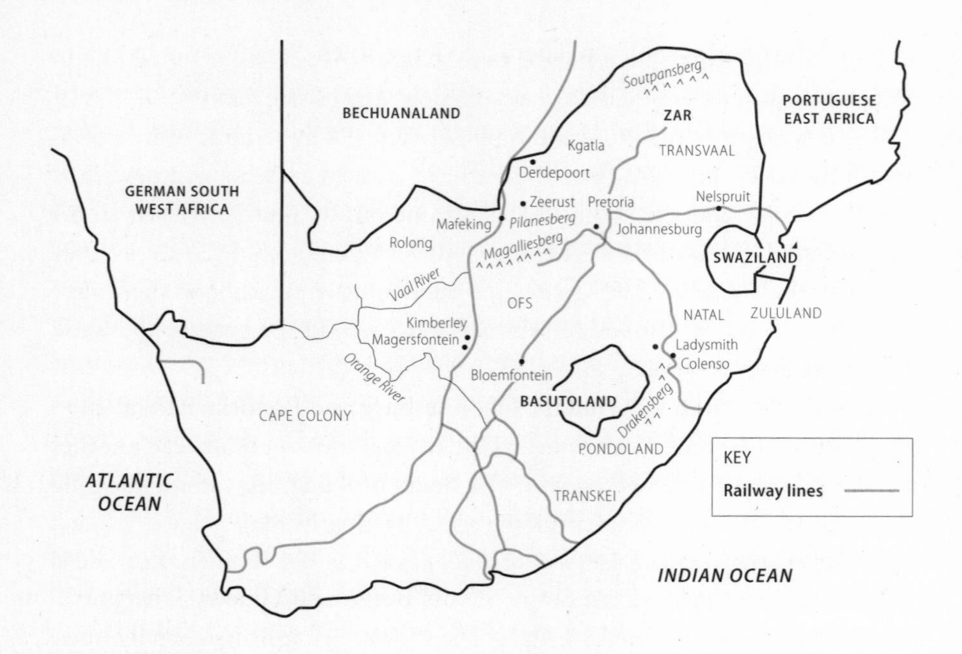

MAP 20 *Sieges and incidents during the Anglo-Boer War, 1899–1902. Key railway lines are also shown.*

quickly over. She did, however, prove her worth during the siege of Mafeking by becoming a war correspondent for London's *Daily Mail*, somehow managing to get her reports out of the besieged town. In one of her reports she describes the Christmas dinner she had made for an elite group, one of whom was Colonel (later Lord) Baden-Powell[15], commander of the regiment in Mafeking. In another, Lady Sarah describes a horse parade celebrating the birthday of Queen Victoria – a grand but somewhat bizarre incident in a besieged southern African town.

In contrast, the young Sol Plaatje[16] described in his diaries the plight of the black people in Mafeking, who outnumbered whites four to one. Sol Plaatje became an interpreter at the court in Mafeking during the siege so he was better fed than most, but in March 1900 he wrote that it was 'a miserable scene to be surrounded by hungry human beings, agitating for your pity – and then to see one of them succumb to his agonies and fall backwards with a dead thud'.[17] A young English nurse, Ina Cowan, wrote that towards the end of the siege, some black people were so hungry they had resorted to digging up the carcasses of dead horses and dogs and eating them.[18]

The British responded to the initial Boer victories by sending more troops to South Africa, and this turned the tide of war. In early 1900, a new chief commander, Frederick Sleigh Roberts, came out to South Africa with his chief-of-staff, Horatio Herbert Kitchener.[19] With additional resources, they conducted a ruthless campaign against the Boers. By March 1900 there were 180 000 soldiers fighting on the British side – almost the entire population of the two Boer republics.

By June 1900 both the capitals, Johannesburg and Pretoria, had fallen to the British. This should have marked the end of the war, but instead another prolonged stage of the war began. The Boers broke up into small guerrilla bands or commandos (small military units, originally established to protect the districts they came from) under leaders such as Ben Viljoen, Koos de la Rey, Christiaan de Wet, Jan Smuts, Louis Botha and Gideon Scheepers.[20] These commandos roamed the countryside destroying British supply lines, sabotaging bridges and railway lines, and generally wreaking havoc.

The war also spread into the Cape Colony. In August 1901, after a long delay waiting for permission, Smuts and his commando of 340 Transvaalers left Koppieskraaldrift on the Vaal River en route to the Cape. After an epic month-long trek of some 480 km they reached the Orange River and from September to November they fought more than a dozen engagements in the eastern Cape and then through the northern and western districts. Some Cape Afrikaners joined Smuts's commando but it was never possible to organise widespread Afrikaner rebellion in the Cape Colony.[21] The British had also declared martial law in the Cape Colony – which was to have important repercussions. Gideon Scheepers, who led a commando of some 150 Cape rebels, was captured by a British column in October 1901, subsequently tried in a British military court and found guilty of murder, arson and sabotage of trains. He was executed by a firing squad in the veld near Graaff-Reinet. He was ill by that time and faced his executioners seated in a chair. Scheepers's execution led to debate about a British military court passing a sentence of death on a prisoner of war while the war was still ongoing. His death made him a martyr to the Boer cause.[22]

The thinking behind the commandos' tactics, especially in the early stages of the war, came mainly from the Boer general Jan Smuts. About 500 commandos operated in the Magaliesberg Mountains; for example, one was commanded by Jan Smuts, who succeeded in repulsing a British force much larger in size. The Magaliesberg was a theatre of war chosen by both sides because of its many hiding places. It was also something of a death trap: lightning is more severe in the Magaliesberg (because of the iron in the mountains) than almost anywhere else on earth, and a lot of British soldiers lost their lives by being struck by lightning.

The commando strategy was unconventional warfare and the British had never encountered anything like it before. During the two world wars that followed, Smuts would also become a much sought-after military consultant for the British, where the British used ideas inspired by the Boer commandos in particular situations.

The Boer commandos were also successful because they were mobile: the Boers had horses, they knew the countryside well and were excellent shots. The British quickly realised that they too needed horses, which were subsequently imported. Some 200 000 horses and mules were sent from Washington in the United States to South Africa for the British war effort.[23] The fodder to supplement the horse feed (because it was winter time in South Africa) was brought in from Argentina, and contained the seeds of the prolific cosmos flower – a weed that now lines the national roads around Johannesburg in autumn. The United States also sent goods such as canned corned beef, boots, gunpowder and firearms for the British troops.

The Boer commandos lived off the land and returned to their farms when they could. This prompted the next stage of the war, which was subsequently criticised by the Liberal Party back in Britain as 'methods of barbarism'.[24] Roberts and Kitchener resorted to a tactic they had used in Asia: they marked off the countryside into about 8 000 sections, built blockhouses,[25] and started burning farms and destroying livestock, making it impossible for the men to come home. The British believed this would bring the war to an end, but the consequences were horrific. In 1901, Roberts returned to England, leaving Kitchener as commander-in-chief of a difficult situation.

Boer women and children who had been displaced, as well as a small number of older men, were rounded up and taken to camps which were hastily erected without proper attention to sanitation and other needs. The concentration of people in these camps led to their being referred to as 'concentration camps'. There were some 50 to 60 camps for white people all over the country, and about 67 camps for black people, mostly along the railway lines from Bloemfontein to Pretoria and Nelspruit. Contrary to popular belief, the camps in South Africa were not the first concentration camps,[26] but they were the most widespread and infamous. Diseases such as measles, diarrhoea, chickenpox and diphtheria spread quickly in the crowded conditions, and the death rate, especially of young children, was appalling. It is estimated that some 28 000 Boer women and children and an unknown but similar figure of black people died in these camps. These figures were in excess of the soldiers who died in the field: an estimated 22 000 British (of whom about two-thirds died of disease) and 7 000 Boers.[27]

The camps varied according to location and the officials administering them, and in some cases conditions were not as bad as in others. Acts of kindness were recorded: one story tells of a British camp official who rode on his bicycle into the nearest town to get ice to put on the throat of a child stricken with diphtheria, and then sat with the mother all night until the fever had passed.[28] The ice helped contract the muscles of the swollen throat and enabled the child to breathe.

Nevertheless, in most cases, conditions were dire. British social worker and anti-war pacifist Emily Hobhouse established a relief fund in England when she heard the news of the camps. She travelled to South Africa with food supplies and clothing, especially for babies, and visited the camps. She then reported back to the British leader of the opposition, Sir Henry Campbell-Bannerman in London, who was appalled at what she described to him.[29] The Cape-based author and feminist Olive Schreiner was another who exposed the cruelties of the camp system.

Emily Hobhouse concentrated her efforts on the camps for whites, but said on one occasion that she wished there was more time to help the blacks, as their suffering was even worse. In the years after the war, she became a heroine to the Afrikaners and when she died in England in 1926, her ashes were brought back to South Africa and buried at the foot of the Women's

Memorial in Bloemfontein. Hobhouse had been too ill to attend the unveiling of the memorial in 1913, but had prepared a speech which she asked to be read out on the occasion: in it, she particularly requested that the women of all races who had suffered in the war be remembered.[30]

In recent times, attempts have been made to find the location of the concentration camps for black people. Proper statistics were never kept and few written records refer to these camps. In 2001, a farmer in Kimberley stumbled over a broken pot and pieces of glass in a remote part of his farm. The archaeological excavations that followed revealed the remains of a concentration camp that was estimated to have held some 1 500 people.[31]

The role of black people in the war

Initial claims were that the war would be fought only by the British and the Boers, but black, coloured and Indian people were ultimately also affected, and played a variety of roles as the war progressed. In the Cape, coloured men served as town guards and scouts protecting communities from Boer commandos, and a coloured man, Abraham Esau, although denied the right to carry arms, defied the odds by recruiting a group to spy and report back to the British on Boer rebel activity. In return, a secret British military force undertook to protect Calvinia where his people lived. His activities made him a marked man and in February 1901, he was executed by Boer forces.[32]

One of the groups that supported the Boers became known as the 'agterryers' – men who rode *agter* (behind) the soldiers. These were trusted black and coloured people who followed the commandos to the front, tended the horses, carried the equipment, did scouting and dispatch riding, and carried the wounded. Some agterryers were mounted and armed, and took part in battle. Altogether, there were about 12 000 agterryers during the war. Every Boer who could afford it, employed an agterryer.[33]

There were also San (Bushmen) agterryers who assisted Boers in the Lake Chrissie area of the eastern Transvaal. The San were expert trackers able to trace the British forces under General Smith-Dorrien. Similarly, the Boer General Piet Cronjé enlisted local Tswana people to help him maintain the siege of Mafeking, and armed black and coloured people guarded outposts at night during the siege of Ladysmith.

On the British side, it is estimated that about 100 000 black and coloured men were employed by the army. Most served as transport workers, camp labourers, scouts, dispatch riders, spies and guards, but there were also some armed combatants. Mohandas Gandhi formed his Natal Indian Ambulance Corps with funding from local Indians. He and his volunteers transported wounded soldiers to the railhead after the Battle of Colenso, and served on the front line at Spion Kop (Spioenkop), in what is now KwaZulu-Natal. Interestingly, three future world leaders were all present in different capacities at Spion Kop: Indian civil rights leader Mohandas Gandhi; future British prime minister Winston Churchill, who was there as a war correspondent for London newspaper, *The Morning Post*; and Boer general Louis Botha, who became the first prime minister of the union of South Africa in 1910.

Throughout the war, the British army relied on chiefs in Basutoland, Bechuanaland, Swaziland and the Transkei to protect their regions from Boer penetration. The local chiefs thought that victory over the Boers would bring them more rights. When parts of Zululand were occupied by Boer forces between January and May 1900, local chiefs kept the British informed about events there. Dinuzulu[34] (the son of Cetshwayo) was one chief who later mobilised a regiment to protect the border.

The historian Bernard Mbenga has shown how the British also used the Kgatla[35] in their campaign in the Pilanesberg (in the now North West province). The Kgatla had their own agenda for assisting the British: they hoped to regain some of the land they had lost to the Boers. The British gave the Kgatla Martini-Henry rifles and they became an effective force in the Pilanesberg, with many Boers vacating their farms in fear. By July 1901, the Kgatla dominated the area of the Pilanesberg down to the Elands River, with the result that the British did not have to use their own forces there. When the war finally ended, the Kgatla believed they would be rewarded for their assistance to the British, and that they would be able to keep the farms they had occupied in the Pilanesberg, which lay on their ancestral lands. They were disappointed. Instead, the British embarked on a reconciliation plan with the Boers, promising to maintain the benefits of their white status. The Kgatla were ordered to return their rifles, but many were smuggled away.

In the Mafeking area, the Tshidi branch of the Rolong sided with the British because they had lost much of their land to the Boers in previous decades. A force of some 500 armed Rolong helped to defend the besieged town of Mafeking from within, and one of their leaders, Mathakgong, conducted raids on the Boers from outside, bringing Boer cattle he had captured into Mafeking to ease the food shortage. He became a legendary figure and one of the heroes of the siege.[36]

Rolong women also played an unofficial role. Towards the end of the siege, when many black people were starving, Rolong women were allowed to leave to find food – pumpkins, wild corn, melons and other fruits, as well as wood – a distance away. The Boers besieging Mafeking mostly let them pass unhindered as the women appeared innocent, but in fact when they came back, they were able to report on Boer positions and movements, and the places where their guns were concentrated.

Like the Kgatla and the others who had assisted the British, the Rolong were destined for disappointment at the end of the war. Early in 1902 their guns were taken away, rendering them helpless when a Boer commando raided their cattle. Despite his fame for founding the Boy Scout movement, Lord Baden-Powell does not come out well in this story. At the Royal Commission on the war in South Africa in 1903, Baden-Powell distorted the record of the Rolong contribution in the defence of Mafeking: when asked whether the Rolong had been used in military operations, he said, 'No, we tried to make them defend their town, but on the first attack they ran away.'[37]

Black migrant workers on the mines were also affected by the war. When hostilities began and the mines closed down, these workers were simply told to go home and were given no protection. For thousands of Zulu workers, this was particularly traumatic: trains were at a standstill and there was no option but to walk the long route home. The men faced pouring rain with no shelter, and often faced great danger as they passed through Boer lines. They also had to find provisions in a war-torn country on a journey that took some eight days.

John Sidney Marwick was a young civil servant whose job it had been to look after the Zulu men working in the Witwatersrand mines. In his personal capacity, he negotiated with the Kruger government to accompany the returning Zulu miners on their journey, which they undertook from 6–14 October 1899. Marwick was given permission as long as the men stayed together. The presence of such a large contingent of Zulu men moving so close to their lines was a cause for concern for the Boers, but Marwick was able to negotiate on the miners' behalf with Boer General Piet Joubert and his commandos, who were waiting on the border to invade Natal. The men were allowed through. Marwick also had a horse that he lent to men who were sick and struggling. He was only 20 years old at the time.[38]

Similarly, when Kimberley was surrounded by Boers and then besieged, Cecil Rhodes sent home some 30 000 black men from the compounds to make the limited food supplies go further. Many of these men were shot by the Boers as they tried to make their way home.

The role of women in the war

Women played a variety of roles in the war. Boer women found themselves having to take charge of farms in the absence of their men, and some resented the British so strongly that they wanted to take part in the war. A Mrs Otto Krantz fought by her husband's side and a young woman, Helena Wagner, fought in the trenches disguised as a man.[39] It is also said that if their men came home or tried to join them in the concentration camps, they denied them sex and urged them to return to their commandos.

When Pretoria fell to the British, a woman called Johanna (Hansie) van Warmelo carried on a spy service under the noses of the British officials. She observed their movements while riding around on a bicycle, and wrote the information in lemon juice on the inside of envelopes that she carried out of the city to the Boer commandos outside. The information could be read when heat was applied to the paper. The British officers did not suspect anything was amiss and she was even sometimes invited to their parties.[40] Such stories of the resilience of Boer women, both during the Great Trek and the Anglo-Boer War, were important factors in the later growth of Afrikaner nationalism.

In Mafeking and the other besieged towns, British women also came to the fore. Women who had never worked outside of their homes before suddenly found themselves fulfilling a number of roles; it was deemed acceptable for middle- to upper-class women to work outside the home as long as it was not for money. They became nurses and relief workers, and some did sewing for the troops. Before the war started there had been very few women in the British medical corps, despite the example of Florence Nightingale in the Crimean War four decades earlier. At first, the Army Medical Department did not think it appropriate that women nurse men, but by the time the war ended, the War Office had sanctioned the establishment of a permanent Army Nursing Service.[41] Young Irish Catholic nuns who had recently arrived in Mafeking to serve in the convent were also obliged to take on new roles. They found themselves becoming nurses of the wounded, most of them totally unprepared for the horrors they saw.

It is regrettable that more is not known about the role of black women during the war. The British scorched earth policy did not discriminate between white- and black-owned farms when they burnt the countryside. Displaced black women and children also experienced the horrors of the camps, but we do not know their stories.

Foreign participation in the war

People from all over the world came to South Africa during the war, as evidenced by the many graves and monuments that still abound – like the monument to the Scandinavians who were killed at Magersfontein outside Kimberley. There were probably at least 2 600 foreigners in the various volunteer corps and Boer commandos. The Empire countries (Australia, New Zealand and Canada) sent troops and aid in support of Britain, while the Netherlands, Germany, France, Italy, Ireland, Russia and others supported the Boers. In Germany, the image of the rugged, poorly dressed Boer on horseback, without all the pomp and insignia of the British army, held appeal, and in Russia, the Boer on horseback was seen as similar to the mounted Cossack.[42] The Irish Republican Army (IRA) would later model its guerrilla tactics on Boer flying columns.

The Americans were also involved. The American business community supported the British because an estimated $150 million was invested in South African gold mines.[43] American engineers had been brought from places like Colorado and Nevada because they had knowledge of hard-rock mining, previously unknown in South Africa, and played an important role as mining-industry consultants. The American engineer Hays Hammond was a key advisor to Cecil Rhodes and contributed American finance to the Jameson Raid. The Americans also sent over much-needed horses for the British troops, who had to traverse vast distances. Interestingly, the American government publicly supported the British but in private many Americans sympathised with the Boers.

The Anglo-Boer War also has the distinction of being the first mass-media war. Foreign correspondents from all over the world, including the young Winston Churchill, later prime minister of Britain (1941–1945 and 1951–1955), arrived in South Africa to cover the war. Winston Churchill was working for the London newspaper *The Morning Post* at the time. On 15 November 1899 he was travelling in an armoured train that came under attack from Boers as it crossed a bridge over the Blaauwkrantz River in Natal. When the train driver heard shooting, he increased speed and crashed into the boulders the Boers had laid across the line. Churchill helped to clear the tracks, despite being under fire. He apparently said, 'This will be good for my paper.'[44] The driver was able to reverse and take the wounded to safety, but Churchill and 70 others were taken prisoner in Pretoria. Churchill escaped by climbing over a wall, and reached safety in Lourenço Marques (Maputo). His reports describing the escape and dangerous trek across Boer territory made him world-famous.[45]

The war was also one of the first whose events were captured by movie cameras, although the films were mostly made in America after the war. Some Boers were later sent to America to feature in the films and add authenticity to the productions, but the cannons that were used were actually from the American Civil War!

The end of the war

The extra troops sent by Britain and deepening misery as the war carried on eventually eroded the will of most of the Boer leaders to carry on, and a negotiated peace settlement, known as the Peace of Vereeniging, was drawn up at Melrose House in Pretoria in May 1902. The terms of this agreement required the Boer republics to surrender their independence, but in return Britain promised economic assistance for post-war reconstruction.[46]

By the later stages of the war, some poorer Afrikaners had lost faith in the republican cause and were serving as scouts in the British forces against their former comrades. The country was also on the verge of civil war. Afrikaners who had started to collaborate with the British were referred to as *hensoppers* by other Afrikaners, especially the *bittereinders*, so named because they were the die-hards, determined to see the war through. *Hensoppers* means 'hands up' because when these men surrendered or defected to the enemy they typically did so with their hands up. *Hensoppers* were despised by other Afrikaners even long after the war ended, a dislike which caused *broedertwis* (brother against brother) and tore families apart. Historian Albert Grundlingh describes the feud between the two brothers, both Boer War generals, Piet and Christiaan de Wet. When Piet de Wet and his staff laid down their arms at Kroonstad, Piet said it was to stop further suffering of his people, but his brother Christiaan did not agree. At a subsequent meeting in Kroonstad Christiaan said that *hensoppers* were 'murderers of their own people,' and when his brother Piet walked into the place where Christiaan was having a drink Christiaan left immediately rather than share space with a man he regarded as a traitor. In his memoirs Christiaan de Wet comes close to blaming *hensoppers* for the Boers' losing the war.[47] He and his brother were never reconciled.

Significance of the war today

In post-1994 democratic South Africa, there have been attempts to make the war image more inclusive. In 1996, the ANC Women's League invited the wives of some prominent Afrikaner politicians to join them in a commemorative walk to 'cement the unity of South African women', because Afrikaner and black women share a history of imperial and colonial brutality. In a similar vein, an ANC judge of the South African Constitutional Court referred to the war as part of the story of the struggle for freedom and – ironically in terms of the events of subsequent years – praised the heroic struggle of the Boer fighters.[48]

There is little evidence that the Anglo-Boer War is a shared history across racial divides. Perhaps it will eventually be seen as a remote episode from a vanished European imperial past.[49]

The Milner Administration, 1902–1905

After peace was signed at Vereeniging in 1902, the British declared sovereignty over the former Boer republics but then, in a show of magnanimity, allowed the Boers free local elections that gave them a measure of self-government again. British administration was by then under Alfred Milner, assisted by young, inexperienced and apparently arrogant graduates from British universities, mainly Oxford, all of whom subscribed to his views on imperialism. They became known as Milner's 'kindergarten of little dolls'.[50] In fact, some of them did some good reconstructive work but their presence did not sit well with the Boers: former Boer War general Jan Smuts, himself a Cambridge graduate and only 32 years old, commented that for Milner it was '... such a comfort to have a little kindergarten show of dolls – all your own, moving at your sweet will, not asking inconvenient questions ...'[51]

Milner embarked on a deliberate policy of Anglicisation and made no secret of the fact that he thought the Afrikaans language and culture was inferior and needed to be suppressed. He was one of the founder members of the Witwatersrand's Council of Education, established in 1895 to promote English-speaking education, even though he had no children of his own.[52] The Council was founded to help meet a genuine need for elementary education on the Witwatersrand, as well as to counter the influence of Dutch in state-aided schools. The first schools for English-speakers sponsored by the Council were both government and private schools, and include such well-known schools as Jeppe Boys, King Edward, St John's College and St Mary's.

Milner and his 'kindergarten' had an enormous task of reconstruction ahead of them after the Anglo-Boer War. They started by bringing back 31 000 Boer prisoners of war from St Helena, Bermuda, Ceylon and other places, and returning them to their farms, if they were still standing. Financial and other assistance was given to those whose farms had been burned down. An estimated 30 000 Boer farms had been destroyed in the course of the war.[53]

The same was not done for black farmers. A commission under Sir

Godfrey Langdon decided that black people would be settled in locations strategically placed so that their labour could be drawn to mines and industries where it was needed. This was the start of official segregation policies that would be extended in future years.

The British administration then set about trying to restore the mining industry to its pre-war levels of production, and to provide the infrastructure to cut down desertions from the mines, and maintain an adequate supply of cheap black labour. Their efforts were largely successful – certainly from the mine owners' point of view. One of the noticeable 'improvements' was that with stricter controls, wages paid to black mine workers could be reduced.

A few years later, in 1910, the almost unthinkable happened. The former adversaries, the British and the Boers, came together in a Union under the British Crown, and the first Union Cabinet had equal numbers of English and Afrikaans-speaking members.

CHAPTER 8

Union, the rise of nationalisms, resistance movements, the First World War (1914–1918), and the PACT government (1924–1929)

The first Union cabinet and the capitals

The long-held federation ambitions of the British in South Africa found fruition in the formation of the Union of South Africa in 1910. The British administrator Alfred Milner played a large part in this before his departure from South Africa in 1905. He persuaded the leaders of all four 'colonies'[1] of the advantages of a union because this would eliminate economic competition between them; to this end, he created a South African Customs Union and a single Central African Railways system, to avoid customs and other taxes paid when goods were moved from one colony to another. His successor, Lord Selborne[2] (high commissioner in South Africa, 1905–1910) continued this policy and urged political unification as well. A National Convention[3] was held to discuss this in 1908 and 1909, and on 31 May 1910, the Union of South Africa came about.

Louis Botha was appointed the first prime minister of the Union, with Jan Smuts as his deputy. The English monarch was represented in South Africa by a governor general, but effective power was put in the hands of the South African Prime Minister and his Parliament. Both Botha and Smuts had been Boer generals in the bitter Anglo-Boer War. Their aim now was to reconcile the Boers and the British. Echoing the words of President Abraham Lincoln at Gettysburg at the end of the American Civil War in 1865, Jan Smuts said it was time to 'forgive and forget, to bind up the old wounds and make the future happier than the past [had] been'.[4] The wounds being referred to were those between the English and Afrikaners: both Botha and Smuts believed that fusion of the white race was essential if they were to survive in a country where they were outnumbered by black people by almost five to one.

The interests of former enemies meant there was disagreement over where the capital of the new Union should be. This was solved by giving three of the provinces (the Cape, Transvaal and Orange Free State) an aspect of the capital and financial compensation to the fourth (Natal) – an arrangement that still stands today. South Africa continues to have three capital cities: Cape Town (the seat of Parliament and the legislative capital), Pretoria (the seat of the president and his cabinet, and the administrative capital) and Bloemfontein (the judicial capital).

Jan Smuts

Louis Botha and Jan Smuts shared a friendship and support for each other that was remarkable in politics at the time. Botha was the more popular of the two with people at home, whereas Smuts achieved fame overseas and was destined to put South Africa on the world map as no statesman had done before.

As a young boy, Smuts had tended cattle on his parents' farm near the village of Riebeeck West in a remote part of the Cape Colony. His ancestors had farmed the land since the late 17th century, and Smuts had grown up a typical *boereseun*.[5] In traditional large Afrikaner families at the time, only the eldest son went to school. In 1882, when Smuts was twelve years old, his older brother died of typhoid, and he took his brother's place and went to school.

Smuts had a brilliant mind and caught up quickly. In 1891, he was awarded a scholarship to study law at Cambridge, where he made English friends and studied a range of subjects, which included the classics, literature (especially the works of Shakespeare, Shelley and Walt Witman), botany and philosophy. It was also during his time at Cambridge that he developed his theory of 'Holism', which he defined as 'the tendency in nature to form wholes that are greater than the sum of the parts through creative evolution'.[6] Smuts believed that small units needed to form larger wholes and that progress lay along that path – hence his belief in the Union of South Africa, the League of Nations and the United Nations, all of which he helped to establish. It was Holism that encouraged his belief that South Africa needed the Afrikaners' old enemy, Britain, in order to be part of the concept that was beginning to take shape: a British Commonwealth of freely associating nations under the British crown. His was unusual thinking for the time, especially for one whose life had started on a simple farm.

Smuts graduated with double firsts at Cambridge and could have pursued an academic career. One of his law professors described him as the most brilliant student he had ever had, and the Master of Christ College Cambridge, Lord Todd, said that in the 500 years of the College's history, of all its members, past and present, three had been truly outstanding: John Milton, Charles Darwin and Jan Smuts.

Smuts was a scholar and would not have chosen a lifetime of war. He would nevertheless live to command forces in three major wars: the Anglo-Boer War (1899–1902), World War I (1914–1918) and World War II (1939–1945). He saw nothing incongruous in the fact that he had been a Boer general fighting against the British in the Anglo-Boer War and then a soldier on the side of Britain in two world wars. In each case, he said, he was fighting for freedom.

His personal bravery was something noted even at the time. In the Afrikaner Rebellion in 1914 and again during the white miners' strike in 1922, he rode in an open car into the midst of the rebels while bullets rained around him. One of his colleagues, General Coen Britz, said Smuts was the bravest man he ever knew, and Winston Churchill wrote a note to congratulate him on his escape. 'Take care of yourself,' he wrote. 'Your life is invaluable to SA and the British Empire.'[7]

The rise of nationalism and resistance movements

The early years of the 20th century saw stirrings of both Afrikaner and

African nationalism, both due to experiences of deprivation and loss that had been experienced in the preceding decades.

In the immediate aftermath of the Anglo-Boer War, Afrikaners were in crisis, especially in the Free State and Transvaal. They had been defeated in war, many had lost their farms and many thousands of Afrikaner women and children had died in concentration camps. The author Olive Schreiner predicted that it was all over for the Afrikaners, and that within 50 years the Afrikaans language would hardly be spoken or heard – except as a curiosity.[8] As things turned out, she was wrong: 50 years later, the Afrikaners would be ruling South Africa having won the elections in 1948. It is a remarkable story of recovery.

There had been stirrings of an Afrikaner nationalist spirit before the war, but the trauma of war was to become the stimulus for an accelerated sense of nationalism. The years after the war saw a rise of Afrikaner nationalist writers and poets, who wrote emotive stories about Afrikaner suffering and heroism. Gustav Preller, for example, collected stories from the descendants of Voortrekkers who were still alive and published them in volumes called Voortrekker Mense ('Voortrekker People'), and poets like Jan Celliers wrote poems like 'Dis al' ('That's all'), which is about a Boer who returns from exile to find nothing left of his farm.

In 1904 the former Transvaal president, Paul Kruger, died in Switzerland and emotion was stirred when his body was brought back to Pretoria for burial. The formation of the Afrikaner National Party in 1914 and the more extreme Purified National Party two decades later, as well as events carefully orchestrated by Afrikaner organisations in the 1930s were to add to a growing nationalist fervour.

Circumstances for black South Africans provided a similar incentive for the rise of nationalist fervour. Nothing much was done to rehabilitate them after the Boer War, and their lot was not likely to be better under a Union than it had been before. No black representatives were invited to the so-called 'National Convention' that met in 1908–9 to discuss the format of the Union. Only a few individual black people had the franchise (the right to vote) in the former British colonies of the Cape and Natal, having qualified on the basis of income or property ownership – this right would be taken away in 1936. No black people had this right in the former Boer republics of the Transvaal and Orange Free State.

The African People's Organisation (APO)

In the early years of the 20th century a number of black political organisations began to emerge. In the Cape, the African People's Organisation (APO) started in 1903. In 1909, nine of its members together with white politician WP Schreiner[9] went to London to protest against the government of the Union, which excluded black people. The delegation was not successful, the most likely explanation being that so soon after the Anglo-Boer War, Britain did not want to strain the fragile peace that existed between the Afrikaners and the British.

In 1905 Dr Abdullah Abdurahman became leader of the APO, a position he was to hold for the next 35 years. Dr Abdurahman's grandparents had been slaves who had managed to buy their freedom at the Cape. He studied at Glasgow University and became a medical doctor in 1888, returning to South Africa in 1893 to set up a practice – the first man of Malay descent in South Africa to do so. Dr Abdurahman served on the Cape Provincial Council and advised on matters pertaining to black and coloured people. He had also noted with concern the implications of comments made by Hendrik Verwoerd, a young professor at the time, who was already advocating ideas that later became the policy of apartheid.

The Land Act and the formation of the SANNC

In 1912, the South African National Native Congress (SANNC) was founded by four lawyers led by Pixley ka Isaka Seme (meaning 'Pixley son of Isaka Seme'). The other three founder members were Alfred Mangena, Richard Msimang and George Montsioa. They had all been educated overseas. Seme's early education was at a mission school in Natal, where he took on the name 'Pixley' from an American missionary, the Reverend SC Pixley, who took care of him after his parents died. Reverend Pixley arranged for him to be educated overseas, and Seme subsequently graduated with a BA degree from Columbia University in New York and a law degree from Oxford. One of the people who influenced him was the black American educationalist and former slave, Booker T Washington. Washington did not advocate confrontation or aggressive resistance against discrimination but rather that schemes be put in place to educate black people and enable them to acquire skills.

The SANNC was more of a pressure group than a political party, and its early members and activists were an elite group of small businessmen, teachers, clerks and clergymen – all distinguished men who had achieved educational success against the odds. They included Solomon (Sol) Plaatje, who spoke several languages and had acted as an interpreter for the British during the Siege of Mafeking during the Anglo-Boer War. He had also written essays and books about African life as experienced by Africans. He became secretary-general of the new organisation, and Pixley Seme's cousin, John Dube, became the first president. In 1903, John Dube had founded the newspaper *Ilanga lase Natal* ('The Natal Sun'), which articulated African aspirations.[10]

Like those of their American counterpart, Booker T Washington, the demands made by the early SANNC leaders to the Union government were reasonable and eloquently expressed. They asked for equal opportunities and gradual inclusion in government, based on merit. Their demands were rejected.

In 1913, the first Act passed by the new Union government concerned land in South Africa. This was the 1913 Land Act, and it reflected the segregation proposals made by a commission appointed during Milner's administration (1903–1905) and headed by the Minister for 'Native' Affairs at the time, Godfrey Lagden. The Act made it illegal for blacks to purchase or lease land except in demarcated reserves. This restricted black occupancy to less than 8 per cent of South Africa's land. It also made it illegal for black farmers to share land with white farmers on a system of 'farming-on-the-halves', which had worked fairly well in the past: the black farmer would work for the white farmer but would also cultivate some land for his personal needs. Under the Act, thousands of black people were forced to relocate.

The Land Act of 1913 laid the foundation for the subsequent Land Acts in 1923 and 1936, and for the segregated homelands policy that followed in the 1950s. The Land Acts and their related policies were restrictive in nature,

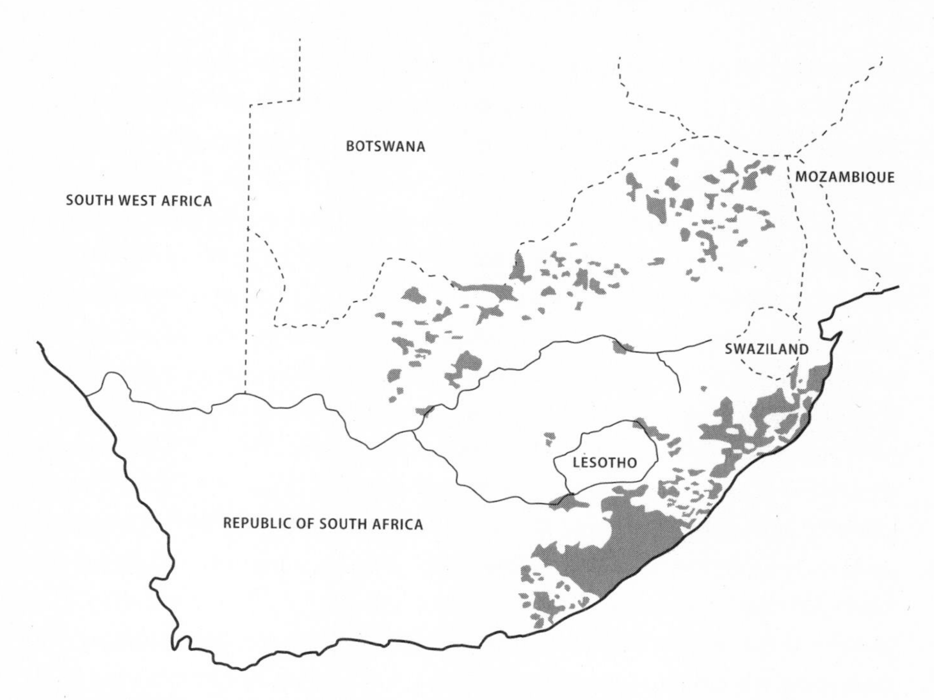

MAP 21 *The effect of the 1913 Land Act. The black shaded areas show the amount of land allocated to black farmers.*

and they left millions of people disadvantaged throughout their lifetimes, creating social and economic problems that have never been solved. In June 1983, on the 70th anniversary of the first Land Act, members of the Black Sash,[11] a white women's resistance movement, organised a week-long nationwide campaign to focus public attention on the effects of that Act.

One of the first projects of the newly formed SANNC was to protest against the Land Act. In July 1913, a month after the Land Act was proclaimed, Sol Plaatje and colleagues rode around the countryside on bicycles noting the distress of people having to leave their former homes, along with their animals and meagre possessions. In the harsh winter conditions, small children died of exposure, as did newborn goats and sheep. Plaatje put the evidence of what he saw in *Native Life in South Africa*, a book published in 1916. The observations he made then have, a century later, received renewed interest.

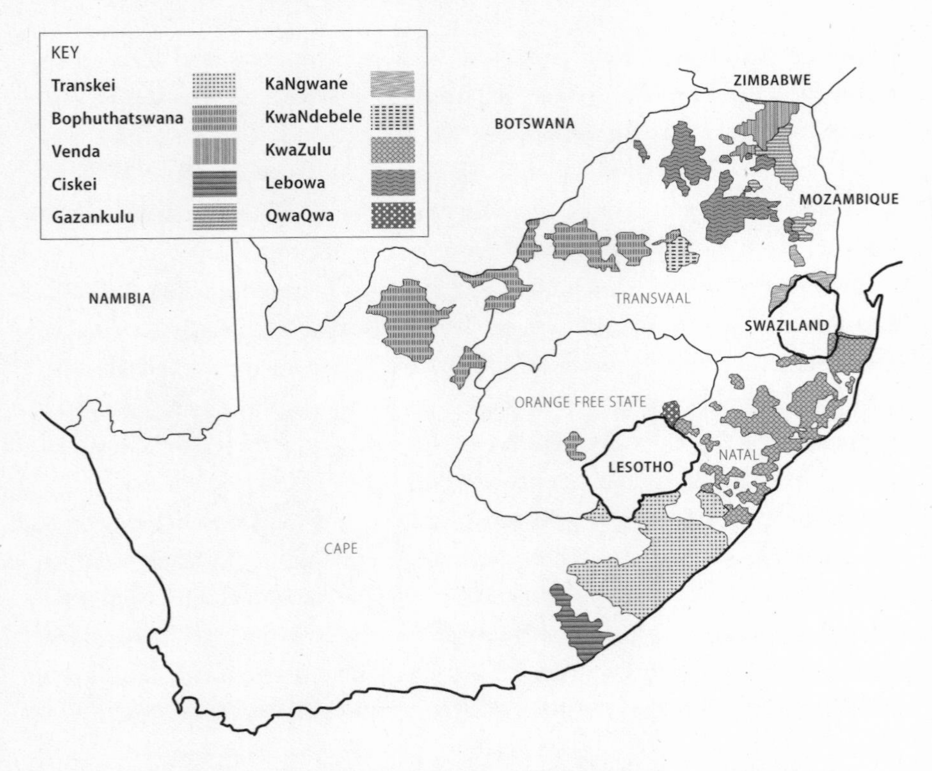

MAP 22 *Land allocated to black people as 'Homelands' in 1976. The original pattern of land allocated to black people in 1913 was still in place but more consolidated and slightly increased. The different patterns show the homelands allocated to the different groups (Zulu, Xhosa, Venda, and so on). The Land Act was only finally repealed in 1991.*

In 1923, the SANNC was renamed the African National Congress (ANC) at a conference in Bloemfontein. By the 1940s, the ANC had become a mass organisation, and within the ANC, the Congress Youth League (ANCYL) had adopted a more militant approach. Early resistance activities were not just male-dominated, however: as early as 1913 there was evidence of opposition movements from women.

The pass system and some early women activists

The system of passes for black people had started as early as 1872, when labour was needed on the diamond fields at Kimberley. [12] Passes were like passports; rural men were registered at labour bureaus and then given passes to look for work in specified areas. The system spread to the gold mines after gold was discovered on the Witwatersrand in 1886. Hut and other taxes were imposed to make it necessary for men to leave the rural areas and work on the mines in order to pay the taxes. The system limited their freedom of movement and was rigorously enforced.

When women started to follow the men into the mining areas, they too, had to have passes, although there were periods when passes for women were relaxed for short periods, only to be reinstated again.[13] In 1913, in what was probably the first women's protest in South Africa, a group of black women led by Charlotte Maxeke burnt their passes, in front of the municipal offices in Bloemfontein.

Charlotte Maxeke was born Charlotte Mannya in Limpopo in 1871, where she received an elementary mission station education. She then went on to become a social worker and leader in the African Methodist Episcopal Church. In 1891, as a young woman of twenty, Maxeke had the unusual distinction of singing for Queen Victoria. She and her sister Katie were members of a choir that went to Britain as part of Queen Victoria's jubilee celebrations. They performed with other choirs at the Crystal Palace, singing songs about work, hunting and social occasions associated with their culture. For part of their performance, they wore traditional African dress, but then changed into Victorian clothes and were introduced to the audience as heathens who had adapted to Christianity.[14]

The choir then went on tour to Canada and the United States, where she met her future husband, Marshall Maxeke, and was sponsored by two Anglican bishops to study at Wilberforce University in Ohio. She graduated in 1903 with a doctorate in the arts and humanities – the first black South African woman to hold a PhD. On return to South Africa, she began to campaign for women's rights.

In 1913, Maxeke and her followers staged protest marches, sang slogans and fought with the police. Many of the women were arrested but their courage did not falter. 'They don't care,' Sol Plaatje wrote in his newspaper, *Tsala ea Batho* ('The Friend of the People'), after visiting some of the women in the Kroonstad prison, 'even if they die in jail.' In 1918, Maxeke led a delegation to Prime Minister Louis Botha's office, again protesting the issue of passes and other grievances. In the same year, she established the Bantu Women's League of the SANNC (a forerunner of the later Women's League of the ANC). Most of the members of the Bantu Women's League were rural, poor and non-literate and the League found little financial support. Money was raised in part through hosting teas and charging pitiful amounts for them.[15]

There were similar protests about passes in 1919 and again in 1920, when Maxeke led demonstrations on the Witwatersrand about low wages and participated in the formation of the Industrial and Commercial Workers' Union (ICU). It might well have been due to her influence that at least during her lifetime (she died in 1939), passes for women were relaxed for short periods, and never quite as rigorously applied to women as they were to men.

Charlotte Maxeke has been called 'the mother of black freedom in South Africa'. In 2008 the former Johannesburg General Hospital in Parktown was renamed the Charlotte Maxeke Academic Hospital in her honour.

Zainunnisa ('Cissie') Gool (1897–1963), daughter of the APO leader Dr Abdurahman, was another early woman activist. As a child she was tutored by the likes of Olive Schreiner and Mahatma Gandhi, who were friends of her father's, and all her life she was guided by their principles. She finished her secondary school education via a correspondence course at London University, and went on to become the first coloured female law graduate in South Africa and the first to be called to the Cape Bar. She represented District Six on various councils, and was referred to as the 'Jewel of District Six', continuing her late father's work as a champion for the marginalised. In subsequent years her participation in resistance movements, notably the 1946 passive resistance campaign, led to her arrest, but it never deterred her from her work.

Afrikaner nationalism and the National Party

Jan Smuts's reconciliatory attitude and admiration for the British did not sit well with some of his colleagues – notably James Barry Munnik Hertzog, another former Anglo-Boer War general, who believed that forgiving the

British so soon meant that Smuts was no longer Afrikaner enough.[16] In July 1914, Hertzog founded the (Afrikaner) National Party in Bloemfontein. By 1915, there were similar Afrikaner national parties in the other provinces.

World War I (1914–1918) and the Afrikaner Rebellion

In 1914, when war broke out between Britain and Germany, South Africa was automatically involved on the side of Britain, because the Union was still under the British Empire. English-speaking South Africans generally responded positively but it was not as easy for the Afrikaners: England was their old enemy. Only 12 years before, Britain had defeated them in war and taken away the Boer republics' independence.

In terms of the Defence Act, members of the Union Defence Force (UDF), which Smuts had inaugurated, were not compelled to serve unless in direct defence of the Union itself. Nevertheless, Smuts called for volunteers to serve on the side of Britain in both German South West Africa (now Namibia) and German East Africa (a region covering what is now Burundi, Rwanda and mainland Tanzania). Initially most volunteers were English-speaking and only about 10 per cent were Afrikaners, but by the end of the war the proportion of Afrikaners serving in the forces had risen to 30 per cent.[17] For some this might have been economic necessity: at least they had jobs in the army.

Initially, however, Afrikaners objected to having to invade German South West Africa, where a number of Afrikaners were living. A rebellion broke out in 1914 that was particularly difficult for Botha and Smuts because it meant they had to resist their own people. A story told at the time illustrates this strange situation: Botha sent a message to General Coen Britz to ask if he would join him, and Britz wired back, 'Yes, but whose side are we fighting on this time?'[18] The rebellion was quickly suppressed, but some important Afrikaner leaders lost their lives – notably General Koos de la Rey.

De la Rey was one of the most astute and celebrated military leaders in the Anglo-Boer War. He subsequently entered politics and was a senator in the Union government when the First World War broke out. He was against participation in the war and was on his way to Potchefstroom to talk to other senior officers about mass resignations as a protest against the attack on South West Africa when he was shot in a police roadblock. Both Botha and Smuts attended De la Rey's funeral without an escort, braving bitter hostility from the mourners. Smuts paid a moving tribute to his fallen comrade, saying that they had been like brothers. But the incident cost Smuts and Botha dearly; it was a divisive influence that played into the hands of Hertzog and his rising opposition.

In 2005, interest in Koos de la Rey was aroused again by a popular song titled 'De La Rey', released by folk singer Bok van Blerk.[19] The song is about a man in the Orange Free State who lost everything in the Anglo-Boer War, and calls on De la Rey to save the Afrikaner people. The lyrics of the song were regarded as subversive by some, while others said it was no more subversive than ANC president Jacob Zuma's song, 'Umshini wami' (Zulu for 'bring me my machine gun').

Another victim of the Rebellion was Jopie Fourie, who had joined the Rebellion without first resigning from his commission. He was shot by a firing squad and became an instant martyr to the Afrikaner nationalist cause.

In 1915, some 67 000 South African troops were sent to invade German South West Africa under the command of General Louis Botha. The German troops stationed there surrendered to the South African forces in July of that year, and in 1920, after five years of military rule, South Africa received a League of Nations mandate to govern the former German colony and to prepare it for independence within a few years.[20]

The next step was the East Africa campaign. Smuts was put in charge of the German East African campaign in 1916 – his success there would have supported his plans for a greater British southern Africa. The campaign went fairly well, but the German forces were not destroyed and Smuts could not capture the German General Paul Von Lettow-Vorbeck. Smuts was clearly the wily German commander's nemesis, however, because one of Von Lettow-Vorbeck's main aims was to lure British forces to Africa, and this was prevented by the presence of Smuts and his Union forces there.

Nevertheless, in East Africa Smuts was criticised by his chief intelligence officer, Colonel Richard Meinertzhagen, for avoiding frontal attacks. In

Meinertzhagen's view, these would have been less costly than the flanking movements which Smuts preferred, and which prolonged the campaign and added to the numbers of soldiers that died of disease. More than 60 000 South Africans served in East Africa and over 1 500 died. Smuts was still regarded by most as a brilliant military strategist and tactician. He was invited to serve on the Imperial War Cabinet in 1917 and played a vital role in decisions concerning the war. He was also instrumental in the creation of the Royal Air Force (RAF) and the air defences of London. South African troops under Smuts also served in France.

Black South Africans in World War I: The incident of the SS *Mendi*

The involvement of black South Africans in the war was largely ignored in the 20th century, and it is only in recent years that some form of recognition is being afforded those who served – and lost their lives in service to – the Union and, by extension, to Britain.

Black South Africans served not as soldiers, but in a variety of non-combatant capacities. Thousands of men were formed into labour corps that assisted General Louis Botha in German South West Africa and General Jan Smuts in German East Africa, and then when the war moved into Europe, a South African Native Labour Contingent (SANLC) was recruited for service overseas.

Between 1916 and 1918, some 21 000 black South Africans – all volunteers – served in France with the SANLC. They were employed in French harbours unloading supply ships; others dug quarries and trenches, and laid and repaired roads and railway lines; and many worked as stretcher bearers on the battlefields, carrying white soldiers to safety at risk to themselves. The black troops were accommodated mainly in closed compounds (like those on the mines back in South Africa) which restricted their freedom of movement and left them vulnerable to attack by enemy planes.[21] Some 333 of these men lost their lives during the war and are buried at the British military cemetery at Arques-la-Bataille.

In February 1917, 607 black troops lost their lives at sea when the SS *Mendi*, the third ship to transport them to France, collided with another ship, the SS *Darro*, in thick fog off the Isle of Wight.[22] Legend has it that some of the black troops stood on the deck and sang as the SS *Mendi* sank, but historical consensus holds that this version of events is apocryphal.[23] The men on the SS *Darro* survived and in July 1917 a formal investigation was held at Westminster. The captain of the *Darro* was found guilty of travelling at a dangerously high speed in thick fog, failing to sound the necessary fog signals and leaving the scene without helping the stricken SS *Mendi* or the soldiers on board who could not swim. His licence was suspended for a year.

After the war, none of the members of the South African Native Labour Corps nor any of the troops on the SS *Mendi* were awarded UK war medals, but the white officers were decorated. In 1995, a memorial to the men of the SS *Mendi* was unveiled by Queen Elizabeth II at Avalon Cemetery in Soweto outside Johannesburg. A similar memorial to them now stands at Hollybrook, Southhampton in England.

In July 2016, an event at Delville Wood in France marked the centenary of the battle that took place there as part of the Battle of the Somme offensive. No black soldiers served at Delville Wood, but most white South Africans who died in World War I died there: of the 3 000 white soldiers who went there, only approximately 700 returned.[24] At the centenary celebrations it was announced that a special wall of remembrance would be erected there, and the names of the more than 6 000 South Africans of all races who were lost or died in France would be listed on the wall.[25] The list would also include those who drowned on the *Mendi*.

The aftermath of World War I

After the war ended in 1918, Botha and Smuts went to the peace conference at Versailles in France. As they had done after the Anglo-Boer War 16 years before, the Boer generals once again sat around a table with British generals and statesmen – but this time they sat on the same side. Significantly, both Botha and Smuts urged caution in the arrangements being made for the defeated Germany. Smuts remembered Britain's magnanimity in allowing the Boers self-government after the Boer War in 1902, and advised the same moderate treatment of Germany for the sake of future security. His advice was not heeded.

Smuts nevertheless played an important role in the drafting of the covenant of the League of Nations, forerunner of the United Nations, and it was he who wrote the preamble to the Charter. It was also Smuts who put forward the proposal in 1917 that the old British Empire, which was disintegrating, be replaced by a British Commonwealth of Nations – a free association of newly independent states or dominions. To help make this possible, he was involved in redefining Britain's relationships with Canada, Australia, India, Ceylon (Sri Lanka), New Zealand, Newfoundland, South Africa, Pakistan and the Irish Free State.

In 1919, soon after returning to South Africa, Louis Botha died unexpectedly at the age of 56, and there was no question but that Smuts would become Prime Minister, as well as Minister of Native Affairs. Smuts had become an internationally known statesman and his opinions were sought in councils all over the world – King George VI was so impressed with his work in the Imperial War Cabinet that he asked Smuts to deliver the address at the opening of the Irish Parliament in 1920. But Smuts had never sought the position of prime minister in South Africa – it had worked well with the more popular Botha running the country while Smuts spent time overseas, advising the British war effort and attending conferences of international significance. These activities brought recognition to South Africa,[26] but at the same time caused animosity back home from people who felt that he was not spending enough time attending to local problems.

Smuts never again found the kind of partnership in politics that he had enjoyed with Louis Botha, and would instead accept some strange alliances based on future circumstances. Many problems lay ahead. Jan Smuts was Prime Minister of South Africa from 1919–1924 and again from 1939–1948, when the Afrikaner Nationalist Party under DF Malan came into power.

White miners' strikes

Almost from the start of the gold mining industry, white mine workers had been a force to contend with. Semi-skilled white workers were protected by the colour bar, earning about half the salary of qualified men, but five times more than black men. But by the early 1900s, many black workers had served several contracts and had acquired significant skills. Mining was taking place at even greater depths, which made it more expensive, and after World War I, the price of gold was low. The mine owners' announcement that they wanted to relax the job colour bar and use black labour more effectively was met with fierce resistance from white workers, and strikes broke out in 1907, 1913 and 1914, and 1922.

By 1922, three quarters of the white workforce were Afrikaners. The white Mine Workers' Union was still controlled by the British, but Afrikaners supported the strike action, set up road blocks and formed commandos much like those used by the Boers in the Anglo-Boer War. The South African Communist Party (SACP) had been formed in 1921 with a mostly white membership;[27] one of the striking units was communist influenced and used the bizarre slogan 'White workers of the world unite'.[28]

During the 1922 strikes, the Smuts government came down heavily on the side of the mine owners and used military force to disperse striking white miners. Bomber aircraft were called in and bombs were dropped on one of the mining centres at Benoni. Nearly 700 people were injured and 153 people died during the turmoil, four of them executed. Smuts said at the time that he'd had to take drastic action as the striking white miners had Johannesburg and its surrounds by the throat and there was madness in their blood.[29]

The move towards the Pact government under JBM Hertzog, 1924–1929

In 1922, in addition to the striking miners, Smuts also used force against two African religious sects: the Israelites and the Bondelswarts (descendents of the Khoisan). The leader of the Israelites, Enoch Mgijima, had told his people the world was coming to an end and that as God's chosen people, only they would be saved. He told his people to assemble at a chosen spot near Queenstown in the eastern Cape and to await the appointed day. Time passed and government authorities became alarmed when the people began to build houses, despite assurances that they would only be there temporarily. After repeated requests for them to move, they were fired on and many killed.[30] The Bondelswarts were fired on for refusing to pay a tax on dogs. More than 200 people were killed in these incidents.

Much of the legislation of the next few years would be detrimental to South African black people. In 1923, the Urban Areas Act was passed, a follow-on from the Union government's 1913 Land Act, which affected mainly rural people. The 1923 Act laid the foundation for residential segregation in urban areas: black people were permitted to come into the urban areas to work for white people, but they could not live there. They had to live in locations outside.

Brilliant man though he was in so many respects, Smuts had shown a lack of understanding of the problems and conflicting interests of an industrialising society in which local whites and immigrants struggled for positions, and both feared competition from other races. Early in his career Smuts had taken the decision that to restore law and order and bring back stability must come first, but this approach cost him dearly in the next elections.

By 1924, JBM Hertzog's National Party had grown in strength and had formed a pact with English-speaking Labourites. When the Pact government defeated Smuts and his South Africa Party, Hertzog became Prime Minister and Smuts the leader of the opposition.

Hertzog's Afrikaner nationalists and the English-speaking Labourites were strange bedfellows, but they achieved their aim, and job reservation for whites continued on the mines. After his election, Hertzog immediately set about passing more legislation in favour of whites, especially Afrikaners. He made more capital available for white farmers through the Land Bank, and in 1928 he established ISCOR (Iron and Steel Industrial Corporation), a state corporation for the manufacture of steel. ISCOR gave jobs to Afrikaners and protected them from black competition.[31] Under Hertzog, unemployed Afrikaners also replaced black men on the railways, and were paid more. These and other moves became known as Hertzog's 'Civilised Labour Policies', the implication being that whites were more 'civilised' and needed to earn more than blacks as they had a higher standard of living, which cost more to maintain.

Hertzog also made moves to promote the Afrikaans language, and in 1925 Afrikaans replaced Dutch as an official language in South Africa.[32] It was also during Hertzog's time, in 1929, that the franchise was extended to white women in the Cape, although this move was less about gender equality than further entrenching racial injustice: it had the effect of reducing the black proportion of voters in the Cape Province from 20 to 10 per cent. It was also largely Hertzog's efforts that resulted in the Statute of Westminster of 1931, which granted legislative autonomy for South Africa and other commonwealth countries.[33]

The first multiracial trade union

South Africans have never constituted a homogenous group, and for most of our history there have been laws prohibiting the mixing of races, but there have also been times when people of different races and classes have worked together. It was, rather incongruously, in Hertzog's time that the first multiracial trade union was established. Despite difficulties, it survived for several years.

In 1928, the Transvaal Garment Workers Union (GWU) was started by a white Jewish man from Lithuania, Emil (Solly) Sachs.[34] It was open to all women employees of the garment industry, irrespective of race or class. Many of its members were young Afrikaner women who had come into the cities looking for work during the global Great Depression of the early 1930s. It was the most active and controversial union of its time. Female workers in the garment industry were notoriously badly paid, and the aim of the union was to improve wages and working conditions.

Several strikes were held in the 1930s, causing much disruption. However, the GWU was difficult to sustain in a society that was so segregated. In addition, Solly Sachs was a member of the South African Communist Party (SACP), and was arrested several times and tried under the Suppression of Communism Act. He finally left South Africa in 1953 and settled in England, saying that his position in South Africa had become untenable.

CHAPTER 9

New political parties, the rise of the Afrikaners, World War II (1939–1945) and the 1948 elections

The formation of two new parties and the 'Native Bills'

The worldwide Great Depression in 1929 led to yet another realignment of political parties. In the wake of Wall Street's collapse in October 1929, South African exports plummeted.[1] Australia and Britain devalued their currencies but Hertzog refused to do the same until 1932, by which time the economy was damaged and many farmers were ruined. Hertzog was also faced with competition from a new maverick politician: Tielman Roos. In response, the two old rivals, Hertzog and Smuts, decided to form a coalition, which won the elections in 1933, and in 1934 they merged to form the United Party (UP). It was a curious turn of events, and very much a matter of political expediency.

A few years before, in 1926, along with his 'civilised labour' policy, Hertzog had introduced what were referred to as his 'Native Bills'. These Bills were designed to remove the vote from the last few black people who had it in the Cape and Natal. In exchange, the land allocated to black people under the Land Act of 1913 was to be increased to 12 per cent. Hertzog did not get a two-thirds majority vote in favour and the Bills were never passed. Smuts was one of the members of parliament who had voted against them. Ten years later, in 1936, when Hertzog reintroduced his Native Bills in a slightly different form as The Natives Trust and Land Act and the Natives Representation Act, Smuts voted in favour, even though the contents were more restrictive.

Smuts's policy towards black people was complex. In 1936 he explained his change of heart by saying that he wished to 'be fair to the black man', but that the black man still needed the white man's guidance; the issues needed time, and should be left to 'the ampler brains of the future'. His motto was 'one step at a time'.[2] But in 1936, Smuts's main concern must have been that he did not want to risk breaking the newly formed coalition with Hertzog. Nevertheless, three years later, when the issue of World War II came up, Smuts did oppose Hertzog, who did not want South Africa to participate.

These infamous Native Bills were euphemistically referred to at the time as 'substance' for 'shadow' – the 'shadow' of the vote in a Parliamentary system said to be alien to black people in exchange for the 'substance' of more land. Black people were completely taken off the common voters' roll, and offered three white representatives in Parliament instead. A Natives Representative Council (NRC) was set up, but it had limited powers. Some distinguished people served on it, notably the white senators Edgar Brookes, Margaret Ballinger and Alan Paton (author of *Cry, the Beloved Country*): they tried to plead the cause of black people but they had little support, and in 1949 the NRC was abandoned. It was said at the time that it was like speaking into a telephone when you knew there was no one listening at the other end.[3] Even the promise of more land was never entirely achieved, and blamed on the outbreak of World War II.

Towards the end of his life, in 1947, Smuts supported the recommendations of a commission led by Judge Henry Fagan, which stated that black people should be accommodated as part of urban life, and not forced to live kilometres away from South Africa's cities. Smuts's government fell from power the following year before anything further could be done. If the recommendations had gone through, it is possible that history might have taken a different turn, avoiding much of the heartache of subsequent years.

The merge of Hertzog and Smuts in the United Party had brought another Afrikaner, DF Malan, to the fore. He objected to the union of Hertzog and Smuts and decided neither was Afrikaner enough. Determined to preserve the exclusive identity of Afrikaners, in 1935, Malan and 19 others formed their own national party called the Gesuiwerde Nasionale Party ('Purified National Party', or PNP). The party would be a force to be reckoned with in the following years, and would sweep into power in 1948.

The rise of the Afrikaners

In the years after the Afrikaners' defeat in the Anglo-Boer War, Afrikaner nationalism had gradually been built through Afrikaner cultural awareness, economic advance and infiltration of the trade unions. At the centre of these endeavours was a society called the Afrikaner Broederbond ('Brotherhood of Men'). This had started in 1918 as a cultural organisation in a house in Kensington, Johannesburg, but became a secret organisation in 1924. Its aim was to promote Afrikaners and help them succeed in all walks of life to the extent that they could influence the media, education, the way history was taught and other important institutions.

Afrikaners were reminded of their cultural heritage and there was an outpouring of nationalist sentiment by the establishment of the Federasie van Afrikaanse Kultuurverenigings ('Federation of Afrikaans Cultural Organisations') in 1929, re-enactments of the Great Trek in 1938 during the centenary of the Battle of Blood River, and the laying of the foundation stone for the enormous Voortrekker Monument outside Pretoria in 1939. People dressed up in the style of the Voortrekkers and exchanged stories about the suffering and hardship of their forefathers.

The Afrikaner economic advance was achieved by the establishment of a fund for Afrikaner people, Volkskapitalisme ('people's capital'), and persuading well-off Cape businessmen to donate to it. The numbers of poor whites (mainly Afrikaners) had grown dramatically during the depression – in 1933 there were an estimated 300 000 poor whites, which constituted about a quarter of the Afrikaner population, and Volkskapitalisme was designed to help these people. Volkskas Bank (now part of ABSA) and insurance company Sanlam were both projects to facilitate Afrikaner economic advance. Afrikaner businessmen were also encouraged to employ Afrikaners rather than English-speaking whites.

The Dutch Reformed Church also played a part in fostering Afrikaner nationalism by encouraging the concept of Afrikaners as 'chosen people', like the children of Israel, and that their hardships thus far had been God testing them. Ardent nationalists frowned on Jews, Catholics and anyone else who might dilute their 'master' race. It is said that this opinion persisted for many years – to the extent that when the Kenridge Hospital (now the Donald Gordon) was opened in Johannesburg in 1970, radical Afrikaners would not go there because it was staffed by Catholic nuns.

In the 1930s, alternative Afrikaner trade unions were also established to wean Afrikaners away from those run by the English. Prime examples were the Mynwerkers Unie (Mine Workers' Union) and Spoorbond (Railway Union).

South Africa in World War II, 1939–1945

The outbreak of war in 1939 had tremendous impact in South Africa, and played into the hands of the Afrikaners. In 1914, South Africans had had no choice but to go to war on the side of Britain. In 1939, thanks to the autonomy achieved largely by Hertzog under the Statute of Westminster, they could make their own decision.

White South Africans were divided on this issue. Smuts was in favour of participation, while Hertzog and most of his supporters were not. Some Afrikaners even wanted a German victory as they thought Britain's defeat would make it possible for South Africa to become a republic again. In the end, it was put to the vote in Parliament: Smuts took South Africa into war on the side of Britain by a narrow margin of 80 votes in favour, 67 against.[4] The fragile alliance between Hertzog and Smuts in their still-young United Party – established only five years before – was split right open over this issue. Hertzog resigned and Smuts became prime minister again.

As it happened, South Africans would play a significant role in the war. There was an amazing response to Smuts's call to arms, and 334 000 South Africans volunteered (approximately 211 000 whites, 77 000 blacks and 46 000 coloureds and Indians). Some 11 023 South Africans are known to have died in World War II, as their names are recorded, but the figure is probably more.[5]

South Africans were badly equipped when war first broke out, but the now elderly Smuts[6] moved quickly to create two active service divisions and an air force. The navy was also brought in to the fray, and South African ships were sent to patrol the coastline from Alexandria through Mersa Matruh in Egypt, to Tobruk in Libya.

At the start of the war, Smuts had undertaken not to send men overseas, preferring that they see service in Africa. Germany no longer had colonies in Africa, but Germany's ally Italy did. Although Italy was not yet in the war, it had colonial interests in North and East Africa, from which Egypt and the oil fields in the Persian Gulf would be threatened. Smuts made it clear that the Union Defence Force (UDF) had to help especially in the Middle East because of the threat to the oil fields in the Persian Gulf and the use of the Suez Canal. Inevitably, as the war progressed, South Africans saw action in both North and East Africa, as well as the Middle East, Italy, the Balkans and other places.

The North African Campaign began in September 1940 with the Italian invasion of Egypt. In 1941 and 1942, the South African First Infantry Division took part in several actions against German and Italian forces in North Africa, notably at Tobruk and Sidi Rezegh in Libya, and El Alamein in Egypt.

In April 1941 some 10 000 Allied troops, including members of the South African First Infantry Division, were trapped at Tobruk by the 'desert fox', German Field Marshal Erwin Rommel, and his Afrika Korps. The siege lasted some 241 days until 8 November, when a military operation known as 'Operation Crusader' by the British Eighth Army took place at nearby Sidi Rezegh. The aim of the operation was to destroy the Axis forces where they stood, and thus relieve Tobruk.

Sidi Rezegh was the first great tank battle in the Western Desert, and it lasted until 30 December. The Fifth South African Infantry Brigade (a section of the First Infantry Brigade) fought with the British Seventh Armoured Division and other forces. They were heavily defeated, and the South African Fifth Brigade was disbanded soon after. Of the approximately 5 800 South Africans who fought at Sidi Rezegh, only approximately 2 000

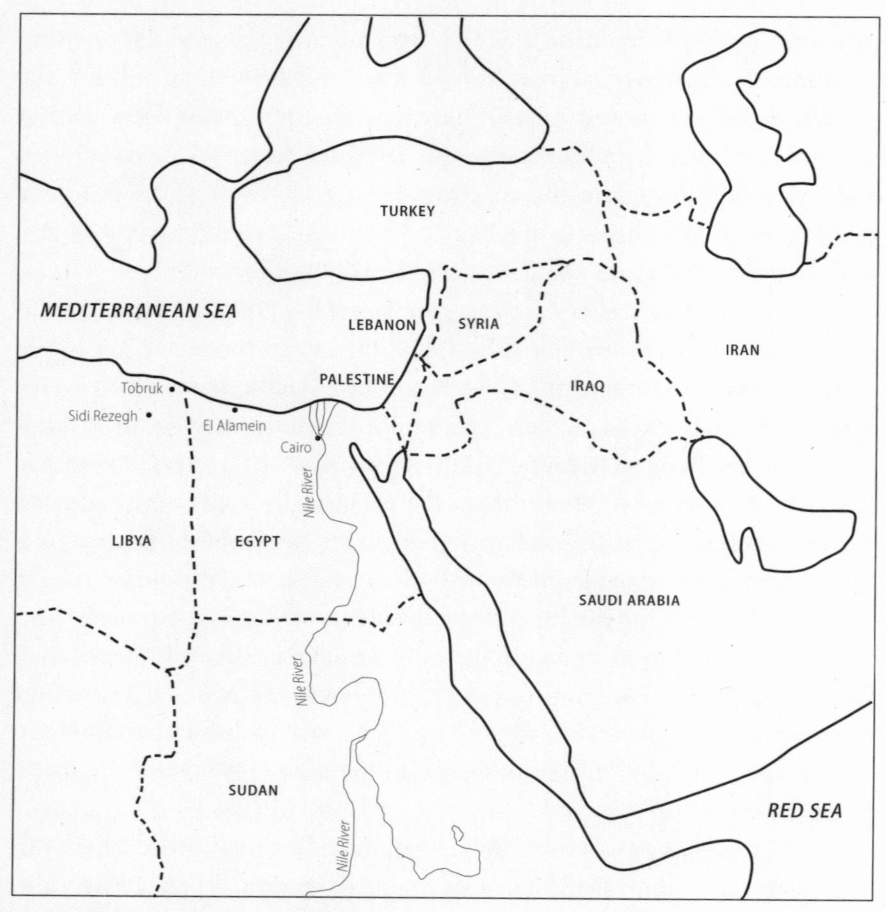

MAP 23 *Battle sites during World War II.*

returned – the rest were killed, wounded or taken prisoner. Smuts said it was one of South Africa's heaviest losses during the war.

A little-known story is that of a young man, Job Maseko, whose home-made bomb, made while he was a prisoner of war in Tobruk, blew up a German ship. His story was researched by Marilyn Honikman after she was intrigued by a painting of a black serviceman at the top of the stairs at the Museum of Military History in Johannesburg. Job Maseko's enterprise was worthy of a VC award but this never happened and his heroic deed was forgotten for almost 50 years.[7]

In 1942, two significant battles took place near the Egyptian railway line at El Alamein in Egypt. The military historian Colonel CJ Jacobs believes the first one, 1–30 July 1942, was the more important because prior to this, it had been thought that the British in the so-called Desert War would never find a way to defeat Rommel and his Afrika Korps – nevertheless, this first battle halted Rommel's advance into Egypt and laid the foundation for his later defeat in the second battle, 23 October–11 November 1942.[8]

In the second battle at El Alamein, Lieutenant Bernard Law Montgomery had taken command of the British Eighth Army, but South African forces also played their part. The Allied victory at El Alamein ended the Axis threat to the oil fields in the Persian Gulf and the Suez Canal. It also restored the morale of the Allied troops after the disasters at Tobruk and Sidi Rezegh.

The South African Air Force (SAAF) made a significant contribution to the air war in East Africa, North Africa, Sicily, Italy and the Balkans. In North Africa, in early 1942, the SAAF squadrons assisted the Allied Desert Air Force in attaining air supremacy over Rommel's air component, and they carried out a series of bombing raids (three a day for weeks on end) on the Afrika Korps. This finally stopped Rommel in his advance towards El Alamein in mid-1942.[9]

Both the South African army and the air force also played major roles in defeating the Italian forces during the 1940/1941 East African Campaign. South African troops took part in campaigns in Ethiopia, and helped the Allies capture Addis Ababa from the Italians. South Africans also took part in the invasion of Italy, helped the Allies capture Madagascar in 1942 and participated in the bombing raids over Poland during the Warsaw Rebellion of 1944. Thousands of South Africans fought in British units, and one of them, a fighter pilot in the Royal Air Force, Adolph (Sailor) Malan, famously led the No. 74 Squadron during the height of the Battle of Britain.

The recruitment of Africans into the UDF was particularly successful; so much so that at the end of the recruitment period, it is estimated that more than 80 000 black men had been recruited into the Native Military Corps (NMC).[10] They were trained in various support functions and then posted to the war zones in east and north Africa, the Middle East, Madagascar and Italy, where they worked, often under heavy fire, as stretcher bearers, drivers, orderlies and trench diggers. They were forbidden by the South African government to carry arms and could only serve in non-combatant roles.[11]

A record states that in El Alamein on 23 and 24 October 1942, Luca Majoli, a stretcher bearer, carried wounded men to safety despite being hit by shrapnel himself when his unit came under heavy fire. He eventually collapsed from loss of blood, but survived. Captain Zietsman, a liaison officer of the 1 SA Division in 1941 testified to the fact that countless men owed their lives to the stretcher bearers. 'They fought like tigers,' he said. 'As one went down, another stepped in to take his place. For a moment they were all South Africans, irrespective of race or creed.'[12]

Black South Africans were also involved in a secret special project to build tunnels and railway links through the mountains between Turkey and Egypt, where the British had a base. The tunnels went through Palestine and Syria, and some of them still exist today. About 420 South African mine workers with special knowledge and experience in underground work were chosen to assist the South African engineers with the project.[13] They built the tunnels in harsh winter conditions and completed them seven months ahead of schedule. After the war, awards and merit certificates were given to black men who had distinguished themselves, but any hope that the government might help them find decent jobs or give them the same rights as whites proved fruitless.

There was activity at home too, where many South African women worked in the Women's Auxiliary Unit (WAU) and the Women's Voluntary Air Force (WVAF). In 1939, a flying school was opened in Witbank (now Emalahleni in Mpumalanga) by British-born Henry Nattrass, who had been a fighter pilot in both world wars. His South African wife, Lorna Nattrass, became one of his first pupils, and was the only woman in the district to obtain her pilot's licence. In 1940, when the WVAF was formed, she became the first commandant of Witbank and what was then the eastern Transvaal.

The WAU and WVAF did wonderful work during the war. They ran first-aid, home-nursing and fire-fighting courses; serviced cars and lorries; knitted and sewed for the troops; packed parachutes; put together and dispatched parcels to the men up north and overseas; and held functions to raise money for war services. Lorna Nattrass flew supply planes in and around her district, and at the end of the war she received the South African medal for war services, signed by Jan Smuts. Her husband commanded three more air-training schools before going up north to pilot aircraft again, and was awarded the O.B.E. (Military) in 1944.[14]

Smuts's influence was very apparent in all stages of the war. He had a firm grasp of military and strategic matters, and the British Prime Minister Sir Winston Churchill sought his advice on several occasions. Once again, as had happened in World War I, he was asked to join the Imperial War Cabinet and given the rank of Field Marshal, the first South African to hold such a position. 'Jan Smuts' became a household name in Britain. Such was his influence that Churchill's secretary apparently even tried to approach King George VI with the suggestion that if anything happened to Churchill, Smuts should be asked to take over as British prime minister.[15] As it happened, Churchill outlived Smuts by several years, and it is doubtful whether Smuts would have accepted such a position: much as he admired the British, he was a South African at heart.

During the course of World War II, Smuts made nine visits to the Middle East to confer with Allied leaders, and at the end of the war he helped to establish the United Nations. Professor Christof Heyns and Dr William Gravett from the University of Pretoria Law School note that Smuts was the first person to use the term 'human rights' in an official document for a world body: in 1945, Smuts wrote human rights into the preamble of the Charter of the United Nations.[16]

The British Royal Tour and Isie Smuts

Smuts had thus been involved in the establishment of two world organisations (the League of Nations and the United Nations), and had placed South Africa firmly on the world stage in a way that would not happen again until the Nelson Mandela era of the 1990s. Smuts's statue still stands in Parliament Square, London – the only Commonwealth leader's statue to be erected there until Nelson Mandela's was added in 2007.

In 1947, the British royal family – King George VI, Queen Elizabeth and their daughters, the princesses Elizabeth and Margaret – visited South

Africa at Smuts's invitation. It had not happened before that a reigning British monarch had visited South Africa, and it would not happen again for another 50 years until 1996, when Queen Elizabeth II, who had been a young princess in 1947, came to visit South Africa at President Nelson Mandela's invitation.

The British royal tour of South Africa in 1947 was a particularly long and successful one. In hindsight, the Smuts government might have organised it not just because of Smuts's friendship and admiration for the British, but also to counter the rise of Afrikaner nationalism. The royal family was welcomed wherever they went with messages in both English and Afrikaans. Nevertheless, a year later, Smuts and his United Party fell from power.

Although she never went overseas with her husband or left the continent of Africa throughout her life, Smuts's wife, Sybella (Isie), played a significant role in the war and post-war era. Affectionately known as Ouma ('grandmother') she was actively involved with the Suid-Afrikaanse Vrouefederasie ('South African Women's Organisation'), the Women's United Party, and the Gifts and Comforts Fund for soldiers during the war. She did not care much for celebrities or formal occasions. On one occasion in Cairo, where she opened a service women's club, an official was making a presentation speech for her. The man had already talked for ten minutes and was showing signs of carrying on for much longer when Ouma tugged his sleeve and said, 'You must stop now. I want to see what is in my parcel.'[17]

When the British royal family visited South Africa in 1947, Isie Smuts did not go to any of the receptions. When the royal family made it clear that they would like to meet her, Isie replied that they would have to come to her. This they did, visiting Isie Smuts at her simple home at Doornkloof, near Irene (about 50 kilometres north of Johannesburg).[18]

Perhaps Isie had never quite forgiven the British, and memories of the Anglo-Boer War loomed large. She had asked to be treated the same as other Boer women and to be sent to a concentration camp,[19] but the British authorities had refused and instead exiled her to a house in Pietermaritzburg (then in a British colony). But Isie had had her share of suffering. Twins born to Isie and Jan Smuts had been born prematurely and only lived a few weeks. A year later, just before the outbreak of the Anglo-Boer War, they'd had a son, Jacobus Abraham (Koosie), who was a strong, healthy child. In August 1900, when he was just 16 months old, he had picked up a childhood ailment and died. It was possible that, had it not been for the war that prevented the supply of medicines, he could have been treated.

Extreme Afrikaner groups

A particularly extremist group during the war was the Ossewabrandwag (meaning oxwagon sentinel or guard). The OB had started as a cultural organisation in 1939 during the centenary celebrations of the Great Trek, but after the outbreak of the Second World War it became a paramilitary body with its own storm troopers modelled on those of the Nazi in Germany. The OB opposed South Africa's participation in the war on the British side, and carried out acts of sabotage against the Smuts government. They wanted a German victory and a nationalist socialist-type government in South Africa. Their leader was JFJ van Rensburg. Two future prime ministers of South Africa, John Vorster and PW Botha, were members of the OB.[20]

Another extremist who hoped for a German victory during the war was Robey Leibbrandt, a South African amateur light-heavyweight boxing champion of German/Irish descent. His father had fought in the Anglo-Boer War. Robey Leibbrandt had represented South Africa at the Empire Games in 1934 and at the Olympic Games in Berlin in 1936, where he was first exposed to Nazi ideology. In 1938 he returned to Berlin, where he trained as a storm trooper and studied sabotage and propaganda methods. When he returned to South Africa during the war, he established the Nasionaal Sosialistiese Rebelle ('National Socialist Rebels'), an extremist group similar to the OB. He made fiery speeches similar to those he had witnessed in Germany, and taught his members about sabotage and bomb making. He was arrested near Pretoria on 24 December 1942 and sentenced to death for high treason, but this was later commuted by Smuts to life imprisonment. When the Nationalist Party came into power in 1948 he was released.[21]

Neither the OB nor the Nasionaal Sosialistiese Rebelle gathered much support as most Afrikaners found their ideas too extreme.

The end of the war

The United Party of Smuts and Hertzog had broken up in 1939, and Smuts had taken South Africa into the war by a narrow majority. South Africa's participation in World War II marked the start of a new political struggle. New political alignments were soon to take place.

In the elections of 1943, Smuts had won comfortably because the war was going well for the Allies, and people felt good about being on the winning side. In 1945, when the war ended in Allied victory, Smuts still rode the crest of the wave for a while. He had distinguished himself in the war and made friends with prime ministers around the world at the various conferences he attended. He still had support in the major cities of the Witwatersrand, the Cape Peninsular, the eastern Cape and Natal, but the remainder of the country was divided into Hertzog and DF Malan supporters.

A post-war situation brings with it inevitable problems and there is often a change in government. This happened in Britain when Churchill fell from power, and it was destined to happen in South Africa, too. The Purified National Party under DF Malan (by now simply referred to as the NP) had started to gain ground. DF Malan had been preaching an extreme form of Afrikaner nationalism for some time already. He and his followers played on post-war grievances of job losses affecting returning soldiers, housing shortages, rising costs and the uncertainties regarding relations between whites and blacks. In 1946 there was a serious strike of black mine workers, adding to the general instability of the times. Then, in 1947, a commission under Judge Fagan appointed by Smuts recommended that influx control be relaxed to allow black people to live in urban areas. Smuts approved and thought the time was right, but many people, especially poorer whites, did not agree. The NP campaigned on the slogan of a swart gevaar ('black danger'), and promised that if the NP came to power there would be a policy of apartheid (apartness or separation of the races) that would protect white people.

Hertzog initially did not go along with Malan's more extreme ideas, but on the eve of the 1948 elections, Hertzog and his followers (who had fallen out with Smuts over South Africa's participation in the war) joined Malan's National Party, swelling the numbers enough to defeat Smuts and his United Party. It was a shocking and unexpected defeat, which no one, least of all Smuts, had seen coming. Smuts was by then quite an old man. He died two years later in 1950, aged 80.

The historian Shula Marks, who is critical of powerful men like Rhodes and Smuts, nevertheless wrote that no single figure had done more to shape South Africa in the first 50 years of the 20th century than Jan Smuts. He was South Africa's most outstanding white statesman, she wrote, and was involved in all the major events in South African, European and Commonwealth history in those 50 years.[22] Jan Smuts's death in 1950 was in many ways the end of an era.

The coming to power of the Afrikaner National Party in 1948

After winning the elections in 1948, DF Malan's Afrikaner nationalist party proceeded to pursue apartheid policies. With few exceptions, black, coloured and Indian people (all generally referred to as 'blacks' by the authorities) were excluded from any active or meaningful participation in government and were disadvantaged in terms of opportunity and education. This system continued until the early 1990s.

Military historian Ian van der Waag dates a period of 'Cold War' in South Africa from this time. He believes this period lasted until about 1959/1960, when a more aggressive 'Hot War' began. The Hot War would last until things changed in South Africa in 1989/1990.[23]

The military

The military is always a reflection of a government's priorities. Likewise in South Africa it has been susceptible to change with changing governments. Soon after South Africa became a Union in 1910, a Union Defence Force (UDF) had been formed. In the reconciliatory spirit of the time (as far as whites were concerned, after the bitter memories of the Anglo-Boer War), members of the UDF were both English and Afrikaans speakers, and to serve in the military was regarded as a noble profession. The UDF went on to serve in both world wars, and when the Allies registered victory in 1945,

Prime Minister and Field Marshal Jan Smuts enjoyed recognition for the UDF's efforts.

In 1948, under DF Malan's National Party government, everything changed. Frans Erasmus was appointed defence minister and made significant changes, mainly in favour of re-establishing commandos and other military traditions of the old Boer republics, and doing away with colonial-influenced UDF formations. He was determined to create a new-look South African Defence Force (SADF). Talented and competent former military leaders were purged in the process as the military also began to promote Afrikaner nationalism and the National Party, and key Afrikaners were appointed to important posts. Military support would prove crucial in the events that followed: when DF Malan's government began implementing their apartheid policies, they would have the military behind them.

CHAPTER 10

The apartheid government

Apartheid policy and the formation of 'homelands'

The theory behind the apartheid policy implemented by Malan and his National Party government was that whites and blacks are so culturally dissimilar that they could never live together as a community, and if they were to try, the numerically stronger black people would swamp the whites.[1]

The solution as they saw it was to divide up the country into areas where whites would have rights and citizenship, and other areas where blacks would have the same. But they then went even further and divided up black people according to ethnic differences: the Zulu were allocated separate land from the Xhosa, the Basotho, the Tswana and so on. The government argued that African people had absolute ethnic and culturally distinct differences that had to be preserved in separate homelands, although it is more likely that the plan was to keep different African communities separate so that they would be unlikely to present a united front against whites.

What the government did not take into account was that while some of black communities were relatively culturally homogenous, others were not. The Basotho, for example, were made up of diverse cultures since the leader Moshoeshoe had over many years incorporated refugees and conquered people of diverse origin into his Sotho kingdom. Of course, history had already shown that people of different cultures could work well together: when the SANNC began in 1912, for example, its founder members were Zulu (John Dube and Pixley Seme), Xhosa (Walter Rubusana) and Tswana (Sol Plaatje).[2]

The policy of apartheid might have seemed to have had some merit[3] until it became clear that black people would be restricted to the reserves that had originally been created under Theophilus Shepstone[4] and others almost a century before; and that the reserves would be extended by very little (only up to about 14% of the total land of South Africa). Black people would not be able to survive on so little land and would still need to come and work in 'white' areas.

The reserves, meanwhile, were to become 'homelands'. Tribal authorities were to be revived and the homelands would be offered self-government and eventually independence. The problem was they were limited in size and had few amenities. They could not justifiably become politically independent until they had economic strength, and this was never achieved. Only a few had applied for independence by the late 1970s.

The force behind the creation of the homelands was Hendrik Verwoerd, the young sociology professor who had advocated apartheid way back in the 1930s. In 1950 he became Minister of Native Affairs, and in 1958, he became prime minister in the NP government. The worst of the apartheid laws were passed under his terms of office, but he made them sound as if they were based on human rights. 'We do not only want to ensure white survival,' he told a London audience in 1961. 'We seek a solution which will ensure survival and full development – political and economic – to each of the other racial groups.'[5]

It seems extraordinary that the architects of apartheid were mostly academics and highly intelligent men. DF Malan had a masters in philosophy and a doctorate in divinity and was an ordained minister of the Dutch Reformed Church. Hendrik Verwoerd had a masters in philosophy and a doctorate in psychology, both cum laude, and other members of his government had a string of doctorates as well.

In 1951, the Bantu Self-Government Act was passed.[6] This created ten homelands based on ethnicity (Zulu, Xhosa, Venda, Tswana, Ndebele, Sotho and others[7]). About 3.5 million black people were forcibly removed to these homelands. Liberal Member of Parliament Alan Paton remarked at the time that it was disappointing that Afrikaners were treating black people this way as they knew what it was like to be discriminated against under the British. The Boers had once been the 'darlings' of the world, he said, for their courage against a stronger force.

The personal effects of some apartheid policies

In the urban areas where black people still came to work, apartheid was enforced in both social and economic life. Notices stating *Slegs blankes* or *Nie-blankes* (whites only or non-whites) appeared on benches in parks and railway stations, separate entrances were created in shops and banks, and Acts were passed which forced the separation of the races. The Separate Amenities Act 49 of 1953 laid down that restaurants, bars, hotels and other public places were for whites only.

In 1950, two Acts passed by the apartheid government, the Mixed Marriages Act and the Immorality Act, made it illegal to marry or have sexual relations across the colour line. People caught doing this were arrested and charged with contravening the Act. The Population Registration Act of 1950 also caused untold suffering. It made it compulsory for everyone over a certain age to be classified as either black, white, Indian or coloured, and to carry an identity document specifying to which race they belonged. Some coloured people were sufficiently 'white-looking' to pass as white and enjoy the privileges that came with it, but everything depended on the classification they were given. A particularly infamous procedure associated with this Act was the 'pencil test'. This was done by pushing a pencil through a coloured person's hair. If the pencil did not fall out – if the person's hair was curly enough to hold it in place – the person was deemed to be coloured.

During the apartheid years the Separate Amenities Act meant that actors and dancers could not perform for white audiences. This also applied to sportsmen and women. People of colour could not play in 'white' teams. The cricketer, Basil D'Oliveira, a coloured man from Cape Town, left South Africa to play in England because he could not play for the (white) South African team although he was good enough. In 1968 he was selected for the English team to play against South Africa. The prime minister of South Africa at the time, John Vorster, believed D'Oliveira's selection was politically motivated and said that the English team was no longer welcome in

South Africa. In 2000, D'Oliveira was nominated as one of ten top South African cricketers of the century, despite not having played for his home country.

Similar discrimation was applied to the Indian golfer, Sewsunker 'Papwa' Sewgolum. He, too, went overseas to advance his career and won several Dutch international competitions. On his return to South Africa, he was the first person of colour to play in a provincial tournament. In the game of golf it was deemed acceptable for a player of colour to participate outside, but not to join his fellow competitors in the whites-only clubhouse afterwards. In 1965, Papwa Sewgolum won the Natal Open Championships but was forced to receive his prize outside in the rain. A newspaper report about this event called it 'The Glory and the Shame'.[8]

These and other incidents led to an international sports boycott of South Africa, which lasted until the 1990s. Countries that sent unofficial 'rebel' teams to play against South Africa were widely condemned. The sports boycotts were also part of a larger international campaign of isolation that eventually included political, economic, cultural and academic boycotts. For example, some academics could not get jobs because of their political views, scholars were denied access to international institutions and the British Actors' Equity Association boycotted the sale of television programmes to South Africa, which meant South African TV was dominated by programmes from the US.[9] These boycotts, too, only ended in the early 1990s.

Sophiatown: an example of forced relocations

Another notorious Act passed in 1950 was the Group Areas Act, which laid down strict segregation rules for different races: whites, coloureds, Indians and blacks all had to live in different areas. Although most races were already living separately, there were a few inner-city mixed-race communities like Sophiatown and Alexandra in Johannesburg, Lady Selborne in Pretoria, District Six in Cape Town and Cato Manor in Durban. The uprooting and relocation of people from these communities caused untold hardship.

The story of Sophiatown is an example of this forced removal policy.

Sophiatown was a suburb of Johannesburg, about 9 kilometres from the city centre. The land was originally owned by Herman Tobiansky, who had named it Sophia (later Sophiatown) after his wife. In 1904, he divided up the land and offered plots for sale. The first stands were bought by whites, but after the municipality established a sewerage works and huge dumping ground in the area, most of the white people moved away. The sewerage works was subsequently moved, but by then Tobiansky had started to offer the stands to other races as well. From 1914 to 1918, black people streamed into Johannesburg because of the increased job opportunities created by the First World War. Many came to live in Sophiatown as it was close to the city centre where they worked. Other races came as well, and by 1955 there were possibly as many as 70 000 black, coloured, Chinese and Indian people living in Sophiatown.

In its heyday, Sophiatown was a vibrant community famous for its musicians and writers; people still reflect on the exuberance of Sophiatown. It was an overcrowded area, but community spirit was strong. As the houses were small, people gathered around braziers in the streets at dusk to talk, gamble and dance, and the dusty streets became synonymous with music. Jazz, kwela, penny whistle, marabi and other distinctive African sounds are associated with Sophiatown and Alexandra in the 1940s and 50s, and the careers of Dolly Radebe, Miriam Makeba, Hugh Masekela, Lemmy Mabaso, Abdullah Ibrahim (Dollar Brand) and other famous singers and musicians are associated with these places. Kwela music is a unique style of street music played with the flute or penny whistle and guitars made from paraffin tins and tea boxes. The word 'kwela' means 'pick up', and referred to the roving police vans that used to patrol the township streets looking for illegal gambling. If a police vehicle was sighted, people would immediately put away their gambling games and start playing their penny whistles.

Many of Miriam Makeba's songs were about her people's suffering and they began to draw the world's attention to what was happening in South Africa. She was banned from South Africa in 1960, and spent the next 31 years in exile in Europe, Guinea and the United States, where she appeared in shows with Harry Belafonte and other popular entertainers of the day.

She believed music had the ability to link people all over the world, and during even her darkest days she said there were three things she would always have: hope, determination and song.[10] Makeba is particularly remembered for "Pata Pata" and "The Click Song". She was married to fellow musician Hugh Masekela from 1964 to 1966, and to the American activist Stokely Carmichael from 1968 to 1978. In 1990, Nelson Mandela personally asked her to come home.

Sophiatown was also home to poet and author Don Mattera, whose grandfather was an Italian immigrant and his mother either a Xhosa or Khoisan woman. His autobiography, *Memory is the Weapon*, won several literary awards. Other famous residents include jazz pianist and journalist Todd Matshikiza, who later wrote music and the lyrics for the stage musical of *King Kong* in London's West End, and Bloke Modisane, an actor and journalist for *Drum* magazine[11] and author of an autobiography titled *Blame Me On History*. For their criticisms of the apartheid government, these and other writers and artists were exiled or compelled to live and work overseas, and their work was often banned.

Sophiatown did, however, have its fair share of crime. Gangs with names like 'Vultures', 'Americans', 'Russians' and others roamed the streets and drove around in flashy American cars. Before his political activism, the young Don Mattera had been one of the gang leaders of the Vultures. He escaped death several times, and carried a walking stick with a sword concealed inside; others used sharpened bicycle spokes as weapons to stab people in the back.

Sophiatown managed to survive as a mixed-race community for a few years after the Group Areas Act, but in 1955 white officials declared it a slum area because it was so crowded. People were told to move to areas designated for their races. There was much resistance. 'We Won't Move' was painted on the walls; people sat down in the streets when the trucks arrived to move their belongings, and a white Anglican priest who lived in Sophiatown, Father Huddleston, tried to plead their case. In the end, blacks had to move to Meadowlands near Orlando in Soweto[12] (about 24 kilometres away), coloureds to Bosmont (11.5 kilometres away) and Indians to Lenasia (30 kilometres away). Houses in Sophiatown were razed to the

The grave of a woman thought to have been a queen at Thulamela in the far north of Limpopo province. (Photograph courtesy of Gold Fields Limited)

Early protest art: Men arriving on horseback with guns. (Photograph from AR Wilcox, *Rock Paintings of the Drakensberg, Natal and Griqualand East*, Max Parrish, London, 1956)

A painting by Charles Davison Bell of Bartholomew Dias erecting a padrao on the Namibian coast in 1488. (Picture courtesy of the South African National Library)

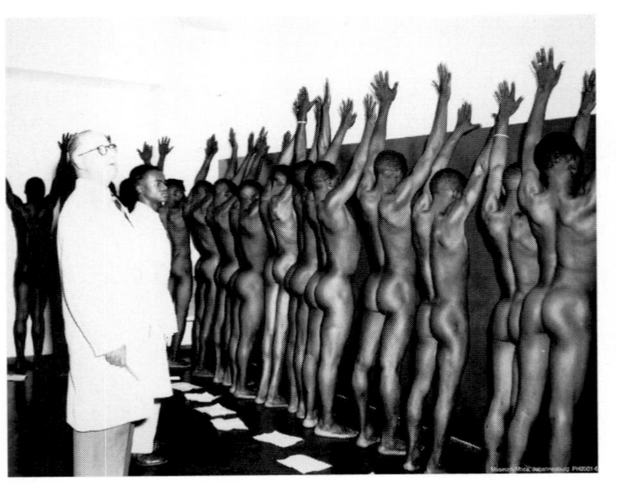

Humiliation: men having to strip for a medical examination on the gold mines in early Johannesburg. (Photograph courtesy of MuseumAfrica)

Nongqawuse (right), the young woman whose prophecies brought catastrophe to the Xhosa. The photo was taken in King William's Town, where she and another young prophetess, Nonkosi, were held captive after the incident. (Photograph courtesy of the South African National Library)

LEFT Migrant workers on their way to the mines. Men walked long distances from the impoverished rural areas to find work on the mines. (Photograph courtesy of MuseumAfrica)

A significant friendship: General Louis Botha (left) and Jan Smuts in 1914. (Photograph courtesy of the Smuts House Museum, Irene, Gauteng)

Zainunnisa (Cissie) Gool addressing a meeting in 1946. (Photograph courtesy of the SS Singh Collection, Documentation Centre for African Studies, UNISA)

Jan Smuts with the British king and queen and their two daughters Princess Elizabeth and Princess Margaret during a visit to South Africa in 1947. (Photograph courtesy of the Central Archives)

RIGHT The Women's March to Pretoria on 9 August 1956. It was led by, from left, Rahina Moosa, Lilian Ngoyi, Helen Joseph and Sophie Williams-De Bruyn. (Photograph © Jurgen Schadeberg/ www.jurgenschadeberg.com)

People publicly burning passes at Sharpeville near Vereeniging in 1960. (Photograph © Terence Spencer/The LIFE Images Collection/Getty/Gallo Images)

Painted on a wall in Sophiatown in the 1950s. (Photograph © Jurgen Schadeberg/www.jurgenschadeberg.com)

Sharpeville. The police open fire and the crowd flees. (Photograph courtesy of MuseumAfrica)

Robert Sobukwe, the founder of the PAC.
(Photograph © Jurgen Schadeberg/www.jurgenschadeberg.com)

Albert Luthuli, teacher, preacher and President of the ANC 1952–1967. (Photograph © Leif Oernelund/Oslo Museum)

Nelson Mandela's wife, Winnie Mandela, leaving the court room after her husband's trial in 1964.
(Photograph courtesy of MuseumAfrica)

LEFT Chris Hani (left) and Joe Slovo in December 1991, during the first legal conference of the SACP in South Africa in 41 years. Chris Hani was assassinated two years later. (Photograph © Walter Dlhadlhla/AFP/Gallo Images)

LEFT A government of national unity: President Nelson Mandela with Thabo Mbeki (left) and FW de Klerk after the inaugural sitting of the first multi-racial parliament, 9 May 1994. (Photograph © Alexander Joe/AFP/Gallo Images)

A traditional praise singer extols the virtues of President Zuma at his inauguration, 9 May 2009.
Photograph © Kim Ludbrook/Reuters/Pool/Gallo Images)

Striking miners and their leader, Mgcineni Noki, known as 'the man in the green blanket', shortly before the massacre at Marikana mine in August 2012 . (Photograph © Katherine Muick-Mere/Sunday Times)

Julius Sello Malema of the EFF and his supporters wearing their distinctive red overalls and berets, marching through the Johannesburg CBD on 27 October 2015. (Photograph © Simone Kley/Beeld/Gallo Images)

ground, and new ones built. The suburb was renamed Triomf ('Triumph') and declared whites-only.

Angus Smith recalls that his family's house was one of the last to be bulldozed. His grandfather was a concert pianist and was often called upon to play for the all-white Johannesburg Symphony Orchestra, until his coloured identity was revealed one night. A newspaper headline the next day screamed the words: '*Kleurling speel met die orkes*' ('Coloured plays with the orchestra'), which put paid to any further performances by the talented man. When the family were forced to move from Sophiatown, Angus's grandfather had to give away his piano as it did not fit through the door of their small house in Bosmont. He did not live long after that – the family believe he died of a broken heart.[13]

Patricia Mokoena Harvey similarly remembers the horror of the removals, and is grateful she was not there at the time. 'I remember the area,' she said. 'Kwela music used to resound through the streets. I remember the gangs; they ruled our pavements. Mostly their fights were over 'cherries' (girls). In Sophiatown we were all mixed up together. Then we had to move to Orlando East. It was far out of the city. We could no longer just catch one tram to get to work. But would I go back to Sophiatown? If the old people were there, if we could recreate it, the ubuntu spirit, then I would go back.'[14]

The trauma of moving all these people to separate areas in the 1950s cannot be overestimated. For many, it was a farewell to friends and people they had grown up with, the loss of stability and social structure, and having to adapt to environments that lacked amenities and work opportunities.

Sophiatown still has an aura of its history. Many of the street names are still the same, but of the original houses, only that of Dr Alfred Xuma, President-General of the ANC (1940–1949), at 73 Toby Street on the corner of Edward and Toby Streets, still stands in its original form. It was considered too beautiful to be bulldozed down when the other houses were demolished in the 1950s, and was declared a National Heritage Monument on 11 February 2006. Bloke Modisane remembers how he and his widowed mother, who ran a shebeen, had looked to Xuma and his house as a model of the good life, which to them meant 'separate bedrooms, a room for sitting, another for eating, and a room to be alone, for reading or thinking, to shut out South Africa and not be black'.[15] The Church of Christ the King, where Father Huddleston practised, is also still there, and the church tower has been declared a national monument. The clock on the tower was visible from afar and used by the whole community, many of whom had no other way of telling the time.

The removal of the last few places where South Africans of any race could live and mix together meant that in the coming decades, few white people ever saw a black home or socialised with black people. White children grew up in isolation from their black peers, and few whites ever learnt an African language. Black and coloured people did not come into contact with white people except in the workplace, and then in generally subordinate positions. In the 1990s, Triomf was re-opened to all races and the old name, Sophiatown, was restored, but it was too late for many.

Black resistance

The ANC Youth League (ANCYL)

Soon after the National Party came to power in 1948, a new generation of black people became prominent in the ANC. They came from the ANC Youth League (ANCYL) and wanted more decisive action.

The ANCYL had been formed in 1944 by young members of the ANC. They were impatient with the approach of the old guard in the ANC and wanted to adopt more militant measures to challenge white rule. Four of these young members were Walter Sisulu, Oliver Tambo, Nelson Mandela and Ashby Mda, all Xhosas from the Transkei (eastern Cape) who had been educated at mission schools. Tambo and Mandela went on to Fort Hare University but were expelled for their political activities. They later qualified as lawyers through Unisa and together set up a practice in Johannesburg. The other early member of the ANCYL was Anton Lembede, who was Zulu. He was the son of farm labourers from the district of Georgevale in Natal. He had worked tirelessly to put himself through school and law school, and was passionate about an African-centred philosophy that he called Africanism.[16] The ANCYL chose him as their first president, but his untimely death in 1947, aged only 33, robbed the league of their future leader.

When the ANCYL was first established, the president of the ANC, Dr Alfred Xuma, was dubious about the more aggressive stance of the young men, who nevertheless quickly won the support of large numbers of people who'd moved to the cities to work in the new factories and industries. In 1944, the ANCYL published a manifesto outlining their plans to mobilise people, and to embark on more militant action.

In 1949, the year after DF Malan's National Party came to power, Oliver Tambo (then aged 31), Walter Sisulu (aged 36) and Nelson Mandela (aged 30) were all elected to the ANC executive, and the ANC officially adopted the ANCYL Programme of Action. The Programme of Action called for more militant action, including strikes, boycotts and defiance, and would subsequently lead to the Defiance Campaign of the 1950s.

The Defiance Campaign and the Treason Trial

For much of its early existence, the ANC did not seek cooperation from other racial groups that were also suffering discrimination. Writing in 1967, the historian Leo Marquard suggested that for a nationalist movement to succeed, it had to be exclusive. This had certainly worked for the Afrikaners in the 1930s and 1940s: their nationalism had excluded non-whites, English-speaking South Africans and Afrikaners who did not support their policies.[17] It seems, however, that cooperation with other racial groups served the ANC well. In 1952 they joined with other liberation movements, notably the South African Indian Congress (SAIC), to organise a Defiance Campaign. This brought ANC leaders like Nelson Mandela and Walter Sisulu into close contact with Indian leaders like Ahmed Kathrada. Many years later, in an interview with Carlos Matos,[18] Ahmed Kathrada recalled what a breakthrough it was when the different resistance organisations began to work together. Before 1950, he said, the ANC was quite exclusivist, preferring to conduct the freedom fight alone. Similarly, former president Nelson Mandela referred to the great role played by Indians in the struggle.

In 1946, the Transvaal and Natal Indian Congresses led by Dr Monty Naicker and Dr Yusuf Dadoo had organised a passive resistance campaign based on the teachings of Mahatma Gandhi. Their aim was to protest against new laws specifically designed to deprive Indians of property and rights of residence. About 15 000 people marched to the municipal grounds in central Durban, where a select group of 17 people set up a camp. The campaign lasted until 1948, during which time some 2 000 resisters had visited the camp. Many of the resisters were abused, attacked and arrested, but the campaign continued and created a unity of purpose among Indian communities. It was also the catalyst for the coming together of the different races in the struggle. In 1947, the 'Three Doctors' Pact' signed by Dr Dadoo, Dr Naicker and Dr Xuma of the ANC set the stage for cooperation between Indians and Africans in the struggle, and the passive resistance approach was adopted by the Defiance Campaign, which followed in 1952.[19] The campaign was launched on 26 June 1952, two months after the 300th anniversary of the arrival of Van Riebeeck and the Dutch at the Cape (on 6 April 1652).

The idea behind the Defiance Campaign was to defy discriminatory laws. Black people were encouraged to board whites-only buses, sit on whites-only benches, stand in whites-only queues and perform other anti-discriminatory acts. The campaign had its desired effect: some 8 000 people were arrested for deliberately breaking the law. The jails were full to overflowing and the authorities embarrassed.

In 1953, members of different black, coloured and Indian organisations (the ANC, CPO, SAIC) as well as the small, predominantly white Congress of Democrats got together at a massive Congress of the People at Kliptown near Johannesburg. It was there that they adopted the Freedom Charter that became the basis of ANC policy; some of its terms are enshrined in our current constitution. It stated that South Africa belonged to all who live in it, black and white, and that no government could justly claim authority unless by the will of the people. It then set out a list of basic rights: equality under the law, the right to vote, schools being open to all races, equal pay for equal work, and minimum wages. It also included some socialist ideas: nationalisation of the mines and the reallocation of land. The aspects of freedom and equality were based on liberal ideas coming from Britain, Europe and the United States, and the fact that some African countries, beginning with Ghana,[20] were starting to win independence from colonial rulers.

The communist ideas in the Charter were a source of alarm to the government, who responded by imposing even stricter legislation. People suspected of collaboration or plotting against the government were arrested and tried for treason. Between 1956 and 1961, 156 people from all racial groups all over the country were arrested on charges of treason. They included Nelson Mandela, Albert Luthuli and Walter Sisulu, as well as doctors, lawyers, teachers, journalists, clergy members and men and women in business. The Treason Trial dragged on for four years, and although the defendants were all eventually found not guilty, many were stigmatised and lost their jobs.

In the 1990s, MuseumAfrica in downtown Johannesburg held an exhibition of the famous Treason Trial. There were pictures of the defendants and under each one there was a little red book in which members of the public could add comments and any additional information they might have about that person. The same approach has been adopted in the former prison cells at Constitution Hill[21] in Braamfontein, where people have had the opportunity to add their own experiences of those times.

More Acts of the apartheid government

Inferior facilities

Until the 1990s, a succession of white-minority governments invested most tax payers' money on facilities (education, roads, hospitals, public transport) used by whites. When it came to non-whites, they favoured coloured people and Indians over blacks, but all were neglected.

In 1953, the Bantu Education Act, later renamed the Black Education Act, enforced racially separated educational facilities. Most of the missionary schools closed down, and education for black people became even more inferior. Children in black schools, for example, were not given the chance to learn mathematics or science. Minister of Native Affairs at the time,

Hendrik Verwoerd, said: 'There is no place for [the Bantu] in the European community above the level of certain forms of labour ... What is the use of teaching the Bantu child mathematics when it cannot use it in practice.'[22] As there were few high schools, black children often left school early. The adverse effects of these policies were immeasurable.

The Tomlinson Commission, the Senate Act and removal of coloured people from the Common Voters Roll

In 1951 a commission under the chairmanship of Professor Tomlinson was appointed to look into the economic conditions of the reserves that were about to become homelands. It was an important move. The commission recommended that a good deal of money (R200 million) be spent over the next ten years to rehabilitate the soil in the reserves and diversify their economy. The recommendations were not accepted by the government and only a fraction of the money was ever allocated.

In 1955, the Senate Act was passed. This enabled the government to appoint more senators and 'pack' the Senate so that a two-thirds majority could be reached to remove coloured voters from the Common Voters Roll and give them four white representatives in the House of Assembly, just as had been done for black people in 1936. The Bill got its two-thirds majority and in 1960 the Senate was reduced to its original size.

The Senate Act and other Acts of the apartheid government aroused both black and white opposition, but the penalties for publicly protesting grew more severe. People lost their jobs and faced banning orders, house arrest and imprisonment. Government response to protests was to harden its policies and impose even more restrictive measures. The police were given wide powers of search and to arrest without warrants, and people were held in prison without trial.

Women in the struggle

Women had been active in the struggle since at least 1913. In 1943, a women's branch of the ANC had been formed, and in the 1950s, when the apartheid government was implementing its discriminatory laws, the women's struggle became more militant. Thousands of black, coloured and Indian women took part in the Defiance Campaign in 1952, and deliberately broke discriminatory laws.

In 1954, the Federation of South African Women (FEDSAW or FDSAW) was established. This multiracial[23] federation was started by Helen Joseph and Ray Alexander (who were white) and Lilian Ngoyi and Florence Mkize (who were black). It aimed to bring the different women's organisations together for the first time, and make women participate more fully in the liberation struggle. A Women's Charter was drawn up, which pledged to bring an end to discriminatory laws.

FEDSAW had the support of the male members of the ANC. At its official launch at the Trades Hall in Johannesburg in 1948, the ANC sent Walter Sisulu as a link between the two organisations; Sisulu said he believed women could play an important role in the liberation struggle. Catering at the launch was done by men to give the women delegates more time to debate political issues. The opening speech was delivered by the president, Ida Mtwana, who said, 'Gone are the days when the place of women was in the kitchen and looking after the children. Today, they are marching side by side with men in the road to freedom.'[24]

Some of the early women leaders came from poor backgrounds. Lilian Ngoyi (1911–1980) worked as a machinist in a garment factory before her gift for public speaking resulted in her leading the ANC Women's League and FEDSAW; author and teacher Bessie Head (1937–1986) was born in a mental hospital because her white mother had been judged insane when it was discovered she was pregnant with a black man's child. Others came from more privileged backgrounds, like Jean Sinclair and her daughter, Sheena Duncan, who led the Black Sash movement, and Norma Kitson, who took part in the Defiance Campaign in 1952.

Norma Kitson was born to a well-to-do part-Jewish, part-Afrikaner family in 1933 in Berea, Durban. She was a member of the SACP, worked as a secretary on a gold mine and acquired skills as a typist and printer, which she put to good use when asked to help collate the demands that became part of the Freedom Charter. She married a fellow activist, Dave

Kitson, and they had two children, Stephen and Amandla (meaning power in Zulu), who also became activists. Dave Kitson joined the ANC underground armed resistance movement, Umkhonto we Sizwe and in 1964 he was jailed for 20 years. Norma Kitson was detained, subjected to menacing calls and threats, and eventually forced to leave South Africa. On one occasion she prepared herself for jail by carrying extra underwear in her handbag, and then sitting on a bench marked 'Nie Blankes – Non-whites' in Joubert Park waiting to be arrested. After leaving South Africa, she became the inspiration behind the City of London anti-apartheid group, which, for several years, mounted a continuous picket on the pavement outside South Africa House in Trafalgar Square. They demanded the release of Nelson Mandela and other political prisoners, including Dave Kitson; when he was released in 1984 and Nelson Mandela in 1990, there were wild scenes of jubilation outside South Africa House. In an obituary after her death, however, it was mentioned that Norma was not a team person, unless she could run the show; this individualism was anathema to other exiled SACP members living in London. There was also a feeling that when a white person was arrested, their case was easily aired in the media; black victims of apartheid were harder to 'sell'.[25]

The Indian peaceful resistance advocate Fatima Meer also came from a privileged background. Her father was a newspaper editor. He made his children aware of racial discrimination from an early age and encouraged them to be free thinking and analytical. Fatima Meer completed bachelor's and master's degrees in Sociology at the University of Natal in the 1950s – remarkable since few Muslim girls even went to high school at the time. She took part in the massive 1946 Indian Passive Resistance Campaign and spoke at several mass gatherings along with other significant activists like Dr Yusuf Dadoo and Dr Monty Naicker. In 1949, Durban was shaken by race riots and Fatima Meer began to work tirelessly to improve relations between Africans and Indians. One of her many projects was a crèche for poor African children in the shanty town of Cato Manor.

The Women's March, 9 August 1956

Over the years, the law about passes for black people, especially black women, was relaxed and then reinstated again and again. As one of the FEDSAW members, Dora Tamana said: 'These passes make the road even narrower for us. We have seen unemployment, lack of accommodation and families broken because of lack of passes. We have seen it with our men. Who will look after our children when we go to jail for a small technical offence – not having a pass?'[26] The issue reached its climax in the famous Women's March on 9 August 1956. On that day, FEDSAW organised some 20 000 women of all races to march up Vermeulen (now Madiba) Street to the seat of government, the Union Buildings in Pretoria, to present a petition against the proposed reintroduction of passes for black women.

Many of the women who took part in the march had babies on their backs. Others walked holding the hands of the white children they looked after. They came by bus and train from all parts of South Africa, those from outside Johannesburg and Pretoria having slept the night before at the Bantu Hall at Lady Selborne just outside the city. The march was led by Lilian Ngoyi, Helen Joseph, Rahima Moosa, Ray Alexander, Amina Cachalia and Sophie Williams-De Bruyn. Lilian Ngoyi was selected to knock on the office door of Prime Minister JG Strijdom to present the petition, but as there was no one there, she had to leave it outside.

The women then stood outside in absolute silence for thirty minutes. The silence was broken by the women singing 'Nkosi Sikelel' iAfrika' (now the national anthem) and a new song in honour of the occasion, the words of which were: '*Wena Strydom, wathinth', abafazi, wathinth' embokotho, uzokufa!*' (You, Strijdom, you have touched the woman, you have struck against rock, you will die!') When the prime minister did, in fact, die soon afterwards, many of the women believed it was their prophesy come true.

The phrase 'You have touched a woman, you have struck a rock,' has come to represent the courage and strength of South African women, and the Women's March is seen as a benchmark in women's fight for justice in South Africa, and an inspiration for the women who came after them. Since the coming of democracy in 1994, 9 August has been celebrated as Women's Day every year. On 9 August 2006, the 50th anniversary of the historic march, Strijdom Square, where the women had gathered before their march, was renamed Lilian Ngoyi Square.

On Women's Day 60 years later, the only surviving leader of the march, Sophia Williams-De Bruyn, recalled that she had only been 18 years old on 9 August 1956, and was the youngest of the leaders. She said that although pass requirements were not applied to coloured and Indian women, she and others supported the march because, as she put it, 'there was a strong sense of unity and empathy among us, because what touched them today could touch us tomorrow.'[27]

The women's march that August day 1956 was the prism through which the women's struggle reached the world. Although it was advanced off the war against passes for black men that had already been in place for 40 years, the Women's March was the fight of the 1950s.[28]

The Progressive Party

The United Party started by Smuts and Hertzog in 1933 had continued to exist as an opposition party throughout the 1940s. In 1953 it joined with Labour in an effort to unseat the National Party in the forthcoming election. The move failed and the nationalists were returned with an even greater majority.

In 1958, the nationalists won the election again and a year later, in 1959, the United Party split and 12 members led by Dr Jan Steytler formed the Progressive Party. This was the party that was to give rise to political greats like Helen Suzman, Colin Eglin, Frederik van Zyl Slabbert and Tony Leon.

Helen Suzman was a Member of Parliament for 36 years, 13 of which (1961–1974) were as a member of the Progressive Party during the worst of the apartheid years. Hers was often a lone voice against injustice in a Parliament dominated by white men, and she opposed every racially oppressive bill that was presented. When a minister accused her of asking questions that embarrassed the country, she replied, 'It is not my questions that embarrass South Africa, it is your answers.'[29]

Helen Suzman used her status as a Member of Parliament to visit Robben Island while Nelson Mandela was imprisoned there, and managed to get a particularly unpleasant warder transferred and some improvement in their conditions. Nelson Mandela said he was surprised by how small she was (only five foot two inches) and how fearless. The prison authorities tried to steer her towards the better aspects of the prison, but she insisted on going to the cells. 'It was an odd and wonderful sight to see this courageous woman peering into our cells and strolling around our courtyard,' Nelson Mandela wrote in his autobiography, *Long Walk to Freedom*. 'She was the first and only woman ever to grace our cells.'[30] Helen Suzman died on 1 January 2009, aged 92.

One of the aims of the Progressive Party was a qualified franchise open to all races, which would have been a solution to South Africa's problems, even if it took some time for everyone to qualify. As it turned out, that was still far from becoming a reality.

CHAPTER 11

The 1960s

The formation of the Pan Africanist Congress (PAC) and Sharpeville

The year 1960 was another turning point in resistance movements, which military historian Ian van der Waag dates as a period of 'Hot War' in South African history.[1]

South Africa had not yet become a republic: this would happen only the following year. On 3 February 1960, British Prime Minister Harold Macmillan, who had just spent a month in Africa, announced to the South African Parliament in Cape Town that the British government was in the process of granting independence to many of their colonial territories in Africa. Ghana (formerly the Gold Coast) had become independent in 1957, Nigeria would follow later in 1960, Uganda in 1962 and Kenya in 1963, amongst others. 'The wind of change is blowing through this continent,' Macmillan said. 'Whether we like it or not, this growth of national consciousness is a political fact, and our national policies must take account of it.'[2]

No such transformation was apparent in South Africa, however, and there was a significant hardening in black resistance to South Africa's apartheid government. In March 1960, Robert Sobukwe broke away from the ANC and established the more radical Pan Africanist Congress (PAC).

Robert Sobukwe had been educated at a mission school at his birthplace, Graaff-Reinet, and had then attended Fort Hare University in the eastern Cape, where he was politically active and became president of the Students Representative Council. He went on to become a teacher and then lecturer in the Department of African Studies at the University of the Witwatersrand, where his interest in literature had led to his completing an Honours dissertation on Xhosa riddles. Sobukwe was an Africanist; he believed advancement opportunities needed to be created for young black people and that the future of South Africa should be in the hands of black South Africans. He did not approve of the multiracial resistance path the ANC had been following in recent years – hence his breakaway to form the PAC.[3]

Their first project was to organise the famous anti-pass demonstration at Sharpeville, south of Johannesburg, in March 1960. The *dompas* that required all black South Africans to carry documents allowing them to 'pass' into urban areas – places many had lived all their lives – had long been a source of contention.[4] In the 1960 demonstration, the plan was for black people to go to the police station at Sharpeville[5] and publicly burn their passes. They believed if enough black people did this and there were too many arrests, the system would be unworkable.

On the morning of 21 March 1960, the movement started when Sobukwe left his home in Mofolo, Soweto,[6] and led a small crowd on an 8-kilometre march to Orlando Police Station, where he intended to give himself up for arrest. Along the march, small groups of men joined him from neighbouring areas like Phefeni, Dube and Orlando West. As the small crowd approached the station, most of the marchers, including Sobukwe, were arrested and charged with sedition.

Meanwhile, an estimated group of 5 000 people had reached Sharpeville Police Station. There are various versions of what happened next. Sobukwe had warned the police in advance that the demonstration was going to take place, but that it would be peaceful. Anything can happen when people group together in a mob: while some witnesses say most demonstrators were peaceful, others say the mood turned ugly. Demonstrations were going on at the same time elsewhere, and only a small contingent of inexperienced policemen was on duty at Sharpeville. According to police reports, stones were thrown, a policeman was knocked over, panic ensued, and a few of the police started firing on the crowd. Sixty-nine people (men, women and children) were killed and about 180 wounded, some of them shot in the back as they tried to run away. The incident made headlines around the world and added to the sanctions already in place against South Africa. It became known as the Sharpeville Massacre.[7]

The government in South Africa responded by declaring a state of emergency, and both the ANC and the PAC were banned. So too was the South African Communist Party (SACP) and other organisations regarded as subversive. Some 10 000 people were detained and harsher measure were introduced to deal with them. Many activists went into exile including future president Thabo Mbeki, who was only 18 years old at the time. Oliver Tambo, who had gone into exile shortly before the ANC was banned, became the young Mbeki's mentor during his exile years.

The Republic of South Africa and the beginnings of the 'Hot War'[8]

The following year, in 1961, South Africa became a republic. Until 1961, South Africa had still been part of the British Commonwealth: when Elizabeth II was crowned Queen of England in 1953, she was also crowned queen of the self-governing Union of South Africa and proteas, the South African national flower, were sewn into her coronation gown. Pieces of the famous Cullinan Diamond[9] also featured in the sceptre she carried and the crown she wore. By 1961, many people (and Afrikaners especially) regarded the position of Queen Elizabeth II as head of state as a relic of British imperialism.

The National Party had been pressing for South African independence for some time. A referendum was held that was restricted to whites: on 31 May 1961, South Africa ceased to be a member of the British Commonwealth and became a republic by a narrow majority, 52.9% in favour. It was a triumph for Afrikaner nationalism. The constitutional ties that had existed between Britain and South Africa since 1806 were broken and would only be restored when the 'new' South Africa[10] came into being and applied to be a member of the British Commonwealth again. It was also in 1961 that decimal coinage was introduced: the South African rand (named after the gold-bearing Witwatersrand) replaced the pound sterling.

When the Nationalist Party government had first came into power in 1948, there had been a loss of confidence by investors, but gradually the economy had gained ground, helped by the opening of more gold fields in the Free State in 1951, the establishment of a uranium plant on the West Rand in 1952, the development of more capital-intensive agriculture and forestry projects, and the expansion of manufacturing and secondary industries (especially with regard to consumer and producer goods) from the 1950s onwards. Transport on land, sea and air also changed beyond recognition, as did retailing with the growth of supermarkets and large chains.[11] Overseas investment increased, especially from the United States and Europe. The National Party increased its parliamentary majority in almost every election between 1948 and 1977, and it was clear that it was not just Afrikaners voting for it.

In 1961, the prime minister of the republic, Hendrik Verwoerd appointed BJ (John) Vorster as Minister of Justice. Vorster believed security of the state was a priority and proceeded to push through a series of laws designed to crush resistance to government policy. These laws included bannings, indefinite detention without trial and house arrest. Robert Sobukwe, whose PAC had organised Sharpeville, was one of the first people to be affected by these laws. In some quarters he was seen as even more dangerous to the apartheid state than imprisoned political leaders such as Nelson Mandela.[12] For his role in Sharpeville, Sobukwe was initially sentenced to three years in prison, but at the end of that term, in 1963, Parliament enacted a General Law Amendment Act, which empowered the Minister of Justice to detain a prisoner for 90 days without trial, and then to extend the time at his discretion. One of the Act's clauses was directed specifically at him, and was called the 'Sobukwe Clause'. Subsequently, Sobukwe was moved to Robben Island,[13] where he remained for an additional six years.

While on Robben Island, Sobukwe was kept in solitary confinement so that he could not influence other prisoners. He was, however, allowed to wear civilian clothes and had access to books. As a result, Sobukwe spent much of his time studying, and obtained a degree in Economics from the University of London.[14] Former inmates at Robben Island described walking past his house when they went to their work tasks: he would stand at the gate and wave to them, but they could not stop to speak. He used secret hand signals to communicate – he would pick up sand and then slowly let it run between his fingers. This was to symbolise that the cause lived in his heart and that freedom would be achieved. [15]

After he was released from prison he was placed under house arrest in Kimberley, and had to get special permission to leave the house for treatment when he developed lung cancer. He died in 1978, aged only 54, and was buried in his home town of Graaff-Reinet. In 2008 his son, Dini Sobukwe, returned to South Africa after 30 years in the United States. With the help of government, he created a trust in Graaff-Reinet in Robert Sobukwe's name: the trust addresses the issues of education and advancement about which Robert Sobukwe cared so much, and helps to keep his memory alive.

The Sobukwe Clause in the General Law Amendment Act was never used to detain anyone else. When it was due to expire on 30 June 1965, the government renewed it. It was renewed every year until 1982, when it was repealed by the Internal Security Act, which nevertheless gave government similar powers of detention. This Act and others of a discriminatory nature were only progressively repealed between 1990 and 1996.[16]

Another victim of the harsh measures taken by the government in the 1960s was Albert Luthuli,[17] the distinguished and widely respected chief of the Zulu people. He was brought up at the Groutville mission station in Natal, trained as a teacher and then become chief of the Groutville reserve in 1935. He believed in sport as a way of maintaining a healthy body and a healthy mind and did much to promote football among his students at Adams College. The sport was widely played as a result of his efforts and the college produced many subsequent soccer stars.

His approach for most of his life was as a pacifist, but his policies had become more militant by the time he was elected president of the ANC in 1952, when he was almost 50 years old. He also took part in the Defiance Campaign in 1952, and publicly burnt his pass in 1960, shortly after Sharpeville. There is no evidence, however, that he ever supported the ANC's decision to resort to an underground armed struggle. In 1960, he was awarded the Nobel Peace Prize for his nonviolent approach to ending apartheid, the first African to receive this award.

In 1962, the government had passed the Sabotage Act, which gave the government the power to place anyone suspected of subversive activities under house arrest without a trial. Chief Luthuli was subsequently banned and arrested several times in the following years. In his autobiography, *Let My People Go*,[18] published in 1962, he describes being woken up in the early hours of the morning by police hammering on his door. His small children stood wide-eyed and fearful as he was taken away. Albert Luthuli died in mysterious circumstances in 1967, ostensibly after being hit by a train while crossing a railway line, but the matter was never satisfactorily resolved.

After Sharpeville and the exile of their leaders, the ANC and PAC went underground and military wings were established: Umkhonto we Sizwe ('The Spear of the Nation', abbreviated to MK) for the ANC, and Poqo ('Pure') for the PAC. Nelson Mandela helped establish MK and his colleague Walter Sisulu was a member. Between December 1961 and July 1963, MK units conducted over 200 acts of sabotage with incendiary home-made bombs. The bomb attacks were carried out on post offices and other government buildings, as well as on railway and electrical installations near industrial towns. Their targets were buildings, not people.[19] Meanwhile Oliver Tambo, who was in exile, began looking for places where MK soldiers could receive guerrilla training.

MK's manifesto drawn up in 1961 stated:

> *The time comes in the life of any nation when there remain only two choices: submit or fight. That time has now come to South Africa. We shall not submit and we have no choice but to hit back by all means within our power in defence of our people, our future, and our freedom.*

The ANC's decision to embark on armed struggle was reached after many decades of nonviolent resistance, which was met by increasingly brutal repression by the apartheid regime. In the words of Ahmed Kathrada some years later: 'We had to switch from non-violence to violence; there were just no more avenues of peaceful resistance left.'[20]

By 1961, the 'Hot War'[21] had begun in earnest. There were police spies and informers everywhere. The government clamped down hard on dissidents and ever stricter measures were applied. On 11 July 1963, 17 MK leaders including Govan Mbeki (father of Thabo Mbeki) and Walter Sisulu were arrested at Liliesleaf, a farm in Rivonia, near Johannesburg. Nelson Mandela and other key ANC leaders had been using the farm as a headquarters and hideout for some time. Mandela had masqueraded as a gardener and cook for the white owner, anti-apartheid activist Arthur Goldreich, and had also used the time there to read up about guerrilla warfare and to plan the initial phase of MK's offensive. Mandela was already in jail at the Johannesburg Fort at the time of the 1963 arrest, having been jailed for inciting workers to strike and for leaving the country illegally, but documents in Mandela's handwriting were found at the farm.

The Rivonia Trial, 1963/1964

In October 1963, the trial began of Nelson Mandela and ten of the arrested men: Denis Goldberg, James Kantor, Rusty Bernstein, Andrew Mlangeni, Elias Motsoaledi, Ahmed Kathrada, Raymond Mhlaba, Bob Hebble, Govan Mbeki and Walter Sisulu. The men were charged with acts of sabotage against the government and for promoting communism, and the trial was named after the suburb of Rivionia, where they had been meeting on Liliesleaf Farm. Before the trial, Harold Wolpe and Arthur Goldreich managed to bribe a guard and escape from the Johannesburg Fort prison. They spent a few months hiding in safe houses and then escaped through Swaziland dressed as priests.

James Kantor and Rusty Bernstein were acquitted, charges were withdrawn against Bob Hepple, who subsequently fled the country without testifying, but the remaining ten had to face a trial that was to drag on for eight months, only ending in June 1964.[22] The accused were defended by Afrikaans lawyer and leader of the SACP, Abram (Bram) Fischer, assisted by Arthur Chaskalson, George Bizos and others. While the trial was in process, photos of Bram Fischer were blacked out in the press, and afterwards he underwent plastic surgery to avoid detection.[23] Arthur Chaskalson later became the first president of the Constitutional Court in 1995 and was Chief of Justice from 2001 to 2005, and George Bizos, amongst many other notable positions, led the team which certified the new Constitution of South Africa in 1996.

At the trial at the Pretoria Supreme Court, 20 April 1964, Nelson Mandela chose to make a statement from the dock rather than the witness stand. This meant he could give a clear statement and not be interrupted with questions and cross examination. He admitted his role in MK and the sabotage campaign and his alliance with the SACP, but said he nevertheless admired Western ways, especially the British parliamentary system, which was the most democratic in the world. He asked for equal rights for black people, for formal education, a living wage and opportunities to learn skills in the workplace. 'All my life,' he said, 'I have fought against white domination and black domination, and cherished the ideal of a democratic and free society. It is an ideal for which I am prepared to die.'[24] His speech made headlines around the world and gave him iconic status.

The trial continued until June 1964. Ultimately, eight of the defendants – Nelson Mandela, Walter Sisulu, Govan Mbeki, Ahmed Kathrada, Denis Goldberg, Raymond Mhlaba, Elias Motsoaledi and Andrew Mlangeni – were found guilty of what the judge decided was essentially treason. The death penalty was requested but the defence team, with the support of global protesters, managed to get this changed to life imprisonment. Because he was white, Denis Goldberg was sent to Pretoria Central Prison, and the others went to the prison on Robben Island.

Christo Brand, a former warder, recalls that when he first went to work on Robben Island, he was told that he was about to meet the biggest criminals in South African history. When he went to the cells he saw old, humble and gentle people who treated the warders with respect: amongst others, these men were Nelson Mandela and Walter Sisulu.[25]

Bram Fischer, meanwhile, continued to support the underground liberation movement against the advice of Nelson Mandela, who thought he should rather support the struggle in the courtroom 'where people could see this Afrikaner fighting for the rights of the powerless'.[26] He went into hiding but was arrested twice. In 1966 he was tried and found guilty of conspiring to commit sabotage with Nelson Mandela and the others he had defended two years before; he was also found guilty of contravening the Suppression of Communism Act. Bram Fischer was sentenced to life imprisonment. He was diagnosed with cancer a few years later and was released to be with his family just two weeks before he died, aged 67, in 1975.

While Nelson Mandela was in prison, Oliver Tambo, from his exiled base in north London, had much to do with the mobilising of international support for the struggle back home. He discussed with other ANC leaders what would have the most impact and it was decided that the campaign should centre on one individual with whom the world could identify. Mandela was seen as the symbol of all the political prisoners in South Africa. Calling for his release would help unlock the doors of all South Africa's political prisons, and this was how the slogan 'Free Nelson Mandela' was born.[27] From 1964 to 1990, millions of people worldwide supported this campaign.

In 2001, more than 30 years after the Rivonia Trial, then-President Thabo Mbeki – whose father, Govan Mbeki, had been one of the ANC leaders arrested at Liliesleaf – announced that a trust would be set up to restore the site. The restoration project was overseen by Nic Wolpe, son of Harold Wolpe, one of the two men who managed to escape from Johannesburg Fort prison. Liliesleaf Farm has now been restored and an interactive museum was opened to the public in 2008.

Activist wives

Winnie Mandela, Zanele Mbeki, Adelaide Tambo, Albertina Sisulu, Ama Naidoo and others spent many years alone, raising their children on their own while their husbands were in exile or in prison. Nelson Mandela was in prison for 27 years, Walter Sisulu was in prison for 26 years, Thabo Mbeki was in exile for 28 years and Oliver Tambo was in exile for 30 years. Many of the activists' wives were also activists in their own right.

Albertina Sisulu and Adelaide Tambo were both nurses as well as political activists, and both were much loved and respected figures. During the long years her husband was in exile, Adelaide Tambo worked double shifts at Baragwanath Hospital to support her family.

Winnie Madikizela-Mandela qualified as a social worker and had a degree in international relations from the University of the Witwatersrand despite the restrictions on black people achieving higher education. During the years of her husband's imprisonment, Winnie was a leading opponent of white-minority rule. For almost 27 years (1964–1990), she was detained, imprisoned, harassed and threatened by government authorities; she was held at the Women's Prison at the Fort (now part of the Constitutional Court complex) in Johannesburg, and then banished to Brandfort in the Free State.

Manonmoney (Ama) Naidoo, together with her husband, Roy, helped build alliances between people of different races who were working towards the same goals during the struggle years. In 1946, Ama Naidoo took part in the passive resistance campaign against the Asiatic Land Tenure Act, which sought to restrict the ownership of land by Indians. She was detained, and in 1952 she was detained again when she took part in the Defiance Campaign. During the Defiance Campaign, her husband died of a heart attack after a confrontation with police.

Ama Naidoo continued his work, taking her five children with her to political meetings and regularly feeding and housing other activists in her small home in Rockey Street, Doornfontein, Johannesburg. Between 1952 and 1956, she took part in demonstrations, marches and candlelight processions. In 1954, she became an executive member of the newly formed Federation of South African Women (FEDSAW). In 1955 she participated in the congress at Kliptown, Soweto, that saw the adoption of the Freedom Charter. In 1956, she marched with 20 000 other women to the Union Buildings in Pretoria to protest against passes for women. In December 1963, she marched to the Union Buildings again to protest against the Group Areas Act with Zainab Asvat.[28]

She also took food to political detainees and prisoners of all races, and was a member of the committee responsible for providing refreshments for the accused in the 1956 Treason Trial. Her children also became activists, and Ama and her children were all detained or banned several times.

One of her sons, Indres Naidoo, was imprisoned on Robben Island for ten years. After his release he was placed under house arrest, and then went into exile in England for almost 15 years. While in exile, Indres, together with lawyer and activist Albie Sachs, wrote a book about their experiences in prison on Robben Island. *Island in Chains: Ten Years on Robben Island*[29] was published in 1982 but banned in South Africa for many years.

Ama Naidoo was a humble person and her nonviolent approach was based on the teachings of Mahatma Gandhi, whom her husband knew personally. Under the Group Areas Act, she was forced to move to the Indian suburb of Lenasia in 1978, leaving her home in Rockey Street, where she had lived for 45 years. In 1983, she was invited to India by Prime Minister Rajiv Gandhi to be honoured for her family's contribution to the struggle. She died in 1993, just months before the first democratic elections, so she did not live to see the new South Africa. In 2006, she was posthumously awarded the Order of Luthuli in Silver for her contribution to the struggle for democracy, equality and justice.

More acts of oppression

The years 1963 to 1967 were significant in terms of oppression. The Federation of South African Women (FEDSAW) collapsed in 1963, and passes again became compulsory for black women, which meant that black women had no secure rights in urban areas – a situation that would only change in 1994.

The reviled 90-day detention without trial law was also causing untold heartbreak. The first person to die under this Act was Looksmart Ngudle, a 41-year-old MK freedom fighter, husband and father of six from a small village in the eastern Cape. He was arrested on 19 August 1963 and never seen again. His family members were told he had hanged himself in jail, but they did not believe it. Some 44 years later, in 2007, journalists Shaun Smillie and Neo Ntsoma took up the story and helped the family find his body. It had been buried in an unmarked mass grave, but DNA tests verified that it was indeed Ngudle, and his body was returned to his village for an emotional burial.

In 1965, the 90-day detention without trial law was increased to 180 days and more if deemed necessary, and in 1967, the Terrorism Act gave the state more power to suppress opposition. New methods of torture were introduced, including extended periods of isolation, standing for long hours, sleep deprivation, assault and psychological torture. Between 1963 and 1977, 45 people died in jail having been imprisoned without trial.

A positive development for the ANC was an increasing tide of independent African states in the 1960s. Amongst others, Ghana had achieved independence in 1957, Nigeria in 1960, Uganda in 1962, Zambia and Tanzania in 1964 and Botswana in 1966. Most of these states were committed to the liberation of the whole of Africa from colonial rule, and the liberation of South Africa from apartheid. The independent African countries supported the liberation struggle through institutions such as the Organisation of African Unity, and most of them hosted ANC leaders fleeing from repression in South Africa. In some countries, South African political exiles were allowed to stay as refugees but were not allowed to establish military bases, while in others – like in Mozambique, Zambia, Botswana and Uganda – they could establish military training camps. MK cadres operated and coordinated the liberation struggle both from these countries and from within South Africa.

In 1967 compulsory military service, or conscription, was introduced for young white men. Before this, military service had been voluntary, or men had been selected for military training by a ballot system, but they generally just did training – they did not see active service. After the Defence Amendment Act of 1967, however, men were conscripted into the SADF – initially for a nine-month period, but in 1977 this was increased to a compulsory two-year period and 30 days annually for eight years.[30] The conscripts were deployed as the military saw fit. Most young white men did this compulsory service straight after school, and many planned careers had to be put on hold.[31] Conscription was said to be reminiscent of the commando system of the Boer Republics, but was more formalised. The young men could be sent anywhere to defend South Africa's borders.[32]

The death of Hendrik Verwoerd, 1966

Despite international criticism after Sharpeville in 1960, the Rivonia Trial in 1963 and 1964 and other turmoil, Prime Minister Hendrik Verwoerd and his National Party seemed to remain unshakeable. In the election of 1966, the NP won 126 of the 166 seats, and 58% of the vote. The liberal Progressive Party suffered a setback and the NP was clearly attracting some of the English vote, as well as that of the Afrikaners.

Then, on 6 September 1966, at the height of his power, Verwoerd was assassinated in the House of Assembly by a messenger named Dimitri

Tsafendas. At the time, it was decided that Tsafendas was deranged and that his motives were not politically motivated. In September 2016, Charalampos Dousemetzis, a doctoral student at Durham University in the UK, produced evidence that in his first statement to the police on 11 September 1966, Tsafendas had said: 'I did not care about the consequences or what would happen to me afterwards. I was so disgusted with his racial policy that I went through with my plans to kill him.'[33] Tsafendas was the son of a Greek mother and African father. He was able to work in Parliament because he could pass for white; jobs in Parliament of the time were reserved for whites only. The death of Verwoerd was one more dramatic incident in an already violent decade.

BJ (John) Vorster was elected as Verwoerd's successor. As Minister of Justice, Vorster had put through some harsh laws, but among his colleagues he was less aloof than Verwoerd, quite popular and a sports lover keen on maintaining international competition. The NP became split between those who supported him and those who did not: on the one side were the 'verkramptes', the conservative, radical right wing, and on the other the more enlightened 'verligtes'. It was a significant crack in the party's base that would widen in the years to come.

In 1967, some positive attention came South Africa's way when Doctor Christiaan Barnard performed the world's first heart transplant on Louis Washkansky.[34] Contemporary histories have thrown light on the work done by Hamilton Naki, an assistant of Barnard's at Groote Schuur Hospital, whose work on dogs[35] was an important component of Barnard's success. Consistent with the apartheid narrative, the story of Naki's contribution to research would remain untold for nearly 40 years.[36]

Journalist Justice Malala also makes the point that 'great achievement though the first heart transplant was in 1967, it nevertheless took place in a country in which many hospitals banned black people from study, service and care … The heart of South Africa,' he adds, 'was inhumane even as it achieved great medical and scientific honours. That is why our current South Africa is so complicated.'[37]

CHAPTER 12

The 1970s and 1980s

Unrest at home and developments in the homelands

In the early 1970s, black labour hit back at apartheid with a series of strikes, starting in South West Africa, which South Africa had ruled by mandate since 1915.[1] The general strike of South West African workers in 1971 posed a threat to South Africa's control of the territory. Within South Africa, the unrest culminated in a wave of strikes in Durban in 1973. South Africa was also facing sanctions and economic boycotts because of apartheid, and becoming increasingly isolated from international sport, which was a source of great frustration for a sports-loving nation. Meanwhile, neighbouring African states had been gaining independence and there were mutterings that South Africa faced a 'total onslaught' in social and economic life.

By the mid-1970s, the economy in white South Africa was taking strain. There had been a sharp increase in energy prices and a fall in the price of gold. The costs of maintaining apartheid were high. The long distances the large black workforce travelled to work because of the Group Areas Act were counterproductive. Also, workers were poorly educated: where mine owners and industry leaders had benefited from the supply of cheap black labour in the early years of industrialisation, technology had improved by the late 1970s, and there was no longer the need for as many unskilled manual workers. Employers now wanted skills.

The development of the homeland policy,[2] which the apartheid government depended on to give it some sort of credibility, was progressing, but slowly. Conditions in the homelands were bleak. In 1970, the Bantu

Homeland Citizenship Act stated that black people would no longer be citizens in South Africa. Each ethnic group had to identify with a homeland, whether or not they had ever lived there, and irrespective of the fact that the ethnicity of many black people had become somewhat blurred. Two of the homelands, the Transkei and Bophuthatswana, became independent in 1976 and 1977 respectively, but were not given much credibility in the outside world.

KwaZulu had become a stumbling block: Chief Mangosuthu Gatsha Buthelezi, the chief minister, rejected the homeland system and in 1975 he started to rebuild a mass cultural movement called Inkatha (meaning 'crown' in Zulu).[3] Buthelezi was born into the Zulu royal family: his mother was a daughter of Dinuzulu and granddaughter of Cetshwayo.[4] He was a Zulu prince and, as the first-born son, he also inherited the title of chief.

The Border War (1966–1989)

The government was also experiencing problems defending its borders. The global Cold War[5] inevitably affected southern Africa as well. In the colonies, those in power tended to look to the West for support, whereas disadvantaged people looked increasingly to the Marxist ideas of the Eastern Bloc. In South Africa, it was inevitable that there would be a link between the ANC and the South African Communist Party (SACP). The SACP was founded in 1921 and declared illegal in 1950, but continued to participate in the struggle against apartheid. It was this ideological dynamic that informed the South African government's stance in the conflicts in Mozambique and Angola, which they felt posed a communist threat.

Until 1974, the Portuguese held both Angola and Mozambique, although there were nationalist movements afoot in both countries from at least the early 1960s. Atrocities were committed on both sides, and fighting in southern Africa intensified from the mid-1970s, with explosives, rockets and automatic rifles becoming increasingly available.

The Mozambique Liberation Front (FRELIMO), a left-wing movement with Marxist leanings, was active in Mozambique. In Angola, liberation forces were divided into three: the socialist Popular Movement for the Liberation of Angola (MPLA), which also had Marxist leanings and was based at the capital, Luanda; the National Liberation Front of Angola (FNLA); and the pro-capitalist National Union for the Total Independence of Angola (UNITA), a large ethnic group in the central highlands, led by Jonas Savimbi. In Angola, the MPLA and UNITA initially cooperated in fighting their common enemy, the Portuguese, but later became opponents in the struggle for power.

The South African government supported Portuguese white-minority rule in Angola. As early as February 1968, the MPLA was reporting that South African helicopters in south-east Angola were attacking MPLA positions. Interestingly, it was just before this, in 1967, that the South African Defence Amendment Act had introduced a system of compulsory national service for white males aged 18 and over.[6] In the coming years, many young men would be sent to Namibia and Angola to defend South Africa's borders, and later they were sent to South African townships to quell the tide of unrest there. Many young lives were lost.[7]

On 25 April 1974, a military coup in Lisbon brought an end to the Estado Novo[8] dictatorship and led to Portugal's withdrawal from its African colonies, Angola and Mozambique, as well as Guinea-Bissau, Sao Tome and Cape Verde.[9] No shots were fired and the coup became known as the *Revolução dos Cravos* ('the Carnation Revolution') because when the population took to the streets to celebrate the end of the dictatorship and war in the colonies, carnations were put into the muzzles of rifles and on the uniforms of the army men. In Portugal, 25 April is a national holiday known as Freedom Day to celebrate the event.

In January 1975, after 14 years of armed resistance against the Portuguese, the MPLA, the FNLA and UNITA signed the Alvor Agreement, paving the way for Angola's independence. But the Portuguese had left Angola without trying to stabilise the country or supervising the build-up to elections. A power struggle ensued between the three liberation movements, and the agreement collapsed. As the elections approached, each of the three liberation movements began to secure Cold War patrons. The MPLA solicited the help of the Soviet Union as well as Cuba, whereas UNITA secured the support of the South African government. The United States sided with the FNLA at this stage, but when it became clear that the FNLA was becoming increasingly inefficient, the United States joined the South African government in support of UNITA.

By mid-July, it seemed the MPLA would assume control. The MPLA controlled less than a quarter of the country's territory but it was being supplied with arms from the Soviet Union, and, as it was based at the capital, Luanda, it had mainly urbanised members. By contrast, the FNLA and UNITA were more rurally based.

The South African government saw the MPLA's rise to power as a threat to their occupation of South West Africa, with which Angola shared a border. The United States feared for their oil companies in the north of Angola if the MPLA gained control. The governments of the two countries then gave their support to UNITA under Jonas Savimbi, and with their support, UNITA became the main opposition to the MPLA. The headquarters of UNITA were moved to Jamba, near South West Africa's border, to be closer to South Africa. As the MPLA was known to be supported by the Soviet Union, the United States and South Africa's support of UNITA was also a front against the spread of communism.

The US Secretary of State, Henry Kissinger, then entered a secret agreement with South African Prime Minister John Vorster that the United States would pay for the war if South Africa sent troops into Angola to stop the MPLA coming into power. He made it clear that the Americans would finance the war but did not want to be seen as the world's 'bully boys' by placing troops on the ground. In exchange, the United States agreed to keep world criticism of apartheid to a minimum.[10] The South African government proceeded to send the SADF into Angola, but they were defeated at Luanda and forced to retreat. On 11 November 1975, Angola became independent and the MPLA seized power with the backing of the Soviet Union and Cuba.

In Mozambique just a few months before, in June 1975, the president of FRELIMO, Samora Machel, had assumed the presidency of the newly independent nation. Prime Minister John Vorster said at the time that South Africa would leave the new Mozambican government in peace as long as it was stable and did not provide bases for South Africa's guerrilla movements.

For several decades, the new governments of Angola and Mozambique would face a severe set of challenges as devastating civil wars broke out in both countries. Ongoing conflicts eventually claimed over 2 million lives and resulted in an even greater number of refugees. Poor planning, inadequate agricultural production caused by power struggles, and attacks on economic targets (especially railways) led to social and economic decline. Much of the infrastructure put in place by the Portuguese was destroyed.

In 1981, the SADF had its revenge on Luanda when some 11 000 troops with sophisticated artillery invaded Angola again and occupied the southern provinces of Cunene and Cuando Cubango. The Angolan army was not prepared for this massive invasion. The provincial capital of Ngiva was sacked and over 100 000 rural people fled their homes. The South African Air Force was also involved; as most other jets flew too quickly to be of use in a bush war, South Africa's Impala jets were found to be very useful 'tank killers'.[11] The SADF kept up the occupation for the next seven years, even though a Resolution of the United Nations condemned it.

In 1987, the Angolans began an effective counter-offensive. They formed a defensive line at Cuito Cuanavale and were supported by the arrival of more Cuban forces. The battle at Cuito Cuanavale involved all the combatants in Angola: on one side were the Angolans, the Cubans, the South West African People's Organisation (SWAPO) and the ANC; on the other were and the SADF, the South West African Territorial Force (an auxiliary arm of the SADF in Namibia), UNITA and mercenaries sponsored by the United States.

By 1988, where South African aircraft had once been successful in the Bush War, it was clear that they were outclassed by Angolan and Cuban MiG 23 aircraft. South African tanks had also been stopped by the presence of mines. After three major ground battles over three months and mutiny by the South West African Territorial Force, the tide began to turn against the South Africans and their allies.

The war had also become more and more unpopular in South Africa when young whites had failed to come home except in body bags.[12] There was also significant world opposition to the invasion and, in a complete about turn,

Kissinger had ordered Vorster to bring SADF troops back to South Africa. During this retreat there was serious fighting with the Cubans, and in June 1988 the SADF and its supporters were convincingly defeated at Tchipa. One South African newspaper called the battle of Tchipa 'a crushing humiliation', and said the SADF 'resembled the trenches of the Somme, rather than the troops of a mobile counter-insurgency force'.[13]

The siege of Cuito Cuanavale only finally ended, however, after the SADF agreed to withdraw from South West Africa as well. The issues that were being fought over in the two countries, Angola and South West Africa, had become inextricably linked.

The Cubans' air superiority towards the end of the war and the vulnerability of the South African supply lines to Cuito Cuanavale must surely have played their part in finally bringing the protracted conflict to an end. Nevertheless, it has been suggested by some military historians that neither the South Africans nor the Cubans could win the war in Angola, which is what forced them to conclude a peace agreement known as the Tripartite (Three Powers) Accord[14] in 1988.

The role of neighbouring countries and Umkhonto we Sizwe (MK)

Angola and Mozambique's independence in 1975 opened up the possibility for other liberation movements in southern Africa to use these countries for military training. Both the Zimbabwe African People's Union (ZAPU) and SWAPO established bases in Angola, and in 1976 the ANC began negotiations with the Angolan government to do the same. The Central Operations Headquarters of Umkhonto we Sizwe (MK) was set up in Angola and for the next 13 years, between 1976 and 1988, Angola served as an MK military training ground.

MK soldiers in the newly set up training camps had the full expectation that once they were trained, they would be deployed back to South Africa to fight the apartheid government. The reality was different. As one MK soldier noted: 'The most traumatic thing in camps was waiting. This became the source of all our frustrations and feelings of despondency. We moved from one post to another, from one camp to another, without ever being deployed to the front.'[15] This sense of frustration led to several mutinous outbreaks in Angola.

Neighbouring countries like Botswana, Lesotho, Swaziland and others further afield like Tanzania, Uganda and Zambia also played an important role in accommodating MK soldiers and supporting the South African liberation struggle. By 1980, large numbers of MK guerrillas were infiltrating South Africa through neighbouring countries, especially Mozambique, Lesotho and Swaziland. The South African government reacted in two ways: by trying to convince Africans of the folly of Marxism, and by asking neighbouring states not to harbour guerrillas and trying to strike security deals with them. It was part of what would later be called the 'total strategy'.[16]

Vlakplaas

The South African government also used force. It bombed ANC facilities in Matola and Maputo (in Mozambique) in January 1981 and Maseru (in Lesotho) in December 1985. In the attack at Matola, 16 South Africans and one Portuguese national were killed by South African forces. In Maseru, six South Africans and three Lesotho citizens were killed in an attack carried out by Unit C-10, a covert South African police death squad that operated from a farm called Vlakplaas near Pretoria.[17]

The notorious 15-man death squad had been established in 1979 to hunt down MK cadres and other opponents of the apartheid system and torture them for information. Vlakplaas was headed by security police commander Dirk Coetzee, who was replaced in 1982 by 33-year-old Eugene de Kock, nicknamed 'Prime Evil'. Unit C-10 and some other apartheid forces also coerced black South Africans, many of them former activists or guerrillas, to become 'askaris', which meant turning against their former comrades.[18] Some of the farm's most high-profile victims included ANC lawyer Griffiths Mxenge, the Pebco Three[19] and freedom fighter Siphiwe Mtimkulu.[20] It is unclear how many victims were tortured and then killed at Vlakplaas as their remains were blown up or burnt. Askaris were also used to kill opponents of apartheid with parcel bombs, as in the cases of Onkgopotse

Abram Tiro (Botswana, 1975), Boy Mvemve (Zambia, 1975) and Philemon Mahlako (1979), Ruth First (1982), and Enoch Reginald Mhlongo (1989) – all in Mozambique.[21]

Ruth First, a prominent academic and activist, and wife of SACP leader Joe Slovo, was killed by a parcel bomb mailed to her home in Maputo, where she was in exile. First had been one of the defendants in the Treason Trial of 1956–1961,[22] and in 1963 she had been imprisoned and held without charge for 117 days under the 90-Day Detention Law – the first woman to be detained under this law. In 1988, leading ANC supporter and activist Albie Sachs would lose an arm and the sight of one eye in a similar way when a bomb was placed in his car.[23] Askaris and other government agents were suspected of the crimes.

During the 1980s, even civilians began to talk in guarded terms about dreaded death squads at the farm Vlakplaas and the Civil Co-operation Bureau (CCB), a military unit staffed by ex-policemen who murdered or severely injured political opponents. There was also a sinister 'Third Force', which ANC leaders believed was mainly responsible for the violence in KwaZulu-Natal and the Witwatersrand, and a top-secret organisation called Project Coast, which experimented with chemical and biological weapons to use in warfare, and poisons to kill civilians regarded as enemies of the state. Project Coast was headed by Wouter Basson, nick-named 'Doctor Death', a cardiologist who was the personal physician of the then South African Prime Minister, PW Botha.[24]

The project had started as a counter to perceived similar methods of warfare used against South African soldiers by Soviet-backed troops in South West Africa and Angola, but then changed during the course of the 1980s to the production of poisons concealed in innocent-looking objects. At the end of 1982, some 200 SWAPO prisoners were drugged with muscle-relaxant pills and their bodies dumped from an aeroplane into the sea.[25] High-profile figures like Ronnie Kasrils, Pallo Jordan and Reverend Frank Chikane[26] were also affected: in London, Kasrils was infected by a modified screwdriver that was carrying what may have been phenylsilitrane and Jordan was injured by a poison-tipped umbrella.[27] In 1989 in the United States, Chikane fell violently ill after wearing poisoned underwear.[28]

By 1984, the pressure on the Machel government in Mozambique was so great that he signed the Nkomati Accord with South Africa. The terms of this were that neither side would give sanctuary to the guerrilla forces of the other or support violence in either state. South Africa had managed to establish a ring of fairly pliant states around it, and these destabilising measures made it difficult for the ANC to pursue its armed struggle. Effectively, it meant that ANC MK soldiers could no longer operate, especially from Mozambique, and there was a general slowing down of the movement. In 1987 the Zulu Chief Buthelezi said that while there had been little progress in the armed struggle, and bridges and factories were still intact, even small hits against the government were keeping up the morale of those involved, but that 'the classical circumstances in which the armed struggle wins the day … are just not present in South Africa'.[29]

Nevertheless, the 'new South Africa' was on its way. When negotiations between the South African government and the ANC got underway in the late 1980s, MK soldiers were rather sidelined. Their headquarters were relocated from Lusaka to South Africa, but cadres were widely dispersed: some were still in exile, unsure of how to get home, and no clear plans or arrangements had been made for them. About half of the 12 000 trained guerrillas eventually got back to South Africa, about a third of whom abandoned their mission, joined the security forces or ended up in jail.

When the ANC and the South African government started to move towards a negotiated transition to democracy in the 1990s, MK suspended the armed struggle. After the 1994 elections, MK forces were integrated into the South African National Defence Force (SANDF). The Vlakplaas farm was formally shut down during the transition to democracy in the early 1990s.[30]

South West Africa (Namibia)

South Africa had ruled South West Africa (SWA) since 1915, after it was taken from the Germans during World War I, and Smuts had hoped that eventually the territory would become a fifth province of South Africa. This was not to be: his 1946 application to the newly formed United Nations was turned down, and after a long legal battle and a protracted struggle between

South Africa and forces fighting for independence in SWA, especially after the formation of SWAPO in 1960, the UN General Assembly unilaterally decided to terminate South Africa's mandate over SWA in 1966. In 1971, this was given validity by the UN International Court.

Resistance to South African occupation of the country had flared up repeatedly over the years, notably in 1959 and again in 1966, when SWAPO's armed wing, the People's Liberation Army of Namibia (PLAN), began guerrilla attacks on South African forces, infiltrating the territory from bases in Zambia. The first attack of this kind was the battle at Omugulugwombashe, Namibia, on 26 August. In 1968, South West Africa had become known as Namibia in terms of a resolution passed by the UN General Assembly, an ethnically based advisory council had been established and there had been talk of independence. South Africa would remain in control, however, for over 20 years, from 1968 until 1990.

After Angolan independence in 1975, SWAPO established bases in southern Angola. This alarmed the South African government as it posed a threat to South African forces defending northern Namibia. Hostilities intensified over the years, especially in Ovamboland.

In 1977, the Western Contact Group (WCG) was formed including Canada, France, West Germany, the United Kingdom and the United States to try to negotiate an acceptable transition to independence for Namibia. There were lengthy consultations with South Africa, Angola, Botswana, Mozambique, Tanzania, Zambia and Zimbabwe, as well as with SWAPO and UN officials. The WCG's efforts led to the presentation in 1978 of Security Council Resolution 435, which called for the holding of elections in Namibia under UN supervision and control, and the cessation of all hostile acts by all parties.

South Africa agreed to cooperate with Resolution 435. Nevertheless, in December 1978, in defiance of the UN proposal, South Africa unilaterally held elections in Namibia, the obvious aim of which was to build an internal counter to SWAPO.[31] Not surprisingly, the elections were boycotted by SWAPO and a few other political parties and a moderate, multiracial alliance known as the Democratic Turnhalle Alliance (DTA) emerged as victor. The result was that South Africa continued to administer Namibia with some multiracial coalitions and an appointed administrator. South Africa seemed determined to win in Namibia, having lost in Angola.

In the early 1980s, South African troops established a buffer zone in the southern part of Angola from which they could launch military attacks on SWAPO bases. By 1988, however, after the SADF had been convincingly defeated at Cuito Cuanavale in Angola, the South African government decided to withdraw its troops from Namibia as well. The cost had been too great.

Also in 1988, the United Nations recognised SWAPO as Namibia's legitimate rulers, and on 21 March 1990, Sam Nujoma became the first president of the independent Republic of Namibia.

Implications of the Border War

The strains of the conflicts in Namibia and Angola on the apartheid government and on the white troops who made up the bulk of the engaged forces was enormous. It was clear that the South African government would fight everything that challenged their racist order, but thousands of lives were lost in the process, and an estimated $30 billion spent.

The defeat of the SADF at Luanda in 1975, and that in Mozambique a year earlier had, however, inspired a generation of young South Africans growing up in the townships: the defeats showed that the SADF was not invincible.

The 1976 Soweto uprising a year later led to the SADF generals formulating what they called the 'total strategy'. This was a multidimensional approach involving political, economic and psychological strategies. The political strategy was to enlist the support of dissident groups to oppose liberation movements all over the region; the economic strategy was to create dependence on South African transport, communications, air traffic, railways, harbours, agriculture and mining; and the psychological strategy was to promote the idea that Africans cannot rule themselves, that Africans are inferior, and that Marxism was not the answer. There would also be a military strategy, but the general idea was that if the other aspects were covered, the military aspect would take care of itself.

Black Consciousness (BC) and the 1976 Soweto uprising

A different kind of black resistance also began in the 1970s. This was the Black Consciousness (BC) movement, which advocated that black people reject feelings of inferiority and be proud of being black.

The movement was inspired by, amongst others, American activists like Malcolm X, who had scorned whites and said he had no wish to be like those 'pale things', and the psychiatrist, Frantz Fanon. Originally from the Caribbean island of Martinique, Fanon used psychoanalysis to explain the feelings of dependency and inadequacy that black people experience in a white world. In his book *Black Skin, White Masks*, published in 1952, he urged black people to shake off feelings of inferiority and to be black. 'I am black,' he wrote, 'and I am in total fusion with the world – and the white man, however intelligent he may be, is incapable of understanding Louis Armstrong or songs from the Congo.'[32] In *The Wretched Earth*, published in 1961, he wrote, 'Each generation must discover its mission, fulfill it or betray it, in relative opacity.'[33]

The BC movement in South Africa was started in 1971 by student leader Steve Biko, who was only 24 years old at the time. Two years before, he had led black students out of the essentially white National Union of South African Students (NUSAS), and founded the exclusively black South African Students Organisation (SASO). Famous for his 'black is beautiful' slogan, Steve Biko was the hope of black youth, and his writings encouraged black people to shake off feelings of inadequacy and be more assertive.[34] He believed that black people needed to fight apartheid on their own because only blacks understood the pain of oppression. Well-meaning white people, he argued, should rather channel their energies into convincing other whites that apartheid was wrong, and leave black people to oppose apartheid the best way they knew how. This ideology was captured in what became a popular slogan within BC circles: 'Black man, you are on your own.'[35]

Biko's teachings were to have a significant effect on liberation movements not just in South Africa but in the rest of Africa and elsewhere in the years to come. In 1977, however, he was arrested for his anti-apartheid activities and died of horrific injuries in police custody when he was just 31 years old.

When the officer in charge was asked where he had got the authority to keep an injured man in chains in a cell for 48 hours, he said he didn't need authority: he could use his discretion in terms of the General Law Amendment Act of 1963 that had been passed to deal with Robert Sobukwe.[36]

By the 1970s, the government's 'Bantu education' policies had resulted in vastly inferior schooling for black children: in 1975 and 1976, a white child's education cost 15 times more than a black child's.[37] Steve Biko's influence was manifest when schoolchildren began what were intended to be protests against such discrepancies in their education. On 16 June 1976, some 20 000 schoolchildren in Soweto began a march to protest against a decree issued by the South African Minister of Bantu Education and Development, MC Botha, in 1974 that Afrikaans was to be the medium of instruction in African secondary schools. This latest move of the government was seen to disempower black people even further.

The march started at Morris Isaacson High School, and was planned to continue to Orlando West Junior Secondary School. In a group that size, it was inevitable that members of the community as well as some of the teachers must also have taken part.[38] A SASO leader, Onkgopotse Abram Tiro, had been expelled from the University of the North for questioning Bantu Education policies and had gone on to teach at Morris Isaacson School, where he may have taught pupils about BC and encouraged them to question Bantu education. Tiro had been a popular teacher, highly respected by his pupils.[39] He was killed by a parcel bomb in Botswana in 1974, two years before the Soweto uprising.[40]

During the march, the police opened fire on the students apparently without warning, and a 13-year-old boy, Hector Pieterson, was killed. The picture of his lifeless body being carried away by his sister and a friend would outrage the world. Many other children also lost their lives that day.[41] Unlike Sharpeville in 1960, by 1976 there was television in South Africa – although it had begun broadcasting only earlier that same year. Scenes from Soweto left little doubt as to the brutality of the apartheid system.

The photo of Hector Pieterson was captured by photojournalist Sam Nzima. In an interview some years later, Nzima said that when he heard the police were coming, he hid the used film from his camera in his sock.

Knowing the police would search him, he then loaded his camera with fresh film and continued to take photographs. The police duly arrived, seized his camera, removed the film and held it up to the light to ruin it, but they did not find the film with incriminating evidence in his sock.

What happened in Soweto in 1976 had lasting repercussions. Violence spread to other townships in South Africa and many more lives were lost. In 1977 the Minister of Justice, Jimmy Kruger, banned all organisations associated with Black Consciousness, as well as the black newspaper, *The World*, and the Christian Institute headed by the Afrikaner Beyers Naudé.

Activist, academic, politician and businesswoman Mamphela Ramphele was 29 years old at the time and the partner of Steve Biko, with whom she'd had two children. On 12 June 2016, as the 40th anniversary of the Soweto riots approached, she recalled that in 1976 and 1977, as the revolt spread across the country, a total security clampdown followed, and in terms of the Terrorism Act, people could be held without trial. Ramphele writes about an activist she knew:

> *Mapetla Mohapi was detained and tortured at the Kei Road police station. On August 5 1976, he became the first prominent Black Consciousness Movement leader to die in detention. He was alleged to have hanged himself with a pair of jeans. I had the painful task of sitting in on his postmortem.*[42]

Ramphele herself was soon to be banished to the Tzaneen area in Limpopo, and Steve Biko was detained and destined to die soon after.

Recalling the uprising some 40 years later in 2016, Ramphele writes:

> *The Soweto uprising shook the foundations of the apartheid regime. The irony of a powerful military regime being challenged by unarmed school children was not lost on us .... it shook passive adults to mobilise for change ... but human rights abuses, including the gruesome practice of necklacing*[43] *scarred our collective spirit... . violence brutalised both victim and perpetrator . . . the wounds of that brutalisation still fester today ... 'the tragedy is that 40 years on we have yet to meet*

> *the demands for accessible quality education ... . and violence has again become the language of those whose voices remain unheard.*[44]

Trouble at home

In 1978, the nationalist government was hit by scandal when it became evident that members had been using public funds for propaganda purposes, to persuade readers of the merits of the apartheid government: a newspaper, *The Citizen*, had been established and funded for this purpose. The scandal became known as the 'information scandal' or Muldergate, named after Dr Connie Mulder, the Minister of Information in John Vorster's government. In September of that year, Prime Minister Vorster resigned and was succeeded by PW Botha whose strategy was 'adapt or die'.[45] He visited the homelands and black townships like Soweto and seemed to be delivering a message of hope, but what followed would be minor reforms without any significant loss of Afrikaner power.

Meanwhile, the SADF was particularly strong in the 1970s and early 1980s. Atrocities like Soweto happened because the South African government's police and army could come down hard on protesters. During that time, a right-wing movement called the Afrikaner Weerstandsbeweging (AWB, meaning 'resistance movement') was also particularly aggressive. Their distinctive badge and flag were reminiscent of the German swastika. In 1979, the AWB interrupted a history conference at the University of South Africa (Unisa), where the Battle of Blood River in 1838 between the Voortrekkers and the Zulu was being debated. Historians and dominees of the Dutch Reformed Church had been invited to give their views, and it was a heated but nevertheless stimulating debate. Suddenly, AWB members stormed the conference hall, and tarred and feathered an eminent historian, Professor FA van Jaarsveld, for questioning the radical Afrikaner nationalist interpretation of the battle: that God had intervened on the side of the Voortekkers and given them a victory. Professor van Jaarsveld was badly burnt in the incident, but returned later that afternoon and resumed his place at the conference.

Sabotage and a few reforms

The 1970s and 1980s were also marked by many more incidents of sabotage and armed attacks. After the 1976 Soweto uprising, hundreds of young people had fled the country and swelled the ranks of MK cadres operating from outside the country. By 1980, some of these MK cadres were starting to come back and to conduct a series of attacks across South Africa. On 1 June 1980, storage tanks at Sasol were attacked; a year later, in July 1981, there was an attack on power stations in the eastern Transvaal, followed in August by an attack on the military base at Voortrekkerhoogte near Pretoria, and in December 1982 by a limpet mine attack at Koevoet Nuclear Power Station near Cape Town. It was clear the country was under siege: the number of recorded incidents increased from 13 in 1978 to 56 in 1983. In 1985, protests broke out again among school children and there were bus boycotts.

At the same time as internal resistance had grown and become more militant, opposition to apartheid had grown around the world, and sanctions and international boycotts were hurting the economy. The South African regime was facing a variety of both internal and external threats from anti-apartheid movements in the UK, Holland and the United States. The UK's Anti-Apartheid Movement (AAM) was the most effective. It came out in support of SASO, political detainees, moves to raise the cost of South Africa's access to North Sea oil, and other measures. Their anti-apartheid campaign also affected art, culture and sport. A list was also made of entertainers who had visited South Africa in the past – artists like Shirley Bassey and Tom Jones, who then undertook not to visit South Africa again while apartheid reigned; and proposed cricket and rugby tours to the UK were cancelled due mainly to the activities of two anti-apartheid activists, Dennis Brutus and Peter Hain.

In August 1985 the Chase Manhattan Bank asked a major bank in South Africa to pay back its loans immediately and a crisis situation emerged. Some $35 billion left the country and complete disaster was only avoided by the agreement among the top five banks in South Africa that they would support each other in times of crisis like this. The following year, in November 1986, Barclays Bank pulled out of South Africa and in the next few years 55 British companies including insurance companies such as Norwich Union and Legal and General followed suit.[46] The effect of apartheid policies on the economy was perhaps the most decisive influence: it was becoming clear to the powers that be in the South African regime that something had to change

At home, more alliances across race and class barriers had started to appear. In 1983, about a thousand delegates of all races representing 575 organisations (trade unions, sporting bodies, community groups and women's and youths' organisations) founded the United Democratic Front (UDF) to coordinate internal opposition to apartheid. One of the founding members was Trevor Manuel.[47]

In response to both international and internal pressure, PW Botha's government began to implement some reforms. In 1984, a constitutional reform allowed for the setting up of a Tricameral (three-part) Parliament which gave coloured and Indian people a measure of power-sharing for the first time. White voters were still dominant, however, and black people, who constituted 75% of the population, had no place in the new dispensation: they were expected to exercise their political rights in the homelands. It was hardly a satisfactory solution.

The government also allowed the registration of black trade unions. By 1986, a powerful national federation, the Congress of South African Trade Unions (COSATU), had been established, which had thousands of members and became quite militant. In 1987 there were 1 148 strikes, the most serious being a strike of the National Union of Mine Workers (NUM) led by Cyril Ramaphosa. Wages and working conditions for black people did improve slightly but not enough, and COSATU would henceforth also play a significant role in the struggle.

By 1986, some segregation laws had also been relaxed. Bans on interracial sex and marriage were relaxed, some aspects of job reservation were repealed, some hotels and restaurants were open to all races and a blind eye was turned to increasing numbers of black people living in apartments in parts of Johannesburg and Cape Town that were meant to be for whites only. Spending on black education had been increasing steadily, but schools remained segregated.[48]

Mangosuthu Buthelezi and the Inkatha movement

But it was not enough. Despite these reforms, violence continued, especially in the KwaZulu homeland, where the Inkatha cultural movement started by Chief Mangosuthu Buthelezi in 1975 was gaining momentum and becoming politicised. In 1990 Inkatha was renamed the Inkatha Freedom Party (IFP). Playing on Zulu military tradition, it had a divisive effect, with some Zulus supporting it while others supported the ANC. There were violent clashes between the supporters of these rival factions, and between Inkatha and the UDF.

In an unexpected twist, Buthelezi's IFP was given support by the NP government because both were against the ANC: the South African army and police units gave the IFP money, training, weapons and personnel.[49] Fierce battles took place, and in 1990 the violence spread to Johannesburg, where there were struggles between the ANC and Inkatha for control of the hostels and townships. In the eight-year period between September 1984 and December 1993, nearly 19 000 people were killed and more than 80 000 injured. Most of the violent deaths were the result of clashes between Inkatha and ANC members.[50] These clashes and the toll they took played into the hands of the apartheid government because they drew attention to the so-called 'swaat gevaar' (black danger) and the need for strong (white) control.

The mid-1980s were also the time when gruesome necklacing incidents took place. Victims were usually people suspected of being informers or selling information to the apartheid government, and their torture and subsequent death was decided on by the people in the townships, in so-called 'people's courts'. People in townships had developed their own judicial system beyond the control of the authorities.[51] It was clear that there were a variety of forces at work to bring about change.

Successive states of emergency

On the back of growing unrest, successive states of emergency were declared, and many people were detained; some were tortured. Some 12% of the detainees in 1986 and 1987 (3 050 people) were women and girls: later, at the Truth and Reconciliation Commission[52] hearings in 1996,[53] former detainees reported body searches, vaginal examinations and other humiliating procedures, as well as assaults on pregnant women that led to miscarriages.

There were also more acts of sabotage. Between June 1986 and September 1988, more than 100 explosions caused 31 deaths and 565 injuries in shops, restaurants, cinemas and other public places in the cities. Most of the ANC leaders were in prison or exile during these years, and church people were forced into playing a bigger role. Prominent among these were Archbishop of Cape Town, Desmond Tutu; the moderator of the Dutch Reformed Mission Church, Alan Boesak; and theologian and general secretary of the Council of Churches, Beyers Naudé, and his successor Frank Chikane.

These men and other church leaders urged people to boycott the elections to elect local segregated authorities that were coming up in October 1988. It would be the first time that black and white people would vote on the same day, although in separate elections. The state hoped that by doing this, it would get a new group of black councillors to support it, and at the same time it could assess the effect of the State of Emergency in stopping resistance. The majority of black electorates followed the call of anti-apartheid forces, however, and largely boycotted the elections, with only an estimated 10–14 per cent of 'eligible' black voters participating.[54] The struggle had by then assumed several dimensions.

Signs of Change: Interracial meetings at Dakar, Switzerland and Zambia

In September 1985, a series of secret meetings began to take place between members of the ANC and church people, white business leaders and other influential whites. The meetings had to be held outside the country because the ANC was banned in South Africa. The first meeting took place in Lusaka, Zambia, and was led by Gavin Relly, chairman of Anglo American, which controlled half the companies on the Johannesburg stock exchange at the time. Oliver Tambo, the ANC president, called him 'Gavin' and asked to be called 'Oliver'.[55] This kind of equal-term basis between different races was a significant change.

In August 1987, a meeting took place in Dakar, Senegal, between 61 white people (mostly Afrikaners) and 17 members of the ANC, headed by Thabo Mbeki, who by then had been in exile in the UK for 25 years. The white delegation was led by former leader of the Progressive Party, Frederik van Zyl Slabbert, and other influential, open-minded people including Breyten Breytenbach, André Brink, Ampie Coetzee, Hermann Giliomee, Max du Preez, Hennie Serfontein, Alex Boraine and Gretha Fox. The talks went on for three days, with both sides bent on finding a peaceful solution to the conflict in South Africa. Thabo Mbeki said of Van Zyl Slabbert that he was an 'Afrikaner pioneer' in this regard:[56] he had paved the way for a negotiated settlement at a time when the opposing forces of African and Afrikaner nationalism were about to explode.

In 1989, a continuation of meetings in Lusaka two years before, secret meetings were held between the ANC and the South African government in Switzerland. They were attended by Thabo Mbeki and Jacob Zuma, both future presidents of South Africa. In 2010, Deputy Transport Minister and Deputy Secretary General of the SACP, Jeremy Cronin, recalled that there had also been peace-seeking delegations to the 'nondescript, run-down offices of the ANC' in Lusaka in 1989. Women's groups, cultural workers, faith-based groups and others all went there – so much so that the South Africa media had dubbed it the 'Great Trek to Lusaka'.[57] These meetings set the scene for what was to follow in 1990.

CHAPTER 13

The momentous 1990s

Nelson Mandela's release

The year 1990 was when things really changed in South Africa, brought about by forces from within South Africa and pressure from the outside world.

In 1989, NP Prime Minister PW Botha suffered a stroke, and FW de Klerk was appointed to succeed him. Botha had been Minister of Defence between 1966 and 1978 and had played a large part in the modernisation of the defence force, but as prime minister he was referred to as '*Die Groot Krokodil*' ('the big crocodile') for his rigid policies; Frederik van Zyl Slabbert referred to him as the last of the real apartheid presidents.[1] Nevertheless, it was under Botha's government that some of the worst discriminatory laws (including the pass laws, and the Immorality Act and Mixed Marriages Act) had been repealed in 1985, and it was he who first made contact with Nelson Mandela and ANC leaders in exile. Nelson Mandela commented later that he had met PW Botha at Tuynhuys ('garden house', the presidential office) seven months before his release, and that after that, there could be no turning back.[2]

PW Botha might have broken the ice, but it is still a subject of debate whether or not he was committed to major change. FW de Klerk was more amenable and, as things turned out, the man most able to keep on course the negotiations for effective change. On 2 February 1990, De Klerk made a historic speech in Parliament.[3] It was time, he said, for a negotiated understanding among representative leaders of the entire population because only this could ensure lasting peace.[4] He then gave his agenda to open negotiations for a democratic constitution, equality before the law and the protection of minority and individual rights. The ANC, PAC and SACP were to be unbanned and their leaders returned from exile; people serving prison sentences for belonging to former banned organisations, including the iconic Nelson Mandela, were to be released.

By then, Nelson Mandela had served 27 years in prison. Most of this time had been spent on Robben Island, but the last two years had been spent in a house at Victor Verster Prison outside Paarl near Cape Town – the house is now a museum called Madiba House. News of Nelson Mandela's pending release captured the world's attention, and those still in exile sat around their shortwave radios all day listening for news.

In South Africa, people rushed into the streets, singing, dancing and ululating. Kwaito musician Arthur Mafokate was a teenager at the time. 'We always thought that when we grew up we would also have to fight for liberation,' he said, 'but suddenly everything was different.'[5]

Trevor Manuel recalled that he and other activists were sitting in a Cape Town coffee shop when the news came through. He had been behind bars several times in the preceding five years, and when he was not in prison he had been under banning orders: security forces would come banging on his door at all hours to make sure he was there. 'Suddenly,' he said, 'activists were defying their banning orders and marching in the streets – and nothing happened … This was a big victory, and we seized the moment.'[6]

Thabo Mbeki recalled that he was in Stockholm as part of a delegation to thank the Swedish government for their support of the ANC. For him, the news of Mandela's release amounted to an 'act of faith' – evidence that the NP had honoured the agreements made in Switzerland and were prepared to 'talk to the ANC'. Years later, Thabo Mbeki would repeat those words, saying, 'We need to learn from those incidents in 1990. If we want to solve difficult problems, South Africans must learn to talk to each other again.'[7]

The day of Nelson Mandela's release was 11 February 1990, a historic and highly emotional day for many South Africans. The feelings of many people were expressed in the words of journalist Audrey Brown, who was a cub reporter for the anti-apartheid newspaper *Vrye Weekblad* at the time.

She recalled that nothing could have prepared her for the exhilaration of seeing Mandela released: 'I laughed with delirious joy,' she said, 'because everything was suddenly possible, just like we knew it was when – as singing children – we threw stones at the staggering giant that was apartheid ... I cried because so many of my friends and family had died trying to make this happen.'

For Brown, Mandela's release was also personal because it heralded the release of other political prisoners, as well as the return of political exiles. Her paternal grandfather, who had gone into exile in the 1950s, would soon come home and she would finally meet him, as well as an aunt, uncles and cousins she did not know; she said she wished her maternal grandmother was still alive to see it.[8]

Other events leading to the 1994 elections

Following De Klerk's announcement in 1990, talks were held between the white government and leaders of the ANC, and power-sharing was discussed. The Land Acts and other old discriminatory laws had already been repealed and there was a freedom that had never been experienced before. The next four years were nevertheless fraught with tension, and at times South Africa bordered on civil war. There were dirty dealings on both sides (the old regime and the proposed new order). In 1990, an underground network led by Mac Maharaj was exposed that was infiltrating arms and had plans to overthrow the apartheid state by force if negotiations failed. Some anti-ANC forces were found to be at work as well. The number of unexplained murders rose alarmingly, with 3 699 deaths recorded in 1990 and similar numbers for the next three years.[9] It seems that there were many forces at work responsible for these murders. Violent clashes between rival Zulu ANC and Inkatha members were increasingly evident in Natal and in townships on the Witwatersrand, but many people believed the murders were mainly political killings, with government forces behind them.[10]

The evidence suggests that many of the killings were carried out by individuals or rogue units within the security forces, and that President FW de Klerk did not know about them until at least January 1990.[11] When he did find out, his government appointed a commission headed by Justice Louis Harms to investigate the killings, but it failed for several reasons: the inquiry was limited to acts committed within the borders of South Africa, despite the fact that many anti-apartheid activists had been assassinated on foreign soil. Government witnesses were not required to produce relevant documents and the information that was submitted was clearly fabricated. Some witnesses turned up to testify in wigs and other disguises, and there was a general lack of cooperation from leaders of the security forces. The Harms report, which was released in November, failed to name any special units of the army or participants in the death squads. No prosecutions resulted.[12] In the months that followed, some individuals were banned and there was a draconian crackdown of the press.[13] The AWB[14] led by Ferdi Hartzenberg and Eugène Terre'Blanche felt betrayed by FW de Klerk, and warned that there would be a violent uprising if the government went ahead with plans to share power and extend the franchise to the black majority.

Almost two years passed between De Klerk's historic speech in 1990 and the start of formal constitutional talks at the Convention for a Democratic South Africa (CODESA) in December 1991. When they did begin, there were clashes between the two main leaders, De Klerk and Mandela. De Klerk criticised the ANC for not disbanding Umkhonto we Sizwe; Mandela was not prepared to do that until an interim government was installed of which the ANC was part, and there was multi-party control of the armed forces. In turn, Mandela criticised De Klerk for not doing more to control the violence that was plaguing the country; De Klerk believed the ANC were complicit in it. Historian Tom Lodge believes neither De Klerk nor Mandela was fully in control of their armed forces, and neither was Inkatha leader Mangosuthu Buthelezi, some of whose followers were deeply involved in the violence.[15]

The men continued to hold meetings. Journalist Abbey Makoe said De Klerk was 'the epitome of courage' during this time. He faced a lot of opposition from his own people, but the talks went ahead.[16]

In 1993 FW de Klerk and Nelson Mandela shared the Nobel Peace Prize for what they had achieved together.

The death of Chris Hani, 1993

Despite the violence and the tensions that persisted, the early 1990s seemed full of promise. Tragedy struck on 11 April 1993, when one of the icons of the struggle was killed in broad daylight outside his home in Boksburg, east of Johannesburg, by a white right-wing group. Until then, many people had thought Chris Hani might follow Nelson Mandela as the next president.

Chris Hani was the protégé of SACP chairman Joe Slovo, and had risen quickly through the SACP ranks. He had studied both locally and abroad at Sussex University, where he had obtained a master's degree in economics. He had then gone for military training in the Soviet Union with other ANC cadres, and had also spent some time in Lusaka, Zambia, in the home of former South African Livingstone Mqotsi, who had been exiled there because of his activities as a leader of the communist-influenced African Unity Movement.[17]

In 1967, while living with Mqotsi, Hani had written a memorandum in which he criticised the luxurious lifestyle of some of the exiled leadership and their reluctance to prioritise the armed struggle. He also referred to the fact that the ANC's security department had been hounding out those who did not agree with their leadership. At one stage, orders were apparently given for Hani's arrest: a group of MK men had come to Mqotsi's house at midnight looking for him. In a second memorandum, Hani referred to this incident and said MK men were looking for him and others who had signed his memorandums. 'Dungeons had been dug in Lusaka for us,' he wrote, 'and that is where we would have been taken if they had found us.'[18]

Chris Hani returned to South Africa when the SACP was unbanned in 1990, and succeeded Joe Slovo as secretary general in 1991. His murder in 1993, when he was 51, plunged the country into its worst crisis since talks between the National Party and the ANC had begun. In 1997 Baragwanath Hospital, the enormous government hospital in Soweto, was renamed the Chris Hani Baragwanath Hospital in Hani's honour.[19]

The 1994 elections

In 1994, black, coloured and Indian people voted in the elections for the first time, and the ANC won an overwhelming majority. South Africans of all races experienced long queues and camaraderie at the various polling stations around the country as the majority cast their vote for the first time. Journalist Barry Ronge recalls with affection the sight of an old woman being wheeled to a voting station in a wheelbarrow, and a group of 'kugels'[20] from an affluent area north of Johannesburg voting in the Zevenfontein squatter camp because the queues were shorter there. These two images sum up for him how special and resourceful South Africans can be, and how funny and determined they are to have their own way.[21]

The ANC leader, Nelson Mandela, became South Africa's first democratically elected president. As arranged during the talks between 1990 and 1994, the new government was to be an ANC-led Government of National Unity (GNU), with Nelson Mandela as president, and Thabo Mbeki and former prime minister FW de Klerk as his deputies. IFP leader Mangosuthu Buthelezi became Minister of Home Affairs; SACP leader Joe Slovo became Minister of Housing; and founding member of MK Joe Modise became Minister of Defence. The GNU also included members of the NP and IFP, as well as members of different races and faiths.

Despite the fears of many that the changeover would be accompanied by more violence, this did not happen. Mandela was determined to foster good race relations and during his time as president went out of his way to nurture reconciliation, even paying a personal visit to the elderly and frail Betsie Verwoerd, widow of the NP leader Hendrik Verwoerd in her old-age home.[22] FW de Klerk and Nelson Mandela's paths would diverge again, but they had found agreement at a crucial time. The peaceful transition to democracy after the pain and bloodshed of the years before was regarded as one of the finest achievements of the 20th century.[23]

A new constitution for South Africa was drawn up and signed into law as Act 108 in 1996. Key negotiators in the process were Roelf Meyer representing the NP, and Cyril Ramaphosa representing the ANC, and the two men proved to work well together. The new constitution reflected many of the aims and aspirations of the Freedom Charter[24] in 1955, and is regarded as one of the most liberal constitutions in the world. South Africa also became a member of the British Commonwealth again.

The new dispensation brought with it a change in the military. In 1994, after the first democratic elections, the country's first national defence force, the South African National Defence Force (SANDF), was established. This replaced the old SADF and integrated forces from the former homelands as well as from former liberation forces, such as the ANC's MK, the PAC's Azanian People's Liberation Army (APLA) and the self-protection units of the IFP. Some personnel from the SADF were retained.

The GNU did not turn out to be as satisfactory as it sounded, however. The enmity witnessed between De Klerk and Mandela at CODESA had never been overcome.[25] The NP's attempt to assert itself in the new government floundered, and almost from the start, De Klerk found himself marginalised and often ignored. The ANC's announcement that it had no plans to nationalise the mines allayed the fears of big business, and gave them confidence that they were getting a government they could work with. White people, especially civil servants, realised they could no longer count on the NP to protect their jobs from the black majority, and the ANC promised that pensions would be safe and there would be compensation if white people were retrenched. All these issues had the effect of scaling down support for the NP. In 1996, when the ANC refused to entrench a power-sharing cabinet in the final constitution, De Klerk took the NP out of the GNU, and in August 1997, after a brief spell in the NNP, he retired from politics, which accelerated the NP's decline.[26]

FW de Kerk and the NNP

In 1997, some conservative former-NP members formed a New National Party (NNP). They said that although they were distancing themselves from the apartheid past, they still wanted their own political home, and were in the process of reinventing themselves as a nonracial federal party. The NNP was first led by FW de Klerk and then by Marthinus van Schalkwyk. The party was largely unsuccessful, and after disappointing results in the 1999 elections, some of its members defected to the Democratic Party (DP)[27] the following year, an ironic twist given that the DP had been one of its greatest critics. The merger ended 86 years of National Party influence on South African politics – it had started in 1914, gone through various changes and finally ended in 2000. In an even more unexpected move, the remnants of the NNP merged with the ANC in August 2004, and the NNP was finally dissolved in 2005.

After his retirement from politics, FW de Klerk continued to participate in the national discourse. On 2 February 2010, on the 20th anniversary of his historic speech announcing Mandela's release, he gave his explanation for the transformation initiative he had started in 1990. He said he had been asked many times in the past why his government had not acted sooner. A core concern was the Afrikaner, he explained.[28] Unlike any other settler group in South Africa, the Afrikaners were a nation. They had developed their own language and throughout their history their main wish had been to rule themselves; their right to self-determination could never have been maintained in a one-man-one-vote situation.

But by 1990, a whole new generation of young Afrikaners no longer held those views. Many were middle class and university educated; they had travelled abroad, watched American TV programmes featuring black people (Oprah Winfrey, Bill Cosby and others), and were becoming increasingly uncomfortable with apartheid. The conservative policies of past white-minority governments had refused to allow TV in South Africa until 1976, but since then it had been part of people's lives, making them more aware of the outside world. Prior to 1990, De Klerk said, he was also concerned about the communist influence in the ANC. Nearly all the members of the ANC national executive were also members of the SACP, and the SACP had advocated revolution. In 1989, however, the global collapse of communism had removed this fear.

Sanctions against South Africa were also a factor. They were counter-productive to industry, and South Africa's economy was becoming increasingly isolated. It was clear too that separate development had not worked: the partition of the country on which it was based (78% of the population allocated 13% of the land) was unfair; more and more black people had been moving to the cities, becoming better educated and occupying more important jobs. The integration of white and black people was already taking place.

A further factor was the successful conclusion of a tripartite agreement in 1988 between South Africa, Cuba and Angola. The Cubans had withdrawn their troops from Angola, and Namibia was given its independence. This had reassured the government that it could negotiate with its opponents and that its borders were secure. Prospects for transformation were favourable in 1990, De Klerk said, and on 2 February 1990, we [South Africans] jumped through the window and landed in a far better country.[29] It has since been said of De Klerk that in 1990, his dramatic U-turn in favour of democracy was a spectacular example of placing country ahead of party.[30]

Nelson Mandela's reconciliatory presidency

South Africa's success in making a peaceful changeover to democracy owes most to its iconic and much-loved president, the late Nelson Mandela. His influence during his term of presidency, from 1994 to 1999, set the country on the path to reconciliation. Mandela promised protection for all cultures and made it clear that he embraced all the people of South Africa. Celebrated all over the world, he showed by example that things move on in history and that even the worst of situations can change.

In 1995 Nelson Mandela was appointed to the British Order of Merit, a dynastic order first established by King Edward VII in 1902, which recognises distinguished service. Admission to this prestigious Order is still the personal gift of the sovereign: in this case, Queen Elizabeth II. At a formal state banquet in London in July 1996, the Queen hailed him as a saviour of his country and praised his willingness to embrace his former captors. Until his death in December 2013, Nelson Mandela was probably the most admired living ex-politician in the world.[31]

In 1995, when the 'new' South Africa was barely a year old, the country hosted the Rugby World Cup for the first time. Because of the worldwide boycott of South African sports teams, the Springboks had been excluded from the previous two Rugby World Cups, in 1987 and 1991. In 1995, they were seeded ninth and no one expected them to win, but in the final game, the Springboks narrowly beat the New Zealand All Blacks 15-12. The euphoria that greeted that victory is something that will live forever in the minds of most South Africans who witnessed it. The occasion was made all the more momentous by the arrival of the new state president, Nelson Mandela, wearing a Springbok jersey with the Afrikaner captain's number six on the back. After years of isolation from world sport, the sight of Afrikaner captain, Francois Pienaar holding the Webb Ellis trophy alongside President Nelson Mandela, who had only been released from prison a few years before, was a powerful moment of hope.[32]

A year after the Rugby World Cup, in 1996, South Africa hosted the Africa Cup of Nations football competition for the first time. Soccer is the most popular sport in South Africa, and the national team is Bafana Bafana.[33] Bafana Bafana had played in the competition for the first time four years before, after the sports boycott on South Africa was lifted, but the team had not done well and failed to qualify for the finals. In 1996, like the Springboks the year before, Bafana Bafana were regarded as the underdogs, but under coach Clive Barker and captain Neil Tovey, they stunned the soccer world by defeating Angola, (1-0), Cameroon, (3-0), Ghana (3-0) and then Tunisia (2-0) in the finals, and were crowned Africa's champions. It was a historic moment for South Africa and African soccer at large. Clive Barker and his team became national heroes.[34]

The match was attended by President Nelson Mandela, who had become famous for his 'Madiba magic' throughout the tournament. It became something of a legend that whenever Mandela attended a match, South Africa always came out victorious. The victory was celebrated nationwide with people (both black and white) taking to the streets to celebrate.[35] These two events – the Rugby World Cup in 1995 and the Soccer World Cup a year later – both won by South Africa, can be seen as symbolic twins in the 'miracle years' of reconciliation.

Nelson Mandela's release from prison was also a chance for him to be reunited with old friends like Helen Suzman[36] and Ahmed (Kathy) Kathrada, the leader of the South African Indian Congress (SAIC).[37] Kathrada had also spent 27 years in prison. Along with Nelson Mandela, he was released in 1990 and became a member of the new GNU government in 1994. Kathrada recalls with affection Mandela's ability to defuse awkward and tense situations in the new South Africa. On one occasion in Parliament, someone from the ANC referred to the Democratic Alliance (DA) led by Tony Leon as a 'Mickey Mouse party'. Tony Leon replied: 'If we are Mickey Mouse, then you are Goofy.' Some time later, Tony Leon took ill and spent a while in hospital. Mandela, in his typically magnanimous style, went to visit him. When he arrived, he knocked on the door and said, 'Mickey Mouse, this is Goofy. May I come in?'[38]

Ahmed Kathrada also recalls Nelson Mandela's love of Pantene hair oil. After 18 years on Robben Island, five of the prisoners, including Mandela and Kathrada, were transferred to Pollsmoor Prison in Cape Town, where they could no longer get Pantene hair oil. Mandela made such a fuss about this that one of the warders, Christo Brand, eventually went around the pharmacies until he found some. Years later, Kathrada organised an 80th birthday party for Mandela, and arranged for Brand to attend the party as a surprise guest. When Brand arrived, he was carrying two bottles of Pantene. Kathrada recalls: 'Madiba laughed like anything.'[39]

It was also Christo Brand who had smuggled in a grandchild to show Nelson Mandela on Robben Island. It was winter and Nelson Mandela's then-wife, Winnie, had come to see her husband with the baby girl, Zoleka, tied in a blanket on her back. She was told to leave the baby in a waiting room while she saw her husband. Christo Brand covered the child in the blanket and took it to show Mandela before Winnie was allowed through. Winnie Mandela didn't know about it at the time – the warders were afraid that if she knew she might tell the press and they would lose their jobs.[40]

Winnie Madikizela Mandela

When her husband became president of the new South Africa, Winnie Mandela became First Lady for two years, from 1994 to 1996, until the couple divorced. She has also held numerous positions in the ANC Women's League and the government. She is, however, a controversial figure.

Admired by many for her bravery and strong anti-apartheid stance, she has been condemned by others for the strong measures she was prepared to support during the struggle. Winnie Mandela was regularly detained by the South African government, subjected to house arrest and kept under surveillance. She was held in solitary confinement for over a year and then banished to Brandfort, a remote town in the then Orange Free State. Despite the restrictions placed on her, she continued to campaign for equal rights and became an icon of the struggle. Her popularity was tarnished, however, by statements she made – for example in Munsieville in the area of Krugersdorp on 13 April 1986, when she said, 'With our matches and necklaces we shall liberate this country.'[41] The horrific practice of necklacing (burning people alive using tyres and petrol)[42] was used against people suspected of being informers. This was done in public as a warning to others about what would happen if they betrayed the cause. Accusations were made against her by her bodyguard, Jerry Musivuzi Richardson, who said that she had ordered the kidnapping and murder of people and that she had committed fraud. She was accused of being an accessory to assault in the death of a 14-year-old boy, James (Stompie) Seipei, an alleged informer whose body was found in a field with stab wounds to the throat on 6 January 1989. In 1992, she was accused of ordering the murder of Dr Abu-Baker Asvat, a family friend who had examined Seipei at Mandela's house.

Graça Machel

Nelson and Winnie Mandela were divorced in 1996, and in 1998, on his 80th birthday, Nelson Mandela married Graça Machel, widow of former Mozambican president Samora Machel, who had died in an aeroplane crash in 1986. They remained married until Nelson Mandela's death in December 2013.

Graça Machel is an international advocate for women's and children's rights, and in 1997 was made a Dame of the British Empire for her humanitarian work.[43] She is the only woman in history to have been First Lady of two separate countries: she was First Lady of Mozambique from 1975 to 1986, and First Lady of South Africa from 1998 to 1999.

The Truth and Reconciliation Commission

In December 1998, the Truth and Reconciliation Commission was set up by the GPU in an attempt to deal with human rights abuses and heal some of the pain of the past. People who had been victims of human rights violations during the apartheid years were invited to give statements about their experiences, and some were selected for public hearings. Perpetrators of violence could also give testimony and request amnesty from both civil and criminal prosecution.[44] The emphasis was on uncovering information – from both victims and perpetrators – and seeking reconciliation, not on prosecuting individuals for past crimes, which is how the TRC mainly differed from the Nuremberg Trials that prosecuted Nazis after World War II.[45] Archbishop Desmond Tutu was appointed as chair by then-President Nelson Mandela.

Winnie Mandela was one of the people selected for public hearing. Archbishop Tutu paid tribute to her role in the anti-apartheid struggle, but asked her to apologise and to admit her mistakes. In a guarded response, she admitted, 'things went horribly wrong'. Hearings concerning her were later adjourned amid claims that witnesses were being intimidated on her orders.[46] Despite the allegations of fraud and corruption against her, Winnie Mandela continued to have a grassroots following, and is still venerated for her role in the struggle.[47] In 2009, she secured fifth place on the ANC's electoral list for the 2009 general election, which suggests the party's leadership still saw her as a valuable asset. Her story has been the subject of an opera, and several books and films.

Thousands of interviews were conducted by the TRC between April 1996 and June 1998, including one with former president FW de Klerk, who apologised on behalf of the NP government for apartheid. Testimonies revealed many cases of rape, torture, deaths in detention, political assassinations, and even human burnings. Tutu wept over many of the stories he heard, and begged people to try to forgive and move on with their lives. The TRC granted amnesty to qualified perpetrators in a gesture of peace and reconciliation. In some cases, relatives of victims forgave individuals who had admitted to killing their loved ones.

The commission concluded that a network of government security and non-security operatives had facilitated most of the violence and targeted killings, but the ANC, PAC and UDF were also responsible for some human rights violations, and that some of the worst violence had taken place between rival Zulu ANC and Inkatha members.

Some people were left frustrated by the Commission. The family of Steve Biko criticised the TRC for failing to bring his killers to justice. It was also pointed out that the TRC only investigated human rights violations, not the 'structural violence' of apartheid, which included racial classification, residential segregation, pass laws, forced removals and much more. Moreover, rape against women went largely unexamined, and relatively few women testified on their own behalf. Young people were also largely absent from the proceedings. The TRC was also criticised for limiting its investigations to post-1960 crimes, which avoided the suffering caused by colonialism, the 1913 Land Act, and other injustices of the segregation period and the first decade of apartheid.[48]

Significantly, major political and military leaders were left off the hook. PW Botha and others refused to take part, with no real sanctions taken against them, and South African and international businesses, foreign governments, religious institutions, the media and other beneficiaries of apartheid were dealt with only in separate and brief 'institutional hearings' toward the end of the proceedings. Despite its shortcomings, former Minister of Justice Dullah Omar believes that allowing ordinary people to tell their stories of human rights abuses began a process of healing for many people who had experienced the brutality of apartheid oppression.[49] The TRC helped reveal the worst excesses of apartheid and achieved a measure of social reconciliation, but the reparations process was neither particularly generous to victims nor efficiently administered.

In 1998, Antjie Krog wrote a book about about the TRC hearings, in which she said she found it difficult to live with the fact that so many of the words used to hurt and humiliate others belonged to the language of her heart, Afrikaans.[50]

CHAPTER 14

The years 1999–2008 and 2009–2016

Presidents post Mandela

Thabo Mbeki

In June 1999, Thabo Mbeki succeeded Nelson Mandela as president. He would go on to serve two terms: from 1999 to 2003, and from 2003 to 2008. Thabo Mbeki is Xhosa, like Mandela, and is widely seen as an intellectual with sound struggle credentials. When the ANC was banned in 1962, Mbeki went into exile in England where, like Chris Hani, he obtained a master's degree in economics from the University of Sussex. He then went to the Soviet Union for military training, and subsequently served as an ANC representative in several African countries before settling at the ANC headquarters in Lusaka, Zambia. While in exile, both his brother Jama and his son Kwanda were murdered, presumably by government security forces.

Where Nelson Mandela stood for reconciliation, Thabo Mbeki emphasised transformation as part of an African Renaissance. The concept of an African Renaissance had been formulated as early as 1946 by Senegalese anthropologist and historian Cheikh Anta Diop. He believed there was a shared cultural continuity across African people that was more important than the different ethnic groups that had developed over time, and that African people could overcome current challenges on the African continent and achieve cultural, scientific and economic renewal.[1] The concept was taken up and popularised by Thabo Mbeki. It represented in part a desire to return to his roots, after what he described as (to all intents and purposes) a 'disconnected', parentless childhood, followed by an itinerant adult life.[2] For Thabo Mbeki, the African Renaissance was not merely a political philosophy, but a call to action, an African recovery programme 'for the reconstruction of the (African) identity and the regaining of self-confidence of the African people'.[3]

On 8 May 1996, on the occasion of the formal adoption of the new constitution for South Africa, Thabo Mbeki gave his famous 'I am an African' speech, in which he said he believed he had many identities and that he had been formed by all the people of Africa. He referred to the pain of the past, but added that people could now celebrate their right to formulate their own definition of what it meant to be African.[4]

Mbeki believed Africa's problems had to be solved by Africans, and that economic rebuilding and growth were essential if Africa was to become a significant player in geo-political affairs. To this end, he was one of the founders of both the New Partnership for Africa's Development (NEPAD), which aimed to develop an integrated socioeconomic development framework for Africa, and the African Union (AU). Mbeki served as president of the AU from 2002 until 2003, and helped broker peace agreements in Rwanda, Burundi and the Democratic Republic of Congo. Yet he was reluctant to intervene in the human rights violations perpetrated by Robert Mugabe in Zimbabwe, and his denialism of the scientific consensus linking HIV and Aids may have directly resulted in the deaths of 330 000 people – the single biggest taint on his legacy.[5] His slowness to implement policy meant that government struggled to stop the mother-to child transmission of the disease.[6]

Opinions about Mbeki's attitude differ. It has been argued that Mbeki was not an Aids denialist but an Aids dissident, and that he asked scientists for evidence that the HIV virus actually existed, not just that it was linked to Aids.[7] This attitude was severely criticised and was seen by some as a reflection of a personal battle with his own demons, or an attempt to reclaim the dignity of his African manhood against what he perceived to be centuries of assault from Western racism.[8]

It was also during Mbeki's time as president that the controversial arms deal was implemented. In November 1998, the South African government approved a R30-billion purchase of weaponry, including submarines, light utility helicopters, lead-in fighter trainer and multi-role combat aircraft. It is believed that the deal diverted funds from Eskom, the country's power supplier, and it is the arms deal that is blamed for the lack of maintenance of the country's electricity supply stations. There were calls from both opposition members of Parliament like Patricia de Lille[9] and ANC member Andrew Feinstein for a full investigation. In 2001 Andrew Feinstein raised the issue again. When the ANC refused, he resigned from his position and moved to London. He has since written his memoirs and a book about the global arms industry in which he criticises the ANC (the political party he once supported) and exposes the secrecy and cover-ups behind weapons deals.[10] The arms deal continues to stand as the biggest symbol in South Africa of the corrupt relationships between government ministers and multinational corporations.[11]

During Mbeki's time in office, the South African economy grew at an average rate of 4.5 per cent per annum. Mbeki created employment in the middle sectors of the economy and encouraged the growth of a black middle class with the implementation of a policy known as Black Economic Empowerment (BEE). By the time his term of office ended, the country had produced the highest sustained economic growth rate in its history. A new class of powerful and wealthy black businesspeople was emerging, but there was also criticism that not enough had been done for ordinary people severely disadvantaged during apartheid.

In 2005, President Mbeki fired his deputy president, Jacob Zuma, after Zuma was implicated in corruption charges mainly to do with the arms deal, and was charged with the rape of a 31-year-old woman who had been staying at his home.[12] Matters came to a head two years later, in December 2007, at the National Conference of the ANC held at Polokwane, Limpopo. In a complete reversal of fortune, Thabo Mbeki was ousted as president of the ANC and replaced by Jacob Zuma: the charges Mbeki had held against the populist Zuma had cost him dearly among Zuma supporters.

Kgalema Motlanthe, the party's secretary-general, was made interim president until the general elections scheduled for 2009. Motlanthe was a former National Union of Mineworkers (NUM) secretary-general and was viewed as someone who could heal the rifts in the ANC, but during his brief term of office (less than a year), he was involved in two controversies. The first was that the Dalai Lama was denied a visa to visit South Africa because the ANC government feared reprisals from the Chinese, and the second was that Motlanthe signed legislation that did away with the Scorpions, an investigative unit that had been investigating the charges against Jacob Zuma.[13]

On 6 May 2009, Jacob Zuma was elected President of the Republic of South Africa and three days later, on 9 May 2009, he was inaugurated at the Union Buildings in Pretoria, with Kgalema Motlanthe as his deputy.

Jacob Zuma

Jacob Zuma started the decade as a sacked deputy president and ended it as an elected president. Zuma is Zulu and thus belongs to the largest ethnic group in South Africa. He has a large following and is a charming man with a down-to-earth appeal, but his presidency has produced some of South Africa's most highly charged controversies.

As a child, Zuma herded his grandfather's cattle in rural KwaZulu. He did not have any formal schooling but he and a few others taught themselves to read with the help of a woman who had passed standard 4 (grade 6). His father died when he was four years old, and his mother moved to Durban to look for domestic work; he was not allowed to visit her at the white-owned house where she worked. As a young man, Zuma took whatever jobs he could find in Durban – polishing the verandahs of white people's houses and other menial jobs. 'We were called "house-boys",' he said in conversation with historian RW Johnson many years later, 'and we wore white calico uniforms with red trim on the sleeves and pants.[14] We were "men-boys," once proud warriors, reduced to this kind of work, and we quickly learnt to appear harmless and quite stupid, because there were still powerful legends attached to the Zulu.'[15]

Zuma became involved in resistance and sabotage incidents during apartheid, and suffered harassment from security forces. He also served time on Robben Island, where he shared a communal cell, sleeping on the floor with a group of between 30 and 50 other prisoners. For the first ten years, the black prisoners were only given cold water to wash with and were fed on a diet of mainly boiled mealies (maize) because the prison authorities had decided that black people did not need bread. Bread was, however, given to coloured and Indian prisoners. During the day the prisoners worked in a stone quarry crushing slate for the construction of more prison cells, but eventually they were allowed sports facilities, and Jacob Zuma became a keen soccer player for the island's Rangers team. He also joined a choral and traditional dance group. It was while he was a prisoner on Robben Island that Jacob Zuma learnt to read and write in English, taught by his cellmate, Zulu teacher and communist Harry Gwala.[16] During all the years he was there, he never had a single visitor; his mother could not afford the fare to visit him.[17]

After Zuma was released from prison in December 1973, he resumed his anti-apartheid activities, and continued to operate for the ANC's underground movement. He became responsible for the ANC's Swaziland/Natal operations, and also worked in Mozambique. There he served as the official ANC deputy chief representative and then as the chief representative after the Nkomati Accord was signed between the governments of Mozambique and South Africa in 1984.[18] In Mozambique, he helped young people who had moved there after the 1976 uprising in Soweto,[19] and he worked with activist Indres Naidoo[20] in the Internal Political Reconstruction Committee (IPRC) set up by the ANC with the idea of rebuilding underground networks. Similar IPRCs were also established in Lesotho, Swaziland and Botswana. The IRPC in Lesotho was run by Chris Hani.[21] The explosions in urban areas of South Africa in 1977 and 1978, although relatively few in number, have been attributed to these IPRCs and to the fact that they were succeeding in getting saboteurs and weapons into the country.[22] During 1978, Zuma also spent three months in the Soviet Union, where he underwent a leadership and military training course.

In 1986, while still living mainly in Mozambique, Zuma was placed in command of the Mandla Judson Kuzwayo (MJK) unit – an underground counter-intelligence unit named after ANC commander Mandla Judson Kuzwayo, who had served a term of imprisonment on Robben Island and died tragically in a car crash the year before.[23] The unit carried out spy activities in companies like Altech,[24] and they infiltrated the security police in Durban and were able to access information relating to informers within the security forces.

The MJK unit had been started by Jayendra Naidoo and brothers Mo and Yunus Shaik, members of the Shaik family, who lived in Greenwood Park, Durban. Four of the five brothers (Schabir, Yunus,[25] Mo and Shamin) became key figures in ANC circles. Many former exiles who subsequently became government members in the 'new' South Africa – including former Transport Minister Mac Maharaj, former Minister of Water Affairs and Forestry Ronnie Kasrils and Jacob Zuma himself – tell stories of how the Shaik brothers helped them to return to the country in the 1980s, and gave them financial assistance.[26] Other activists concurred: 'When things were hard and we had no money or nowhere to hide, we would turn to the Shaiks.'[27]

In January 1987, as a result of pressure applied by the apartheid government on Mozambique to expel ANC activists, Jacob Zuma was forced to leave Mozambique. He moved to the ANC Head Office in Lusaka, Zambia, where he was appointed Head of Underground Structures and shortly thereafter Chief of the Intelligence Department.

In February 1990, the ANC was unbanned in South Africa, and the following month Zuma returned to the country, where he worked alongside Penuell Maduna, Mathews Phosa, Thabo Mbeki and Oliver Tambo (who was president of the ANC at the time) to identify and remove obstacles in the way of negotiations between the government and ANC. Zuma was also involved in negotiations concerning returning exiles and the release of political prisoners. In July 1991, at the first ANC conference held in South Africa since 1959,[28] he was elected Deputy Secretary General, and in November of the same year he chaired the ANC's negotiations commission[29] at the Convention for a Democratic South Africa (CODESA).[30] He had by then ceased to be a member of the SACP. As a senior intelligence officer and negotiator, Zuma was thus a key ANC figure in the years just prior to the unbanning of the party, and in the volatile period leading up to the first democratic elections.

In 1994, after Nelson Mandela was elected president and Thabo Mbeki his deputy, Zuma became the MEC for Economic Affairs and Tourism in his home province of KwaZulu-Natal. In December 1997 he was elected deputy president of the ANC, two years before becoming deputy president of South Africa in June 1999.

After his return to South Africa from Mozambique, Schabir Shaik became Zuma's financial adviser and is said to have given him large sums of money and interest-free loans. In 1999, when arms were being purchased, it was 'payback time'.[31] With Zuma's help, two of Schabir's companies, Nkobi Holdings and African Defence Systems, were among the beneficiaries of billions of rands' worth of arms purchases. Zuma was apparently promised R500 000 a year to protect the company from investigation.[32]

The reputable corruption and crime-fighting unit called the Scorpions investigated the arms deal, and both Zuma and Shaik were accused of corruption and fraud. Shaik was also charged with tax evasion relating to alleged bribes and payments from himself and his companies to Zuma. The state alleged that Zuma had used his position in government to enrich himself by benefiting from Shaik and that he had violated the 'Code of Conduct in Regard to Financial Interests', to which all cabinet members are bound.[33] But the National Prosecuting Authority's (NPA) decided not to prosecute Zuma. Shaik, however, was tried in the Durban High Court and sentenced to 15 years' imprisonment. He began his sentence on 9 November 2006, but on 3 March 2009, after serving just over two years, and just before the elections that brought Zuma to power, Shaik was released on medical parole. Just a few months before, in October 2008, Parliament had officially disbanded the Scorpions and replaced it with the Hawks, headed by a man of Jacob Zuma's choice. The Hawks proceeded to shut down the probe the Scorpions had been conducting into bribery among Zuma allies, especially the Shaik brothers.

These incidents caused much controversy at the time. There were accusations that Zuma had interfered with the process of law, and that Schabir Shaik had feigned his illness and violated the terms of his parole. He was seen playing golf on several occasions and visited Thanda Private Game Reserve for three nights in June 2009.[34]

It was also a taste of what was to come. Zuma and his supporters remained largely unaccountable for their violation of the constitution. By 2015, the Shaik brothers' influence had been largely replaced by that of another wealthy family: the Indian-born Guptas were given carte blanche in business enterprises and even influenced cabinet appointments. In April 2016, the Constitutional Court cracked down on them and banks followed suit. When called to account, President Zuma has said on several occasions that he solves problems the African way, no doubt recalling the power that traditional chiefs once held.[35]

Jacob Zuma has married six women: Gertrude Sizakele Khumalo in 1973, Kate Mantsho in 1976, Nkosazana Dlamini-Zuma in 1982, Nompumelelo Ntuli in 2008, Thobeka Madiba in 2010 and Gloria Bongekile Ngema in 2012. In keeping with Zulu tradition, he paid lobola (bride wealth) for all his wives. It is estimated that he has fathered 22 children, 14 of them with his wives and seven with other women. He says this behaviour is in keeping with Zulu culture and many people support him on this, but he also has critics who are concerned about the cost to tax payers of his large family, and some who condemn it on moral grounds.

President Zuma has faced problems during both terms of his presidency (2009–2013 and 2014–time of going to print). In his pre-election speeches he made promises about solving unemployment and reducing poverty that have thus far proved impossible to keep. In 2009, economic recession affected South Africa, as it did in the rest of the world. President Zuma had promised to create 500 000 new jobs by the end of the year,[36] but between June and September the number of unemployed rose by 70 000, and it is estimated that a million jobs were lost over the year. Poverty and a lack of economic opportunities increased the crime rate, and economic problems inherited from the apartheid era worsened.

By 2010, the recession was past its worst, but severe problems remained. Maintenance of the main power stations had not been sustained so plants were breaking down, and Eskom (the main electricity supplier) was unable to keep up with demand. For the next few years, South Africans were subjected to long periods of 'load shedding'.[37] People were urged to make other arrangements for power, but many small businesses were unable to invest in alternative sources of energy and had to close down. In the long term, the country's Nuclear Energy Corporation (Necsa) in Pelindaba, 30 kilometres west of Pretoria, has offered some relief: they have announced an Integrated Resource Plan for Electricity (IRP), which aims to deliver a nuclear generation fleet to produce low-cost and low carbon-base-load electricity supply by the year 2030.

Also in 2010, South Africa was admitted to BRIC, a trade organisation that had been established the year before,[38] and made up of four major emerging national economies: Brazil, Russia, India and China. Its aim is to promote trade between its members and create financial institutions to compete with the Western-dominated International Monetary Fund (IMF) and the World Bank. When South Africa joined, it became BRICS. Global economist Jim O'Neill voiced the concern that South Africa, with a population of under 50 million people, was just too small an economy to join the BRIC ranks.[39]

In subsequent years, there has not been much economic integration, as the member countries have very different political systems and vulnerable currencies; in terms of GDP (Gross Domestic Product) China contributes the most (41%) and therefore has the biggest political say.[40] Nevertheless, most economists are generally optimistic that membership of BRICS will be good for South Africa, and that it will mean increased business and trade opportunities.

Despite this hopeful development internationally, by April 2016, it was clear the ruling party was losing support in South Africa, and there was mounting criticism of President Jacob Zuma from all quarters, and even from within the ANC itself.[41] Zuma had also aroused criticism from women's organisations, who saw some of his pronouncements on women as offensive and contributing to gender inequality. At the local-government election results ceremony in Pretoria in August 2016, Zuma remained silent while his bodyguards forcefully removed four young women who were standing in front of the podium silently protesting rape culture in South Africa.[42]

Significant changes have nevertheless taken place in the last 60 years, including that of the role of women in politics. In photos taken of the Cabinet in 1953 and 2014 respectively, the earlier photo shows all white men, while in 2014 all members were black and three were women. A year later there were significantly more women in these important positions. On Women's Day, 9 August 2015, President Zuma said that female representation in the National Assembly had been only 2.7% prior to 1994; it was then 41%, and both the speaker in Parliament and the chairperson of the National Council of Provinces were women.[43] Despite this acknowledgement of the role of women, gender issues are vexed when it comes to Zuma's private life.

Just prior to going to print with this book, another crisis befell the Zuma presidency when President Zuma announced a major cabinet reshuffle, which included axing respected finance minister Pravin Gordhan and his deputy Mcebisi Jonas. The ensuing political turmoil caused the Rand to weaken rapidly.[44] Despite increasing public pressure and sometimes ridicule, Jacob Zuma appears to manage these and other challenges, and at the time of writing retains enough ANC members to support him.

Forces in opposition

The Democratic Alliance (DA)

Since June 2000, the official opposition party to the ANC has been the Democratic Alliance (DA), which has a large following in the Western Cape. It traces its roots to the Progressive Party in 1959,[45] with many mergers and name changes in between. The DA was founded by Tony Leon on 24 June 2000. Leon had by then served in Parliament for almost 20 years, but first entered as a Progressive Party member in 1999, when Helen Suzman[46] retired and he won her seat. 'She was my idol,' he has said.[47]

From 1990 to 1994, Leon chaired the Democratic Party's Bill of Rights Commission, served as an adviser to CODESA and took part in the multiparty negotiations that led to the end of apartheid and the establishment of a nonracial democracy in 1994. Leon retired as Party leader in 2007, and was succeeded by Helen Zille, who served as both mayor of Cape Town and leader of the party until 2015. Before she entered politics, Helle Zille was a journalist and anti-apartheid activist. She worked with the Black Sash and drew attention to the appalling circumstances surrounding the death of Black Consciousness leader Steve Biko in 1977

In 2010, the DA merged with a smaller party, the Independent Democrats (ID), founded by Patricia de Lille in 2003 – the first South African political party founded by a woman. When De Lille wrote her matriculation examinations at the end of her schooling, she'd had to produce an identity book, which white children were not required to do. Her race was described as 'mixed', which angered her as she felt no one had the right to tag other people in that way. She took pride in the words of PAC leader, Robert Sobukwe, who said he believed there is only one race and that is the human race. Sobukwe's belief that an African was anyone who gave allegiance to Africa, regardless of their skin colour, resonated with De Lille. She said, 'It gave me an identity and a home.'[48]

In 2009, Patricia de Lille challenged the controversial arms deal that implicated Jacob Zuma and other political and business figures when Zuma was about to become president. She called for a full judicial investigation into the alleged corruption in South Africa's purchase of weapons costing R30 billion, and was consequently accused of being unpatriotic and embarrassing the country. The charges were dropped, as she predicted they would be. Patricia de Lille succeeded Helen Zille as mayor of Cape Town in 2011.

In May 2015, Mmusi Maimane became the new leader of the DA, a clear attempt to transform the perception of the DA as a 'white' political party.[49]

Julius Malema and the Economic Freedom Fighters (EFF)

Jacob Zuma's government also faces opposition from a former president of the ANC Youth League, Julius Malema. In July 2013, Julius Malema founded an opposition group, the Economic Freedom Fighters (EFF), the most aggressive opposition movement yet. According to their manifesto, the EFF positions itself as a revolutionary party which draws its inspiration from the broad Marxist–Leninist tradition. It is critical of both the ANC and the DA for their allegedly pro-capitalist stances which it claims have sold out the black people of South Africa to capitalism as cheap labour. It is currently the third-largest party in parliament. Members of the EFF wear distinctive red overalls and berets to identify with the working classes.

Their demands include land redistribution, nationalisation of the mines, an end to retrenchments and better salaries.

On 2 February 2015, one of the most dramatic incidents in parliamentary history took place. While President Zuma was giving his State of the Nation address, members of the EFF began to raise points of order related to the huge amount of tax payers' money (R246 million) that had been spent on renovations to Zuma's rural homestead, Nkandla, in KwaZulu-Natal. The protestors held up placards saying, 'Pay Back the Money'. The protest became violent and the agitators were forcibly removed by plain-clothes security forces. Some DA members also walked out in protest.

On Friday 1 April 2016, President Zuma was finally called to account. A full bench of 11 judges of the Constitutional Court ruled that remedial action recommended by the public prosecutor, Thuli Madonsela, was binding, and that President Zuma was required to pay back money spent on non-security aspects of his Nkandla homestead. There were calls for President Zuma to resign, but he stood firm. On September 2016, it was announced that a bank had given President Zuma a R7.9 million load to pay back the money, but the controversy continued, with Zuma the subject of continued abusive comments from EFF members in Parliament.

Public prosecutor, Thuli Madonsela

Thulisile (Thuli) Madonsela is an advocate and human rights lawyer. In October 2009 she was appointed by Jacob Zuma to be public prosecutor for a non-renewable seven-year term.

During the apartheid years, Madonsela worked for the ANC and UDF, and was one of the technical advisers who drafted the new constitution for South Africa in 1994–1995. During her term as public prosecutor (2009 to 2016), she was not afraid to investigate complaints about government spending, especially those related to the private homestead of President Zuma in Nkandla. Thuli Madonsela also regularly reminded people of what is at stake if the rule of law were to be manipulated to suit those in power, and she called for transparency and accountability in all matters of state. When her seven-year term ended in October 2016, Madonsela was replaced by Advocate Busisiwe Mkhwebane.

The unions

In the struggle years, the unions were a great support to the activities of the ANC and other liberation movements. As has happened elsewhere in Africa, however, once independence has been achieved, unions are often marginalised because of their ability to garner mass support, which governments see as a threat. Unions then have either to kowtow to the ruling elite, or break away. South Africa's biggest trade union federation, COSATU, faces this dilemma.

When political organisations were unbanned in early 1990, the ANC, SACP and COSATU had agreed to work together as a Revolutionary Alliance (Tripartite Alliance), each member committed to the objectives of democracy and the desire to unite the largest possible cross-section of South Africans behind these objectives.[50] In the 1980s and 1990s, the three alliance members had much in common. All three were equally committed to ending white minority rule. All three were led by revolutionaries – people willing to lose their lives for the freedom of all South Africans. All three had members in prison.[51]

Since then, circumstances have changed. South Africa now has majority rule and a constitution that has ended racism, but problems remain. Some people have found personal wealth and security, but millions have not, and poverty endures.[52] The three parts of the alliance have started to pull in different directions: the ANC is a party divided, and both the SACP and COSATU are full of contradictions, partly the result of their commitment to the tripartite alliance and the fact that they cannot operate freely.

COSATU has some two million members but is restricted in what it can do in terms of wages and working conditions because of the affiliation with the Tripartite Alliance. Some of COSATU's biggest unions – the National Education, Health and Allied Workers' Union (NEHAWU) and the South African Democratic Teachers' Union (SADTU), for example – are in the public sector.[53] Thousands of these members work in dilapidated classrooms or clinics, without clean toilets, but their bosses are ANC government minsters. There has been little improvement in many of these places.[54]

On 28 June 2013, a summit meeting of the Tripartite Alliance was held in Pretoria. Key issues listed for discussion were organisational weaknesses driven by factionalism, corruption and self-enrichment among members, and complacency in government. COSATU president Sdumo Dlamini said COSATU was the first organisation to admit up front that they are faced with challenges; he said he believed in the alliance and would welcome 'constructive criticism'.[55] Others are of the opinion that the country would be better served if the different organisations followed their own agenda instead of shielding each other.[56]

COSATU remains split on this basis: some members are still willing to align with the ANC, while others have demanded stronger concessions from the government, and have left when these are not forthcoming. This kind of in-fighting consumes the energies of both sides, and the real economic issues that they should be dealing with are neglected.[57] Regular strikes affect the economy and the issues behind the strikes are seldom satisfactorily resolved – this has resulted in South Africa having one of the highest number of working days lost to industrial action in the world, and our strikes rank among the most violent.

On 6 August 2013, Chamber of Mines president Mike Teke acknowledged that the nation was facing an increasing number of strikes and that the duration of the strikes was also lengthening, leading to greater impacts on companies and employees.[58] Strike action is also often not just an outlet for workers' frustration, but also of citizens' frustration at continued poor service delivery and difficult living conditions.[59]

Marikana

By far the worst incident involving union activity in the period post 1994 took place at a platinum mine owned by Lonmin in the Marikana area close to Rustenburg in North West in August 2012. The issues at stake were a growing disparity in earnings between management and workers, dissatisfaction with poor living and working conditions for the workers, and the migrant labour system in general. Rock drill operators were at the centre of the protests.

There seems to be an unfortunate perception in South Africa that unless strikes are accompanied by violence, nothing will be achieved. The drama at Marikana started as a wildcat strike,[60] but developed into a series of violent incidents between the South African Police Service, Lonmin security and the leadership of the National Union of Mineworkers (NUM) on the one side, and the strikers on the other.

The striking miners believed NUM was siding with Lonmin management and were outdated in their negotiating approach. There was also growing inter-union rivalry between NUM and the Association of Mineworkers and Construction Union (AMCU). The violence at Marikana continued for several days and led to the deaths of 44 people, 39 of whom were striking miners. A worker who was not striking, as well as two Lonmin security guards and two policemen were also killed, and at least 78 people were injured.

Marikana was the worst massacre committed by South African police since Sharpeville some 50 years before.[61] There were some 718 policemen at the scene, and about 3 000 striking miners; the police defended their actions by saying the miners had become a dangerously frenzied mob, and they feared for their lives. Nevertheless, some of the striking miners had been shot in the back as they were trying to run away. President Zuma also initially defended police action by saying the striking miners had become killers[62] and that harsh action had to be taken. His words were reminiscent of what Jan Smuts had said about white striking miners in 1922: Smuts justified police action on that occasion by saying there was madness in their (the strikers') blood.[63]

The massacre at Marikana led to a further wave of wildcat strikes on mines, particularly the gold and coal sectors across South Africa, and attracted worldwide attention. The aggregate losses to the mining industry reached some R15.3 billion, and some R7 billion was lost in workers' wages, compared with the R1 billion recorded in 2011.[64]

After a long process, it was decided that the police had to shoulder most of the blame because they had acted before the striking miners had been given a chance to discard their weapons, but it was also concluded that none of the policemen could be charged with murder: the bullets they had used disintegrated when entering the victims' bodies, making it impossible to determine who had fired them.[65] Families of the deceased and injured were left frustrated with the results, and it was anticipated that it would take several years for individual cases to be heard and compensation paid.

NUM lost out heavily over Marikana. Once the largest union in the country, by June 2016 it had lost 40% of its members, many of whom had joined the rival union, AMCU.[66] In June 2016 it was reported that COSATU was similarly in decline, with less than 30 per cent of South Africa's work force unionised.[67] This spells disaster for the working class because apart from the benefits of belonging to trade unions for individual employees, unions should be presenting a united campaign against unfair labour practices.

There is real concern that ordinary people have not benefited enough from the new democracy. In June 2015, deputy minister of public works and SACP general secretary Jeremy Cronin said the main beneficiaries of South Africa's hard-earned democracy have not been the workers, but the capitalists. In the 1970s and 1980s, he said, capitalists were adversely affected by sanctions against South Africa because of apartheid, but all that has now gone and monopoly capital is flourishing. He has urged mine owners and the government to improve conditions for workers, especially for migrant workers. 'Not only is this a democratic right,' he said, 'it is also directly linked to re-building worker unity and effective trade union organisation.'[68] The previous year, on 6 August 2014, Chamber of Mines president Mike Teke had said that mining companies were undertaking 'a lot' of initiatives and injecting hundreds of millions of rands to ensure the well-being of their workers, but that the challenges were too big for a company to face alone.[69]

One of the biggest obstacles to unionisation is the growing casualisation of the workforce. The number of informal workers is growing and is difficult to protect. In 2015, it was estimated that over 5 million workers were employed under limited or unspecified contracts. Domestic workers and farm workers were among the most vulnerable and hard to organise.

Hope seemed to be on the horizon when a workers' summit was held on 30 April 2016, attended by 1 406 representatives of 51 unions, in an attempt to form a kind of union federation to address these and other issues pertaining to labour practices. The general secretary of NUM, Irvin Jim, said the time had come for action: the new federation needed to do more than simply write good articles and make fine speeches; union officials needed to leave their offices and see what was happening on the streets; and unions needed to ensure that they were not the mouthpiece of government. The main task of the unions would be to protect the working classes.[70]

CHAPTER 15

Prospects and challenges

The maturing of the ANC

The ANC has been the ruling party in South Africa since 1994, and is one of the oldest liberation movements in the world. It started as the SANNC in 1912, a small elitist organisation[1] with modest demands, but became more aggressive as those demands were ignored. Having survived nearly a century of harassment, bannings and exile, bloodshed and pain, the ANC celebrated its 100th anniversary in 2012.

As first president of the 'new' South Africa after 1994, Nelson Mandela had played a reconciliatory role, and seen the country through a difficult changeover of power. His successor, Thabo Mbeki, also had statesman-like qualities and conducted some successful foreign policy moves, but he was never as popular as Mandela. Nor was Mbeki's successor, Jacob Zuma – although he has always had a large, mainly Zulu following. Under all three presidents, the ANC government has tended to put ideology ahead of practical decisions and efficiency. Their years in either prison or exile made all three men inclined to close ranks and favour former 'comrades' from the struggle, rather than people most suited for important jobs. In 1967, when South Africa was ruled by the NP apartheid government, historian Leo Marquard said that the fundamental mistake of any national party is to confuse the party with the state.[2] His words still apply today under the ANC government.

A sense of entitlement and extravagant spending among some ANC leaders is still prevalent. Thabo Mbeki, addressing students at the Thabo Mbeki

African Leadership Institute in Pretoria, said that the problem of self-enrichment in the ANC was raised as early as the party's 1997 conference in Mafikeng by former president, Nelson Mandela, who 'dedicated time to eradicating the problem'.[3]

Court cases involving senior officials accused of corruption are also generally allowed to drag on at tax payers' expense, and people are not brought to book. Nor are the rules of international law followed: in June 2015, the Sudanese President Omar al-Bashir came to South Africa to attend an AU conference in Sandton. President al-Bashir was wanted by the International Criminal Court for charges of genocide (the deaths of some 300 000 black Africans) and crimes against humanity. He should have been arrested in South Africa, but he was allowed to leave.

The military has also not been an entirely successful story. The South African National Defence Force (SANDF) has been subject to criticism and allegations of corruption, mainly as a result of the controversial arms deal. By 2014, the SANDF was described in the Defence Ministry's Annual Defence Review as being 'in a critical state of decline'.[4] In December 2016, new programmes were announced that should improve the situation: job cuts and retrenchments should trim down the bloated wage bill[5], and the focus will be on maintaining younger and more active personnel. A military skills development system (MSDS) was also introduced: during this two-year voluntary service system, members do basic as well as specific functional training, with the long-term goal of enhancing the SADF's deployment capability.

Other civil service budget cuts have also been announced recently,[6] but it remains to be seen if this will be enough to steer the country out of its economic woes. Criticism continues to be levelled against the ANC for its mismanagement. Under Zuma, the ANC has not progressed from a liberation movement to that of a successfully functioning government.

Nevertheless, for many people the ANC is South Africa. It is the party that delivered South Africa out of a period of darkness and is therefore the one party that can lead the nation. This attitude is not unlike that of Afrikaner nationalists in the 1930s and 1940s: they saw themselves as 'a chosen people'[7] who supported an exclusivist nationalist party ordained by

God. Interestingly, though the ANC claims not to be faith-based, Zuma has said that the ANC will rule until the 'second coming of Christ'.[8]

Until recent times it seemed nothing could shake the ANC's hold on South Africa. The DA, EFF[9] and other fairly young parties did not have the history or the weight behind them to make a real challenge, and the SACP and COSATU have been alliance partners at best. But in 2016, three significant events took place that might well have strong repercussions in the future.

On 30 April 2016, the EEF launched its local government election manifesto at Orlando Stadium in Soweto. The 40 000-capacity stadium was filled with thousands of young people tired of being told about the liberation struggle, and desperate for change. It seemed that South Africa was entering a new era in which no one party could claim dominance. For many of the young people in that stadium, a substantial number of them unemployed, Julius Malema's modern-day socialism policy, although extreme, seemed to offer a better life. One 26-year-old graduate from a technical college summed it up when he spoke of his struggle to get a job. He said he was still being supported by his mother, who was a domestic worker, because he was not well connected to the powers that be. His story is typical of thousands more young people like him[10]: by June 2016, one in four South Africans was unemployed, and half of all young South Africans were without jobs.

The second incident was the local elections in August 2016, when long-held frustrations with the ruling party came to a head. It became clear that the ANC had lost support because of its inability to deal with everyday problems, especially service delivery, health, education, conditions for workers, wage gaps, unemployment and much more. In results that shocked the country, President Zuma's ANC lost three key urban metros as well as his rural homeland of Nkandla to other parties. It was clear that opposition parties, especially the DA and EFF, had gained significantly in support. Cape Town mayor Patricia de Lille and her DA team posted the biggest win of any party in any city, winning more than 66% of the votes. It was also the first time the DA had beaten the ANC by a two-thirds majority. The shock result of Nkandla falling to the IFP in KwaZulu-Natal was evidence that its leader, Mangosuthu Buthelezi, was still very much on the scene. The ANC still held the majority, but it was clearly not as strong as before. It is cause for concern that close to 3.3 million people did not vote, and that key parties fought over Nelson Mandela's legacy and campaigned mainly on the grounds of race.

Tensions in the country had grown, not just because of unemployment, power cuts and other issues mentioned above, but also because of opposition between the ANC and other political parties, and tension within the ANC itself. This led to the third incident – an extraordinary situation on 5 September 2016, when ANC members who opposed President Zuma and his NEC (National Executive Committee) tried to storm Luthuli House, the ANC headquarters in Sauer Street, Johannesburg. Many of these protesters were 'born-free'[11] ANC members,[12] who said they were tired of state looting, corruption and President Zuma's leadership style, which has veered from one scandal to the next. They wanted President Zuma to step down. They were met with fierce resistance from stalwart former MK veterans, women loyal to the ANC, and members of the ANC Youth League. ANCYL president Collen Maine accused the protesters of not being members of any of the structures of the ANC, and therefore not being credible. The chaos lasted four hours, with police heavily in attendance, but little was achieved.

Frederik van Zyl Slabbert, who had played an influential role in the negotiations with the ANC in the late 1980s, made the comment in 1992 that he had never doubted that democracy would eventually come to South Africa. Far more disturbing to him were the expectations that people would have of what a democracy could deliver – that for him was the real burden of democracy.[13]

Many questions remain. Will the 2016 election results herald a meaningful shift of power? Will South Africa see efficient socio-economic development at community level, so that businesses and individuals become empowered to make a real difference to South Africa's overall economy? And will there be better service delivery to take care of the basic needs of South Africans across the board?

Mining

The mining industry worldwide underwent challenges in recent years when it was affected by high volatility of commodity prices and uncertain demand.[14] Big projects soured when metal prices collapsed, and analysts at Investec estimate that billions of dollars were lost.[15] South Africa was inevitably affected, and the local mining industry, once so profitable, faced especially bad times in the three years from 2013 to 2016.

Apart from volatile global issues, South African mines also had problems with electricity supply and rising electricity costs, as well as labour disputes. This resulted in some mines no longer being profitable, and very little exploration for new deposits has been done. At the annual mining indaba held in Cape Town in February 2017, however, leaders in the mining industry commented that there was hope on the horizon: the price of gold had recovered and cost cuts were taking effect; there was also a resurgence of exploration to counter the fact that the lifespan of current mines' assets was getting shorter.[16]

In the long term, it is anticipated that increased technology will create the possibility of mining at ever greater depths. In August 2015, AngloGold Ashanti reported that 48 holes had been drilled as deep as 5 kilometres into the earth, and that samples confirmed that there were gold deposits that far down. Although this news in encouraging, advanced technology has implications for employability as human labour will increasingly be replaced by mechanisation.[17]

Also speaking at the mining indaba in Cape Town, Minister of Trade and Industry, Dr Rob Davies, warned against the oversupply of a commodity like steel by the major producers around the world. This, he said, was an example of the negative effect of globalisation. He believed this could be countered by revitalizing manufacturing and fast-tracking market integration in Africa. There needed to be more collaboration between the mining and manufacturing sectors, measures which would also create work opportunities and close the inequality (wage distribution) gap.[18] But former president, Thabo Mbeki, who was also present at the conference, was skeptical. He commented that an African Mining Vision (AMV) had been adopted by all 54 African countries at the AU in 2009 in anticipation of cooperation between the private and public sector. He was not convinced this was being realised.[19]

The mining industry employs some 460 000 people and contributes about

8% directly to South Africa's GDP,[20] but more needs to be done, especially in the field of job creation. Symptomatic of the dire straits some people find themselves in are the stories of the zama zamas.[21] These illegal miners go into disused mines, like Langlaagte in the south of Johannesburg, at great risk in search of ore containing gold. The men and sometimes young boys live underground for days or weeks on end without seeing daylight, saying that if they find a promising area they dare not leave it because rivals will move in. Stabbings and deaths from rival groups are a regular occurrence, and there are problems with ventilation in these dangerous old mines, as well as the constant risk of rock falls. Despite efforts by the police to stop them, the number of zama zamas is growing.

Agriculture

Issues regarding agriculture are a bit more positive. Most of South Africa's food needs are still supplied by white commercial farmers, but since the repeal of the Land Acts in June 1991, the number of black farmers is increasing, and government has been working towards redistributing land that was appropriated from black farmers in the early years. Schemes are also afoot to develop small-scale farming, although there is still a long way to go.

It is also anticipated that South Africa will be able to sell more agricultural produce, especially wine and fruit, to the United Kingdom once it leaves the EU because the UK will no longer have the same objections from other European countries to trade with South Africa. South Africa and Spain are major suppliers of oranges and other citrus fruits globally, but South African exports have in the past been regularly blocked because of competition from Spain.[22]

Climate change

Like the rest of the world, South Africa is affected by climate change.[23] South Africa follows the Kyoto Protocol, which asks countries to limit their greenhouse gas emissions, especially in the waste and transport sectors. The country is also poised to conserve and use energy efficiently and undertake sustainable forms of agriculture where possible. The implementation of a carbon tax to reduce emissions has been suggested, but this has not currently proven a successful alternative.[24] The largest contributor to carbon emission is the burning of fossil fuels, but at present there are few alternatives and those that are available are expensive.

On the horizon is the creation of 'fuel cells' that will use platinum as a catalyst rather than carbon. Africa's first fuel-cell component plant using platinum will start production in December 2017 either in Johannesburg or Durban. As South Africa is the world's top platinum producer, with the largest reserves of the metal,[25] the success of the plant could be an important breakthrough; it would also boost the mining industry and be a source of much-needed job creation.

Education

In January 2016, South Africa's Education Minister, Angie Motshekga, admitted that South Africa's education system, which should be the answer to the devastating unemployment situation, was in crisis.[26] In 2016, South Africa's education ranked only eighth out of 15 African countries.[27]

In October 2015, serious student protests arose over the proposed increase in university fees. In Johannesburg on 22 October thousands of students from the University of the Witwatersrand (Wits) and the University of Johannesburg (UJ) marched to the ANC headquarters, Luthuli House, in the Johannesburg CBD to hand over a memorandum, and in Cape Town, university students stormed the parliamentary precinct.[28] Student protests began again at the beginning of the academic year in 2016, and again in August, September and October of that year. By then, students were demanding not just a reduction in fees, but a no-fees policy. The protests also opened heated discussions around the decolonisation of university curricula,[29] lack of transformation in the promotion of black academics, and issues around student housing. The protests at universities in 2015 and 2016 caused an estimated half a billion rands in damages to libraries and buildings, and have been described as the most significant disuption of the country's education system since the uprising in Soweto in 1976.

DA spokeswoman for higher education, Professor Belinda Bozzoli, commented that the government should have seen this coming: there had been a decline in student subsidies in real terms, and this concern had been raised in parliament many times. The DA felt millions of rands could be redirected to higher education if the cabinet was reduced from 33 to 15 members, and if some government departments were closed altogether. The EFF has also continuously reminded government of shortcomings in education and has called for action. A number of non-governmental organisations have also played an important role.

Many see the legacy of colonialism as the reason for many of the problems in education, and the call for decolonisation has become an increasingly important element of transformation. It is not just a matter of changing the names of buildings and removing statues associated with colonialism, says Professor Emeritus George Devenish: it also involves a process of renewal of educational institutions that impacts curricula, course content, language and management. This does not mean that Western scholarship must be abandoned, but rather reinterpreted from an African perspective. This will take time, he adds, and must not be confused with radical racial agendas; it should be done within the framework of universal human rights and non-racialism.[30]

Trade within Africa

The South African economy is only expected to grow by 1.3% in 2017 and by 2% in 2018.[31] Since the inauguration of a populist president, Donald Trump in the United States in January 2017, there has been concern that developing economies are at risk of capital flight: President Trump made it clear in his pre-election campaign that he intends to place the United States first, suggesting less aid for developing economies. A similar kind of inward-looking nationalism is becoming evident in some European countries since Brexit.[32]

But since South Africa's admission to BRICS in 2010,[33] there has been more urgent discussion about improving trade opportunities within Africa itself. As far back as 2002 and 2003, then president Thabo Mbeki said there needed to be more integration and free movement of goods within Africa, and he was instrumental in the formation of the African Union (AU)[34] in 2001 to that end.[35] On 5 June 2015, former prime minister of Britain and chairman of the World Economic Forum (WEF), Gordon Brown, told forum delegates that Africa's growth could be 2% higher if it solved its infrastructure problems. 'Africa has great mineral resources, great uncultivated farmland and a population of young people who want to work,' he said, 'but we have to find a way to speed things up.'[36]

On 27 January 2017, the AU commissioner for economic affairs, Anthony Mothae Maruping, and the AU commissioner for trade and industry, Fatima Haram Acyl, said that the productive capacities of the 54 countries of Africa needed to be strengthened and diversified, and 'the mindset needs to change from thinking as individual countries to that of Pan African'. Events in other parts of the world, they added, have left Africa's countries no choice but to integrate to attract investment.[37] At the mining indaba in Cape Town in February 2017, Thabo Mbeki reminded delegates that this kind of African vision had been discussed as far back as 2009, but little had been achieved. It was time to go forward.

In the 1990s, South Africa enjoyed 'soft power' on the world stage as a result of the iconic Nelson Mandela, but this has been in decline, as has our real political and economic influence. If more trade within Africa could be achieved, and if it could happen quickly, South Africa could also play a more significant role in BRICS, and the economy would benefit.

But will this happen and when?

Implications of the last 20 years of democratically elected presidents

Leading political commentator Justice Malala says that there is much analysis of South Africa's problems, but few solutions are offered. The debates still centre mainly around race and equality. In South Africa, he says, a majority liberation movement is in power, and with that power they should be able to formulate policies that begin to solve our problems.[38] We have one of the most democratic constitutions in the world, but sluggishness and inefficiency, and the way the values of the constitution and the rule of law are manipulated remain a cause for concern.

In 1977, during the worst of the apartheid years, Emeritus Fellow of Magdalen College, Oxford, RW Johnson published a book called *How Long Will South Africa Survive?* Now, after more than 20 years of ANC rule, he feels the question must be posed again. Yes, apartheid is over, he says, but our economy is in a dire state and we need a change in regime. The big question about ANC rule, Johnson adds, is whether African nationalism which elsewhere conquered only poorer agrarian economies can cope with the challenges of running a modern industrial economy. The last 20 years have shown that the ANC is ill-equipped for the task and South Africa is slipping backward. In his opinion, South Africa can either choose to have an ANC government or it can have a modern industrial economy. It cannot have both.[39]

What South Africans can do, Professor Jonathan Jansen proposes, is use our vote rather than vote for the same people over and over and then complain when the job does not get done. Our vote is a powerful weapon, he says – we must use it.[40] Justice Malala concurs: saying that we must vote for delivery, not history.[41]

In 1967 Leo Marquard, prophesied that if the ruling party did not adapt to the changing circumstances in South Africa, he was afraid that South Africa would sink into oblivion, a classic example of a multiracial society that failed. He ended by quoting Dryden: 'There seems yet to be room for compromise; hereafter there may only be pity'.[42] Fifty years later, the circumstances have changed but Marquard's words still ring true, and once again we are reminded of the old adage that the more things appear to change, the more they stay the same.

Postscript

The old adage that it is the people who make a country is as true of our country as anywhere else. Our people have generally remained resilient and resourceful throughout the traumas of the past and the challenges of the present, and many have achieved great things despite the odds against them.

The gap between the haves and have nots remains impossibly high.[1] Opulent, spacious homes in areas like Sandton in outer Johannesburg are barely six kilometres away from crowded townships like Alexandra, where chickens and cow heads are sold along the roads and shacks and small houses have been built right onto the pavements to use the space available. But South Africans are generally warm-hearted, friendly people and a typical greeting is accompanied by the question: How are you?

Most of our people are still a fascinating combination of the 'old' and the 'new'. We carry the traces of our diverse ancestors as well as the changing modern environment in which we live. Jacob Zuma, for example, wears mostly Western suits but changes to traditional clothes when addressing meetings of traditional leaders in the rural areas; he refers to Christianity, but also still calls on the ancestors,[2] and praise singers were in attendance at his formal inauguration as president.

People from all walks of life have contributed to our story: businessmen like Harry Oppenheimer, Anton Rupert and Patrice Motsepe who have given generously of their personal fortunes to community development; entrepreneurs like Mark Shuttleworth and Elon Musk who have brought recognition to our country with their technological projects; musicians like

Miriam Makeba, Johnny Clegg, Ladysmith Black Mambazo and Mango Groove, whose African rhythms and harmonies fascinated the world; and cartoonists, satirists and comedians like Zapiro, Dov Fedler, Rico, Pieter-Dirk Uys and Trevor Noah, whose humour nevertheless exposes the bizarre and often cruel aspects of our past.[3] Much like the San protest artists of the past, these modern people record what is happening in South Africa, play on the consciences of people and help bring about change.

South Africans generally love to laugh, and they can laugh at themselves; despite the clandestine nature of much of our past history, some things were always transparent. The satirist, Pieter-Dirk Uys, for example, said he didn't have to look far for material for his shows, our politicians provided it.

We have a history that is complex and full of contradictions. Our population is so diverse that there will always be conflict as well as cooperation and goodwill, but whatever race, culture or religion we come from, there will always be links between us, based on the shared experiences of being South African.

Notes

Introduction

1 Adapted from a comment by Ian van der Waag in *A Military History of Modern South Africa*, Jonathan Ball Publishers, Johannesburg & Cape Town, 2015, p2.
2 Archbishop Emeritus Desmond Tutu coined the term 'rainbow nation' to describe South Africa's multiracial society.
3 Alan Parks, Senior Manager of Technical Support and Training at Johannesburg City Parks, https://joburg.org.za.
4 Basutoland had been a British Crown Colony since 1884, due to the Cape Colony's apparent inability to control the territory.
5 The name Lesotho roughly translates as 'land of the people who speak Sesotho'.
6 Swaziland had become a protectorate, which approximated to Crown Colony status, in the 1880s. The British had decided that some form of control was necessary because the king, Mbandezi, had been granting concessions of land, grazing and mineral rights to European entrepreneurs.
7 See *The Star*, 26 August 2016. *The Times*, 31 October 2012, gives the suggested breakdown.
8 From Statistics South Africa, http://www.statssa.gov.za/census/census_2011/census_products/Census_2011_Census_in_brief.pdf. These were the latest figures available at the time of going to print.
9 In this book I use the racial categories 'white', 'black' (or African) and 'coloured' not because I subscribe to biological opinions on race but because these racial 'identities' assumed considerable importance in South African history and are understood in this context. The terms are not meant to be derogatory. It should also be noted that all black people – the San, Khoikhoi, and black farmers who came later (between AD 300 and AD 900, possibly earlier) – can be described as indigenous as they arrived in South Africa centuries before white immigrants.
10 The correct ethnic terms are isiZulu, isiXhosa, Sepedi, Sesotho, Setswana, Siswati, Tshivenda and Xitsonga.
11 From Statistics South Africa, http://www.statssa.gov.za/census/census_2011/census_products/Census_2011_Census_in_brief.pdf. These were the latest figures available at the time of going to print.

12 See Jonathan Jansen, *The Times*, 5 June 2015.
13 The queenship of the Balobedu tribe in Limpopo dates back to the 1800s, when Maselekwane Modjadji became the first queen, commonly called the Rain Queen. On 31 March 2016, President Jacob Zuma gave official recognition to this position in terms of the Traditional Leadership and Governance Framework Act. The queen, Masalanabo Modjadji, is currently only 11 years old. She will be crowned when she turns 18. Her uncle meanwhile acts as regent. See *The Times*, 30 May 2016.
14 See Tom Eaton, *The Times*, 13 October 2015.
15 'Apartheid' means apartness or separation.

Chapter 1 How it all began

1 For years scientists have referred to the 'missing link', but Wits professor and paleoanthropologist Lee Berger says the term is misleading because it implies a chain of evolution, whereas he prefers the concept of branches. He nevertheless agrees that this skull represents a transitional stage. See Prega Govender, *Sunday Times*, 11 April 2010.
2 Adapted from an interview with Professor Clarke by Heather Dugmore, *The Star*, 16 October 2006.
3 Ibid. The delay in removing the whole skeleton could also be due to a gentleman's agreement among archaeologists that a site is never completely excavated: part must be left for future archaeologists with superior technology.
4 Adapted from *The Star*, 10 September 2015, and *The Times*, 11 September 2015. Articles by Angelique Serrao, Shaun Smillie and Katharine Child.
5 See Tanya Farber, *Sunday Times*, 24 April 2016.
6 See Shula Marks and Anthony Atmore, quoted in William Kelleher Storey, *Guns, Race, and Power in Colonial South Africa*, Cambridge University Press, Cambridge, 2008, p1.

Chapter 2 Early settlers from about 1000 BC to AD 1500

1 The origin of this name is uncertain, but the term 'San' is still used in the Nama language to describe hunter-gatherers. The derivation of the word is 'sa', which means 'to inhabit' and suggests that it refers to the San as the original inhabitants of southern Africa. Nama is one of the few surviving languages of herders; it is still spoken in parts of South Africa, Botswana and Namibia. Adapted from Christopher Saunders, ed., *An Illustrated Dictionary of South African History*, Ibis Books, Sandton, 1994, p208.
2 Partly adapted from https://en.wikipedia.org/wiki/Khoikhoi-Dutch_Wars.
3 Bantu languages are interrelated and spoken over a large area of Africa, from the southern part of Cameroon, eastwards to Kenya and southwards to the southernmost tip of Africa.
4 Click sounds are produced by an ingressive stream of air when the tongue is drawn sharply away from the roof of the mouth.
5 The term 'Bantu', when used to refer to black people, is regarded as offensive nowadays because it is associated with the discriminatory laws of the apartheid era.
6 Interview with Sian Tiley-Nel, Curator, Mapungubwe Museum, University of Pretoria, 13 November 2015.
7 Soldering is a process by which two pieces of metal are melted and then joined together with a filler metal that has a lower melting point.

8 The time period of 200 years is accepted by most historians, but Professor André Meyer from the Department of Archaeology, University of Pretoria, believes the period was shorter than that – possibly only about 60 to 80 years, because the onset of a mini Ice Age made agricultural conditions impossible for such a large number of people. Information taken from Franz Kruger, *Sunday Times*, 27 February 2000.
9 Amulets are little objects believed to protect the wearer from harm.
10 Smelted gold means gold extracted from the ore using extreme heat.
11 Dry-stone walling refers to stones fitted together without wet mortar or anything resembling cement.
12 Anita Allen, *The Star*, 7 August 1996. 'Thulamela' is a Venda word meaning 'place of giving birth'.
13 See http://www.sahistory.org.za/article/kingdoms-southern-africa-thulamela.
14 Interview with archaeologist John van Ewyk, Cape Town, December 2004.
15 HM Friede, 'Notes on the composition of pre-European copper and copper-alloy artefacts from the Transvaal', *Journal of the South African Institute of Mining and Metallurgy*, February 1975, pp187–188.
16 Gail Nattrass, *The Rooiberg Story, 75 Years: 19 May 1908–1983*, Gold Fields of South Africa, 1983.
17 Ibid. The handwritten records were destroyed in a fire, but in 1981 the author spoke to Anneci van Rensburg and Hans Beukes, who farmed in the area of Rooiberg and who saw them at the time.
18 *Mining Weekly*, 2 April 2014; interview with Tim Williams, Mineral Resources Management Executive at Metorex, Johannesburg, 15 September 2016.
19 'Lobola' is originally a Zulu word, but is commonly used among the Sotho. The Sotho term 'bohali' means 'home of the husband's family, to which cattle, etc., are paid in bride price'. See http://www.mountainvoices.org/l_glossary.html.

Chapter 3 Settlers from out of Africa

1 The Dutch East India Company was considered the largest and most extensive maritime trading company at the time and held a virtual monopoly on strategic European shipping routes westward through the Strait of Magellan, and eastward around the Cape. See https://en.wikipedia.org/wiki/Dutch_Empire.
2 For more about the Slave Wrecks Project, see https://www.slavewrecksproject.org.
3 Malcolm Turner, *Shipwrecks and Salvage in South Africa: from 1505 to the Present*, Struik, 1988, p36; see also Lawrence Green, *Harbours of Memory*, Howard Timmins, Cape Town, 1969, p123.
4 Green, *Harbours of Memory*, p124.
5 Ibid.
6 Ibid.
7 Ibid., pp121–122 & 124.
8 Ibid., p121 & 128. These lighter-skinned people inhabited the area of the Wild Coast around present-day Port St John's in the Eastern Cape; they were clearly the ancestors of liaisons between Portuguese, Dutch, British and Indian castaways with the local Mpondo people from the 16th century onwards. For further reading on these survivors of shipwrecks and the Mpondo people, and the story of a white child named Bessie who grew up with the Mpondo and became something of an African queen, see also Hazel Crampton, *The Sunburnt Queen*,

Jacana Media, Johannesburg, 2004.

9 The Afrikaans word 'trek' means 'move', and 'boer' means 'farmer'.

10 See Map 13 later in this chapter.

11 See Leonard Thompson, *A History of South Africa*, Jonathan Ball Publishers, Johannesburg & Cape Town, 2009, p36.

12 Interview with Katie Jacobs conducted by a journalist for the African People's Organisation (APO) newspaper, 1910: https://slavery.iziko.org.za/katiejacobs. See also Nigel Worden, *The chains that bind us: A history of slavery at the Cape*, Juta, Cape Town, 1996, pp89–91.

13 Ibid.

14 Ibid.

15 Richard Elphick and Hermann Giliomee, eds., *The Shaping of South African Society, 1652–1840*, Maskew Miller Longman, Cape Town, 1990, pp133 & 161.

16 For more about 'black ivory', see Chapter 4.

17 For more on Indian indentured labour, see Chapter 5.

18 Adapted from Tanya Farber, *Sunday Times*, 3 July 2016.

19 William Wilberforce was a Member of Parliament for Yorkshire, a philanthropist and a leader of the movement to abolish the slave trade. He also founded the Royal Society for the Prevention of Cruelty to Animals.

20 There were missionaries from France, the United States and Germany. It does not seem as if the Dutch did any missionary work at this stage.

21 Adapted from Storey, *Guns, Race and Power in Colonial South Africa*, p2.

22 Hermann Giliomee in Hermann Giliomee and Bernard Mbenga, eds., *New History of South Africa*, Tafelberg, Cape Town, 2007, pp59 & 79. These figures were based on the first proper census taken in 1795.

23 MD Nash, 'The 1820 Settlers', in Trewhella Cameron and SB Spies, *A New Illustrated History of South Africa*, Southern Book Publishers, Johannesburg, 1991, p97.

24 Guy Butler, 'The Dispersion and Influence of the 1820 Settlers', in Cameron & Spies, eds., *A New Illustrated History of South Africa*, p100.

25 Port Natal was renamed D'Urban after Sir Benjamin D'Urban, governor of the Cape 1834–1835, on 23 June 1825. It was founded by merchants from the Cape led by British lieutenant FG Farewell, accompanied by Henry Francis Fynn.

26 During the apartheid era, South Africa did not honour the Rule of Law. Section Six of the Terrorism Act, for example, enabled men to be detained without trial. A considerable body of arbitrary (unrestrained) power was exercised by government agents who were responsible to no one.

27 See André Odendaal, *The Story of an African Game: Black Cricketers and the Unmasking of One of Cricket's Greatest Myths, South Africa 1850–2003*, David Philip, Cape Town, 2003, p23.

28 See John Nauright and Charles Parrish, eds., *Sports Around the World: History, Culture and Practice*, ABC-Clio, Santa Barbara, CA, 2012.

29 See Floris JG van der Merwe, 'Rugby in the Prisoner-of-War Camps of the Anglo-Boer War', Department of Human Movement Studies, University of Stellenbosch, April 2016. The prisoner-of-war camps in the Cape were full and at risk of attack, so the decision was made to send some of the prisoners to British possessions like St Helena, Ceylon (Sri Lanka) and Bermuda.

30 See Albert Grundlingh, André Odendaal and SB Spies, *Beyond the Tryline*, Ravan Press, Johannesburg, 1995, pp33 & 89.

31 See Odendaal, *The Story of an African Game*, p32.
32 Ibid.
33 Ibid., p39.
34 *The struggle for the land, South African History Series No. 1, Life on the Land to 1913*, Economic History Research Group, Salt River, no date, p10.
35 The so-called Great Trek of Boers into the interior – see Map 15 in Chapter 4.
36 For further reading on this, see Isaac Schapera, ed., *Apprenticeship at Kuruman: Being the journals and letters of Robert and Mary Moffat 1820–1828*, Chatto & Windus, London, 1951.
37 See 'The Diary of Francis Owen', in John Bird, ed., *The Annals of Natal, Vol 1*, Struik, Cape Town, 1965.

Chapter 4 Migrations within South Africa

1 The Highveld is the high plateau region in the interior of South Africa. It includes most of Gauteng and the northern Free State and parts of Mpumalanga, the North West, the Northern Cape and Limpopo.
2 See Richard Cope, ed., *The Journals of the Rev TL Hodgson: missionary to the Seleka-Rolong and the Griquas, 1821–1831*, Witwatersrand University Press, Johannesburg, 1977, where Hodgson reports on cannibalism among the Rolong. He describes coming across people roasting a human leg and other examples.
3 See JPR Wallis, ed., *The Matabele Journals of Robert Moffat, Vol 1*, Chatto & Windus, London, 1945, pp6–9 & 99–100.
4 See Adulphe Delegorgue, *Voyage dans l'Afrique Australe, Vol 2*, Paris, 1847, quoted in Norman Etherington, *The Great Treks*, Pearson, Cape Town, 2001, p299.
5 See http://www.sahistory.org.za/article/zulu.
6 This was a system whereby both young men and women were put into regiments according to age. Women performed labour tasks for the king and men were in the military. Marriage was forbidden until the men had served time in the army and 'washed their spears in blood'.
7 Nathaniel Isaacs, *Travels and Adventures in Eastern Africa, Descriptive of the Zoolus, their Manners, Customs, etc. etc. with a Sketch of Natal*, revised and edited by Louis Herman and Percival R Kirby, Struik, Cape Town, 1970, p148. Isaacs uses the spelling 'Chaka'.
8 'The diary of Anna Steenkamp' in Bird, ed., *The Annals of Natal, Vol 1*. Anna recorded that her faithful female slave had run away during the night because she had heard the Zulus were coming.
9 Adrienne Sichel, *The Star*, 17 May 1995.
10 Basotho is the ethnic term. It refers to members of the Sotho community.
11 Giliomee & Mbenga, eds., *New History of South Africa*, p131.
12 This refers to people who sought his protection and/or services.
13 Saunders, ed., *An Illustrated Dictionary of South African History*, p178 gives his estimated kingdom as between 60 000 and 80 000 people.
14 'Bergenaars' means 'mountain people', and they were a branch of the Griqua. The Bergenaars, Griqua, Korana and Kora were all mixed-race descendents of the Khoikhoi.
15 Philippolis is the oldest town in the Free State province. It was founded for the Khoisan in 1823 by the London Missionary Society. In 1826, a group of Griqua under the leadership of Adam Kok III settled there and stayed until about 1862, when they moved to what is now Kokstad. Many of the old houses at Philippolis have been declared national monuments.

16 Sun City is a holiday resort with casinos, golf courses and hotels. It is in North West, about 200km from Johannesburg and Pretoria.
17 This battle led to the story of Thaba Nchu that is described later in this chapter. 'Voortrekkers' (meaning people who move/trek forwards) is the name given to groups of Dutch/Afrikaners who migrated into the interior from the eastern Cape.
18 See Vincent Carruthers, *The Magaliesberg*, Southern Book Publishers, Johannesburg, 1990, p238.
19 See Wallis, ed., *The Matabele Journals of Robert Moffat, Vol 1*, pp95, 97 & 143.
20 Ibid., p368.
21 See CJ Beyers, ed., *Dictionary of South African Biography (DSAB), Vol 4*, Butterworth and Co, Durban and Pretoria, 1981, p390. One of Mzilikazi's favourites was the hunter Henry Hartley, who also brought the German geologist Karl Mauch to investigate gold-mining prospects in Zimbabwe.
22 Sorghum is a tall, coarse grass similar to corn, but with better resistance to drought. It was known historically as 'kaffir corn'.
23 See Beyers, ed., *DSAB, Vol 1*, p562. Today's Lesotho was formerly known as Basutoland.
24 See Etherington, *The Great Treks*, p320.
25 Adapted from Thompson, *A History of South Africa*, p77.
26 Giliomee & Mbenga, eds., *New History of South Africa*, p177.
27 Ibid., p112.
28 See Tim Couzens, ed., Sol T Plaatje, *Mhudi*, Francolin Press, Sefika Series, Cape Town, 1996, pp409–410.
29 It was believed that witches on broomsticks would circle an area overhead before swooping in.
30 Jacob Hlambamanzi had been imprisoned for stealing cattle in the Cape. He then accompanied surveying expeditions in Natal before ending up at Shaka's kraal. He had learnt English and acted as interpreter for whites, as well as for Shaka first and later Dingane. He also accompanied delegations to the Cape on Dingane's behalf.
31 A laager was a typical way of arranging wagons in an oval shape for the purposes of protection. Branches of trees and other reinforcements would be put between the wagons, and animals would be kept in the middle. Today one hears of a 'laager mentality': when people close ranks and withdraw into a protective mode.
32 BJ Liebenberg, 'Mites rondom Bloedrivier en die Gelofte', paper presented at the SAHJ conference, University of Pretoria, 21–22 January 1988, p13.
33 Ibid.
34 The Venda are descendants of the people at Thulamela (see Chapter 2). Archaeological and linguistic evidence suggests that they absorbed a number of immigrant Shona groups from Zimbabwe, and that a large, clearly identifiable Venda state existed in the area around Schoemansdal by the early 18th century, if not before.
35 Interview with Dirk de Witt at the Schoemansdal site, September 1994.
36 Tsetse refers to a dreaded parasitic disease commonly called sleeping sickness and caused by the blood-sucking tsetse flies that inhabited much of rural sub-Saharan Africa.
37 Mphaya Nemudzivhadi, 'The conflict between the Mphephu and the South African Republic, 1895–1899', unpublished MA thesis, 1977, p17.
38 Other Voortrekker towns include Potchefstroom, Lydenburg, Origstad and Pretoria.
39 Paul Kruger would later become president of the ZAR (Transvaal) in 1883.
40 Interview with Dirk de Witt at the Schoemansdal site, September 1994.

41 Sidney Miller and Johann Templehoff, 'The Romance of a Frontier', *Fauna and Flora*, No 47, Transvaal Directorate of Nature and Environmental Conservation, 1990, p34.
42 Peter Delius, *The Land Belongs to Us: The Pedi Polity, the Boers and the British in the Nineteenth Century Transvaal*, Ravan Press, Johannesburg, 1983, pp138–140.

Chapter 5 The mineral discoveries

1 In 1981, West Driefontein merged with the eastern part of the mine to become Driefontein Consolidated.
2 Ed Prior, BBC News, quoting Thomson Reuters GFMS, World Gold Council Annual Gold Survey, 1 April 2013.
3 Today, no single country supplies more than 14% of the world's gold. In 2010, China was still the largest producer with 13%, followed closely by Australia with 10%, the United States with 9%, and both Russia and South Africa with 8%. See http://www.goldsheetlinks.com/goldhist.htm and 'The Evolving Structure of Gold Demand and Supply', Bloomberg, LBMA, Thomson Reuters GFMS, World Gold Council, p9. This information was made available by Russell and Associates, in conjunction with the Chamber of Mines, on 16 December 2016.
4 In diamond weights, a single carat is equivalent to 0.2 grams.
5 In 1980, Western countries, especially in North America and Europe, accounted for a combined share of 56% of the global gold market. This had fallen to 14% by 2010, whereas the share bought by India and East Asia had risen from 22% in 1980 to 66% in 2010. See 'The Evolving Structure of Gold Demand and Supply', p3, Russell and Associates in conjunction with the Chamber of Mines, 16 December 2016.
6 Interviews with Minette Jacobs, financial planning consultant, Alexander Forbes, Sandown, 28 October 2015, and Derrick Willcock, CEO of Micromation, Johannesburg, 15 December 2016.
7 Ian Phimister, 'Frenzied Finance: Gold mining in the globalising south, c. 1886–1896', in B Mountford and S Tuffnell, eds., *A Global History c.1848–1910*, Oxford, 2017, forthcoming publication.
8 Jan Smuts quoted by Mark Irvine, *Arena*, April 1996, p2.
9 Business Report, *The Star*, 29 April 2016.
10 For further reading on this, see Brian Roberts, *Kimberley: Turbulent City*, David Phillip, Cape Town, 1976.
11 To annex a territory means to add that territory to one's own territory by appropriation.
12 A bi-plane is an airplane with two sets of wings, one above and usually slightly forward of the other. This particular aircraft was named after the British aircraft designer Crompton Paterson, who established the South African Aviation Corps in Kimberley and trained the first South African pilots.
13 It has not been possible to identify this woman beyond identifying the house where she lived in Bulawayo; interview with Vic Jansen (who visited the house), Carletonville, 8 May 1972.
14 A hole in the septum (the wall that separates the heart's left and right side) is commonly called a 'hole in the heart'. It causes oxygen-rich blood to mix with oxygen-poor blood, and affects breathing. It is a birth defect that can correct itself over time, but is otherwise quite easily corrected nowadays with surgery.
15 Young women can now also qualify for these scholarships.
16 Dineo Faku, Business Report, *The Star*, 2 December 2015. Diamonds with a touch of blue in them are formed when boron is mixed with carbon when the gem is created.

17 The story follows the adventures of a puppy, Jock, who was the runt of a litter and about to be drowned in a bucket before being saved by Percy FitzPatrick. It has been reprinted many times in several languages. The book was made into a movie in 1986, and featured the music of Johnny Clegg and South African actors and actresses, notably Jonathan Rands as Percy FitzPatrick. The movie did not prove popular with American audiences, primarily due to its sad ending; a fictional version with a more palatable ending was released in 1995.
18 Charles van Onselen, *Studies in the social and economic history of the Witwatersrand 1886–1914, Vol 1: New Babylon, Vol 2: New Nineveh*, Ravan Press, Johannesburg, 1982, p2.
19 Gwen Watkins, writing on the 130th anniversary of Johannesburg, *The Star*, 3 October 2016.
20 Charles van Onselen discussing his latest book, *Showdown at the Red Lion: The Life and Times of Jack McLoughlin, 1859–1910*, in the *Sunday Times*, 29 May 2016.
21 Giliomee & Mbenga, eds., *New History of South Africa*, p149.
22 For more reading on Mohandas Gandhi, see Eric Itzkin, *Gandhi's Johannesburg*, Witwatersrand University Press in association with MuseumAfrica, Johannesburg, 2000.
23 Libby Husemeyer, 'Johannesburg – One Hundred Years', *Mining Survey, Vol 2* (4), 1986, p7.
24 Giliomee & Mbenga, eds., *New History of South Africa*, p190.
25 Charles van Onselen, *The Fox and the Flies: The World of Joseph Silver, Racketeer and Psychopath*, Jonathan Cape, London, 2007, p151.
26 Van Onselen, *New Nineveh*, pp11 & 46.
27 Van Onselen, *New Babylon*, pp16 & 112. 'Frenchfontein' was the area between Bree Street in the north, Anderson Street in the south, Kruis Street in the east and Sauer Street in the west, where there were some 95 brothels. Van Onselen cautions that some of the women labelled 'French' were French-speaking but not necessarily from France – there were also German and other nationalities and coloured prostitutes from the Cape.
28 Van Onselen, *New Babylon*, pxv, and a guest lecture at the School of Education at Wits, June 1982.
29 Ibid., p7.
30 Olive Schreiner to Edward Carpenter, Johannesburg, 13 November 1898, quoted in Van Onselen, *The Fox and the Flies*, p145; see also p159.
31 See Van Onselen, *The Fox and the Flies*.
32 It has lost this position now, and is ranked about third. China is the first (October 2015).
33 Interview with Professor Ian Phimister, University of the Free State, 18 December 2016.
34 The gold price is determined twice each business day (at 10h30 and 15h00) on the London Bullion Market (LBMA). This provides a rate that is used as a benchmark for pricing the majority of gold products throughout the world's markets.
35 See Robert Kubicek, 'Finance capital and the South African gold mining industry 1886–1914', *Journal of Imperial and Commonwealth History, Vol 3* (3), May 1975, p386 onwards.
36 Luli Callinicos, *A People's History of South Africa, Vol 1: Gold and Workers; Vol 2: Working Life*, Witwatersrand University Press, Johannesburg, 1994, p71.
37 Elaine Katz, *The White Death: Silicosis on the South African Gold Mines 1886–1910*, Witwatersrand University Press, Johannesburg, 1994.
38 East Coast fever affected livestock. The disease originated from Rhodesia in 1901.
39 '"Mduduma": A migrant worker's story', adapted from Callinicos, *Working Life*, p35. The bride wealth he refers to was the customary lobola a man had to pay for a bride. This was usually in cattle, paid to the bride's father.
40 In rural areas, women traditionally did the agricultural work, but men looked after the cattle and other animals; this herding work would then have to be done by young boys.

41 Callinicos, *Gold and Workers*, p73.
42 Elaine Katz, 'Revisiting the origins of the industrial colour bar in the Witwatersrand gold mining industry, 1891–1899', *Journal of Southern African Studies, Vol* 25 (1), March 1999, p73.

Chapter 6 The decline of the African chiefdoms and the rural areas

1 The Fingo were a branch of the Xhosa. Fingoland was the name given to the territory where they lived: it was in the south-west portion of what is now the Eastern Cape.
2 Land in rural areas was 'owned' by chiefs who allocated land to their subjects; when the British annexed these areas, large sections were opened up for white farming, which reduced the amount of land left for black farmers.
3 The Korana were also a pastoral people but distinct from other Khoikhoi groups because they had their own language. By 1932, they had virtually died out. See also the section on Mzilikazi in Chapter 4.
4 The other British High Commission Territories were Swaziland, which gained independence in 1968, and the Bechuanaland Protectorate (now Botswana), which became independent in 1966.
5 For more on the Griqua, see Chapter 4.
6 See Map 16 in Chapter 5.
7 For more on the Difaqane, see Chapter 4.
8 See Map 16 of the diamond-fields dispute in Chapter 5. The map also shows Stellaland and Goshen, which even had their own flags at one time.
9 See Giliomee & Mbenga, eds., *New History of South Africa*, p173.
10 Dinuzulu is the preferred spelling; Dinizulu is the colonial version.
11 Theophilus Shepstone was later knighted for his services in South Africa in 1876.
12 This gave the impression that Cetshwayo had a standing army, which was not completely true. It nevertheless made him seem like a threat, and was used against him.
13 British central government.
14 For more reading on this, see Richard Cope, *Ploughshare of War: The Origins of the Anglo-Zulu War of 1879*, University of Natal Press, Pietermaritzburg, 1999.
15 The British troops were also referred to as the 1st Battalion, 24th Foot. Statistics estimated from http://www.britishbattles.com/zulu-war/isandlwana.htm and Saunders, ed., *An Illustrated Dictionary of South African History*.
16 Martini-Henry rifles were breech-loading, single shot, lever-activated rifles first introduced in 1871 and used by the British army throughout the British Empire for the next 30 years. They were the best in the world at the time, despite their limitations.
17 This story was told to me on 15 July 2008 at Isandlwana by a Zulu guide trained by the late David Rattray, the distinguished specialist historian of the Anglo-Zulu War.
18 For more reading on this, see Ian Knight, *Zulu Rising: The Epic Story of iSandlwana and Rorke's Drift*, Pan Macmillan, Johannesburg, 2010.
19 Ibid.
20 Ian Knight, *The National Army Museum Book of the Zulu War*, Pan Books, 2004
21 Ibid.
22 The distance between Ulundi and Isandlwana is approximately 102 kilometres.
23 Ibid.
24 Frank Emery, *The Red Soldier: The Zulu War 1879*, Hodder and Stoughton, London, 1977. This quote inspired the book.

25 John William Colenso (1814–1883) was the first Anglican Bishop of Natal. His wife, Frances Colenso, wrote letters back to their sons and friends in England and have become an important historical source.
26 Jeff Guy, *The Destruction of the Zulu Kingdom: The Civil War in Zululand 1879–1884*, Ravan Press, Johannesburg, 1982, p130.
27 In the mid-1850s, Cetshwayo had been head of a young Zulu group known as the Usuthu; these people were still his main supporters.
28 For more on Dinuzulu in the Second Anglo-Zulu War, see Chapter 7.
29 An 'induna' is a kind of headman or overseer, often an adviser to the chief.
30 The 2/24 regiment was based in Brecon in South Wales, although very few of the men in the regiment were actually Welsh. Nevertheless, the image of Welshmen fighting at Isandlwana persists, and descendants of those soldiers still visit the battle site.
31 Teignmouth Melvill and Nevill Coghill are buried on a farm belonging to the family of David Rattray. They were the first two British soldiers to be posthumously awarded the VC (Victoria Cross) for their gallant conduct.
32 Emery's book *The Red Soldier* is based on the letters these men wrote home. See, for example, p101.
33 David Downe, *Isandhlwana and all that*, Serendip, Lyme Regis, 1980.
34 In the ritual of 'pig', a soldier would run through the barracks while the others gave chase. The practice was meant to build team spirit.
35 Gerald French, *Lord Chelmsford and the Zulu War*, The Bodley Head, London, 1939, p144.
36 These are those who supported the Bonaparte claim to the throne.
37 A pretender is an aspirant or claimant to a throne that has been abolished, suspended or occupied by another. Since 1999, the Bonaparte pretender has been Jean Christophe, a direct descendant of Napoleon's youngest brother, Jerome Bonaparte. He also has a Bourbon mother.
38 For more issues affecting the Pedi, see Delius, *The Land Belongs to Us*.
39 Redwater fever is a usually deadly disease borne by ticks; cattle suffering from it are generally seen lying on the ground, grinding their teeth and involuntarily moving their legs.
40 Rinderpest is a viral disease that affects cattle as well as buffalo, wildebeest, giraffe, warthog and other animals. It is closely related to measles and canine distemper. There have been regular outbreaks of rinderpest in South African history, but in 2011 the United Nations Food and Agriculture Organisation announced that the disease had finally been eradicated. It is only the second disease to be completely eradicated – the first is smallpox. A pioneer in the recognition of the dangers of rinderpest was a black man and the first qualified veterinary surgeon in South Africa, Dr Jotella Soga (1865–1906). Dr Soga was born in the then Transkei (now Eastern Cape), and qualified as a veterinary surgeon in Edinburgh. In 1886 he returned to the Cape Colony, where he was appointed veterinary surgeon for the colonial government. He gave lectures on the recognition and treatment of rinderpest, and was among the first to warn of the dangers it posed: 'Our new Colonial enemy is rinderpest,' he wrote in 1892, 'Lung Sickness and Redwater are simple fools to it.' See http://www.library.up.ac.za/vet/soga.htm.

Chapter 7 The Two Anglo-Boer Wars, 1880–1881 and 1899–1902

1 Adapted from http://www.sahistory.org.za/article/first-anglo-boer-war.
2 See Giliomee & Mbenga, eds., *New History of South Africa*, p206.
3 The Geneva Conventions between 1864 and 1949 and the Hague Conventions of 1899 and 1907

were among the first formal statements of the laws of war and war crimes. These conventions were signed by world leaders at international peace conferences in Geneva and The Hague respectively, for the purpose of ameliorating the effects of war on both soldiers and civilians.

4 Adapted from Bill Nasson, 'A Capitalist War for Gold?', in Giliomee & Mbenga, eds., *New History of South Africa*, p210.

5 The Baring Brothers Bank was established in 1792 and was the second oldest bank in the world after Berenburg in Germany.

6 For more on this, see Chapter 5.

7 'Uitlander' (literally 'outsider', someone from 'out of the land', or 'foreigner') referred to immigrants from Britain living in the Transvaal. Uitlanders were not allowed to vote and could not become citizens of the Transvaal.

8 George Albu was of German-Jewish descent. He was born in Brandenburg in 1857. He emigrated to South Africa in 1876 and first made money in Kimberley. In 1895, he and his brother Leopold founded the mining house which became General Mining and Finance Corporation, later part of Gencor and then BHP Billiton, one of the largest mining houses in the world.

9 Wayne Graham, 'The Randlord's Bubble 1894–6: South African Gold Mines and Stock Market Manipulation', *Discussion Papers in Economic and Social History, No 10*, University of Oxford, August 1996, pp7–8 & 29.

10 Interview with Charles van Onselen, Johannesburg, 23 September 2016.

11 Dr Leander Starr Jameson was a renowned doctor who had come out to South Africa from Britain for health reasons. He treated both President Paul Kruger and the Matabele king Lobengula, who honoured him with the rare status of induna (councillor) for curing his gout, and he was in contact with Cecil Rhodes. Jameson's leadership of the Jameson Raid was a disaster, but in Britain the general feeling was that he was not to blame and that he had shown great courage. Elizabeth Longford states that Rudyard Kipling wrote the poem 'If' with Jameson in mind – as an example and inspiration for the young. The poem celebrates heroism, stoicism and courage in the face of disaster; the last two lines are addressed to Kipling's son. See Elizabeth Longford, *Jameson's Raid: The Prelude to the Boer War*, Jonathan Ball Publishers, Johannesburg & Cape Town, 1982.

12 Alfred Milner is generally referred to as Lord Milner. After retiring to England he became a member of the House of Lords, and he was a member of David Lloyd George's war cabinet (1916–1921). For his services in southern Africa, he was made a baron in 1901 and a viscount in 1902.

13 Johannes Meintjies, *President Paul Kruger: A Biography*, Weidenfeld & Nicolson, London, 1974, pp226–228; see also Giliomee & Mbenga, eds., *New History of South Africa*, p209.

14 Today's Mahikeng takes its historical spelling, Mafeking, when used in the context of the Anglo-Boer War.

15 Baden-Powell used young boys as messengers during the siege, a practice that is said to have given rise to the international Boy Scout movement.

16 Sol Plaatje went on to become one of the founders of the SANNC, which became the ANC.

17 See Brian Willian, 'The Siege of Mafeking', in Peter Warwick, ed., *The South African War*, Longman, London, 1980, p155.

18 This was the evidence of a nurse, Ina Cowan, in a letter written to her sister on 30 December 1899. See Trevor Davies, ed., *Mafeking besieged: The Diary of Civilian Nurse Miss Ina Cowan, 12 October 1899–17 May 1900*, Roberts, Berkshire, 1995.

19 These men had numerous awards bestowed on them. Frederick Sleigh Roberts had been created a baron in 1892, and Horatio Herbert Kitchener was created a viscount in 1902, and an earl in 1914. When they returned to England, both men were also made knights of the Order of the Garter, the world's oldest national order of knighthood, founded by King Edward III in 1348.
20 Both Louis Botha and Jan Smuts would subsequently become prime ministers of South Africa: Louis Botha in 1910 and Jan Smuts in 1919, after the early death of Louis Botha.
21 SB Spies and Gail Nattrass, eds., *Jan Smuts: Memoirs of the Boer War*, Jonathan Ball Publishers, Johannesburg & Cape Town, 1994, pp27–28.
22 Warwick, ed., *The South African War*, pp306–307. See also http://www.sahistory.org.za/dated-event/gideon-scheepers-executed.
23 Richard Hull, 'American enterprise and the South African war 1895–1902', paper presented at Rethinking the South African War, Unisa Library Conference, 3–5 August 1998, p12.
24 See SB Spies, *Methods of Barbarism? Roberts and Kitchener and Civilians in the Boer Republics: January 1900 – May 1902*, Human & Rousseau, Cape Town, 1977.
25 Blockhouses were small forts built mainly along strategic railway lines, bridges, etc. to impede the free movement of the British forces. Some of them can still be seen today, especially in the Magaliesberg area.
26 The Americans put Filipino civilians into 'protected zones' and concentration camps ('reconcentrados') during the Filipino-American War of 1899–1902, just ahead of the Anglo-Boer War.
27 Warwick, ed., *The South African War*, pp62 & 220.
28 These and other stories were told to students at the School of Education at Wits by a descendant of a woman who survived the concentration camp in Krugersdorp, September 1991. The woman only wanted to be remembered as 'Maria'.
29 It was Sir Henry Campbell-Bannerman who first coined the phrase 'methods of barbarism', based on Emily Hobhouse's evidence.
30 Adapted from SB Spies, 'Women and The War', in Warwick, ed., *The South African War*, p182. See also Elsabé Brits, *Emily Hobhouse: Beloved Traitor*, Tafelberg, Cape Town, 2016, p201; and https://www.theguardian.com/theobserver/1999/oct/10/focus.news.
31 Jana Engelbrecht, *Saturday Star*, 12 April 2008.
32 Giliomee & Mbenga, eds., *New History of South Africa*, p220.
33 For more on this, see Pieter Labuschagne, *Ghostriders of the Anglo-Boer War (1899–1902): The Role and Contribution of Agterryers*, Unisa Press, Pretoria, 1998.
34 For more on Dinuzulu, see Chapter 6.
35 A branch of the Tswana people in present-day Botswana. Warwick, ed., *The South African War*, p223.
36 Adapted from Brian Willan, 'Siege of Mafeking', in Warwick, ed., *The South African War*, p151.
37 Warwick, ed., *The South African War*, p160.
38 See Elsabé Brink, *1899: The Long March Home*, Kwela Books, Cape Town, 1999.
39 Warwick, ed., *The South African War*, p163.
40 For further reading about women in the Anglo-Boer War, see Ann Harries, *No Place for a Woman*, Bloomsbury, London, 2005. The book is based on a diary kept by her grandmother during the siege of Ladysmith. See also Brian Roberts, *Those Bloody Women: Three Heroines of the Anglo-Boer War*, J Murray, London, 1991.
41 Adapted from SB Spies, 'Women and the War', in Warwick, ed., *The South African War*, pp179–180.

42 Cossacks were skilled Russian horsemen. See Apollon Davidson and Irina Filatova, *The Russians and the Anglo-Boer War*, Human & Rousseau, Cape Town, 1998, p287.
43 Richard Hull, 'American enterprise and the South African War 1895–1902', Rethinking the South African War, Unisa Library Conference, 3–5 August 1998, pp4, 12 & 14
44 Adapted from Giles Foden, *Mail & Guardian*, October 1–8, 1999. Also adapted from David Buckerfield, 'Churchill's Capture, Imprisonment and Escape', in http://www.britishempire.co.uk/article/churchillscapture.htm.
45 Ibid.
46 Bill Nasson, 'The South African War, 1899-1902', in Saunders, ed., *An Illustrated Dictionary of South African History*, p227.
47 Max du Preez, quoting Albert Grundlingh's work on hensoppers in *Of Warriors, Lovers & Prophets: Unusual stories from South Africa's past*, Zebra Press, Cape Town, 2004, p129. See also Mike Coghlan, 'The Other De Wet: Piet de Wet and the Boer "Hendsoppers" in the Anglo-Boer War', *Military History Journal, Vol 11* (6), December 2000: http://samilitaryhistory.org/vol116mc.html. Coghlan adds that the hero-worship of Boer generals like Christiaan de Wet and Koos de la Rey, and the demonisation of 'joiners' such as Piet de Wet, was prevalent as late as 1990. See also Jacques Malan, *Die Boere Offisiere 1899–1902*, JP van der Walt, Pretoria, 1990, p 28; and Emanoel Lee, *To the Bitter End: A photographic history of the Boer War 1899-1902*, Viking, 1985, p172. Lee says of the collaborators: 'Amongst Afrikaners they are remembered to this day with such hatred that it is almost impossible to get any information about them'. See also Kobus du Pisani and Louis Grundlingh, 'Volkshelde: Afrikaner nationalist mobilisation and representation of the Boer warrior', paper presented at Rethinking the South African War, Unisa Library Conference, 3–5 August 1998, p18. Kroonstad, where Piet de Wet surrendered, is in what is now the Free State.
48 Adapted from Bill Nasson, 'The war 100 years on', paper presented at Rethinking the South African War, Unisa Library Conference, 3–5 August 1998, pp5–6.
49 Ibid., p10.
50 Adapted from Giliomee & Mbenga, eds., *New History of South Africa*, p224.
51 Ibid.
52 Milner married for the first time aged 67. The masculine nature of the imperialist enterprise has been noted by many historians, notably SB Spies, who in his chapter 'Women and the War' in Warwick, ed., *The South African War*, p177, says that 'Many of the leading imperialists, including Rhodes, Milner, Baden-Powell (who married at age 55), Jameson and Kitchener were all bachelors'. He adds: 'the empire was not acquired in a fit of absence of mind as much as in a fit of absence of wives – and it has to be speculated whether the history of South Africa would have been different had it been otherwise'.
53 Warwick, ed., *The South African War*, p61.

Chapter 8 Union, the rise of nationalisms, resistance movements, the First World War (1914–1918), and the PACT government (1924–1929)

1 At the end of the Anglo-Boer war, the British had declared sovereignty over the former Boer republics of the Transvaal and Orange Free State, but then allowed them to hold free elections. Their own local parties had got in, so they were not 'colonies' in the full sense of the word.
2 His name was William Palmer, the 2nd Earl of Selborne, but he was more commonly known as Lord Selborne.

3 It was called a 'national' convention, but only white leaders were invited to attend.
4 Spies & Nattrass, eds., *Jan Smuts: Memoirs of the Boer War*, p31.
5 Farmer's son.
6 Jan Smuts, Holism and Evolution, Macmillan, London, 1926, p88.
7 Richard Steyn, *Jan Smuts: Unafraid of Greatness*, Jonathan Ball Publishers, Johannesburg & Cape Town, 2015, p239.
8 Brian Lapping, *Apartheid: A History*, 1987, Paladin Books, London, 1987.
9 WP Schreiner was the brother of Olive Schreiner, who had taken up the cause of Boer women and children in concentration camps during the Anglo-Boer War – projects that would contribute to the rise of Afrikaner nationalism in the years to come.
10 Newspapers or publications by African people in the late 19th and early 20th centuries played a critical role in black people's struggle for recognition and political rights. Other significant publications were Sol Plaatje's newspaper *Tsala ea Batho* ('The Friend of the People') and his book *Native Life in South Africa*, published in 1916. Information partly adapted from http://www.sahistory.org.za/topic/history-abantu-batho-newspaper-1912-1931.
11 The Black Sash was started in 1955 by six white women led by Jean Sinclair, and headed later by her daughter, Sheena Duncan. In protest against discriminatory laws, they held vigils and silent demonstrations on street corners, wearing black sashes as a sign of mourning about injustice. The women also helped people affected by land appropriation and the dreaded pass laws. Nowadays the Black Sash concerns itself mainly with issues related to poverty.
12 Passes were also referred to as 'dompas', literally meaning in Afrikaans the dumb (or stupid) pass.
13 The pass system continued throughout the next several decades and was particularly dominant during the apartheid era, from 1948 to approximately 1986, when political change was imminent and the pass laws were finally repealed.
14 The queen enjoyed their singing so much that she asked them to sing for her again at her summer palace on the Isle of Wight. See Zubeida Jaffer, *Beauty of the Heart: The Life and Times of Charlotte Mannya Maxeke*, Sun Press, Cape Town, 2016.
15 See http://www.anc.org.za/content/women-and-african-national-congress-1912-1943.
16 James Barry Munnik Hertzog was born in 1866 during an emergency caesarean section performed by an Irish surgeon, James Barry. It was the first successful caesarean in Africa. Both mother and child survived, and the baby was named after the surgeon – hence the Afrikaner leader's unusual name.
17 Statistics adapted from Van der Waag, *A Military History of Modern South Africa*, p108. He adds that the Afrikaners were renowned as light cavalrymen and distinguished themselves in the South West Africa campaign, so were well suited for the next stage in East Africa, especially in the area of Tanganyika (today's Tanzania).
18 Leo Marquard, *The Story of South Africa*, Faber and Faber, London, 1955, p228.
19 Words in the song include: 'my huis en my plaas tot kole verbrand (my house and my farm burned to ashes) … De La Rey, De La Rey, De La Rey, sal jy die Boere kom lei? (De La Rey, will you come lead the Boers?)'. See https://en.wikipedia.org/wiki/Koos_de_la_Rey.
20 The German cultural influence in Namibia remains to this day.
21 See Brian Willan, 'The South African Native Labour Contingent, 1916–1918' in *Journal of African History, Vol 19* (1), 1978, pp61–68; also Albert Grundlingh, *Fighting their own war: South African blacks and the First World War*, Ravan Press, Johannesburg, 1987, p114.
22 Nine white officers and 33 white crew also died.

23 Albert Grundlingh, 'Mutating Memories and the Making of a Myth: Remembering The SS Mendi Disaster, 1917–2007', *South African Historical Journal, Vol 63* (1), 1 March 2011, pp20–37.
24 Professor Emeritus Kathy Munro, lecture on Delville Wood to U3A, Northwold, Johannesburg, 6 September 2016.
25 See *The Times*, 5 July 2016.
26 In this regard, parallels could be drawn between Botha and Smuts, and Nelson Mandela and Thabo Mbeki after 1994.
27 After 1922, the SACP began to pay more attention to disadvantaged blacks and by 1928 most of its members were black.
28 Steyn, *Jan Smuts: Unafraid of Greatness*, p64.
29 Charles van Onselen describing Smuts's actions in 1922 to students at the former Johannesburg College of Education, August 1983.
30 This religious group drew on both Jewish and Christian doctrines and modelled their dress on the Israelites of the Old Testament. Information adapted from Saunders, ed., *An Illustrated Dictionary of South African History*, p146.
31 ISCOR no longer exists in its original form, but was the predecessor to today's ArcelorMittal Group.
32 Mike Boon, *The African Way: The Power of Interactive Leadership*, Zebra Press, Cape Town, 2001, p156.
33 This statute had important repercussions for South Africa because when the Second World War broke out in 1939, South Africa was not automatically at war on the side of Britain. South Africa's own Parliament could decide.
34 His son, Albie Sachs, would also later take up the struggle cause and become an activist. Albie Sachs became a judge of the Constitutional Court in Johannesburg.

Chapter 9 New political parties, the rise of the Afrikaners, World War II (1939–1945) and the 1948 elections

1 Australia was the main wool-producing country at the time, but South Africa was also a major producer.
2 Steyn, *Jan Smuts: Unafraid of Greatness*, pp218 & 223. In the second comment Steyn is quoting one of Smuts's biographers, WK Hancock.
3 Adapted from JD Fage, Michael Crowder and Roland Anthony Oliver, *The Cambridge History of Africa*, Cambridge University Press, Cambridge, 1984, p282.
4 See http://www.sahistory.org.za/dated-event/sa-joins-world-war-ii.
5 Statistics from the Commonwealth War Graves Commission: http://www.cwgc.org.
6 Smuts was nearly 70 when World War II broke out.
7 MJ Honikman, *There Should Have Been Five*, Tafelberg, Cape Town, 2016.
8 See Colonel CJ Jacobs, 'The role of the First South African Division during the first battle of El Alamein, 1–30 July 1942', *Military History Journal*, Vol 13 (2), December 2004.
9 Van der Waag, *A Military History of Modern South Africa*, pp200–201.
10 WK Hancock, *Smuts: The Fields of Force, 1919–1950*, Cambridge University Press, Cambridge, 1968, p370.
11 Ibid.
12 *Upbeat Magazine*, No 1, February 1997.

13 S Horwitz, 'The Non-European War Record in South Africa', in Ellen Hellman, ed., *Handbook on Race Relations in South Africa*, 1949, pp542. See also http://samilitaryhistory.org/vol101jm.html.
14 Both Lorna and Henry Nattrass's log books of air miles and other personal records are in their family's possession.
15 Information supplied by Richard Steyn, Johannesburg, 6 January 2017. He referred to *The Fringes of Power: Downing Street Diaries 1939–1955* by Churchill's private secretary, Jock Colville. Colville apparently did not approach the king directly; he wrote to his mother, a lady in waiting to Queen Elizabeth, asking her to mention the idea to the Queen in the hope that she would pass it on to the king. No one knows whether she did or not. Smuts's son, Jannie Smuts, in his biography of his father, also mentions that Churchill wanted Smuts to act as PM when he was out of the country on business. See also Steyn, *Jan Smuts: Unafraid of Greatness*, p143.
16 Hermann Giliomee, quoting Christof Heyns and William Gravett in 'Jan Smuts reconsidered', *Politicsweb*, 26 January 2016: http://www.politicsweb.co.za/news-and-analysis/jan-smuts-reconsidered.
17 Marquard, *The Story of South Africa*, p239.
18 When Smuts became prime minister, he turned down the mansion in Pretoria that went with the position. He preferred to live on his farm at Doornkloof, where he said his wounds healed and he found peace.
19 Spies & Nattrass, eds., *Jan Smuts: Memoirs of the Boer War*, p27.
20 John Vorster was prime minister of South Africa from 1966–1978 and state president of South Africa from 1978–1979; PW Botha was prime minister from 1978–1984 and state president from 1984–1989.
21 See https://www.supersport.com/boxing; https://en.wikipedia.org/wiki/Robey_Leibbrandt; and https://en.wikipedia.org/wiki/Ossewabrandwag.
22 Shula Marks, 'Jan Smuts, Race and the South African War'. Lecture given at the Institute of Economic and Social History and the Institute of Africanistic Studies, both at the University of Vienna, and at the Southern Africa Documentation and Co-operation Centre (SADOCC) in Vienna, 24 October 2000.
23 See Van der Waag, *A Military History of Modern South Africa*.

Chapter 10 The apartheid government

1 Marquard, *The Story of South Africa*, p242.
2 See Chapter 8 for more on the SANNC.
3 Until he realised the parallelism the NP had in mind was unjust, even the liberal senator Edgar Brookes, who was one of the three representatives of black people in the NRC (Natives Representatives Council), thought the principle of parallel development and differential development was a possible solution.
4 For more on Shepstone, see Chapter 6.
5 Adapted from Giliomee & Mbenga, eds., *New History of South Africa*, p324. 'When the white man is given full authority only in his own areas,' Verwoerd said, 'the Bantu will acquire full authority elsewhere in the course of time.' He added: 'There must not only be justice to the Black man in Africa, but also to the White man . . . for these Europeans there is no other home, Africa is their home now too, and they are also a strong stance against communism, for their ways are grounded in Christian values.' Historian Saul Dubow suggests that 'The unintended

effect of the speech was to make two hitherto separate strands of Verwoerd's political career seem mutually reinforcing: republican nationalism on the one hand and apartheid ideology on the other.' Saul Dubow, 'Macmillan, Verwoerd, and the 1960 "Wind of Change" Speech', *The Historical Journal, Vol 54* (4), 2011, pp1087–1114. The speech itself is housed in Oxford University's Bodleian Library and can be accessed at https://en.wikipedia.org/wiki/Wind_of_Change_(speech).

6 The word 'Bantu' refers to the linguistically related people of central and southern Africa. The term is regarded as offensive due to its use by the apartheid regime and is seldom used now.

7 See Map 22 in Chapter 8.

8 The story of Papwa Sewgolum is summarised and adapted from Paul Murray's review of Maxine Case, *Papwa: Golf's Lost Legend*, Kwela Books, Cape Town, 2015.

9 https://en.wikipedia.org/wiki/Academic_boycott_of_South_Africa; https://en.wikipedia.org/wiki/Television_in_South_Africa; South Africa only got television in 1976. The delay was because the Afrikaner government (especially Prime Minister Hendrik Verwoerd and Minister of Posts and Telegraphs Albert Hertzog) saw the new medium as a threat to Afrikaans, giving undue prominence to English; they regarded television as the 'devil's box', over which parents would have no control and which would encourage immorality and temptation because there would inevitably be films which showed races mixing.

10 http://www.azquotes.com/author/9313-Miriam_Makeba. For further reading about Miriam Makeba, see Miriam Makeba and James Hall, *Makeba: My Story*, New American Library, New York, 1988.

11 During the 1950s, *Drum* magazine became an important platform for urban black journalists and photographers, and grew many significant names in what became referred to as the 'Drum school'.

12 Soweto was a segregated township for black people laid out in 1956. The word stands for South Western Townships, because the area was south-west of Johannesburg.

13 Interview with Angus Smith and his mother, Laura, Johannesburg, October 1999.

14 See *The Star*, 31 January 1996. 'Ubuntu' means 'humanity' or 'compassion'.

15 See Bloke Modisane, *Blame Me on History*, Ad. Donker, Johannesburg, 1986, pp27 & 36.

16 Adapted from Robert R Edgar and Lyanda ka Msumza, eds., *Freedom in our Lifetime: The collected writings of Anton Muziwakhe Lembede*, quoted in Ayabonga Cawe, *The Star*, 16 September 2016.

17 See Marquard, *The Story of South Africa*.

18 *Sunday Times*, 30 June 2013; In fact Ahmed Kathrada and Nelson Mandela had had acrimonious disagreements in the past about Nelson Mandela's extreme form of African nationalism and Ahmed Kathrada had urged him to change it. The two men became close in later years. Chris Barron, 'Ahmed Kathrada: Principled icon of the ANC old guard who put struggle loyalty first', *Sunday Times*, 2 April 2017. This was an obituary to Ahmed Kathrada after his death on 28 March 2017.

19 Jackie Clausen, *The Times*, 14 June 2016, and Zaakirah Vadi, *The Star*, 14 June 2016.

20 Ghana was the first African country to win independence from a colonial ruler (Britain) in 1957.

21 The Constitution Hill site in Kotze Street, Braamfontein, Johannesburg, is a former prison and military fort. It now houses the Constitutional Court but part of it has been retained as a museum in which tourists can visit the old prison cells where many were imprisoned for political and other crimes.

22 Nancy L Clark and William H Worger, *South Africa – The Rise and Fall of Apartheid*, Seminar Studies in History, Pearson Education, New York, 2004, pp47–52.
23 Although FEDSAW was multiracial, most of its members were black.
24 Cherryl Walker, *Women and Resistance in South Africa*, David Philip, Cape Town, 1991, p154.
25 Partly adapted from an obituary by Denis Herbstein, at https://www.theguardian.com/news/2002/jul/12/guardianobituaries.
26 Walker, *Women and Resistance in South Africa*, p154; see also http://sahistory.org.za.
27 Delani Majola, 'Sophie Williams-De Bruyn – A lifetime of activism', *The Star*, 10 August 2016.
28 Adapted from Janet Smith, *The Star*, 9 August 2016.
29 Milton Shain, *Helen Suzman, 1917–2000*, Jewish Women's Archive. This famous comment was repeated in tributes to Helen Suzman after her death in January 2009, aged 91. See also https://www.da.org.za/campaign/know-your-da/helen-suzman-2/.
30 Nelson Mandela, *Long Walk to Freedom: The Autobiography of Nelson Mandela*, Macdonald Purnell, Johannesburg, 1994, p423.

Chapter 11 The 1960s

1 Historian Ian van der Waag identifies a period of 'cold war' affecting Berlin, Korea and South Africa (1945–1966), and a period of 'Hot War' in southern Africa (1959–1989). For more reading on this, see Van der Waag, *A Military History of Modern South Africa*, pp215 & 245 onwards.
2 Carl Peter, 'The "Wind of Change": British Decolonisation in Africa, 1957–1965'. *History Review* (71), pp.12–17, December 2011, accessed at https://en.wikipedia.org/wiki/Wind_of_Change_(speech).
3 Adapted from https://www.brandsouthafrica.com/south-africa-fast-facts/history-facts/robert-sobukwe-overview.
4 Ibid.
5 Sharpeville Police Station is in Vanderbijlpark, near Vereeniging in the Gauteng Province.
6 Soweto, which stands for South Western Townships, was created in the 1930s as a predominantly black township on the outskirts of the city of Johannesburg. Orlando is a part of Soweto.
7 See http://www.sahistory.org.za/topic/sharpeville-massacre-21-march-1960.
8 This is the terminology used by Van der Waag in *A Military History of Modern South Africa*.
9 For more on the Cullinan Diamond, see Chapter 5.
10 The period after the first democratic elections in 1994, which brought a majority black government into power for the first time, has been referred to as the 'new' South Africa.
11 See Stuart Jones, 'Economic Development', in Saunders, ed., *An Illustrated Dictionary of South African History*, p107.
12 See https://www.brandsouthafrica.com/south-africa-fast-facts/history-facts/robert-sobukwe-overview.
13 Robben Island (named after the Dutch word for seal) is located in Table Bay near Cape Town. It was used at various times between the 17th and 20th centuries as a prison, a leper colony and a military base. It became a high-security prison for political prisoners and criminals in 1961. Three future South African presidents served time there: Nelson Mandela, Jacob Zuma and Kgalema Motlanthe, although the latter's term was temporary. The maximum-security prison closed in 1991; the medium security prison some five years later. Robben Island is now a

South African National Heritage Site as well as a UNESCO World Heritage site. Adapted from https://en.wikipedia.org/wiki/Robben_Island and http://whc.unesco.org/en/list/916.

14 See http://www.sahistory.org.za/people/robert-mangaliso-sobukwe.

15 Adapted from https://en.wikipedia.org/wiki/Robert_Sobukwe.

16 See https://en.wikipedia.org/wiki/Internal_Security_Act,_1982.

17 His name is also spelled Lutuli, as in his autobiography, but is more commonly seen as Luthuli.

18 Albert John Lutuli, *Let My People Go: An Autobiography*, Collins, London, 1962.

19 Giliomee & Mbenga, eds., *New History of South Africa*, p338.

20 Radio interview with Ahmed Kathrada, 24 March 2007.

21 As identified by military historian Ian van der Waag, see above.

22 See https://en.wikipedia.org/wiki/Rivonia_Trial.

23 Mary Benson, 'A True Afrikaner', *Granta 19: More Dirt*, 1986, p26, accessed at http://pzacad.pitzer.edu/nam/newafrre/writers/fischer/Benson%20on%20Fischer.pdf.

24 Giliomee & Mbenga, eds., *New History of South Africa*, p339.

25 Interview with Christo Brand by John Carlin: http://www.pbs.org/wgbh/pages/frontline/shows/mandela/interviews/brand.html.

26 See https://en.wikipedia.org/wiki/Bram_Fischer.

27 Mike Terry, 'Some personal recollections of the "Free Nelson Mandela" campaign': http://www.anc.org.za/content/some-personal-recollections-free-nelson-mandela. See also: http://www.history.com/topics/nelson-mandela.

28 Information about Ama Naidoo based on an interview with her grandson, Mayan Naidoo, Johannesburg, 1989, and http://v1.sahistory.org.za/pages/people/bios/naidoo-ma.htm.

29 Indres Naidoo, *Island in Chains: Ten Years on Robben Island*, Penguin, London, 1982.

30 See http://www.sahistory.org.za/dated-event/military-service-becomes-compulsory-white-south-african-men.

31 Adapted from Graeme Callister, 'Patriotic duty or resented imposition? Public reactions to military conscription in white South Africa, 1952–1972', *Scientia Militaria: South African Journal of Military Studies, Vol 35* (1), 2007.

32 For more on the Border War, see Chapter 12.

33 Charalampos Dousemetzis was a doctoral research student in the School of Government and International Affairs at the University of Durham at the time. For an article about his research see Monica Laganparsad, 'Hendrik Verwoerd's killer a freedom fighter?', *Sunday Times*, 11 September 2016.

34 The transplant was performed in December 1967 on 54-year-old Louis Washkansky. He received the heart of a 25-year-old woman, Denise Darvall, who was declared brain dead after a car accident. Washkansky's body did not reject the new heart because he had been given heavy doses of immunosuppressive drugs, but these strong drugs weakened his immune system and he contracted double pneumonia and died 18 days later. Dr Barnard nevertheless considered the operation a success. Over the next several years he performed more transplants, with his patients surviving for increasing periods of time. One patient, Dorothy Fisher, survived for 24 years after receiving a new heart in 1969. Heart transplants are now a fairly regular procedure. See https://www.wired.com/2007/12/dayintech-1203/. For information about the Transplant Museum at Groote Schuur Hospital, where the world's first heart transplant was performed, see https://en.wikipedia.org/wiki/Heart_of_Cape_Town_Museum.

35 Christiaan Barnard and Hamilton Naki together performed 40 transplants on dogs before attempting the human transplant.

36 Marius Barnard, *Defining Moments: A Memoir*, Random House Struik, Cape Town, 2011.
37 Justice Malala, *The Times*, 9 January 2017.

Chapter 12 The 1970s and 1980s

1 For more on South West Africa, see the section on World War I in Chapter 8.
2 The policy of creating different homelands for black people started in 1951. See Chapter 10.
3 For more on Buthelezi and Inkatha, see later in this chapter.
4 For more on Dinuzulu (1868–1913) and Cetshwayo (1826–1884), see 'Isandlwana' in Chapter 6.
5 The Cold War was the ideological struggle between the Soviet Union and the West, which started after World War II in 1945 and lasted until approximately 1990.
6 For more on conscription, see Chapter 11.
7 Graeme Callister, 'Patriotic duty or resented imposition? Public reactions to military conscription in white South Africa', 1952–1972, *Scientia Militaria: South African Journal of Military Studies, Vol 35* (1), 2007.
8 The Estado Novo ('New State') was an authoritarian regime that had been established in Portugal in 1933, after a coup d'état against the democratic and unstable First Republic. Conservative, Catholic and nationalist in nature, the Estado Novo was opposed to communism. Adapted from https://en.wikipedia.org/wiki/Estado_Novo_(Portugal).
9 Portugal had been the first modern European power to establish a colony in Africa when it captured Ceuta (in present-day Morocco) in 1415, and it was one of the last to leave. The former Portuguese territories in Africa became sovereign states.
10 Interview with Derrick Willcock, CEO of Micromation, Johannesburg, 10 August 2016.
11 Ibid.
12 Horace Campbell, 'The Military Defeat of the South Africans in Angola', *Monthly Review: An Independent Socialist Magazine, Vol 64* (11), April 2013: http://monthlyreview.org/2013/04/01/the-military-defeat-of-the-south-africans-in-angola/.
13 Ibid.
14 The Tripartite Accord was mediated by the United States. It ended the direct involvement of foreign troops in the Angolan Civil War and was signed by the Foreign Ministers of Angola, Cuba and South Africa. Cuban and South African military personnel were then withdrawn from Angola and South West Africa respectively. Geoff Harris, ed., *Recovery from Armed Conflict in Developing Countries: An Economic and Political Analysis*, Routledge Books, Oxfordshire, 1999, pp262–264. See also https://en.wikipedia.org/wiki/South_African_Border_War.
15 James Ngculu, *The Honour to Serve: Recollections of an Umkhonto Soldier*, David Philip, Cape Town, 2009; see http://mg.co.za/article/2010-03-05-from-the-classroom-to-battlefield.
16 For more on the 'total strategy', see 'Implications of the Border War' later in this chapter.
17 Giliomee & Mbenga, eds., *New History of South Africa*, p392.
18 Askaris were traditionally defined as local soldiers in the service of a colonial or European power; https://www.merriam-webster.com/dictionary/askari. In the context of this period of South African history they were black people (including former guerrillas or activists) who had changed sides or been coerced into serving white power (in this case the apartheid government forces).
19 The Pebco Three were Sipho Hashe, Champion Galela, and Qaqawuli Godolozi, members of the Port Elizabeth Black Civic Organisation (PEBCO).
20 See http://www.enca.com/look-vlakplaas-apartheids-death-squad-hq.

21 See http://overcomingapartheid.msu.edu/multimedia.php?id=65-259-14 and Giliomee & Mbenga, eds., *New History of South Africa*, p392.
22 For more on the Treason Trial, see Chapter 10.
23 In 2010, Ruth First's former high school, Jeppe High School for Girls in Johannesburg, set up a scholarship in her name, with Albie Sachs as patron.
24 Historian Tom Lodge in Giliomee & Mbenga, eds., *New History of South Africa*, pp397 & 399.
25 This evidence was supplied by a counter intelligence officer in the special forces, Colonel Johan Theron, at the trial of Wouter Basson in 1999. He said Wouter Basson had supplied the drugs. In a controversial judgment, the court found Basson innocent. See https://en.wikipedia.org/wiki/Project_Coast.
26 Ronald 'Ronnie' Kasrils was a founding member of MK, and later became Minister for Intelligence Services (2004–2008); Pallo Jordan became a member of the National Executive Committee of the ANC, and a cabinet minister (1994–2009); Frank Chikane is a cleric, writer, and member of the ANC.
27 Little is known about this drug, but in experiments on rats and baboons at the Roodeplaats research laboratories it produced muscle spasms and eventually suffocation. See https://wikileaks.org/gifiles/attach/33/33200_Roodeplaat%20Research%20Laboratories.pdf.
28 An exhibition of South Africa's poisoned past was held at the Nelson Mandela Foundation in Johannesburg in October 2016. See https://www.businesslive.co.za/bd/life/arts-and-entertainment/2016-10-06-poisoned-pasts-exhibition-shows-horror-of-apartheidsas-project-coast/.
29 Giliomee & Mbenga, eds., *New History of South Africa*, p370.
30 See http://www.enca.com/look-vlakplaas-apartheids-death-squad-hq.
31 Giliomee & Mbenga, eds., *New History of South Africa*, p369.
32 See https://en.wikipedia.org/wiki/Black_Skin,_White_Masks.
33 Ten Quotes from Frantz Fanon accessed at http://thisisafrica.me/10-quotes-from-frantz-fanon and https://www.goodreads.com/author/quotes/37728.Frantz_Fanon.
34 *I Write What I Like*, first published in 1978, contains a selection of Biko's writings from 1969, when he became the president of SASO, to 1972, when he was prohibited from publishing. The book's title was taken from the title under which he had published his writings in the SASO newsletter under the pseudonym Frank Talk; see https://en.wikipedia.org/wiki/I_Write_What_I_Like.
35 Giliomee & Mbenga, eds., *New History of South Africa*, p354.
36 For more on Robert Sobukwe, see Chapter 11.
37 Giliomee & Mbenga, eds., *New History of South Africa*, p362.
38 A list with the ages of people injured and killed that day shows that some were older than students and were either members of the community, members of the Black Consciousness Movement or teachers. See list on http://www.sahistory.org.za/topic/june-16-soweto-youth-uprising.
39 Giliomee & Mbenga, eds., *New History of South Africa*, p355.
40 See https://en.wikipedia.org/wiki/Abram_Onkgopotse_Tiro.
41 There are varying opinions about how Hector Pieterson died. It has been suggested that he was caught in cross fire. A museum honouring Hector Pieterson and other victims has been built in Orlando West, Soweto, near the spot where he was killed.
42 Mamphela Ramphele, *Sunday Times*, 12 July 2016: http://www.timeslive.co.za/sundaytimes/opinion/2016/06/12/Soweto-Uprising-The-struggle-was-shaken-out-of-its-moribund-state1.

43 Necklacing was a form of torture by which a rubber tyre, filled with petrol, was placed around a victim's chest and arms, and set on fire. Adapted from: https://en.wikipedia.org/wiki/Necklacing. See also Chapter 13, p230.
44 Ramphele, *Sunday Times*, 12 July 2016.
45 See https://en.wikipedia.org/wiki/P._W._Botha.
46 Interview with Derrick Willcock, whose company, Micromation, tested the telephone lines of the bank system for bugs; Johannesburg, 13 January 2017. See also http://www.sahistory.org.za/topic/british-anti-apartheid-movement.
47 In 1996, Trevor Manuel would become Finance Minister in the new democratic government.
48 Thompson, *A History of South Africa*, pp221–222.
49 Thompson, *A History of South Africa*, p242.
50 Giliomee & Mbenga, eds., *New History of South Africa*, p397.
51 Adapted from https://en.wikipedia.org/wiki/Necklacing.
52 For more on the Truth and Reconciliation process, see Chapter 13.
53 Information on the 1970s and 1980s partly adapted from Beth Goldblatt and Sheila Meintjes, *Gender and the Truth and Reconciliation Commission: A submission to the Truth and Reconciliation Commission*, May 1996: http://www.justice.gov.za/trc/hrvtrans/submit/gender.htm.
54 See http://www.sahistory.org.za/dated-event/blacks-boycott-municipal-elections.
55 Giliomee & Mbenga, eds., *New History of South Africa*, p387.
56 Thompson, *A History of South Africa*, p237.
57 Article by Jeremy Cronin in *The Star*, Special Supplement, 2 February 2010. In 1990, Jeremy Cronin worked for the ANC's internal political committee, which was responsible for monitoring and engaging with the mass movement back home.

Chapter 13 The momentous 1990s

1 Frederik van Zyl Slabbert quoted in *The Star*, 1 November 2006, on the death of PW Botha. Van Zyl Slabbert was leader of the parliamentary opposition party, the Progressive Federal Party (PFP), through much of Botha's rule.
2 Ben Maclennan quoting FW de Klerk in *Business Day*, 2 November 2006; and John Carlin quoting Nelson Mandela in *The Sunday Independent*, 5 November 2006.
3 Historian Annette Seegers makes this comment in Giliomee & Mbenga, eds., *New History of South Africa*, p395.
4 Adapted from FW de Klerk's speech at the opening of Parliament, 2 February 1990, authored by Padraig O'Malley, the Nelson Mandela Centre of Memory: https://www.nelsonmandela.org/omalley/index.php/site/q/03lv02039/04lv02103/05lv02104/06lv02105.htm.
5 See the *Saturday Star*, 30 January 2010.
6 Interview with Trevor Manuel in *The Star*, Special Supplement, 2 February 2010. Trevor Manuel was Finance Minister from March 1996 to 2009 and Cabinet Minister in the Presidency in charge of the National Planning Commission, 2009 to 2014.
7 Article by Thabo Mbeki in *The Star*, Special Supplement, 2 February 2010.
8 Audrey Brown, 'Remembering the day Nelson Mandela was freed', Focus on Africa Magazine, BBC World Service, 11 February 2010. Audrey Brown worked as a journalist in South Africa before joining the African News and Current Affairs department of the BBC World Service. See http://news.bbc.co.uk/2/hi/africa/8421444.stm.

9 Lodge in Giliomee & Mbenga, eds., *New History of South Africa*, p397. He says that between 1984 and 1993, there were close to 19 000 deaths and more than 80 000 violent incidents.
10 Thompson, *A History of South Africa*, p241.
11 Lodge in Giliomee & Mbenga, eds., *New History of South Africa*, p397.
12 Supreme Court Judge Louis Harms issued his report on 13 November 1990. Despite the assassinations of opponents of the government that were going on in the country, notably the deaths of activists David Webster and Anton Lubowski in May and September 1989, the commission found no evidence to back up the allegations of army and police involvement. The testimony of three former police officers Dirk Coetzee, Almond Nofomela and David Tshikalanga was dismissed as untrustworthy. Accessed at http://v1.sahistory.org.za/pages/chronology/thisday/1990-11-13.htm.
13 Dr Melanie Chait recalling those years in the *Saturday Star*, 11 June 2016.
14 For more on the AWB, see Chapter 12.
15 Lodge in Giliomee & Mbenga, eds., *New History of South Africa*, p403.
16 Abbey Makoe, *The Star*, 4 February 2010.
17 The African Unity Movement (or The Non-European Unity Movement, NEUM), was established by activists against the racist policies of the white government in South Africa. It was founded in Bloemfontein in 1943 and had branches around the country. Its members were influenced by the teachings of Trotsky, and many of its members were teachers, or former teachers. Livingstone Mqotsi campaigned against inferior Bantu education, was banned from teaching, imprisoned under the Suppression of Communism Act and eventually obliged to leave the country. In 1957, the Unity Movement split and went into decline but was revived for a while in the 1980s. Accessed at http://www.sahistory.org.za/people/livingstone-mqotsi.
18 Quoted by Ayabonga Cawe in *The Star*, 16 September 2016.
19 Chris Hani Baragwanath Hospital is the third largest hospital in the world.
20 'Kugel' is a slang word with somewhat critical but nevertheless affectionate connotations. It refers to South African women with predilections for material goods and ostentation. Taken partly from http://thejewniverse.com/2014/did-you-know-that-kugel-is-south-african-for-jap/.
21 Barry Ronge, quoting images from Martin Pope and Robbie Botha in *The Star*, 11 May 1994.
22 Giliomee & Mbenga, eds., *New History of South Africa*, p412.
23 Thompson, *A History of South Africa*, p234.
24 For more on the adoption of the Freedom Charter, see the section on 'The Defiance Campaign and the Treason Trial' in Chapter 10.
25 Lodge in Giliomee & Mbenga, eds., *New History of South Africa*, p403.
26 Giliomee & Mbenga, eds., *New History of South Africa*, p413.
27 The Democratic Party was established in 1989 by the merger of the Progressive Federal Party with two smaller liberal parties: the National Democratic Movement and the Independent Party.
28 The explanation that follows is adapted from his article in *The Star*, Special Supplement, 2 February 2010.
29 Article by FW de Klerk in *The Star*, Special Supplement, 2 February 2010.
30 Tony Leon, quoted in *The Times*, 11 November 2015.
31 Giliomee & Mbenga, eds., *New History of South Africa*, p433.
32 The story has been immortalised in the movie *Invictus* (2007), directed by Clint Eastwood and starring Morgan Freeman as Nelson Mandela and Matt Damon as Francois Pienaar.
33 'Bafana Bafana' is a nickname given to the national side by its fans. In Zulu,

it means 'the boys, the boys' or 'Go, boys!'; see https://en.wikipedia.org/wiki/South_Africa_national_football_team.

34 In the true spirit of the new South Africa, it was a mixed-race team: http://www.sahistory.org.za/dated-event/bafana-bafana-sa's-national-soccer-team-wins-africa-cup-nations-final.

35 Ibid.

36 For more on Helen Suzman, see 'The Progressive Party' in Chapter 10.

37 For more on the SAIC, see 'The Defiance Campaign and the Treason Trial' in Chapter 10.

38 Interview with Ahmed Kathrada by Carlos Amato, *Sunday Times*, 1 June 2013.

39 Ibid.

40 Zoleka is the daughter of Zindzi, the younger of Nelson and Winnie Mandela's two daughters. See http://www.dailymail.co.uk/news/article-2560199/The-moment-I-smuggled-baby-Nelson-Mandelas-jail-cell-prisoner-friend-Robben-Island-guard.html.

41 See https://en.wikipedia.org/wiki/Winnie_Madikizela-Mandela.

42 For more on necklacing, see Chapter 12.

43 See https://en.wikipedia.org/wiki/Graca_Machel.

44 See https://en.wikipedia.org/wiki/Truth_and_Reconciliation_Commission_(South_Africa).

45 Adapted from https://en.wikipedia.org/wiki/Truth_and_Reconciliation_Commission_(South_Africa).

46 See https://en.wikipedia.org/wiki/Winnie_Madikizela-Mandela.

47 Adapted from http://www.biography.com/people/winnie-mandela-9397037#freedom-and-charges-of-violence.

48 Dullah Omar, 'Exploring the Truth and Reconciliation Commission': http://overcomingapartheid.msu.edu/unit.php?id=65-24E-3.

49 Ibid.

50 Antjie Krog, *Country of My Skull: Guilt, Sorrow, and the Limits of Forgiveness in the New South Africa*, Random House, Johannesburg, 1998. See also Giliomee & Mbenga, eds., *New History of South Africa*, p414.

Chapter 14 The years 1999–2008 and 2009–2016

1 Cheikh Anta Diop's ideas were expressed in his book *Towards the African Renaissance: Essays in Culture and Development, 1946–1960*, http://www.africaspeaks.com. See also https://en.wikipedia.org/wiki/Cheikh_Anta_Diop. The African Renaissance has also been described as the 'third moment' in post-colonial Africa, following decolonisation and the spread of democracy across the continent during the early 1990s. This comment was made by Vusi Maviembela, an adviser to Thabo Mbeki, in June 1997. See https://en.wikipedia.org/wiki/African_Renaissance.

2 This was said in conversation with Mbeki's biographer, Mark Gevisser, at his official residence, 'Mahlamba Ndlopfu', Pretoria, in August 2000, the year after he became president. See http://markgevisser.bookslive.co.za/book-excerpt/.

3 Zukiswa Mqolomba, *Mail & Guardian*, 16 February 2016.

4 Mbeki said, 'I am an African … I was born of the peoples of the continent of Africa.' For the full speech, see https://en.wikipedia.org/wiki/I_Am_an_African.

5 Mark Gevisser, *A Legacy of Liberation: Thabo Mbeki and the Future of the South African Dream*, Palgrave Macmillan, New York, 2009, p277. The statistics are based on a Harvard study.

6 Thabo Mbeki's views on Aids have been roundly disputed and government policy since 2010 is to provide antiretroviral drugs to HIV-positive people. On 26 August 2016 it was recorded in *The Star* that the number of people living with HIV in South Africa had dropped to 6.19 million, compared to 7.03 million the previous year.

7 See Gevisser, *A Legacy of Liberation*, Chapter 41, quoted in *The Weekender*, 17–18 November 2007.

8 *The Weekender*, Weekend Review, 17–18 November 2007; see also https://www.markgevisser.com/images/pdf/weekender_karimabrown.pdf.

9 Patricia de Lille was Chairperson of the Parliamentary Committee on Transport at the time.

10 For further reading on this, see Andrew Feinstein, *After the Party: A personal and political journey inside the ANC*, Jonathan Ball Publishers, Johannesburg & Cape Town, 2007, and *The Shadow World: Inside the Global Arms Trade*, Hamish Hamilton, London, 2011. In *The Shadow World*, Feinstein reports that the trade in weapons accounts for around 40% of all corruption in all world trade, and that the manufacturers of weapons are closely tied in to governments, militaries, intelligence agencies and, crucially, political parties. South Africa is included in the list of countries he names. See https://en.wikipedia.org/wiki/Andrew_Feinstein. See also Ashley Smith, 'Band of brothers in the thick of things', IOL, 22 November 2003: http://www.iol.co.za/news/politics/band-of-brothers-in-the-thick-of-things-117369.

11 The arms deal is discussed further in this chapter.

12 The woman was Fezeka Ntsukela Kuzwayo, but before her death in 2016 she was known only as 'Khwezi'. She was the daughter of Judson Kuzwayo, after whom the MJK unit (discussed in the section on Jacob Zuma later in this chapter) was named. She accused Zuma of rape but he said the sex had been consensual. Khwezi and her mother were vilified and forced to leave the country. See https://www.dailymaverick.co.za/article/2016-10-09-rememberkhwezi-zumas-rapeaccuser-dies-never-having-known-freedom/#.WI4rHjeKCtE.

13 For more on this, see the section on Jacob Zuma in this chapter.

14 Van Onselen, *New Nineveh*, p31, shows how white people in early Johannesburg felt threatened when they saw their servants wearing 'white' clothes.

15 Adapted from RW Johnson, *How Long Will South Africa Survive? The Looming Crisis*, Jonathan Ball Publishers, Johannesburg & Cape Town, 2015, ppix–xi. Johnson gave some lectures on Marxism/Leninism at Lakhani Chambers in Grey Street, Durban in 1961 on behalf of his friend, Rowley Arenstein, who had been banned as a communist and placed under house arrest after Sharpeville. Johnson recalls that he did not know much about the communist manifesto at the time, but his lectures were enthusiastically received by a roomful of young Zulu men. He only discovered years later that one of them had been Jacob Zuma. The two then exchanged memories of that time, and Jacob Zuma told him about working as a 'house boy'.

16 Johnson, *How Long Will South Africa Survive?*, px. It is assumed that the elementary knowledge of reading he had previously acquired was in Zulu. For more about Harry Gwala and their time on Robben Island, see http://www.sahistory.org.za/people/jacob-gedleyihlekisa-zuma.

17 See http://www.sahistory.org.za/people/jacob-gedleyihlekisa-zuma.

18 Ibid. For more on the Nkomati Accord, see 'The role of neighbouring countries' in Chapter 12.

19 For more on the 1976 Soweto uprising, see Chapter 12.

20 Indres Naidoo was an anti-apartheid activist and son of Manonmoney (Ama) Naidoo. For more on both Indres and Ama Naidoo, see the section on 'Activist wives' in Chapter 11.

21 For more on Chris Hani, see Chapter 13.

22 Janet Cherry, *Spear of the Nation: Umkhonto weSizwe, South Africa's Liberation Army*,

1960s–1990, Jacana Media, Johannesburg, 2011, pp41–56. Janet Cherry gives examples of the bomb attacks that took place outside the Bantu Affairs offices in Port Elizabeth; a bus terminus in East London; Church Street, Pretoria; Magoo's Bar in Durban; and Ellis Park rugby stadium in Johannesburg. She makes the point that the people killed were often MK cadres themselves: they had either been inadequately trained to handle explosives, or their organisations had been infiltrated and their devices tampered with.

23 Mandla Judson Kuzwayo was the chief representative of the ANC in Zimbabwe. He died on 1 May 1985 after his car overturned on his way to Lusaka. See more at http://www.sacp.org.za/main.php?ID=2326.

24 Shamin (better known as Chippy) Shaik was chiefly responsible for the infiltration of Altech. The Altech/Altron group is a telecommunications, multimedia and information-technology company. See http://www.iol.co.za/news/politics/band-of-brothers-in-the-thick-of-things-117369.

25 The name is also spelt Younis and Yunis in some sources.

26 See http://www.iol.co.za/news/politics/band-of-brothers-in-the-thick-of-things-117369.

27 Marlan Padayachee, 'The Story of Movers and Shaikers in South Africa', 30 June 2008: http://wordsmith-commissar.blogspot.co.za/2008/06/story-of-movers-and-shaikers-in-south.html.

28 When the ANC was banned after Sharpeville in 1960, it was forced to go underground and to hold meetings in countries sympathetic to the cause. See Chapter 11 for more.

29 See http://www.sahistory.org.za/people/jacob-gedleyihlekisa-zuma.

30 For more on CODESA, see 'Other events leading to the 1994 elections' in Chapter 13.

31 Padayachee, 'The Story of Movers and Shaikers in South Africa'.

32 See http://www.sahistory.org.za/people/jacob-gedleyihlekisa-zuma and http://www.corruptionwatch.org.za/timeline-of-the-arms-deal/.

33 See http://www.sahistory.org.za/people/jacob-gedleyihlekisa-zuma.

34 See https://en.wikipedia.org/wiki/Schabir_Shaik.

35 He told a meeting of traditional leaders that rather than turning to the courts, African problems should be solved in an African way. See Gia Nicolaides and Barry Bateman, *Eyewitness News*, 8 April 2016: http://ewn.co.za/2016/04/08/Before-turning-to-the-court-we-should-solve-things-Africa-way.

36 Political analyst Nkosikhulule Xhawulengweni Nyembezi, *The Star*, 10 February 2015: http://www.iol.co.za/the-star/mr-president-where-are-the-jobs-1815939.

37 A system in which residential, industrial and commercial areas have their electricity switched off on a rotation basis as a way of coping with limited electricity supply.

38 The foreign ministers of these four countries first met to discuss the formation of such an organisation at the UN General Assembly in New York in 2006, but the first formal summit was held in 2009. Since 2009, the BRICS nations have met annually at formal summits. See https://en.wikipedia.org/wiki/BRICS.

39 See https://en.wikipedia.org/wiki/BRICS.

40 At the 8th annual summit in India in October 2016, the group called on BRICS's New Development Bank to focus on funding specific development priorities and to create a network of angel investors. These are usually private investors who provide starting or growth capital in promising ventures. Other agreements at the summit included to set up research centres in the fields of agriculture, railways and a BRICS sports council. The Chinese leader, Xi Jinping warned, however, that the global economy was still going through 'a treacherous recovery', which meant that BRICS countries had also slowed down in economic growth. He added that

some countries were becoming more inward-looking in their policies and protectionism was rising. See https://en.wikipedia.org/wiki/8th_BRICS_summit and https://en.wikipedia.org/wiki/BRICS.

41 This is dealt with at greater length in Chapter 15.

42 The women aimed to remind the country about the accusation against Zuma of the rape of Khwezi in 2005. Khwezi left the country to avoid the witch-hunt against her; she returned to Durban, where she died aged 41 in October 2016. See http://mg.co.za/article/2016-08-09-jacob-zuma-and-his-sexism-as-laid-out-in-the-presidents-own-words.

43 Baldwin Ndala, *The Star*, 10 August 2015.

44 Pravin Gordhan was replaced with Malusi Gigaba (former Minister of Home Affairs) and his deputy Mcebisi Jonas with Sfiso Buthelezi. President Zuma said the move was to replace older MPs with younger talent, but this and other changes were hotly disputed and there were major calls from all sides, including initially some members of the ANC executive, for Zuma to step down as president.

45 For more on the history of the Progressive Party, see Chapter 10.

46 For more on Helen Suzman, see 'The Progressive Party' in Chapter 10.

47 Tony Leon said this to the Deutsche Presse-Agentur. His comment was that when he was a 17-year-old schoolboy helping out in Helen Suzman's 1974 election campaign, she was his idol. See http://www.news24.com/SouthAfrica/News/Suzman-disappointed-with-govt-20021105.

48 Yazeed Kamaldien, 'Retracing apartheid-era footsteps in Cape Town', *Weekend Argus*, 3 April 2016. Accessed at https://yazkam.wordpress.com/2016/04/03/retracing-apartheid-era-footsteps-in-cape-town/.

49 S'thembiso Msomi, *Mmusi Maimane: Prophet or Puppet?*, Jonathan Ball Publishers, Johannesburg & Cape Town, 2016.

50 See http://www.anc.org.za/kids/tripartite-alliance.

51 See http://www.cosatu.org.za/show.php?ID=2051#sthash.CT514ZkF.dpuf.

52 See https://www.dailymaverick.co.za/article/2013-07-11-the-tripartite-alliance-is-ananachronism/#.WIpd7zeKCtE.

53 Ibid.

54 Ibid.

55 See https://www.enca.com/south-africa/tripartite-alliance-summit-continues.

56 See https://www.dailymaverick.co.za/article/2013-07-11-the-tripartite-alliance-is-ananachronism/#.WIpd7zeKCtE.

57 Adapted from an article by Ian Ollis in *The Star*, 28 May 2015.

58 See http://www.engineeringnews.co.za/article/sa-one-of-the-worlds-most-violent-strike-pronecountries-2014-08-06.

59 Bowman Gilfillan consultant and dispute resolution specialist John Brand quoted. See http://www.engineeringnews.co.za/article/sa-one-of-the-worlds-most-violent-strike-prone-countries-2014-08-06.

60 A wildcat strike is a strike action undertaken by unionised workers without union leadership's authorisation, support, or approval. See https://en.wikipedia.org/wiki/Wildcat_strike_action.

61 For more on Sharpeville, see Chapter 11.

62 See http://www.iol.co.za/news/crime-courts/marikana-miners-were-killers---zuma-1875560.

63 For more on these strikes, see Chapter 8.

64 See http://www.engineeringnews.co.za/article/sa-one-of-the-worlds-most-violent-strike-prone-countries-2014-08-06.

65 An investigation by the South African Human Rights Commission reported that it was most likely that R5 rifles with hollow point bullets were used because these bullets tend to disintegrate when entering the body of a victim. They added that this provided the clearest illustration of why military assault rifles should be banned in public order situations even if fired in self-defence. See http://www.iol.co.za/news/south-africa/north-west/marikana-cops-wont-face-charges-1877367; information about R5 assault rifles and hollow point bullets supplied by Derrick Willcock, Johannesburg, 31 January 2017.
66 *The Star*, 3 June 2016.
67 Irvin Jim, *The Star*, 10 July 2016.
68 Adapted from http://www.news24.com/Tags/People/jeremycronin, and http://www.politicsweb.co.za/news-and-analysis/multidimensioned-attacks-on-num-no-accident--jerem. Jeremy Cronin was addressing delegates at the 15th annual congress of the National Union of Mineworkers (NUM). He said the mining houses, local government, local traditional leaders, and national government have let mine-workers down. Very little decent affordable housing, proper family accommodation, viable mining communities with clinics, crèches, schools, parks and public transport had been delivered to replace the old single-sex hostels.
69 See http://www.engineeringnews.co.za/article/sa-one-of-the-worlds-most-violent-strike-prone-countries-2014-08-06.
70 Irvin Jim, *The Star*, 10 July 2016.

Chapter 15 Prospects and challenges

1 See Chapter 8. The four main founders of the SANNC were all lawyers, and the members were an elite group of businessmen, teachers, clerks and clergymen.
2 Marquard, *The Story of South Africa*, p257.
3 George Matlala, *The Times*, 4 October 2016. See https://www.pressreader.com/south-africa/the-times-south-africa/20161004/281539405455593.
4 http://citizen.co.za/news/news-national/385566/delay-in-sandf-review-costing-armed-forces-minister/.
5 On 11 December 2016, the National Treasury instructed that almost R3 billion had to be cut from the SADF's salary bill over the next three years: http://www.timeslive.co.za/sundaytimes/stnews/2016/12/11/Defence-force-told-to-cut-troops-by-16000.
6 Finance Minister Pravin Gordhan announced in February 2016 that the Treasury would trim the public sector wage bill by at least R25 billion over three years: http://www.timeslive.co.za/sundaytimes/stnews/2016/12/11/Defence-force-told-to-cut-troops-by-16000.
7 See 'The Rise of the Afrikaners' in Chapter 9.
8 See http://www.news24.com/elections/news/anc-will-rule-until-jesus-comes-zuma-says-again-20160705.
9 For more on the EFF and Julius Malema, see Chapter 14.
·o Dominic Mahlangu, *The Times*, 3 May 2016.
The term 'born-free' describes South Africans born in the early 1990s, when the 'new' South frica was already taking shape.
Herskovitz, 'ANC risks losing South Africa's "born free" voters', 28 January 2013. He says any older South Africans still feel grateful to the ANC for winning their freedom, but ı frees" are not as swayed by history as their elders: http://www.reuters.com/article/ ınc-idUSBRE90R0GH20130128.

13 Adapted from a tribute to Frederik van Zyl Slabbert after his death in 2010, *Mail & Guardian*, 14 May 2010.
14 Mineral Resources Minister, Mosebenzi Zwane, speaking at the Investing in African Mining Indaba in Cape Town, 6–9 February 2017, quoted in Business News, *The Star*, 9 February 2017.
15 Kevin Crowley, 'Gold mines emerge from survival mode', *The Star*, 9 February 2017. Kevin Crowley was reporting on issues raised at the 'Investing in African Mining Indaba', in Cape Town, 6–9 February 2017. Investec is an international banking and asset management group. Its three principal markets are the UK, South Africa and Australia.
16 Ibid.
17 Palesa Vuyolwethu Tshandu and Lutho Mtongana, *Sunday Times*, 23 August 2015.
18 Ibid.
19 'Mbeki queries Africa Mining Vision progress', *The Star*, 9 February 2017.
20 Minister Mosebenzi Zwane quoted in *The Star*, 9 February 2017.
21 In colloquial terms, zama zama means trying your luck or taking a shot at fortune. It is estimated that after more than a century of mining, there is a labyrinth of underground passageways extending across the Witwatersrand, from Roodepoort in the west to Springs in the east. Mine officials and security personnel estimate that overall there may now be as many as 15 000 zama zamas, compared to 120 000 people employed in South Africa's formal gold mines. Greg Mills, *Daily Maverick*, 5 July 2016: https://www.dailymaverick.co.za/article/2016-07-05-take-achance-welcome-to-the-golden-underground-world-of-zama-zamas/#.WI-LIDeKCtE.
22 Trade and Industry Minister Rob Davies quoted in *The Times*, 26 January 2017.
23 The burning of fossil fuels (oil, coal, natural gas) and forest clearing increases the concentration of greenhouse gases in the atmosphere and leads to warmer temperatures. Warmer temperatures affect rainfall, which in turn affects human and animal health, plant life, grazing livestock and forestry.
24 Ettiene Retief, chairperson of the National Tax and SARS Stakeholders committees, quoted in *The Star*, 9 February 2017. He explained that experiments in Australia and Norway had not suggested that a carbon tax would work. In Australia, implementation of the carbon tax affected employment in the energy sector and energy-intensive industries, and in Norway carbon taxes had only yielded modest reductions in gas emissions.
25 Wendell Roelf, *The Star*, 9 February 2017.
26 Milton Nkosi, BBC News, 29 January 2016: http://www.bbc.com/news/world-africa-35427853.
27 Katharine Child, *The Times*, 14 September 2016.
28 See GT Maqhubela, 23 October 2015, https://www.wsws.org/en/articles/2015/10/23/safr-o23.html; and 'Thousands of protesting students have clashed with police on the stairs of the National Assembly in Cape Town', http://www.enca.com/south-africa/live-stun-grenades-chaos-stairs-parliament-feesmustfall.
29 The issue of decolonisation of education has aroused much controversy and one might argue that the students have generally not defined exactly what they mean by this.
30 George Devenish, *Cape Times*, 23 January 2017: https://www.pressreader.com/south-africa/cape-times/20170123/281852938279637. George Devenish was also one of the people who drafted the Interim Constitution in 1993.
31 Kabelo Khumalo, *The Star*, 25 January 2017.
32 Brexit is an abbreviation for 'British exit', which refers to the referendum on 23 June 2016, whereby British citizens voted to exit the European Union (EU).

33 See Chapter 14.
34 The African Union (AU) is a union consisting of 54 countries in Africa. It was established on 26 May 2001 in Addis Ababa, Ethiopia. See Thabo Mbeki's role in its formation in Chapter 14.
35 See Chapter 14.
36 Craig Dodds, *The Star*, 6 June 2015. Gordon was speaking about Africa in general, but his words are pertinent to South Africa.
37 Anthony Mothae Maruping and Fatima Haram Acyl quoting the AU objectives in its Agenda 2063, *The Star*, 27 January 2017. Pan-Africanism is the idea that all people of African descent share a common history and destiny, and should be unified.
38 Justice Malala, *The Times*, 16 November 2015.
39 Adapted from Johnson, *How Long Will South Africa Survive?*.
40 Adapted from Jonathan Jansen, *The Times*, 5 May 2015: http://www.timeslive.co.za/thetimes/2015/06/05/Light-the-way-in-a-darkling-SA.
41 Justice Malala, 'How to Stop South Africa Losing its Way', *We Have Now Begun our Descent*, Jonathan Ball Publishers, Johannesburg & Cape Town, 2015.
42 Marquard, *The Story of South Africa*, p267.

Postscript

1 Research data in October 2016 revealed that 10% of South Africa's population owned 90–95% of its assets. Anna Ortforer, *Natal Mercury*, 10 October 2016.
2 In the build-up to local elections in August 2016, sensing that the ANC might be losing out to opposition groups especially in Gauteng and the Eastern Cape, Jacob Zuma appealed to people not to disappoint their ancestors by not voting for the ANC. See http://www.iol.co.za/news/politics/ancestors-will-turn-against-those-who-dont-vote-anc-2050807.
3 Zapiro (Jonathan Shapiro) and Dov Fedler are well-known cartoonists whose work appears in several publications, and the cartoonist Rico created the 'Madam & Eve' cartoons, based on the experiences of a white 'madam' and her domestic servant, Eve.

Acknowledgements

This book has been several years in the making and many people have helped me along the way. The staff at our universities, archives, libraries and newspapers must get many odd requests on a daily basis but were always gracious. I would like to thank them all, but especially: Anthony Paton, Jeff Rikhotso and Mags Pillay at the Cradle of Humankind World Heritage Site; Sian Tiley-Nel at Mapungubwe Museum, University of Pretoria; Diana Wall at MuseumAfrica; Francis Thackeray and the late Tim Couzens at the University of the Witwatersrand; Annie and Jannie Gagiano, University of Stellenbosch; Ammi Ryke at Unisa Library Archives; Marise Bronkhorst and Erika le Roux at the Western Cape Archives and Records Service; Michelle Loock at the National Archives and Records Service, Pretoria; Phillip Kgaphola at Times Media; Kevin Ritchie and Karen Sandison at *The Star*; Etna Labuschagne at the War Museum, Bloemfontein; Annemarie Carelson and Anton Joubert at Smuts House Museum, Irene; Amy van Wezel at Albany Museum, Grahamstown; Claudia and Jurgen Schadeberg; Melanie Geustyn and Laddy McKechnie at the South African National Library, Cape Town; Lailah Hisham at Iziko Museums, Cape Town; Susanne Blendulf and Phindile Madida at the South African Museum of Military History; Renate Meyer at the University of Cape Town; Alison Chisholm and Mark Sandham at the School of Education, University of the Witwatersrand; and Leigh Benson, Kate Sun and Kim McCarthy at Gallo Images.

The following special people have influenced my work: Luli Callinicos and Charles van Onselen, whose books on early Johannesburg greatly inspired my teaching; Ian Phimister, student from many years back in Mufulira, whose achievements as a historian have been my great joy; my students in Johannesburg, especially Angus Smith and Mayan Naidoo who shared their stories of Sophiatown and the Naidoo family with me; my son-in-law Tim Williams who helped with mining aspects in the story; Derrick Willcock who gave me information about communication systems, military aspects and the border wars; Sudipa Balgobind who did the first draft of the maps, often from very vague instructions; my son Errol Nattrass who, from his home in Vermont, USA, sorted out my on-going computer mishaps; and my late husband, Brian, who supported me always, and knew how much this project meant to me.

Most of all, my thanks go to the wonderful Jonathan Ball who took on this project, my two superb editors, Nicola Rijsdijk and Ester Levinrad, and the whole Jonathan Ball Publishers team, especially Valda Strauss, Marius Roux of MR Design, Kevin Shenton of Triple M Design, George Claassen, Janto Gildenhuys and Ceri Prenter, all of whom were experts in their fields and a pleasure to work with.

Gail Nattrass, June 2017

Index